YOUR STORY IN THE STARS

YOUR STORY IN THE STARS

*Using Astrology to Uncover
the Hidden Narrative of Your Life*

Trish MacGregor

ST. MARTIN'S GRIFFIN ⚊ NEW YORK

www.stmartins.com

Book design by Ellen Cipriano

Library of Congress Cataloging-in-Publication Data

MacGregor, T. J.
    Your story in the stars : using astrology to uncover the hidden narrative of your life /
Trish MacGregor.—1st ed.
        p. cm
    Includes index (page 331).
    ISBN 0-312-29135-3
    1. Astrology. I. Title.
BF1708.1 .M295 2003
133.5—dc21

                                                                        2002042573

First Edition: March 2003

10 9 8 7 6 5 4 3 2 1

With love, for Megan and Rob,
the double Virgo and the double Taurus
who always have something new to teach me

A special thanks to Al Zuckerman and Marian Lizzi.
Without these two, there wouldn't be a book.

I would also like to thank the people who allowed
me to use their stories as examples of how story lines
unfold: my husband, Rob, Vivian Ortiz, Vicki Webber,
Phyllis Vega, Sharon Garcia, Carol Bowman, and Barb
Haldeman.

CONTENTS

PART THREE:
PARTING THOUGHTS

INTRODUCTION:
THE WORLD OF STORIES

When I was fifteen, I left home to go to boarding school in New England. High schools in Caracas, Venezuela, where my family lived at the time, weren't very good and my parents felt I would have a better shot at college if I finished my high school education in the States. I didn't want to go. Venezuela was my home, my friends were there, my life was there.

But in the fall of that year, I joined the league of teenagers born to Americans living abroad who left for U.S. boarding schools every fall and returned to their adopted countries every Christmas and summer. In retrospect, it was a strange and wonderful time, filled with new experiences, new people, new challenges. But I don't think I ever really overcame my homesickness for the life I had vacated. I missed the mountains, the soft trill of Spanish on the streets. I missed the clatter of the horse-drawn cart filled with vegetables and fruits that passed our apartment every morning. I missed all the small things, the nuances. And when I returned at Christmas and for summer, my heart filled up again.

In the fall of my junior year, I returned to school, already planning my trip home at Christmas. In November, shortly after the Kennedy assassination, I got a letter from my parents explaining that my father was retiring from the company, *we were moving* and would be celebrating Christmas in Florida. In other words, I wouldn't be going home again.

I was devastated. Not long after I learned about our move, I discovered astrology. I guess I was looking for answers about why this happened. I knew the superficial reasons—the political situation had become unstable, my father could take early retirement, other Americans were leaving because Caracas was no longer safe. But I was looking for the larger context. I wanted the *evolving story*.

In those days, there were no PCs, no astrology software, not very many books on astrology—and I was terrible in math. But I gradually learned to construct my birth chart by hand and saw it as a blueprint of potential. I discovered that the daily movement of the planets—the transits—affected my chart in the most immediate and personal way. The day I learned that my parents had decided to leave Venezuela, four planets were hitting my ascendant and first house, and Uranus was conjuncting my vertex. This is astrospeak for a major life change that is sudden and unexpected, and has the feel of something destined.

From that point on, I was hooked. Here was a *symbolic system* as ancient as Babylon, based on your date and place of birth, fine-tuned by the moment you drew your first breath, that provided not only the larger picture of your life but also its story line. Here were the characters, the plots, the subplots, the events, the secondary characters. Here was an oracle that could supply information about what might be coming up. Here was a *pattern*, a *matrix*.

Over the years, my love affair with astrology waxed and waned, depending on what was going on in my life at the time and how difficult I found the mathematical computations necessary to erect a birth chart by hand. There are purists who insist that computers have made things too easy, that every astrologer should know how to construct a birth chart the old-fashioned way. Quite frankly, I don't see the point. We live in the computer age, and if a software program can distill the math and erect a chart in a matter of seconds, why should anyone spend three or four hours putting one together by hand? It's like saying that writers who scribble novels on yellow legal pads are somehow better novelists than those who use word-processing programs. On the other hand, I'm a Gemini who uses whatever tools are available to cut to the chase. So if astrology hooks you and you're good in math, then be my guest. Learn to erect charts without an astrology program.

Around 1981, my love affair with astrology was in a good place. I was teaching Spanish to Cuban refugees through a federal program that had been set up after the Mariel boat lift that brought hundreds of thousands of Cubans into south Florida. I was working on my sixth unpublished novel. I had an agent and Jupiter, the planet that represents luck and expansiveness as well as publishing and education, was hitting my ascendant. And one night a journalist came to our center to find out if the refugees were really learning English. He was interested in the stuff that interested me, the stuff that people, at least back then, talked about in whispers. I did his chart and was intrigued by what I saw.

A year and a half later, we got married, and fourteen months after that, my first novel sold to Ballantine books.

By then, it was already apparent to me that novels and certain aspects of astrology share some uncanny parallels. Both deal with stories and characters, events and emotions. When I did natal charts, I attempted to interpret them as stories that possessed all the elements of a novel. When you speak to people about their lives as a story, something happens in their faces, their eyes. Lights blaze, pieces slam into place. They *get* it.

Just as writing fiction broadened my understanding of astrology, the reverse was also true. I started erecting natal charts for the main characters in my novels, and the first step was to decide on their sun signs. Since the sun is the total expression of who we are, the fundamental archetype of our personalities, this decision was pivotal in the construction of the characters.

In a novel called *Vanished,* for example, my antagonist is a female marine biologist who trains dolphins for a dolphin defense program for the military. She is a deeply conflicted woman whose relationship with another marine biologist colors everything she does. As soon as I started writing about her, I knew she had to be a Scorpio, because her personality archetype is about deep transformation. She was born in Havana, Cuba, to American military parents, so I had the longitude and latitude of her birth, and I played around with her time of birth until I had a chart that seemed to fit what I perceived her to be. Once I had her natal chart, I was able to run transits for important events in her life, which provided the evolution of her story over the course of the novel.

In real life, transits serve the same purpose. Whether you're a Scorpio or a Virgo, a Gemini or a Sagittarian, the motion of the planets in relation to your sun sign describes your evolution as a human being from birth to death. Once you understand the nature of the planets and the broad themes of the sun signs, astrology becomes another way of telling a story. And in this story, you're the protagonist, the main player.

If you develop an expertise in reading your story line as it unfolds, you can spot challenges and opportunities before they happen, and you can predict thematic possibilities for a specific time period. When you're informed, you can act decisively to mitigate and even alter the possibilities. This ability essentially makes you your own astrologer.

While there are other astrological techniques that yield valuable information, transits are the most personal. They represent the events and people and situations that we encounter in our daily lives and illuminate our stories. Transits from the slower-moving planets—Uranus, Neptune, and Pluto—impact our lives for years.

Everyone has a story. And astrology is a way to see how that story is unfolding now and how it might unfold in the future. If you can see the patterns forming before they manifest themselves fully in your life, you can be prepared. If you're prepared, you are empowered. If you are empowered, you are the master of your own destiny, able to live your life more fully and happily.

Using This Book

The heart and soul of any astrological predictive work is the ephemeris, a list of the daily motion of the planets over the course of a particular length of time. The sign and degree of the planet are given for every day of every year. The ephemeris also includes information on the phases of the moon, the signs, and degrees of eclipses, and lists numerous other pieces of information that are valuable to an astrologer.

A five-year ephemeris is included in Appendix A of this book. For Pluto and Neptune, the two slowest-moving planets, the positions are listed by the month, at the beginning of each month. The positions for Uranus, another snail that moves slightly faster than Neptune and Pluto, and for Saturn are listed for every two weeks. For the faster-moving planets—the moon, Mercury, Venus, Mars, and Jupiter—the daily planetary positions are listed. The moon's nodes are listed for once a week. There's also a new moon ephemeris, which lists every new moon during this five-year period. The sun moves about a degree a day, so to calculate its position you simply start at the beginning of the sign's cycle and add a degree for each day.

This book is interactive. There are plenty of activities that give you practice in using an ephemeris and finding story lines. With enough practice, though, you won't need the description in the book because you'll have a clear understanding of how *your* story is evolving. You'll know which transits you're most sensitive to and will be able to predict possible events and experiences before they happen. Even better, you won't have to read your daily horoscope in the newspaper to find out what's coming up in your own life!

PART ONE

ASTROLOGY AND STORIES

Stories sustain us.

—ANONYMOUS

STORIES AS EMPOWERMENT

*A beautifully told story is
a symphonic unity in which structure, setting,
characters, genre, and idea meld seamlessly.*

— ROBERT MCKEE, *STORY*

If you had a crystal ball, what might it look like?

The first image that probably comes to mind is the typical crystal ball associated with gypsies, as round as a globe and made of plain, transparent glass. With this type of crystal ball, the gypsy or crooked little woman in the fortune-teller's tent leans in close, gazing into the depths of glass and light, seeking images or colors or faces or whatever it is that speaks to her about you. *Long life, health, and happiness,* she says, and you roll your eyes and if you're smart, not long after that you get up and leave.

There are other types of crystal balls that aren't shaped like globes or made of glass or crystal and that, well, have some substance to them. We call them oracles, and they're the oldest predictive device on the planet. Nearly every culture, from the Celtics to the Cubans, has used oracles. The ancient Greeks had their Delphic oracle; the ancient Chinese had the *I Ching*. The Haitians have their voodoo priests and priestesses; the Hopi Indians have shamans; the Mayas, Babylonians, and ancient Chaldeans had astrology.

Of these, the *I Ching* and astrology are actual *symbolic systems* that anyone can learn. Both systems are based on thousands of years of observation and experimentation. Even though neither system is "scientific" in the way that science is currently defined, both possess an intuitive order and cohesion that is readily apparent to anyone who learns the symbolism.

In the *I Ching,* the symbols consist of sixty-four hexagrams based on complex mathematics. In astrology, the symbols consist of signs, planets, and aspects or the geometric angles that the planets form to each other. Over the centuries, various kinds of astrology have evolved. This book deals with predictive astrology based on transits or the daily movement of the planets and their effect on your natal sun—that is, your sun sign. This is the type of astrology at work when you open your daily newspaper to the horoscope section and run your finger down the columns, looking for your astrological fortune cookie for the day.

Some days, that fortune cookie doesn't amount to much more than what the gypsy says as she leans over her crystal ball. But other times, the information is specific enough to your life so that you're taken aback. *Where'd that come from? How'd the astrologer know that?* Transits, that's how. The daily motion of the planets is the most personal and immediate predictive device in astrology.

The beauty of this type of astrology is that anyone can learn it without devoting twenty years to studying it. The secret lies in the "story line" that is revealed as the daily motion of the planets influences your sun sign, your primal pattern.

Astrologically speaking, your sun sign represents the protagonist in a story, and the transiting planets symbolize secondary characters who enter the picture, plots, and subplots that unfold over the course of a given period of time. Once you learn the symbolism, the story is easy to read.

In his memoir, *On Writing,* Stephen King pinpoints Mother's Day 1973 as the day he found out that the paperback rights to *Carrie* had just been sold for $400,000. King was to get half of that.

This event didn't just transform King's career; it transformed his life. In August of that same year, his mother died. This is the power of a Pluto transit to your sun, which in King's case was close to a conjunction with his Virgo sun. It gave him wealth and took away his mother. Pluto symbolizes profound transformation and any time it conjuncts your sun sign by transit, some aspect of your life will be profoundly changed.

This doesn't mean that everyone who experiences this aspect can expect wealth and the death of a parent. It's just one possible expression and depends to a large extent on what you have been doing in your life before you experience the transit. And since we don't live in a social vacuum, your experience of the transit also depends on what's going on in the lives of the people around you.

Another woman, who was going through a Pluto transit to her sun, was asleep one night when gas began to leak somewhere in her house. She was near death when a friend found her and rushed her outside. That's another possible plot with a Pluto transit (and not one that you're likely to find in a newspaper horoscope!).

In the 2000 presidential election, the planet Mercury, which represents communication, was moving retrograde—an apparent backward motion that often results in communication snafus—at the time the networks announced that Al Gore had won Florida. About ten minutes after Mercury switched directions and began to move forward again, the networks announced that Gore *hadn't* won Florida. This is typical of what happens when Mercury changes directions. If you know ahead of time when a Mercury transit is going to affect your sun sign, you can prepare for it. It's best not to sign contracts or make travel plans under a Mercury retrograde. It's also best not to schedule elections under a Mercury retrograde!

Once you understand the symbolism of the planets and the aspects, you can be your own astrologer. You can see something beneficial as it approaches and prepare yourself to take full of advantage of it. Or you can see a risky period as it approaches and prepare yourself for that. In either case, you're *informed*. If you're informed, you can act. If you can act, you're *empowered*. And that's really what this kind of astrology is about: self-empowerment.

STORIES AND SOLAR ARCHETYPES

Good movies, like good stories, have recognizable themes. Their archetypes speak to us. *Star Wars* is ultimately about the father/son relationship. *E.T.* is about love and compassion. *The Sixth Sense* is about life and death and alternative realities. Good stories, like good movies, are a delight to astrologers because they usually encompass an *astrological archetype,* symbolized by the sun signs.

Take the movie *Gladiator.* Times are brutal, life is savage, war is all there is. The gladiator himself, Russell Crowe, is fearless, strong, independent, a true warrior. And beneath all that courage beats the heart of a man with a passion for life. This is pure Aries, the sign ruled by Mars, the god of war. (And sure enough, Crowe is an Aries.)

In the movie *The Gift,* Cate Blanchette plays a Southern psychic who comes up against the closed-minded establishment when she helps a cop on a murder case. This movie has strong water sign themes—notably mystical Pisces and transformative Scorpio.

Sleepless in Seattle fits the Gemini and Libra archetypes— Gemini for the communication themes and chameleonlike characters and Libra for the love theme.

Both the book and the movie version of *The Firm* entail Capricorn themes about ambition—how ambition can corrupt, destruct, or collapse into unmitigated greed. This doesn't mean that every Capricorn is corrupt, but every Capricorn is ambitious in some area of his or her life.

By now, just about everyone in the universe has heard of Harry Potter. So what is it about the boy wizard that is so incredibly appealing to both kids and adults alike? It's not just Harry and Hermione and Hogwarts. It's the *world* they inhabit and the worldview they come to embrace, a Sagittarian (truth seeker, foreign society or place) archetype. But the idea that magic can be taught within a school setting, according to ancient codes and rules, encompasses Gemini (learning, communication) and Capricorn (structure) archetypes. Rowling didn't stop there. The books have a few other solar archetypes mixed in: Aquarius for the visionary aspects of the stories, Scorpio for the deep transformation that Harry himself undergoes, and Pisces for the mystical and magical qualities of the stories and characters.

In the *Handmaid's Tale,* Margaret Atwood's dark portrayal of a future society in which most women are chattel used for procreation, Scorpio (transformation) and Cancer (nurturer, the mother, emotions, the womb) archetypes emerge as the strongest themes. In *Fahrenheit 451,* Ray Bradbury's classic tale of a totalitarian society in which books are burned, the most prevalent themes are Gemini (books), Sagittarius (foreign society or place), and Capricorn (authority).

Stephen King's books seem to swing from things that go bump in the night *(Salem's Lot, The Shining, Christine)* to childhood angst *(Hearts in Atlantis, Stand by Me)* to other worlds and realities *(The Dreamcatcher, Green Mile, The Black Tower).* It's impossible to assign just one solar archetype to each grouping because the characters themselves, the events they experience, and the emotions they feel span the spectrum from Aries to Pisces.

But King brings the archetypal energy of his sun sign to every book he writes—he's a Virgo, the Perfectionist and Analyst. When he creates a story, you are usually *there,* breathing the air of the 1950s or hearing the music of the 1960s. You are nostalgic (Cancer) for bygone days, scared of what you can sense but can't see (Scorpio, Pisces), enraged, saddened, and caught up in the antics of his heroes (Leo).

You get the idea. Our favorite books and movies are stories with strong archetypal themes. In the table below, key words are provided for each sun sign archetype. In the activity section that follows, list your top five favorite books or movies and the archetypal theme that fits each one.

SUN SIGN ARCHETYPES

SUN SIGN	ARCHETYPE
Aries	Warrior and Pioneer
Taurus	Realist and Sensualist

SUN SIGN	ARCHETYPE
Gemini	Communicator and Networker
Cancer	Nurturer and Intuitive
Leo	Actor and Hero
Virgo	Perfectionist and Analyst
Libra	Artist and Mediator
Scorpio	Alchemist and Detective
Sagittarius	Traveler and Truth Seeker
Capricorn	Achiever and Strategist
Aquarius	Innovator and Visionary
Pisces	Mystic and Healer

ACTIVITY:

Your Favorite Stories

List five of your favorite books or movies, along with their dominant solar archetypes. You may want to do this in a journal you can use specifically for the various activities in this book.

BOOK OR MOVIE	ARCHETYPE
1. _____	_____
2. _____	_____
3. _____	_____
4. _____	_____
5. _____	_____

YOUR NATAL CHART

Even though you don't need your natal chart to use the information in this book, its worthwhile to have one done. You can get a computerized copy of your natal chart from most New Age bookstores for about five dollars. If you have access to the Internet, there are several good sites that offer free natal charts. You'll need your exact time of birth.

One of the best sites for free natal charts belongs to astrologer Jan Spiller: www.cosmicpath.com. At http://astro-software.com you get a chart and a brief analysis. The wheel used on the site is somewhat difficult to read, however. You can also try: http://0800-horoscope.com/birthchart.html or www.1horoscope.com/natal_lite.html.

2

SOLAR STORY LINES

A coughing chuckle filled his throat.
He turned and leaned against the wall
as he swallowed the pills.
Full circle, he thought, while the final lethargy crept into
his limbs. Full circle. A new terror born in
death, a new superstition entering the
unassailable fortress of forever.
I am legend.

—RICHARD MATHESON, *I AM LEGEND*

Sun-sign story lines are simple, but they aren't always obvious. I recently attended an alternative health seminar given by Eric Pearl, a former chiropractor. I had read Pearl's book, *The Reconnection: Heal Others, Heal Yourself,* and was intrigued by his personal story.

For twelve years, he ran a successful chiropractic practice in Los Angeles. One day in 1993 his patients began reporting that they felt Eric's hands on them even though he hadn't touched them physically. Then his patients began to report miraculous healings from cancer, AIDS-related diseases, Chronic Fatigue Syndrome, birth disfigurements, and other serious afflictions. His healings have been documented in five books and have elicited interest from physicians and medical researchers. Pearl's exploration of this ability eventually led him to conclude that anyone can tap into the energy he uses when these healings occur. So a friend and I attended the two-day workshop to learn how to do this.

I wasn't sure what to expect of this guy and was really puzzled when he first came out onto the stage to greet the two hundred attendees of the workshop. With his biting wit and casual, irreverent manner, he had the audience in the palm of his hand within two minutes. A Leo, I figured, a born actor who worked the audience like a pro. But over the course of the weekend, as Pearl directed two hundred people through personal and immediate experience with this healing energy, I changed my mind several times. If he wasn't a Leo, then he had to be one of the other fire signs, a Sagittarius or an Aries, truth seeker or pioneer. Of course, I could have done the obvious thing and asked Pearl himself what sign he was, but by then I was determined to figure it out on my own.

During the breaks, I talked to people who claimed to have been healed by Pearl. One man had been diagnosed with throat cancer the year before and the doctors had given him just a few months to live. His daughter told him about Pearl and he flew out to Los Angeles for a healing. After two sessions, he flew home again and his doctors told him the tumor had shrunk enough so that they could operate. Just as important, the man's excruciating pain had disappeared. He subsequently went through chemo and radiation and is now cancer free. He attributes his initial healing to Pearl.

Another man had had a valve in his heart replaced and couldn't walk more than a few hundred feet without stopping to rest. The day after he was reconnected, he walked three miles. Mainstream medical thinking says these kinds of healings can't happen. Yet I experienced this tangible energy during the workshop so I knew it wasn't phony. But I still couldn't figure out Pearl's sun sign.

Finally, on Sunday evening when the workshop was over, I asked his assistant what sign he was. "Oh, he's a Scorpio."

Well, hey, of course, dumb me. It made perfect sense. What

could be more Scorpio than a mysterious healing energy that *trans- forms* bodies and lives at the deepest levels?

The story lines—the archetypes—of the sun signs are straight- forward. But because we are complex creatures, they find expression in many ways. Each sign is grouped according to its element and its quality or modality, and these two groupings are an intimate part of every sign's story line.

THE ELEMENTS

We learned about them in grade school, the four cornerstones of physical existence: fire, earth, air, and water. In astrology, the ele- ments describe the basic energy of the signs. The element that rules *your* sign explains not only your temperament but also the primary thrust of your story line. Are you more intuitive than action ori- ented? You're probably a water sign. Do you love ideas? You're prob- ably an air sign.

Read on.

Under each element heading is the title of a book or movie with a story line that fits that element.

Fire: Aries, Leo, Sagittarius

Clan of the Cave Bear by Jean Auel

Years ago (and I'm probably dating myself here), there was a group of comedians who called themselves The Fire Sign Theater. They used an old-time radio show format for their routines, and I remember sit- ting around listening to their albums and howling with laughter. Everyone in the group was supposedly a fire sign, and whether they were or not, the energy they radiated was pure fire—creative, pio- neering, impulsive, completely original.

Fire sign people are dynamic, action oriented, enthusiastic, and completely spontaneous. When they're angry, you know it. When they're happy, you know that, too. They are natural leaders, do their best work independently, and love being the center of attention. Their natural warmth attracts other people, and they never lack for friends and companionship. They excel at launching projects and trends.

They are the zodiac's natural leaders and aren't the least bit shy in letting you know that. If you're looking for the next trend or cutting edge in any field, ask a fire sign. He or she is probably already aware of it.

Aries initiates. Leo acts out. Sagittarius speaks his or her mind.

Earth: Taurus, Virgo, Capricorn

The Shining by Stephen King

Earth signs are the builders of the zodiac. And they can build anything—a strategy, a budget, a political campaign, a novel, a garden, a power base, an empire. Their grounded realism gives them a unique perspective on the world and how it really works. Their insight is like the eye of a camera. It misses nothing.

Earth signs are extremely responsible; they always get the job done. They may not do it fast, but they do it thoroughly and well. Earth signs can take a fire sign idea and make it tangible and useful, then improve on it again and again. They're ambitious, but the ambition is often quiet and measured. They're not in a hurry. They wait patiently, like Buddha.

Earth signs are also sensual. They appreciate comfortable surroundings, good art, good food, good sex, good everything. They usually take care of their bodies and are scrupulously attentive to their health. They're good money managers and make terrific parents.

Taurus stabilizes. Virgo perfects. Capricorn achieves.

Air Signs: Gemini, Libra, Aquarius

You've Got Mail, Meg Ryan and Tom Hanks

Their minds are their castles. These cool intellectuals of the zodiac *think* their way through life and pride themselves on their logic and ability to reason things out. Their intellects are sharp, insightful.

Air signs have the gift of gab. They can talk with anyone about anything, and if they don't have any idea what *you're* talking about, they'll fake it. They can do it convincingly, too, because their steel trap minds are archives of information, bits of this and that, trivia the rest of us might dismiss. This ability to talk, to *communicate,* makes them the socialites of the zodiac, the people who connect other people.

Despite all the socializing, air signs need time alone to regenerate their energies. Many of them can burn their candles at both ends and not stop until they drop.

Gemini gathers and disseminates information. Libra connects people. Aquarius relates every experience to a higher source.

Water Signs: Cancer, Scorpio, Pisces

Resurrection, Ellen Burstyn

Sensitive, moody, emotional, psychic. Water signs feel and intuit their way through life, which makes them naturals at comforting and nurturing other people. They sometimes cling to people and situations longer than they should. Their memories are usually excellent, perhaps because there are such strong emotional components to what they remember. Even though they try to hide their feelings, they have deep reserves of compassion.

Water signs are so highly attuned to the emotions of others that they sometimes act like psychic sponges, absorbing the emotional texture of their environments. For this reason, it's important that they keep their own energy as positive as possible. My friend Vivian, a Cancer and a psychiatric RN, has a message on her answering machine that typifies water signs: "Please leave a positive message."

Given their sensitivity, water signs need time alone to regenerate themselves. Their solitary times are enormously creative and healing.

Cancer nurtures. Scorpio penetrates. Pisces heals.

THE QUALITIES

Signs are also classified according to quality or modality, and there are three groupings: cardinal, fixed, and mutable. The quality of a sign describes how energy is used, the types of activities that sign may engage in, and the ease or difficulty in adapting to a change in circumstances.

Whenever I meet someone, I try to grasp the *quality* of his or her sign first, then the element. After that, it's easier to figure out the individual's sun sign.

Cardinal: Aries, Cancer, Libra, Capricorn

The Firm by John Grisham

They're enterprising, quick, focused. If you want to launch anything, tap a cardinal sign. They are natural pioneers and have enormous energy, and when their passion is ignited, *nothing* can stop them. And when that passion fizzles out, get a fixed sign in to continue what the cardinal signs started.

Cardinal signs aren't crazy about change, unless they initiate it. When change is thrust upon them, they may react by tightening their control over elements in their lives that they *can* control. They're innovators who bring originality to anything they think, do, and believe. They are often identifiable by eccentricities, unusual interests, odd turns in their speech. But don't be fooled. What you call eccentric today will become, under the influence of a cardinal sign, business as usual for you tomorrow. It's called the power of persuasion, and cardinal signs have made an art of it.

Fixed: Taurus, Leo, Scorpio, Aquarius

24 (TV show with Kiefer Sutherland)

Endurance, persistence, and a kind of dogged determinism typify fixed signs. Their patience is legendary and is one of the secrets of their ultimate success. They can outwait anyone.

They are among the most stubborn people in the zodiac, are slow to alter their viewpoints and beliefs, and don't readily embrace change. They tend to be self-assured loners with emotions that run deep. The rest of us may never know how deeply they feel because they're generally reticent about their emotions. Some fixed signs are downright secretive. Their fixed nature is precisely what makes them loving and loyal mates.

Even though they are often slow workers, they always get the job done.

Mutable: Gemini, Virgo, Sagittarius, Pisces

Mind of My Mind by Octavia Butler

Of the three groupings, mutable signs are the most adaptable to change. Their flexibility is their best coping mechanism. They are the communicators and teachers of the zodiac, rarely keep their feelings to themselves, and possess a chameleonlike quality that allows them to fit into almost any social situation and to get along with anyone. Routine bores them.

At times, the mutable signs may become *too* flexible, *too* malleable, until they reach a point where they don't have any idea who they are anymore. But when they're balanced in their flexibility, they always find ways to circumvent obstacles. Where a fixed sign will plow through an obstacle, a mutable sign views it as a challenge and finds another way of coping with it.

ANOTHER PIECE OF
THE STORY: RULING PLANETS

Every sun sign has a ruler, a planet assigned to it. The ruler's characteristics color those of the planet it rules. In fact, when talking about solar story lines, the ruling planet is as important as the sign itself.

Take Mercury. In mythology, he was the messenger of the gods, the guy with wings on his shoes who served the same purpose as the white owl in *Harry Potter*. So in astrology, Mercury rules communication and language, intelligence and the mental processes, travel, the gathering and dissemination of information, education and learning, and news and contracts. It rules mutable air sign Gemini and mutable earth Virgo.

Gemini, the seminal communicator and networker, gathers information and then disseminates it; Virgo's analytical, razor-sharp mind moves with lightning quickness. Even though Virgo is an earth sign, he or she's as brainy as Gemini and just as much of a communicator.

Venus rules both Taurus and Libra, one a fixed earth sign, the other a cardinal air sign. What could these two signs possibly have in common that would warrant a joint rulership by Venus, the goddess of love? Several things, actually. Venus doesn't just rule love and romance; she also symbolizes friendship, joy, and social interactions, and is patron of the arts. Both Taurus and Libra have an artistic bent and a deeply spiritual connection to something larger than themselves. Taurus often finds that connection in nature, and Libra finds it in social relationships.

Mars rules Aries, which explains the impulsiveness and impatience of Aries, as well as the aggression and independence. Back in the days when people believed there were only seven planets—and still had twelve signs—Mars ruled Scorpio, too, a rulership that's tough to understand. Even though Mars is a frozen planet, we called it the "red" planet and associate it with war, fire, and action, all of which fit Aries, not Scorpio. At any rate, it's still considered to share rulership of Scorpio with Pluto. Mars represents our physical energy, our sexual drive, combat, fire, the military, and anything associated with traditionally "masculine" pursuits.

Jupiter rules Sagittarius. This one fits like the proverbial glove. As the largest planet in the solar system, ruler of things like the higher mind, spiritual beliefs, higher education, foreign cultures and countries, and the law, it seems only just that it should rule the most expansive sign in the zodiac. But there's a co-rulership here, too, that dates back to our lack of knowledge about the solar system: Jupiter as ruler of Pisces. This fits in the sense that Pisces is a mystical, right-brain sign, and Jupiter rules ephemeral elements like luck, serendipity, and our spiritual beliefs, and relates to our creativity.

Saturn rules Capricorn. They were made for each other, these two. Saturn symbolizes responsibilities, discipline, authority, restrictions, the building of foundations, structures. Saturn is serious, just like Capricorn. If you want to achieve, which Capricorn does, you need Saturn. Once again, though, we have a co-rulership: Saturn as ruler of Aquarius. This is another co-rulership that isn't self-evident. Aquarius is one of the most freedom-loving signs around, the very antithesis of everything that Saturn represents. But when you have twelve signs and only seven planets, as the ancients did, you have to squeeze to make things fit.

Uranus rules Aquarius, an ideal fit. Uranus represents individuality, the process of individuation, electricity, the unexpected, new paradigms, genius, thinking out of the box. All of the rapidly developing technology falls under the rulership of Uranus. Aquarians are visionaries who value individual and personal freedom above all else, but they are also able to relate to "the family of man."

Once Neptune was discovered, it became the ruler of Pisces, a perfect fit. Neptune represents our visionary selves, our illusions and ideals, our imaginations and inspirations, all the right-brain stuff that is Piscean territory. As the higher "octave" of Venus, Neptune also rules poetry, idealism, clairvoyance. It symbolizes all forms of escapism and addictions.

Then there's Pluto, that tiny devil spinning at the edge of the

Rulers, Elements, and Qualities

SIGN	RULER	ELEMENT	QUALITY
Aries ♈	Mars ♂	Fire	Cardinal
Taurus ♉	Venus ♀	Earth	Fixed
Gemini ♊	Mercury ☿	Air	Mutable
Cancer ♋	Moon ☽	Water	Cardinal
Leo ♌	Sun ☉	Fire	Fixed
Virgo ♍	Mercury ☿	Earth	Mutable
Libra ♎	Venus ♀	Air	Cardinal
Scorpio ♏	Pluto ♇	Water	Fixed
Sagittarius ♐	Jupiter ♃	Fire	Mutable
Capricorn ♑	Saturn ♄	Earth	Cardinal
Aquarius ♒	Uranus ♅	Air	Fixed
Pisces ♓	Neptune ♆	Water	Mutable

galaxy. The god of the underworld. He rules Scorpio, a match so ideal that it's astonishing anyone ever dared to make Mars the ruler of Scorpio. Pluto knocks your house down, sends the IRS sniffing at your door, ignites cancer in your cells. But if you manage to live through all that, his rewards are vast and profound. Your life is forever changed. The transformer: Scorpio understands all that. He lives it daily.

The Moon rules Cancer. This one is a good fit, too. The moon rules emotions, Mom, intuition, all the stuff hidden away in your psychic cellar, your subconscious mind. It describes what you need to feel secure within yourself and represents important females in your life. It also represents your memories, the deeper layer of memories, which is one reason why Cancers have such strong memories.

Then there's the Sun, brilliant and dramatic, flamboyant and essential. It's the primal force, where it all begins. It rules Leo, another great match. The sun is our primal pattern, the force that keeps us going. Without it, we are barren darkness, a void. Just ask Leo. He knows.

In the next chapter, we explore planets in depth.

ACTIVITY:

Working with Partners or Groups

Astrology is certainly something you can learn on your own. When working with story lines, though, it's often more insightful to work with another person or with several other people. You can brainstorm with each other for other archetypes that fit your sun sign, for emerging plots and story lines, for the kinds of characters and the many possibilities the transiting planets may bring into your life.

An activity you may want to try with your partner or group is to jot down the person's strengths in your journal, with his or her sun sign at the top of the page. If you're working with people you don't know well, then write your first impressions. Stay positive. You're going to share your impressions with the group when you finish, and besides, this isn't the time or place to attack anyone's negative attributes.

When you've shared your impressions, turn to the respective sun signs in Part Two of this book and find out how your impressions fit with the description of the sign.

3

PLANETARY PLOTS
AND PEOPLE

*To build a scene, we constantly break open
these breaches in reality.*

— ROBERT MCKEE, *STORY*

Think about one of your favorite books or movies. If you were describing the story to a friend who wasn't familiar with it, how would you do it in just a couple of sentences?

". . . the end of the world is just the beginning of mankind's ultimate struggle." From the back cover of *Swan Song* by Robert McCammon.

"A child wounded in body and spirit, a horse driven mad by pain, a woman fighting to save them both, and the man who is their only hope . . ." From the back cover of *The Horse Whisperer* by Nicholas Evans.

These are examples of how novels are distilled into their essential story lines. Granted, cover copy is written to sell books—and with astrology, you're not *selling* anything. It's the distillation process you're after. Even if you know what the planetary energies mean, if you understand the solar themes, houses, aspects, you still need a story line to connect them. Without that connection, you're just stumbling around in the dark, hoping that someone turns on the light.

Before I write a word on a new novel, I write an outline, and it usually begins with a two- or three-sentence summary of the idea. "A family on a camping trip in the Florida Everglades stumbles into a secret project on invisibility that renders *them* invisible." That's the first sentence in the synopsis I wrote for *Out of Sight*. It's the basic story line out of which everything else evolved. If I can find that story line, I can write the book. Yes, the characters and plot change, new elements enter into the story, and the ending is rarely where I think it's going to be at the onset. In the actual writing, the characters take on a life of their own. But without that story line, I may write five hundred pages that lead me to the story line, to the nugget of what the novel is about, and everything before that point gets tossed out. Even though I may spend weeks or months looking for the story line, it saves time to find it first and then write the novel.

This same process is at work in astrology. An astrologer might say, "Mars is approaching a conjunction with your sun." Unless you're familiar with astrology, the sentence means absolutely nothing to you. But if you know the story line—that in the next few weeks you should watch your temper and your attitudes toward authority, and know that you better think before you act—the prediction is useful.

THE PLANETS

In grade school, we learn about the solar system, and the teacher usually has some mnemonic that helps us remember the names and order of the planets, such as *My Very Elegant Mother Just Sat Upon Nasty Prickles*: Mercury, Venus, Earth, Mars, Jupiter, Saturn, Uranus, Neptune, Pluto. In astrology, we add the sun and the moon and, because we live on Earth, we don't include it in the lineup of planets.

The meaning of each planet remains constant regardless of the kind of astrology you're doing. Transits, the daily movement of the planets, act as triggers that set off events and situations, and the meanings of the transiting planets are pertinent only for the length of the transit.

The sun and the moon always move forward through the signs. Every other planet, however, has two types of motion in relation to us here on Earth—direct and retrograde. In direct motion, a planet moves forward through the signs. In retrograde motion, a planet appears to be moving backward through the signs. The direct motion of a planet permits outward expression of its energy. With retrograde motion, the energy is less obvious and, quite often, more internal.

The table on pages 38–41 is a handy reference about the planets and the areas they rule. You'll be referring to it frequently.

The Sun
Rules Leo

The Forever King by Mollie Cochran and Warren Murphy

It all starts here. The sun symbolizes the primal force, the foundation of who you are. It represents your personality, ego and individuality, and creative talents. It's your flame, the spirit that drives you, where you shine in your life. It often describes what you do—or should do—professionally. It provides vital clues about your temperament, your overall health and outlook on life, and your self-esteem. It represents your *archetype*.

In terms of people, the sun symbolizes authority figures and masculinity. In a woman's chart, this would include the father or father figures, bosses, and significant others—boyfriend, lover, or spouse. In a man's chart, the sun represents any important male figure.

The transiting sun has the same meanings, but because it moves about 1 degree a day, its impact is fleeting. With transits, think of the sun as a bonus. The transiting sun to watch for happens around your birthday. At this time, the transiting sun invigorates you physically, boosts your energy, and may result in encounters with people in authority. Your father or significant other may play a vital role in your life at that time.

Moon
Rules Cancer

Woman on the Edge of Time by Marge Piercy

It represents our emotional, intuitive selves, our inner beings. It is yin, receptive, feminine, where the sun is yang, active, masculine. The moon symbolizes everything that happens beneath the surface— our dreams, subconscious mind, habits and instincts, imaginations. In Western astrology, its importance is second only to the sun. In Vedic astrology, however, its importance is second to none.

The moon symbolizes your mother and your experience of her as well as how *you* mother and nurture other people. It also represents what we need to feel secure in our lives. Is it money? A loving family? A job we love? The moon often represents important women in a woman's life—sisters, friends, sometimes mentors—and the mother and women in a man's life. It symbolizes our connection to the collective unconscious.

In transits, the moon changes signs every two and a half days, so the impact of lunar transits is brief. If we notice them at all, it's through fleeting moods, transient encounters with others, or our habitual actions and motives. The two exceptions are lunar eclipses and the new and full moon phases.

A new moon phase is the perfect time for beginnings, to plant the seeds for whatever you are trying to manifest during a given month. Certain types of manifestation spells are done under a new moon. It's a propitious time for meditation, creative visualization, and creating goals. Two weeks later, when the moon is full, the energy of whatever you planted during the new moon culminates.

A friend of mine needed to find an agent. He had done the grunt work—written a book, sent out queries and outlines—and now he was ready to attract the right agent. During a solar eclipse, which happens only during a new moon, he focused intently on his wish. He also planted fourteen watermelon seeds—one for every day to the full moon—in a ceramic pot in his backyard. The seeds sprouted within several days, around the same time he found an agent.

A skeptic would balk at something like this, dismiss it as unscientific bunk or, at the very least, as an interesting coincidence. My response to skeptics is don't knock it until you've tried it.

In Appendix A, you'll find an ephemeris that gives the date and sign of every new moon from 2003 to 2007. To find the full moon, just add fourteen days to the date. The sign of the full moon is always opposite the sign of the new moon. If the new moon is in Gemini, then the full moon will be in Sagittarius. When you attempt to manifest anything, the most powerful energy is that of a new moon that falls in your sun sign. But any new moon will work the magic.

Look in the new moon ephemeris and jot down when the next new moon will occur.

Date and sign of next new moon: _____

Mercury
Rules Gemini and Virgo

Sleepless in Seattle, Tom Hanks and Meg Ryan

Remember Mercury in Roman mythology? He was the messenger of the gods, the guy who flitted around, delivering messages in much the same way as the white owl in Harry Potter. That's why Mercury rules communication, travel, the mind. Take a look at Mercury's list in the table at the end of the chapter. You can see that this planet is especially important to anyone in the communication business— writers, publishers, publicists, salespeople—and in education and travel.

In a natal chart, the sign of your Mercury describes how your intellect works, what types of communication skills you have, how you assimilate daily experience. It can represent children or siblings, too, and your particular way of communicating with others and with yourself. Are you a fast talker? An intuitive thinker? A gossip? Are your friends foremost in your life? Look at Mercury's sign and placement in your natal chart.

Transiting Mercury describes the same things and indicates how these issues are likely to be expressed. Once every three months or so, Mercury goes retrograde and tends to foul up our lines of communication. Your fax quits working. Your computer gets a virus. Your travel plans fall apart. You revise, revisit, rework.

Astrologers usually advise people that it's best not to engage in certain activities under a Mercury retrograde. Don't sign contracts unless you're prepared to get into all that fine print and, even then, you may have to rework the terms. Don't schedule a move under a Mercury retrograde, unless you're prepared to deal with delays and snafus. If you travel, be flexible, roll with the delays, the sudden cancellations. Even then, you may end up in Toledo instead of LA.

Geminis and Virgos, who are ruled by Mercury, tend to be the most sensitive to Mercury retrogrades, as do individuals in the communication and travel industries.

When Mercury is moving direct and is in the same sign as your sun, your communication skills are sharpened. Your mind works with lightning-quick efficiency. Ideas flow. It's an excellent time to plan and strategize. You may find you have more contact with neighbors and relatives, with brothers and sisters. Your daily routine is intensified, you may be busier than usual. If you're stressed, problems can manifest themselves in the physical areas ruled by Mercury—the hands, fingers, and shoulders, and sometimes in the eyes.

Now take a look through the Mercury ephemeris and note when the next Mercury transit occurs in your sun sign. If it's going to be retrograde, note that, too. Geminis and Virgos should pay special attention to periods when Mercury is in their sign. In the ephemeris, look for transits in the sign opposite yours and in signs of the same quality. If you're a Scorpio, for example, look for Mercury transits in other fixed signs: Taurus, Leo, and Aquarius. These transits will also affect you in some way.

Date and sign of next Mercury retrograde: _____
Date of next Mercury transit in my sign: _____
Date of next Mercury transit in a sign of the same quality as my sun sign: _____

Venus
Rules Taurus and Libra

Cowboy by Sara Davidson

Even young children who don't know anything about astrology seem to understand what Venus represents: love, romance, stars in your eyes. It also symbolizes pleasure and parties, socializing, your artistic tastes and aesthetic sense. In a natal chart, the sign of your Venus usually describes what you're looking for in a mate or significant other, your capacity to appreciate art and fine foods, your social self, your capacity for love, your creative inspiration. It can describe your friends.

Transiting Venus draws the qualities of this planet into your life: romance, love affairs and new friendships, financial opportunities, artistic inspiration, spiritual buoyancy. Although Venus moves quickly, staying in a sign from three to four weeks, her transits are nearly always pleasant. Under a Venus transit to your sun sign, for instance, the check isn't just in the mail; it's in your mailbox. The guy next door isn't just a neighbor; he may be the next love in your life. The novel that has given you fits for months suddenly flows out of you in exactly the right way. But even this pleasant transit requires something from you.

When you spot a Venus transit that's in your sun sign, take advantage of it. Prepare ahead of time. If you're planning a party, schedule it when Venus is in your sun sign. If you're looking for a new job, make appointments during the time that Venus is in your sun sign. Stack the deck in your favor by spotting windows of opportunity before they're on top of you.

Venus goes retrograde far less frequently than Mercury. In 2003, for example, there are no retrograde periods for Venus. In 2004, it goes retrograde in mid-May in Gemini and doesn't go direct again until the end of June. If you're a Gemini, Sagittarius, Virgo, or Pisces, make note of this retrograde in the space at the end of the Venus section. During a Venus retrograde, you tend to be more reticent in social situations, financial delays sometimes occur, and there can be misunderstandings in friendships and romantic relationships or in dealings with female bosses and siblings.

Taurus and Libra individuals, who are ruled by Venus, should pay special attention to the periods when Venus is in their sun signs and when Venus is retrograde.

Date and sign of next Venus retrograde: _____

Date of next Venus transit in my sign: _____

Mars
Rules Aries, co-ruler of Scorpio

Gladiator, Russell Crowe

Without Mars, not much would happen. It symbolizes our physical energy and sexual drive, our aggression and individuality, our ability to get things done. Mars is passionate and forceful, aggressive and bold, the god of war. It is ego, yang, purely masculine. There is nothing spiritual or ephemeral about this planet's energies. It deals with what exists here and now, in the physical world.

The meaning of Mars in a natal chart isn't any different from the meaning of transiting Mars. Transits are simply more immediate and more fleeting. In either case, Mars is all about the energy at your disposal to survive and maintain yourself in your environment. As long as that energy has plenty to do, to keep it occupied, it probably won't manifest itself in combativeness. But if it does, you have to roll with whatever happens and let the drama unfold. Resistance only makes things worse.

In terms of people, Mars transits tend to attract individuals who reflect some hidden part of ourselves that we don't like, who force us to clarify our point of view or our ability to survive and maintain ourselves in our environment. We went to war with Afghanistan when Mars was in Capricorn, a sign that is all about authority, rules and regulations, and slow, steady progress. Put that definition together with "military" or "god of war," and it spells everything in which this country is now embroiled.

When Mars is moving direct, it remains in a sign for six to eight weeks. The retrograde period usually lasts from two to three months, and then Mars is in a sign for as long as seven or eight months. In 2003, Mars goes retrograde in Pisces at the beginning of August and doesn't go direct again until the end of September. During any retrograde period for this planet, its tremendous energies are turned inward and can sometimes manifest themselves as accidents, injuries, or high fevers. These types of experiences can be averted if you see the transit coming and make sure that you have sufficient outlets for the energy.

When Mars transits your sun—and right now we're talking primarily about conjunctions, when Mars is in the same sign as your sun—your ego is really *out front.* You can stand up for yourself against nearly any opponent. You're like the rooster that struts through the chicken coop, just daring another rooster to take you on. You'll work long and hard during this transit and will have the energy to accomplish whatever goal you set for yourself. The main risk is combativeness. You'll be ready to argue with anyone, anywhere, over virtually anything.

Take the time now to check the Mars ephemeris for the dates when Mars will be retrograde or in your sign.

Date and sign for the next Mars retrograde: _____
Next date for Mars in my sign: _____
Next date for Mars transit in a sign of the same quality: _____

Jupiter
Rules Sagittarius, co-ruler of Pisces

Coincidence by David Ambrose

Luck, serendipity, synchronicity, your spiritual beliefs, your world-view, expansion, the primary thrust of your creativity—all of these elements belong in the domain of the largest planet in the solar system. Without Jupiter, our capacity to imagine and to philosophize would be nil. Religion and spirituality might not exist. This is the planet that helps us see and define the bigger picture—of our lives, our society, and the world in which we live.

In a natal chart, Jupiter indicates your innate capacity for these various traits. Transiting Jupiter describes opportunities for vast growth and expansion in your life according to the nature of the planet or the planets that are affected. If Jupiter is transiting in the same sign as your sun, everything in your life works more smoothly. Your creativity expands exponentially. You buy a winning lottery ticket, your spiritual life deepens, you meet the right people at the right time. Sometimes you expand physically, too, the most literal manifestation of a Jupiter transit to your sun!

Transiting Jupiter often brings foreign trips or encounters with foreign-born individuals. For writers, these transits are especially rewarding because Jupiter rules the publishing industry. It also rules the sign of Sagittarius, which is one of the reasons these people are so buoyant and generally optimistic.

I keep a close eye on transiting Jupiter in my chart and those of my husband and daughter. To give you an idea of how a Jupiter transit to your sun works in real life, here's an example. When Jupiter went into my sun sign (Gemini) at the tail end of June 2000, it signaled a time of incredible expansion. We moved into a larger house, we got several new pets, I had plenty of writing projects, we traveled to South America, our finances improved. It also signaled a time of introspection: My mother had died, my ailing father lived with us, our daughter had started middle school. My spiritual beliefs deepened. My story lines embraced many facets of Jupiter's energy.

Jupiter stays in a sign for about a year. Like the other planets, it can go retrograde, and then its tenure in a single sign is extended by several months. This is usually a good period to think and reflect, to delve into spiritual matters, and to travel to foreign countries to discover whatever they have to teach you.

A Jupiter transit brings people into your life who are right in line with the areas this planets rules. Look at the table on pages 38–41 again. Lawyers, judges, government authority, professors, priests or ministers, and spiritual leaders—all of these individuals are associated with Jupiter.

Glance through the Jupiter ephemeris to note the upcoming transits that are pertinent to your sign.

Date of next Jupiter transit in my sign: _____

Date and sign of next Jupiter retrograde: _____

Date of next Jupiter transit in a sign of the same quality: _____

Saturn
Rules Capricorn, co-ruler of Aquarius

Wall Street, Michael Douglas; *Dune* by Frank Herbert

This planet is like the relative no one wants to talk about. Yet Saturn is one of the most important planets astrologically. Without his energies, we would still be living in caves and eating with our fingers. We wouldn't have civilizations, cultures, arts, sciences, inventions. We would have no *structure.*

In a natal chart, Saturn represents many characteristics, but foremost among them is our capacity *to build*—a career, a family, a dream, a goal, a book, a movie, a house, a corporation, a business. It symbolizes our responsibilities to ourselves and others and how we fulfill those responsibilities. It represents authority and structure, the power of manifestation, physical reality.

Transiting Saturn—its daily motion through a horoscope or theory—tends to clarify what you need to confront and what you really want. It fosters patience, discipline, responsibility, control. It does this in ways that may not be particularly pleasant. But if you negotiate a transit of Saturn step by step, it helps you manifest your dreams and teaches you to recognize and appreciate who you are.

Transiting Saturn usually brings authoritarian figures into your life. Father issues may come up. You may have dealings with the elderly. In each instance, though, these people and situations help clarify where you have been in your life, where you are now, and where you may be headed. Quite often during Saturn transits, relationships and situations that no longer serve a purpose in your life end. This purge is necessary to make space in your life for new people and experiences that are more in line with who you are and who you are becoming.

It takes Saturn twenty-nine and a half years to get around the zodiac, so it spends about two and a half years in a sign. When it moves retrograde, its transit in a particular sign can take well over three years. Around the ages of twenty-nine to thirty and fifty-eight to sixty, we all experience a Saturn return, when Saturn returns to the sign and place it occupied in our natal chart. Life changes often happen during these cycles. People get married or divorced. A parent dies. Professional achievements are attained. Professional or personal goals and directions are altered.

Saturn transits that occur in the same sign as your sun are also important. Like the returns, they happen once every twenty-nine to thirty years and can bring satisfaction and achievement or difficulties and disappointment. It depends on what you've been doing with your life and how well you have dealt with your issues and responsibilities. These transits usually coincide with a lot of hard work, additional responsibilities, and the failure or successful completion of activities and projects.

When you check the Saturn ephemeris, also look for the dates when Saturn is in the sign that is opposite yours and when it's in a sign of the same quality. These periods will also signal the emergence of profound developments in your life.

Next date that Saturn is in my sign: _____

Next date when Saturn is in a sign of the same quality: _____

Next date when Saturn is opposite my sun sign: _____

Uranus
Rules Aquarius

Powder, Sean Patrick Flanery, Jeff Goldblum

So your life is humming along just fine. Maybe it's a bit predictable, but hey, there's comfort in habit. Then, seemingly out of the blue, *wham.* Everything familiar and predictable collapses. Your life appears to be in utter chaos. Welcome to the world of Uranus transits.

Astrologically, Uranus is a fascinating planet. In a natal chart, it indicates your special genius, an area where your individuality shines, where you can trailblaze and pioneer, and where and how you move against the status quo. It represents your individuality in the purest sense of the word.

Transiting Uranus brings sudden, unexpected change that whisks you out of your ordinary life. In the areas where you are rigid, Uranus collapses the spine of that rigidity. In areas where your life is predictable and habitual, you face the opposite.

This planet also rules lightning, all the new technology from the Internet to digital photography, as well as cutting-edge medical research. It rules space exploration, homeopathy, the mind-body connection, computers, and astrology. Anything innovative and futuristic falls under the rule of Uranus. Here is where we find the sudden flash of intuition, astonishing originality, the moment of epiphany when everything falls into place.

When you experience a Uranus transit in your sun sign, you're in for a wild, chaotic ride. Your life suddenly breaks open at the seams and all the old baggage is seared away. If you resist, you're in for a difficult time. If you go with the flow, you'll embrace the adventure. Either way, your life won't be the same at the end of the transit. People who enter your life during a Uranus transit are likely to be harbingers of change or individuals you meet as a result of change. Any love affairs begun under a Uranus transit are likely to be exciting but unstable.

Uranus moves slowly. It takes eighty-four years to travel around the zodiac and spends about seven years in a single sign. Its initial impact when it goes into your sun sign is apt to be tremendous. Whether it's positive or negative will depend on your capacity to embrace change. If you were born in the latter part of a sun sign, its impact will become stronger as it approaches a conjunction with your sun. As with the other planets, you should check the ephemeris for dates when Uranus will enter the sign that is opposite yours or when it enters a compatible sign.

Regardless of where Uranus is in your natal chart, most of us feel its impact in seven-year increments, at the ages of seven, fourteen, twenty-one, twenty-eight, thirty-five, and so on to the end of our lives. If you're an Aquarian, the sign ruled by Uranus, the pattern this planet etches against the template of your life will be obvious if you give it some thought.

In the ephemeris, Uranus's position are listed every two weeks. It moves only forty-two seconds a day, or 4 degrees a year, so you can always interpolate if you have to.

The dates when Uranus will be in my sun sign: _____

The dates when Uranus will be in the sign opposite mine: _____

The dates when Uranus will be in a sign of the same quality: _____

Neptune
Rules Pisces

Dead Again, Emma Thompson

Idealism. Imagination. Self-sacrifice and selflessness. Dreams and illusions. The right brain. Compassion, confusion, escapism, and addictions. Neptune embraces all of these qualities. In a natal chart, it represents the area of your life where you are most idealistic and selfless and pinpoints your blind spot. It also describes your intuition, your psychic ability, your openness to mystical beliefs and experiences.

Neptune spends about fourteen years in a sign, so it's considered to be a generational planet. In other words, anyone born around the same time you were has Neptune in the same sign. Neptune went into Libra in 1942 and stayed there until 1956, affecting many of the baby boomers who came of age during the sixties. At this time, the Neptune in Libra energy manifested itself in the culture of the hippies, an idealization of relationships and, in later years, a spiritual renaissance. The generation of children born between November 1984 and the end of November 1998 have Neptune in Capricorn and are likely to idealize work, duties, and responsibility (all of which are Capricorn's domain). They may not be especially practical individuals, but they are probably going to be tremendously creative and funnel that creativity into new structures.

Neptune's transits don't encompass sudden, unexpected events as do transits from Uranus. Instead, these transits tend to dissolve ego barriers and may leave you feeling discouraged and deeply confused. At times, these transits can result in various forms of escapism, from alcoholism to drug addiction, and can bring out the martyr in your personality. But spiritual bonuses are another aspect of this transit, times when you feel a sense of oneness with the universe or really understand the interconnectedness of everyone and everything.

The people associated with Neptune transits fall into several distinct areas. In the spiritual arena, you can expect contact with preachers and priests, spiritual teachers and leaders, or individuals who awaken spiritual potential in you. There can also be contact with people who work in institutions like nursing homes, hospitals, charitable organizations, prisons. Psychiatrists and psychologists often come into the picture during Neptune transits.

People with a sun in Pisces, the sign that Neptune rules, should be especially aware of this planet's transits. Any time Neptune transits your sun sign, the opposite sign, or any sign in the same quality, you'd better pay attention. It's a good time to take up meditation or some other spiritual discipline so that you are in touch with your inner self. You may consider getting involved in charity work or doing something for other people; this helps channel Neptune's energy.

Neptune went into Aquarius in 1998 and will be there until April 2011. After a short stint in Pisces, it goes retrograde and travels back into Aquarius in August 2011. In November 2011, it goes direct again in Aquarius and stays there until February 2012, when it goes into Pisces again. Even though Neptune doesn't change signs for the five years of transits this book covers, the ephemeris lists Neptune's positions at monthly intervals and notes the retrograde periods, important because it means that certain issues will surface more than once.

The ephemeris is useful for those of you who have their natal charts and can track Neptune's progress as it transits through Aquarius and for how Neptune's transits affect your sun sign. Obviously, this Neptune transit is important for Aquarius and the opposite sign, Leo, as well as Pisces, the sign it rules. It impacts the rest of us according to the section of the natal chart that is being hit and the geometric angles it makes to our natal sun.

Notable dates for Neptune's transits: _____

Pluto
Rules Scorpio

One Flew Over the Cuckoo's Nest by Ken Kesey

Power. Profound transformation. The creator and the destroyer. Death and regeneration. Heavy-duty stuff. That's what Pluto is about. And it's never subtle.

In a natal chart, Pluto symbolizes how you deal with the power you hold over others, whether you use this power in a positive or negative fashion, and how you cope with transformative experiences throughout your life. It also describes the depth of your ambition and your need to affect the world in some way.

Pluto moves at a snail's place, circling the zodiac in 248 years. Since its orbit is erratic, it spends as few as twelve years in Scorpio and as long as thirty years in Taurus. Pluto went into Sagittarius in 1995 and will be there until the end of November 2008, when it moves into Capricorn. Pluto's transit through 2008 has an impact on Sagittarius and its opposite sign, Gemini, as well as the other mutable signs—Virgo and Pisces.

Even though Pluto's transits are slow, its effects are deep, inevitable, and necessary in the evolution of you life.

Date of significant Pluto transits: _____

Areas the Planets Rule

Some areas are listed under the rulership of more than one planet.

PLANET	AREA
Sun ☉	Your primal force
	Basic physical energy and health
	The men in your life
	The ego, your overall archetype
	Authority and your attitudes toward authority
	Overall personality
	Bosses, heroes, monarchs
	Public officials
	The heart and the blood
Moon ☽	Your emotions, your moods
	Intuition, psychic ability, imagination
	Your connection to the collective unconscious
	Your nurturing parent, your parental style
	Babies, women in your life, wife in a man's chart
	The unconscious mind
	Habitual behavior
	Moves
	Fertility
	The past
	Emotional memories, connective to the collective mind
	Tides, ocean
	Stomach and breasts
Mercury ☿	All types of communication
	Your rational mind, intellect, language
	Learning, teaching, writing, books, manuscripts, speeches
	School/education, workshops, skills and competence, language
	Travel, primarily short trips; transportation
	Moves
	Daily routine
	Siblings, relatives, neighbors

Sales, contracts
Childhood
Pets, small animals
Hands, fingers, shoulders, eyes, arms

Venus ♀
Romance, love, marriage for a woman
Creative thrust
Significant women in a woman's life, spouse or significant
    women in a man's chart
Social contacts, friendships
Fame
Fertility
Small animals
Art, music, appreciation for all kinds of beauty
Beneficial for financial matters
Pleasure
Femininity, adornment, jewelry
Neck, fingers, hands, throat, thyroid, kidneys, ovaries,
    veins, small of the back

Mars ♂
Physical and sexual energy
Aggression, anger, hostility, war, military strategy
Physical strength, ego strength
Accidents, especially by burning or fire
Sharp instruments, knives, surgery and surgical
    instruments
Masculinity, men
Marriage for a man
Spouse or significant other in a woman's chart
Soldiers, war, the military
Ironworkers, pirates, surgeons, thieves
Fevers, hemorrhages
Explosives, weapons in general
The head, musculature, red corpuscles

Jupiter ♃
Luck, success, expansion
Serendipitous encounters
Creative view, worldview, philosophy, idealism

Higher education, spiritual and religious beliefs
Ministers, priests, reverends
Law, lawyers, judicial system, government, judges
Professors, universities
Excess, weight gain, profligate spending
Foreign people, cultures, countries, foreign travel
Wealth and financial gain
Publishing
Hips and thighs, arteries, liver and hepatic system

Saturn ♄

Structure, restrictions, rules
Where and how you are being "tested"
Your challenges and obstacles
Your responsibilities and how you handle them
How you manifest what you want
The elderly, bricklayers, builders, fathers or husbands,
   authoritarian figures, plumbers
Depression, emotional heaviness
The rules of the game in physical reality
Karma
Bones and joints, skin, teeth

Uranus ♅

Individuality
Unusual, unexpected events
Sudden change
All that is new, unusual, eccentric
Your particular genius
Your capacity to embrace change
The occult, psychic ability
Electricity, computers, astrology, inventions, and people in
   those professions
Earthquakes
Breakdown of structures, habits, old behavioral patterns,
   the end of what no longer works
Revolution

Neptune ♆

Your highest dreams, profound inspiration
Psychic ability, intuition, dreams, the unconscious

Dissolves your sense of reality, confusion, doubt
Illusions, your blind spot
Ego denying
Poetry, fiction, otherworldly art, beauty in its highest form,
    inspired music or art
All forms of escapism: alcoholism, drug addiction, etc.
Narcotics, drugs
Psychics, mediums, poets, saints, martyrs
Hypochondria, accidents by drowning
Places of confinement: prisons, hospitals, nursing homes
The feet, illnesses that are difficult to diagnose

Pluto ♀
Creator and destroyer
Power
People who have power over you and over whom you
    have power
The Mafia
Subversive groups
Metaphorical death
Decay
Profound transformation
Destruction, death, regeneration, rebirth
Witchcraft, black magic
"Higher" occult powers
Atomic power

Moon's Nodes ☊ ☋
The north node ☊ symbolizes the direction you should move toward in this life to evolve spiritually; the south node ☋ symbolizes what is familiar and habitual, what you should release.

Vertex Vx
A point in a chart that symbolizes a destined encounter or experience agreed upon before you were born

The following table lists opposite signs, which are known as oppositions, an aspect discussed in Chapter 5.

OPPOSITE SIGNS

Aries ♈	Libra ♎
Taurus ♉	Scorpio ♏
Gemini ♊	Sagittarius ♐
Cancer ♋	Capricorn ♑
Leo ♌	Aquarius ♒
Virgo ♍	Pisces ♓

4

REAL-LIFE
STORY LINES

*. . . readers don't turn pages to get to the end.
They turn pages to get to the next page.*

—GARY PROVOST

Astrologers who create daily horoscopes use different techniques to arrive at their predictions for the individual sun signs. Let's take a look at two of those techniques.

The first technique involves the use of a horoscope chart. In a natal chart, the structure of the horoscope wheel is set up according to your time of birth, which determines the sign that was rising when you were born. In the blank chart on the next page, the rising or ascendant is the horizontal line just under the numbers 12 and 7. It represents the horizon of the sky. On the left side of that line, jot down **ASC** for ascendant. On the right-hand side of that line, between numbers 6 and 7, jot down **DES** for descendant.

The vertical line that cuts down the center of the chart, between numbers 9 and 10 and numbers 3 and 4, is known as the MC/IC axis. The MC, between numbers 9 and 10, stands for *medium coeli* and is known as the midheaven. It forms the border between the ninth and tenth houses and is the highest point in the chart. The IC,

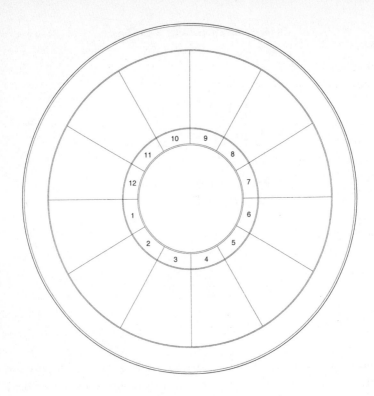

between numbers 3 and 4, stands for *imum coeli* and is the cusp of the fourth house, the "basement" of the chart.

Each of the twelve pieces in that circle symbolizes a specific area of your life. The space just under the ascendant on the left side of the horoscope wheel is the first house. Moving counterclockwise, number the houses sequentially, then jot down key words for the meanings of the houses:

Ascendant. Your physical appearance, your general health, and how others perceive you. It's sometimes referred to as the "mask" because it's the face you wear in public. It's considered to be one of the four "critical" angles of a chart and is superseded in importance only by the sun and the moon. When planets transit any of the four angles of a chart, their impact is usually felt strongly.

First house: Personality. You. Your creative voice. Your early childhood. Physical health and appearance.

Second House: Personal values and material resources. Money—how you earn it, how you spend it, and what you think about it. Your personal possessions. What you value personally. How you meet your financial obligations.

Third house: Communication. Your intellect, how you learn, your siblings and neighbors, reading and writing, how you think and communicate. Short journeys go here.

IC and fourth house: "The basement." Your deepest roots, personal environment, attitudes toward your family, real estate, early childhood conditioning. Mom or her equivalent. Beginnings and endings. Your link to the collective unconscious. This is the another of the four "critical" angles of a horoscope.

Fifth house: Creativity and pleasures. Your children, your love affairs, what brings you pleasure, your creativity. Gambling, financial speculation, risk taking. I also include small animals—pets—here because they bring us pleasure. In the old days of astrology, pets and small animals were placed in the sixth house, as chattel.

Sixth house: Your daily bread. Your daily work environment and your day-to-day health. Your experience of employees and employers. Your skills. Services you perform for others.

Descendant and seventh house: Partnerships. Marriage or any committed relationship. Your partner. Contracts. Open enemies. Business partnerships. Any one-to-one relationship. This is the third "critical" angle of a horoscope.

Eighth house: Your support system. Transformative experiences. Sexuality, death, taxes, inheritances, resources you share with others or that they share with you. Your instincts. With the first and fourth houses, a health house. Metaphysics. Reincarnation. Rebirth.

Ninth house: Your worldview. Your spiritual or religious views, philosophy, publishing and publishers, the judicial system, higher education, foreign travel, cultures, foreign-born people. Your higher mind. Intuition. Long-distance travel.

MC or tenth house: Your profession and career. Your public self. Your creative and professional achievements. Your father or his equivalent. Authority in your life. Your career. Authority and authority figures. Politics and politicians. CEOs. This is the fourth of the "critical" angles in a horoscope.

Eleventh house: Ideals. Peer groups. Social groups. Your aspirations. Your wishes and dreams.

Twelfth house. Personal unconscious. Power you've disowned. Institutions. Hidden enemies. Karma. Psychic abilities. Spies and anything clandestine. Nursing homes, hospitals, mental institutions. Issues brought over from past lives. Suicide. Anything behind the scenes.

DAILY HOROSCOPES

When astrologers create daily horoscopes, which have to apply generally to the twelve signs, they put the sun sign on the horizon, so that it becomes the ascendant. Then they note the transiting planets and their signs for that particular day. Some columnists take special note of the transiting moon, whether it's changing signs or its phase, or whether it's involved in a lunar eclipse. Others look to the position of the planet that rules that sun sign. Then they create their story lines.

To personalize this process (and in lieu of a natal chart), let's say you're a Virgo. On one of the blank horoscope wheels in the back of the book, put Virgo on the ascendant. Then, moving counterclockwise around the chart, put the subsequent signs on each of the cusps. Libra will go on the cusp of the second house, Scorpio on the cusp of the third, Sagittarius on the IC or cusp of the fourth, and so on around the horoscope.

Assume you're born on September 19. You know that the Virgo cycle runs from August 24 to September 22 and that the sun moves about 1 degree a day, so a birth on the 19th means that your sun sign is about 26 degrees Virgo. Assume that the cusp of each house in the horoscope is 26 degrees. That means that as you're going around the chart, putting the sign on each cusp, 26 Virgo will go on the ascendant; 26 Libra on the cusp of the first house, 26 Scorpio on the cusp of the third, and on around the chart. This is called an equal house system. In a natal chart, the degrees on each house cusp vary according to the time you're born, but the equal house system is fine for our purposes.

You want to know what's coming up for you on January 1, 2004. So what do you look for first? Since Virgo is ruled by Mercury, start there. In the Mercury ephemeris at the back of this book (pages 257–271), the positions for that planet are listed daily for five years. On January 1, 2004, the entry for Mercury is 01-01-2004,28°SgRx. Mercury is at 28 degrees Sagittarius and is moving retrograde (Rx). Since it's at 28 degrees and the cusps of your houses are at 26 degrees, place Mercury just inside the fourth house, close to the cusp (IC).

By January 7, Mercury is at 26 degrees Sagittarius and the symbol for retrograde motion is no longer there. That means Mercury is now direct or moving forward once more through the zodiac, so until it goes retrograde again, it will continue to move counterclockwise through the fourth house and into the fifth.

Right now, you've got quite a bit of information about some of the story lines that may evolve on January 1, 2004. Glance back at the table on pages 38–39 to refresh your memory about the areas that Mercury rules. One of the things you can expect for that day is news concerning any of the areas under Mercury rule: communication, your mind, contracts, siblings and relatives, travel, your daily routine. To some extent, the *type* of news depends on your focus in life and what you do for a living. If you're a writer or a teacher, perhaps a new contract is in the offing. If you're an editor, you may have manuscripts that don't come in on time or snafus in the production of a book or books.

Take a look at the earlier section on houses, starting on page 44. The fourth house rules your deepest roots, Mom or her equivalent, your personal environment, anything related to your home. This broadens the interpretation somewhat. Mercury in the fourth house may relate to a visit to your mother or your childhood home, thoughts about rearranging your home (or home office) in some way, or communication related to your home and personal environment.

However, in early January, Mercury is retrograde. That means that if you're going to be traveling, you can expect delays, schedule changes, snafus. This isn't always negative, by the way. Under one Mercury retrograde, my family and I elected to be bumped from an overbooked flight and got three free tickets that were good for a year. Under a Mercury retrograde, it's best not to sign any contracts. But if you have to, make sure you read the fine print very carefully. Confirm and reconfirm any changes in schedules.

Mercury retrograde, especially when you're a Gemini or a Virgo, can be a strange time. The annoyances can range from problems with computers, appliances, cars and travel plans, siblings and relatives, to unexpected revisions on books and contracts, to simple misunderstandings. During one Mercury retrograde in her fourth house (the home), a friend had trouble with all her appliances and electronics. One of my astrologer friends swears that if you travel somewhere under a Mercury retro, you'll be returning when Mercury is direct. So just keep all that in mind, Virgo, as you're going through your ephemeris.

Now look for planets that might be in Virgo. There's just one, the best one—Jupiter. Break out the champagne, celebrate! You're in for a wonderful ride that happens once every twelve years and lasts about a year, a Jupiter conjunction with your sun. In fact, Jupiter goes into Virgo around August 26, 2003, and stays there until around September 25, 2004. On January 1, 2004, Jupiter is at 18 degrees Virgo, approaching a direct hit on your sun. According to the horoscope we've set up, with the ascendant at 26 degrees Virgo, Jupiter at 18 degrees goes into the twelfth house.

Jupiter, like every planet except for the sun and the moon, also goes retrograde periodically and usually remains retrograde for about four months. In the ephemeris, you'll see that it goes retrograde on January 3, 2004, and continues to move that way until early May 2004. On May 5, it begins to go direct once more at 8 degrees Virgo.

Take a look at the meanings for the twelfth house, then glance at pages 39–40 to find the areas that Jupiter rules. During the period that Jupiter is in the twelfth house, you'll experience expansion and luck through anything that is behind the scenes. Since it's retrograde, its expansiveness will be directed inward. Your psychic abilities may blossom. You may experience an expansion in your beliefs and worldview or your spirituality. You may find that you're more interested in foreign cultures and people and may even travel to another country, but the journey may be spiritual rather than just a trip or a vacation. Since Jupiter also rules creativity, publishing, the judicial system, and higher education, you may be successful in some creative endeavor in one of those areas.

As Jupiter approaches the 26 degrees of the Virgo ascendant set up in the horoscope, you'll become more expansive, more outgoing, more social and optimistic. Since the ascendant also symbolizes how other people see you, you'll find that other people perceive you as lucky and successful. The ascendant also governs your physical appearance, and with Jupiter approaching your ascendant, the planet's expansiveness can translate quite literally into an expansion of your waistline!

In a transit to one of the four critical angles, you'll feel the planetary energy when it's within 5 degrees of the degree on that angle. Look in the ephemeris to find when Jupiter will be about 21 degrees Virgo. On August 14, 2004, Jupiter is at 21 degrees Virgo. On September 7, 2004, it makes a direct hit on your Virgo sun at 26 degrees Virgo, and on October 6, it will be at 2 degrees Libra. This means that you'll feel the greatest impact of this transit between mid-August and early October. A Jupiter conjunction to your sun brings expansion, luck, and success in all areas governed by either your sun sign or Jupiter or both. However, you may find that money goes out as fast as it comes in or that some other area of your life expands in an undesirable or unexpected way.

The next thing you want to check is the position of the transiting sun for January 1, 2004. It's in Capricorn, a fellow earth sign, a cycle that begins on December 22 and ends on January 19. You know that the sun travels about 1 degree a day, so on January 1, it should be 9 or 10 degrees Capricorn. Capricorn is on the cusp of the fifth house in the chart you're using, but because we're using an equal house chart, the degree on the fifth house is 26. So the 9- or 10-degree Capricorn sun goes into the fourth house, and toward the end of the Capricorn cycle, it will be moving into the fifth.

With the transiting sun in your fourth house, you should be feeling pretty good about things in general. Issues with men or authority figures may come up. Your health should be good, since the fourth house is often involved in health issues. The story line with the transiting sun is that whatever house it touches increases your health and vigor as it pertains to the issues of that house. As the transiting Capricorn sun makes its way toward your fifth house of creativity and kids, those areas of your life will be highlighted.

What about the transiting moon? It moves so quickly that its effects are felt, at most, for a couple of hours. However, it changes signs every two and a half days and when it goes into your sign, you will feel either more emotionally invigorated or more sensitive and vulnerable. Astrologers also use the changing phases of the moon, especially the new moon and full moon phases, in predictions. During a transiting new moon, you "sow seeds," beginning things that you harvest about two weeks later, during the full moon phase.

Appendix A contains an ephemeris for every new moon between 2003 and 2008. About two weeks after each of those days is a full moon. You might consider tracking its impact on your chart for a couple of months.

Since water signs are compatible with Virgo's earth element, look for any planets in water signs on January 1, 2004. You'll find two: Saturn in Cancer and Uranus in Pisces. On January 1, 2004, Saturn is at 9 degrees Cancer, and it's retrograde. The eleventh house has Cancer on the cusp. But since Saturn is at only 9 degrees, place it in your tenth house. Uranus is at 0 degrees Pisces, so it will go in your sixth house. Now you've got even more information at your fingertips. With Saturn moving retrograde through your tenth house of profession and careers, the story line until March 7, 2004, when it goes direct again, is likely to be one of increased responsibility. You have to be more disciplined in your profession and may be called on to do more than your share of the work. But you're building foundations for the future and, somehow, that will make it more worthwhile.

Even when Saturn begins to move direct, its movement is so

slow—about 1 degree a month—that it won't reach the degree of your Virgo sun until early October 2004. You'll feel its impact most as it approaches your sun to within 5 degrees. Sometimes, this Saturn/sun transit feels as if you're so burdened you have no idea how you're going to get up in the morning. But other times, it brings utter and total glory, a culmination of everything you've worked for.

What about Uranus? If you look back at the table on pages 38–41, you'll see that Uranus is about sudden, unexpected change, genius, new insights. Maybe you get fired from a job that you hated and were reluctant to leave because of the regular paycheck. But on the other side of that event, you find your true passion. That's how Uranus works. It knocks everything down, then provides the tools for you to rebuild something even better out of the rubble.

It's also a good idea to look for planets in signs that have the same quality as yours. Since Virgo is a mutable sign, you're looking for planets in other mutable signs: Gemini, Sagittarius, and Pisces. We already mentioned Pisces, there aren't any planets in Gemini for the rest of that month, but Pluto is in Sagittarius at 20 degrees. Sagittarius is found on the cusp of the ninth house in our example, but because it's at 20 degrees, place it in the eighth house. Now look at the meanings for Pluto on page 41 and at the meanings for the eighth house. At the very least, you can expect some sort of deep change in your support system and shared finances.

By looking at transits for January 1, 2004, you now have a pretty clear idea about events, situations, and people who may play a part in that day's story line.

Now let's see how transits play out with a natal chart. In Appendix C is a natal chart for a Virgo writer born on September 19, 1945. Using the same transits, place the planets for January 1, 2004, outside the horoscope wheel, in their respective houses. Start with the position of the transiting sun for that date (10 degrees Capricorn) and place in the third hour of the writer's natal chart. Then proceed in the same way with the rest of the transiting planets.

WHAT'S MY LINE?: TRANSITS
TO THE WRITER'S NATAL CHART

The chart on page 323 is the writer's actual natal chart. Keep it handy as you go through this section. Her Virgo sun at 26♍16 is in the twelfth house. Her Aquarius moon at 25♒03 lies in the fifth house. Libra is her ascendant at 18 degrees 56 minutes. Immediately, you see that any fast-moving planet that hits her sun will be hitting her ascendant shortly afterward. Notice that Capricorn is on the cusp of her fourth house (IC) at 21♑47, that Aries is on the cusp of her seventh house or descendant at 18♈56, and that the cusp of her tenth house (MC) is in Cancer at 21♋47.

We already know that in early January, Jupiter in Virgo is at 18 degrees, getting ready to go into the writer's twelfth house. It's moving retrograde, though, so it will be crossing back and forth over the twelfth house cusp until May 2004. This indicates that the writer will enjoy Jupiter's luck in two areas of her life: the wishes and dreams of the eleventh house and the personal unconscious of the twelfth house. Some of the luck will come to her through her peer group—other writers and people in publishing (which Jupiter rules). Since Jupiter also rules our worldview and spiritual beliefs, it's likely she will experience an expansion in this area.

During this Jupiter transit, she will benefit from any work that she does behind the scenes. As both a fiction and a nonfiction writer, this woman may expand creatively by using large spiritual themes in her books. She will be able to tap easily into her personal unconscious for whatever she needs creatively during this period. There may be serendipitous experiences related to eleventh and twelfth house affairs that she can use in her writing.

In January 2004, Jupiter is close enough to her Mercury in Virgo in the eleventh house (☿ 15♍25) that she can expect expansiveness and luck in everything related to communication. Mercury rules not only her sun sign, it also rules what she does for a living. This will be a great creative time for her. She will speak and write with great eloquence. Mercury, however, will be retrograde for part of that period (and for about two weeks in December 2003), which points to revisions in her writing and perhaps some travel related to her writing.

As Jupiter gets within 5 degrees of her sun in mid-August 2004, her physical energy increases, her optimism flourishes, and, if she doesn't watch what she eats, she may gain weight, too. What's beautiful about her chart is that she feels the influence of transiting Jupiter for quite a while because she has Jupiter and Neptune in Libra in that twelfth house, and they're in the same degree. Neptune relates to imagination, deep inspiration, and also to fiction, so she can expect to tap into new areas and more profound depths in her fiction writing at this time.

When Jupiter conjuncts itself in a natal chart, which it does every twelve years, it's called a Jupiter return. The actual time when the transit is exact is relatively brief, just several days, but as it gets within 5 degrees of the natal Jupiter, the impact can be tremendous. Because the transiting Jupiter hits her natal Neptune and Jupiter simultaneously, she should be prepared to take full advantage of the benefits this transit will bring. Success, an expansion in the way other people perceive her, luck, and serendipitous experiences.

Jupiter will keep moving toward her Libra ascendant through early February 2005, when it then goes retrograde. In early June 2005, it goes direct at 8 degrees Libra. Even though it doesn't go back far enough for a direct hit on her natal Jupiter and Neptune, it gets close enough so that she may revisit some of the same story lines that she experienced in October 2004. By late August and early September of 2005, Jupiter is making another hit on her ascendant. This is like a cosmic gift, particularly because this woman is very aware of the patterns that operate in her life.

About the same time that Jupiter is crossing back and forth between her eleventh and twelfth houses, Saturn will be approaching the same position it is in her natal chart—22 degrees Cancer. This is known as a Saturn return and is always an important astrological event. It happens about every twenty-nine to thirty years, and whether its impact is positive or negative depends on how you've been living your life. Based just on Jupiter and Saturn's transits through the fall of 2004, this writer has a major year in store for her, filled with surprises, serendipitous experiences, and success related to her career.

Uranus in Pisces will be transiting her fifth house on January 1, 2004. Since Uranus is such a slow-moving planet, it will be in her fifth house until April 2008, beyond the scope of this book. Since the cusp of her fifth house is 20 degrees and 47 minutes Aquarius (20≈47), the planet actually entered the fifth house in February 2001, so she's been feeling its impact for some time. It's likely that her approach to writing during this transit has undergone dramatic and perhaps profound change and will continue to do so, surprising even her. There may be professional recognition during this time and financial rewards. She may experience upheavals and changes related to her children, the things she does for pleasure, and everything related to her creativity.

Looking at the possible story lines for the single day January 1, 2004, actually provides evolving story lines over a nine-month period. The writer now has specific target dates that she can prepare for so that she can take maximum advantage of the opportunities that will come about.

ACTIVITY

Planets in the Horoscope Wheel

Practice finding daily narratives in your own life, following the instructions below and using one of the blank charts in Appendix C.

1. Pick a date that's coming up in the near future.
2. Using one of the blank charts at the back of this book, put your natal sun sign and degree on the ascendant or rising.
3. Go counterclockwise around the chart and place the subsequent signs on the house cusps.

4. Find the house position of the planet that rules your sun sign (refer to the table on page 19).

5. Look for planets that are in the same sign as your natal sun for the date you selected. If there aren't any planets in that sign, then look for planets in compatible signs. If you're an air sign, for example, then you would look for planets in other air signs or in fire signs.

6. Number the houses and jot a note to yourself about the meaning of each house. The first house, for instance, could be tagged simply as *Self*, the second as *$*.

7. Use the planetary meanings on pages 38–41, and the meanings of the houses to come up with each story line.

8. Place the other planets in their respective houses, according to their sign and degree for the day you've selected. Expand your story lines.

9. Check the ephemeris for each planet to see how long the impact of that planet's influence is going to last. The slower-moving planets will have the longest effect.

10. Pinpoint dates that look beneficial and mark them on your calendar.

5

DEEPER LAYERS

*You won't be aware of your body coming into
contact with inanimate objects.
You will walk, stand, sit, brush against them,
but will feel nothing. Don't worry.
The very fact that you can move without
sensation is half the wonder.*

—DAPHNE DU MAURIER,
HOUSE ON THE STRAND

As the transiting planets make their solitary journeys through the sky, they form angles to your sun (and to the planets in your natal chart) called aspects. Each aspect creates a distinct kind of energy and story line.

Five major aspects are used in this book for determining story lines. The conjunction ☌ occurs when two or more planets occupy the same sign and degree; the opposition ☍ is when two or more planets are 180 degrees or six signs apart; a square ☐ occurs when two or more planets are 90 degrees or three signs apart; the sextile ✶ happens when planets are two signs or 60 degrees apart; and the trine △ is the name given to planets that are four signs or 120 degrees apart. Aspects add depth and subplots to your story lines.

The table below provides a quick reference to the aspects for each sign.

SO WHAT'S IT ALL MEAN?

When astrologers calculate aspects, they allow themselves orbs, or a certain latitude of degrees. A square, for example, is a 90-degree angle between two or more planets. But astrologers allow from 3 to 5 degrees on either side of that exact square, particularly when the aspect is being made to the sun or moon.

The only aspect in this list is the quincunx, for which I use a 1-degree orb. It's considered a less important aspect, so it wasn't included in the table.

The Conjunction: 0°, same sign, fusion and power

Fusion is what happens when diverse elements merge into a unified whole. The energy of all the elements become greater. In astrology, this is known as a conjunction.

A conjunction of two or more planets, whether in a natal chart or through transits, *intensifies and focuses* the combined energies. Take another look at the writer's chart on page 323. In the twelfth house, her Neptune and Jupiter (♆ ♃) are exactly conjunct at 5 degrees Libra. This combination expands (Jupiter) her imagination (Neptune) and gives her a distinctive spiritual (Jupiter) and idealistic (Neptune) bent. These qualities are with her throughout her life. But if transiting Jupiter were conjuncting her natal Neptune, these qualities would be most noticeable when Jupiter was exactly at 5 degrees Libra or within 5 degrees on either side of it.

Conjunctions are considered beneficial. By transit, they signal a new phase or cycle in a person's life and usher in new opportunities and individuals who help make things happen.

Under conjunctions, there are cycles known as returns when a

Aspects

SIGN	CONJUNCTION ☌	OPPOSITION ☍	SQUARE □	SEXTILE ✳	TRINE △
Aries	Aries	Libra	Cancer, Capricorn	Gemini, Aquarius	Leo, Sagittarius
Taurus	Taurus	Scorpio	Leo, Aquarius	Cancer, Pisces	Virgo, Capricorn
Gemini	Gemini	Sagittarius	Virgo, Pisces	Leo, Aries	Libra, Aquarius
Cancer	Cancer	Capricorn	Aries, Libra	Virgo, Taurus	Scorpio, Pisces
Leo	Leo	Aquarius	Scorpio, Taurus	Libra, Gemini	Aries, Sagittarius
Virgo	Virgo	Pisces	Gemini, Sagittarius	Scorpio, Cancer	Taurus, Capricorn
Libra	Libra	Aries	Cancer, Capricorn	Leo, Sagittarius	Aquarius, Gemini
Scorpio	Scorpio	Taurus	Leo, Aquarius,	Capricorn, Virgo	Cancer, Pisces,
Sagittarius	Sagittarius	Gemini	Virgo, Pisces	Aquarius, Libra	Leo, Aries
Capricorn	Capricorn	Cancer	Aries, Libra	Scorpio, Pisces	Virgo, Taurus
Aquarius	Aquarius	Leo	Scorpio, Taurus	Aries, Sagittarius	Libra, Gemini
Pisces	Pisces	Virgo	Gemini, Sagittarius	Taurus, Capricorn	Scorpio, Cancer

transiting planet returns to the position it held when you were born. In other words, a transiting planet conjuncts its natal position. The most important returns are the Jupiter return, a twelve-year-cycle, and a Saturn return, a twenty-nine- to thirty-year cycle. Under a Jupiter return, your life expands tremendously in some area. Opportunities flow into your life, you lay new groundwork, start new projects, make new friends. During this return, people get married, start a family, move to larger homes, start new professions and careers. So mark the years twelve, twenty-four, thirty-six, forty-eight, sixty, and onward.

The first Saturn return happens between the ages of twenty-six and thirty, and the second occurs between the ages of fifty-four and sixty-two. During the first, people get married or divorced, have children, change jobs or lose jobs, find new career paths, go back to school or graduate from school. In other words, something in the external world occurs that causes you to alter your personal course. It's often a time of introspection and review, where you look back to see what you have achieved and what you would like to achieve from this point forward. Although good things *do* happen during the first Saturn return, this return isn't a feel-good transit overall. Instead of placing blame, however, think of it as the reality you have created according to our deepest beliefs. Change the beliefs and go forward.

The second Saturn return encompasses the same themes of introspection and review. If you learned whatever you were supposed to learn during your first Saturn return, then the second return can be a period of culmination and recognition.

The Sextile: 60°, two signs apart, ease and harmony

In the writer's chart on page 323, her sun is in Virgo in the twelfth house. Her Saturn (♄) is in Cancer (♋) in the tenth house. Her sun and Saturn are sextile to each other.

In a natal chart, a sextile suggests ease between the planetary energies and indicates a buffer against instability. The sextile between the writer's sun and Saturn tells us that although her ambition (Saturn) is strong, it won't ever overshadow everything else in her life. She plans carefully and structures her life so that all things are balanced.

A transiting sextile also means ease and often provides opportunities for positive group interaction and a chance to take the initiative. It's also a good time to review changes you've made in particular areas of your life and to figure out how to fine-tune these changes so that you can achieve what you really want. Your inner and outer world tend to flow seamlessly together because you don't encounter outside resistance.

Sextiles are considered beneficial. They don't require much from you, though, so they don't strengthen areas where you are weak. By being alert for their approach, you can take advantage of them.

Square: 90°, three signs apart, friction and challenges

Take another look at the writer's chart. She has an almost exact square between Mars (♂) in the ninth house and Jupiter (♃) and Neptune (♆) in the twelfth. Even though this book deals primarily with transits to the sun, what story line would you assign to this square?

You know that Mars represents physical and sexual energy, as well as the capacity for aggression, and that the ninth house symbolizes, among other things, publishing and your worldview. Jupiter represents luck and expansion, and the twelfth house symbolizes institutions, what goes on behind the scenes. Even if we didn't know that this woman is a writer, one possible story line for this natal square might be: *You funnel enormous energy into your spiritual beliefs and benefit from anything done behind the scenes. You express your idealism as well as your spirituality through your creative endeavors.*

Transiting squares create just as much friction as natal squares, but they last only for the period of the transit. When your sun is hit by a transiting square from one of the slow-moving planets, though, it can feel like a lifetime! Transiting squares rarely feel good. They tend to attract people and circumstances into your life that force you to stand up for what you believe or to prove yourself in some way. They demand that you examine some area in your life that is uncomfortable to look at. However, *squares often create events.* There's a good example of this in the Chapter 17.

Yes, squares are challenging and create a deep, sometimes painful itch for change in some area of your life. But, hey, transiting squares build character!

Trines, 120°, four signs apart, inner harmony and balance

This is another feel-good aspect. Our writer has one very close trine, between her Uranus (♅) in her tenth house and her Libra ascendant. Notice that they are both in air signs—Gemini and Uranus—and lie four signs apart (counting the ninth house as the first and moving counterclockwise to the ascendant).

In a natal chart, a trine is a point of inner ease and balance, a place where things work smoothly and effortlessly. Think of trines as magnetic attractors—they attract what you need, when you need it, without any effort on your part. Like squares, they don't do much to build character and if there are too many of them, you may spend your life in a hammock sipping margaritas. But they sure feel good.

In transits, a trine works much the same way. The advantage to knowing when you're going to experience a transiting trine to your sun is that you can prepare for this window of immense opportunity and creative expansion. Transiting trines are good times to take vacations and get away for a while to enjoy the lack of stress.

Quincunx, 150°, five signs apart, adjustment

Astrologers are somewhat divided on whether this is a major or minor aspect. It isn't referred to very often in this book, but I mention it so that you will have the option of looking for it. It lies roughly five signs apart. In the writer's chart, the easiest Quincunx to spot is between the sun and the moon. The aspect indicates that an adjustment of some kind is called for. It sometimes pertains to health issues or an adjustment in your attitude or thinking. The orb to use is small, 1 or 2 degrees.

Oppositions, 180°, six signs apart, confrontation and culmination

This aspect is nearly as easy to spot as a conjunction. In the writer's chart, her Aquarius moon in the fifth house forms a nearly exact opposition with her Venus in Leo in the eleventh house. Sometimes, a certain extravagance goes along with this opposition in a natal chart. There may be mother issues (the writer's moon) or emotional difficulties with a sister or some other woman who is close to the individual. It nearly always involves relationships.

In transits, oppositions often involve confrontations with other people that probably won't ever be resolved to your satisfaction without some intense inner work. Change comes about because of self-awareness. Some type of culmination is likely. Oppositions don't feel too good, either. But exciting change and movement can come about during transiting oppositions. In fact, if you see an opposition approaching your sun, preparation for it is nine-tenths of the battle.

ACTIVITY

Using What You Know

Given what you know now, you should be able to come up with plots and subplots for your overall story line. This is fun to do with a partner or group, too, where someone else in the group does your story lines and vice versa.

Use one of the blank charts in the back of the book and put your sun sign and its degree on the ascendant, just as you did before. Move counterclockwise around the horoscope and fill in the rest of the signs on the cusps of the houses.

Now pick a date and turn to Appendix A. Begin with the ephemeris for Pluto, the slowest-moving planet, and look up the date you've selected. Place it in the appropriate house. Work your way forward through each of the planets and place them in their appropriate houses. Which planets are making aspects to your sun sign on the ascendant? Use the chart below to record what you find and create a story line to go with each aspect for the date you've selected.

You can also do this with your partner or group, making up story lines for each other. This is a terrific way to deepen your understanding of emerging story lines.

My Story Lines for (date) _____

Conjunction to my sun by (planet): _____

Possible story lines:

_____

_____

_____

Sextiles to my sun by (planet): _____

Possible story lines:

_____

_____

_____

Squares to my sun by (planet): _____

Possible story lines:

_____

_____

_____

Trines to my sun by (planet): _____

Possible story lines:

_____

_____

_____

Oppositions to my Sun by (planet): _____

Possible story lines:

_____

_____

_____

MULTIPLE HITS

As you begin to track transits to your Sun, you'll find that sometimes you're being hit by more than one transiting planet. This can be especially difficult when one of those transits involves an outer planet—Saturn, Uranus, Neptune, or Pluto—that goes retrograde in your Sun sign, then moves forward again. When this happens, it's possible for your sun to be hit as many as three times. A triple transit.

Debbie, a Taurus friend, was hit by a Uranus transit three times. During the first hit, the people who lived in the downstairs apartment got a karaoke machine and the noise reverberated through the floor of her apartment at all hours of the day and night. She developed a deep intolerance to noise, her sleep was constantly disrupted, and she began to feel physically ill. "I would feel dizzy all the time, my heart raced, I really believed there was something seriously wrong with me." Her doctor ran numerous tests, but didn't find anything physically wrong with her.

The noise level in her apartment became intolerable. She decided to move and since her family was in Florida, she left her job and New York City and headed south. This move coincided with a second hit from Uranus.

During the third hit, she had to confront the noise issue again, but this time it wasn't as bad and, besides, there were other things going on. Her father was ill and died under Uranus's third hit.

This process unfolded over a lengthy period of time because Uranus moves so slowly. The first hit was the beginning of a process— her sensitivity to sound that would force her to move. The second hit was a culmination of what started during the first transit—the actual move. The second transit forced her to deal with the specific problem or issue. During the third transit, noise was still an issue, but because she had dealt with it under the second transit, it wasn't as bad. Since the Sun often represents the father or an important male figure in a woman's life, the death of her father was one *possible* story line when Uranus hit her Sun for the third time.

In Debbie's case, the triple transit was a square to her Sun. This doesn't mean that every Uranus square to your Sun will result in a move, the death of a parent, or a change in jobs. But these are three possible story lines to consider for a transiting Uranus square to your Sun. Uranus's bottom line, after all, is to shake up the status quo.

A LITTLE KNOWLEDGE

Remember the adage about a little knowledge being a dangerous thing? It's certainly true with astrology. There you are, flipping through one ephemeris after another, and you notice that during a particular week or month, you'll have—*gasp*—four planets hitting your sun. Before you panic, keep in mind that the ways transits manifest themselves have everything to do with how you've been living your life.

Even if you have a lot of knowledge about astrology and see potentially difficult transits coming up, it's tough not to panic. One astrologer friend was going through a divorce and had to have a hysterectomy. She cast multiple charts, looking for the best time to have the surgery, and suddenly saw numerous other potential problems. She came up with every dire scenario from death to permanent coma to abject poverty. Instead, her divorce was amicable, her surgery turned out fine, and then she sold four books and fell in love.

We create our lives from moment to moment, working from our deepest beliefs. When our beliefs change, our reality changes. Astrology's role in this process, especially predictive astrology (or any other predictive system) is to show us *potential.* Maybe all the terrible story lines the astrologer saw were distinct possibilities and frightened her so deeply that her beliefs changed, so the potential story lines unfolded much differently and far more positively than she had foreseen.

As you become more deeply involved in predictive astrology, the best course is to stick to the most basic, simplest story lines. If Pluto and Saturn are going to be hitting your sun next month, then you know that some type of transformation (Pluto) is going to occur. It may involve your father or a fatherlike figure or your attitudes toward authority (Saturn), and it's definitely going to impact your essence (the sun) in a profound way. But it isn't necessarily *negative.* It doesn't mean your father is going to die. It doesn't mean your life is going to collapse. It may mean you're going to find the work you were meant to do, a soulmate who is older than you are, and that your life is finally going to be on track.

In the next chapter, we're going to cover the possible aspects that the planets can make to your sun, what those story lines may be, and how you can make the most of them. In the sun sign sections that follow, you'll have a chance to put all the information to use for your particular sign. The activities are designed to use by yourself or with a partner or group. As you move through the activities, allow your intuition to guide you. Astrology, after all, is a symbolic language, the language of the soul.

6

CONTACTS WITH YOUR SUN SIGN

Betty put the binoculars up to her eyes
and focused carefully.
What they were about to see was to
change their lives forever, and as some observers
claim, change the course of the history of the world.

—JOHN G. FULLER, *THE INTERRUPTED JOURNEY:*
TWO LOST HOURS ABOARD A FLYING SAUCER

This isn't a chapter about alien contact. But with some of these transits, you may feel as if you've been thrust into an alien world, arriving with nothing more than the clothes on your back and a lifetime of memories. Other transits will feel more familiar, more comfortable. But with any transit to your sun the heart of its impact on your life depends to a great extent on how *you* react to it, whether *you* use its energy to *your* advantage or whether it uses you.

As discussed in the previous chapter, positive contacts to your sun sign are the *conjunction* (when a planet is in your sign), the *sextile* (when a planet is forming a 60-degree angle to your sun or is two signs from it), and the *trine* (when a planet forms a 120-degree angle to your sun or is four signs from it). The challenging contacts are the *square* (90 degrees or three signs from your sun) and the *opposition* (180 degrees or opposite your sun). As you read through these descriptions and story lines, it will be helpful to refer to the table on page 58, where the aspects for each sign are delineated. You also may want to use some of the blank charts in the back of the book so you can visualize each of these aspects.

In the sun sign sections in Part Two, many of these aspects are explored in depth, through stories and anecdotes.

MOON TRANSITS

Story lines: *Intuition, the unconscious, emotions. Mother issues, home. Contact with people you've known in other lives. Intuitive ability.*
Movies/fiction: The Gift; Shattered Moon *by Kate Green*, The Family Tree *by Sheri S. Tepper*, Divine Secrets of the Ya-Ya Sisterhood *by Rebecca Wells*

The moon moves so quickly that you probably won't feel every transit to your sun. The exception may be Cancer, ruled by the moon. In any case, the moon to watch for is the one that's conjunct your sun sign, and the new moon, the best time to start new projects and to sow seeds for the next month.

Positive Moon/Sun Contacts

Story lines: *Home life is highlighted. Think: Mom or her equivalent, old gunk rising to the surface, harmonious relationships with women, equilibrium between inner and outer selves.*

For the conjunction, sextile and trine, you feel pretty good about yourself and life in general. Any of these contacts are excellent times for dream work and plundering your unconscious. Your home life and personal space are emphasized in some way, and you may be more emotional or sensitive than usual. Your inner and outer lives seem to be in sync. Your nurturing talents—how you nurture and mother others or how you nurture yourself—come to the forefront. Generally, though, these contacts are pleasant. Any of them can bring people into your life whom you have known in previous lives.

Challenging Moon/Sun Contacts

Story lines: *Unconscious habits and behavioral patterns surface. Emotional issues you've been avoiding now must be dealt with.*

When the squares and oppositions are difficult, you may take solace in the fact that they last, at the most, only a couple of days. Confrontations with bosses and employers are likely; tensions that have been building at home now burst. Your inner and outer selves don't feel in sync. Just remember: *You* create your reality through your deepest beliefs, so if things happen that you dislike, get to the root of the belief that has caused the problem.

MERCURY TRANSITS

Story lines: *Communication, siblings, relatives, neighbors. Your intellect. Faxes, E-mails, phone calls crowd your days.*
Movies/fiction: You've Got Mail, Sleepless in Seattle; Gravity *by Tess Gerritsen*

Mercury transits affect everyone but are of special interest to Geminis and Virgos. Use these transits to become more conscious of how you communicate and how you think on a daily level, and to become aware of how you fill your day. When dealing with Mercury transits, always check whether Mercury is retrograde.

Positive Mercury/Sun Contacts

Story lines: *Heightened communication skills. Sharp mind. Restlessness. Travel. Learning. Favorable for group work.*

Any of the positive contacts are great for taking workshops, seminars, or classes. The sextile is especially beneficial for any kind of group work, and with the trine, your inner and outer selves work well together.

Under any of these contacts, your mind is sharp, eager to absorb. There's a lot of running around, calls to return, faxes to answer, E-mails to read. When Mercury is retrograde during the positive contacts, things get a bit more frantic. You run run run until you drop, you revise and refurbish, you feel mentally exhausted when you fall into bed at night. If possible, don't negotiate or sign contracts under a Mercury retrograde. If you travel, check and recheck your plans and reservations.

If you're a Gemini or a Virgo, take time for yourself. Chill out. Get a lot of sleep. Sounds like advice from your mother, doesn't it?

Challenging Mercury/Sun Contacts

Story lines: Don't go looking for trouble. Possible confrontations with authority. Keep your own counsel. A test.

Most squares are a test, and most oppositions involve some sort of turbulence. With challenging Mercury transits, the test and the turbulence focus on your communication skills. Your best way to navigate the challenging contacts is to think before you speak. In fact, if you can take a couple days off work, you will benefit tremendously and avoid some of the hassles of this transit.

If that isn't possible, be aware that a square or an opposition can get you into trouble by speaking out before you think about what you're saying. Or you may be so intent on saying what you have to say that you really aren't listening to what anyone else is saying.

VENUS TRANSITS

Story lines: Romance, the arts and creativity, women. Love in all of its mystery and intrigue. Parties, socializing, friends.
Movies/fiction: Sleepless in Seattle, Titanic; Love Story *by Erich Segal,* Bridges of Madison County *by Robert James Waller,* Old Yeller *by Fred Gipson.*

This one is a no-brainer. Venus transits, even those that are "challenging," are pleasant. The big drawback is that you may not feel like doing anything except stealing off with your significant other for a candlelit dinner and the promise of terrific sex afterward. Venus transits also often bring animals into our lives that we grow to love as much as or more than we love other human beings. Venus transits should be of particular interest to Taurus and Libra, the signs it rules.

Positive Venus/Sun Contacts

Story lines: Easy flow of creative ideas. Stars in your eyes. Excellent for interviews, applying for loans, partying with friends. Life is fun but a bit shallow.

Venus transits are a break from the routine. If you're an introvert by nature, this is the time to get out and have fun. If you're an extrovert, Venus transits give you the excuse to get together with friends and party. The positive contacts are also excellent times to do some creative brainstorming as long as you understand that you may not feel like doing the actual creating. That's okay, too. Just have a journal handy. Keep track of your ideas so you can implement them during a Mars transit, when work and productivity will come to the forefront.

Challenging Venus/Sun Contacts

Story lines: Social activities. The arts. Lack of motivation. Excess.

Venus squares and oppositions aren't all that challenging. Your best bet is to take a vacation or a long weekend with your significant other or even with friends. If getting away isn't possible, indulge yourself in something you really enjoy: a movie, a good book, Internet exploration, even a hot, relaxing bath. Excess and lack of motivation may dog you through the challenging transits, but if you're aware that a square or an opposition is coming up, you can practice moderation before the transit arrives. You may also want to schedule a visit to an art museum, always a good thing to do under any Venus transit.

MARS TRANSITS

Story lines: Individuality and physical energy are heightened. Assertiveness, self-confidence, restlessness. I can do anything.

Movies/fiction: Gladiator, Spartacus, Saving Private Ryan; A Kiss Before Dying *by Ira Levin*

These transits should be of special interest to Aries, ruled by Mars, and to Scorpio, coruled by Mars. They invariably highlight your physical and sexual energy, your temper, your capacity for risk, your aggression, and your capacity for action.

Positive Mars/Sun Contacts

Story lines: *High energy, volatile disposition, group work, confrontation with bosses or other authority figures.*

You may be feeling so cocky during the conjunction that you sabotage yourself. Even though you're filled with self-confidence right now and believe absolutely in what you believe and what you're doing, being too forceful with others about your viewpoint will only turn them off.

During the sextile, you get along well with groups or in a group setting. Your energy, like your health, is good and you feel as if you can take on anything and achieve it. Better yet, you're right. Opportunities come up during both the sextile and the trine. If you seize them, they bear fruit later. You're able to strategize now and are clear about your goals.

Challenging Mars/Sun Contacts

Story lines: *Tests your individuality and your ability to stand up for yourself. Irritability, anger. Confrontations.*

Mars squares and oppositions sometimes feel as if you permanently get up on the wrong side of the bed. You may be irritable and aggressive, short-tempered, and not especially pleasant to be around. You may have to stand up for yourself or defend some pet project or endeavor in which you're involved. Tread carefully and be aware of the kind of energy these challenging aspects bring.

The opposition can bring you into serious conflict with bosses or authority figures, or it can result in a triumphant culmination of something you've been working on for some time. To a great extent, the expression of this transit depends on where you are within yourself.

JUPITER TRANSITS

Story lines: Expansion, luck, success, creativity. A "feel good" transit.
Movies/fiction: Sliding Doors; Memoirs of a Geisha by Arthur S. Golden, This Perfect Day by Ira Levin, Song of Kali by Dan Simmons.

What's there not to like about a Jupiter transit? Like transits of Venus, even the challenging ones aren't very challenging. Also like Venus transits, the biggest drawbacks are excess—too much of a good thing?—and not much motivation. That said, think of Jupiter transits as gifts and the universe's way of fortifying us for the very challenging Saturn transits. However, these transits, as good as they are, sometimes bring confrontation with authority, bureaucracy, and our own fears.

I include *This Perfect Day* under Jupiter transits because it's about a perfectly "Jupiter" idea—life in a so-called utopian society. *Song of Kali* is here because of its depiction of foreign cultures and beliefs.

Positive Jupiter/Sun Contacts

Story lines: Optimism, excellent health, expansion in professional or personal life. Serendipitous encounters. Spiritual issues.

Jupiter conjunctions feel so good that even if things go slightly askew, you barely notice. Your spirituality usually deepens during the positive contacts, and with the sextile you may even do some type of group spiritual work. The sextile favors group work of any kind, whether it's a workshop, seminar, or just a class about a topic that interests you.

The positive contacts also favor contact with publishers, attorneys, college professors, anyone connected with the areas that Jupiter rules. Your optimism is exuberant and infectious. A possible drawback is that you may be so optimistic that you are blind to the reality of a situation.

The trine is especially conducive to feeling good. In fact, you may feel so good you won't feel like doing much of anything at all. It's important, though, to take advantage of these Jupiter contacts. They represent windows of opportunity.

Challenging Jupiter/Sun Contacts

Story lines: *A test about self-restraint. Luck and expansiveness, but luck isn't inexhaustible.*

Okay, you know all the good stuff about Jupiter transits, and all that good stuff holds true for the challenging contacts. So let's look at the shadow side: excess (again) and lack of discipline. You may spend more money than you actually have in your checking account. Or, in anticipation of an end-of-the-year bonus, you spend what you don't have yet and then, if the bonus doesn't arrive and your bills come due, you don't have the money. You may take on more than you can do in some area of your life.

Any Jupiter transit can result in a weight gain—the literal translation of expansion—so this may be a good time to start a regular exercise program.

SATURN TRANSITS

Story lines: *Increased responsibility, burdens, hard work. Also opportunities, rewards, insight.*
Movies/fiction: Memoirs of a Geisha *by Arthur S. Golden,* Gravity *by Tess Gerritsen,* The Firm *by John Grisham or the movie version with Tom Cruise*

Yes, I know. The story lines sound like a contradiction. But in many ways, Saturn transits *are* contradictions. Whether a Saturn transit affects you positively or negatively ultimately depends on what you've been doing with your life, whether the path you're on is the right path in the cosmic scheme of things, and whether you've owned up to the contract you agreed on before you were born. That's why they call Saturn the planet of karma.

Positive Saturn/Sun Contacts

Story lines: *Requires enormous patience. Achievement or collapse, triumph or defeat. A paring away of what is nonessential. Hard work, additional responsibility.*

It doesn't sound like much fun, except for the part about achievement and triumph. In fact, under Saturn transits, you may feel the way a teenager often feels, as if the entire universe is stacked against you. But actually, you're laying the foundation for a whole new cycle of growth.

With the conjunction, you get hit with added responsibility in one or several areas of your life. You may feel burdened, depressed, tired. You may wonder how you're going to keep doing what you're doing. Yet at some level the conjunction helps you get rid of things in your life that no longer work or don't serve your highest good. The conjunction also warns you not to take on anything new that adds to the burden; finish what you're doing before moving on to something else. If, however, the path you're following is the right path for you, then you may reap rewards.

The sextile and trine both provide opportunities—but you still have to be aware enough to recognize these opportunities and seize them. Saturn never dumps a good thing in your lap; you have to earn it.

Challenging Saturn/Sun Contacts

Story lines: *A test. Confrontation with authority figures. Delays. Ambitions meet with opposition. Heavy responsibilities.*

Can you do what is required of you now? That's the test. The best way to navigate the energy of the square is to understand that it's part of the evolutionary cycle of life. It helps you get rid of relationships and situations that you've outgrown or that no longer work. The harder you fight against it, the worst it will be. Try to go with the flow.

The opposition can make you feel that you're up against a concrete wall, trapped, with nowhere to go. It seems that your boss and other people in authority are against every idea you have, every project. There can be problems with a parent or an older relative. You may be physically tired, with low energy. You may have to rethink your goals and will need to develop a lot of patience. But the transit *will* end, and when it does, your life will be more in line with your deepest desires.

OUTER PLANET TRANSITS

Due to the slowness with which Uranus, Neptune, and Pluto move, it's unlikely that you'll experience all of the aspects in your lifetime. This is covered in more depth in the sun signs chapters in Part Two.

URANUS TRANSITS

Story lines: *Sudden, unexpected change. Disruptions.*
Movies/fiction: Sliding Doors, The Terminator, Jacob's Ladder; What Dreams May Come *by Richard Matheson,* The Running Man *by Richard Bachman (Stephen King)*

The purpose of these transits is to break up rigid patterns and beliefs. In whatever area your life is rigid and predictable, Uranus comes along and blows it all apart, releasing you to find new and better ways of living and being. Aquarians should pay close attention to Uranus, which rules their sign.

Positive Uranus/Sun Contacts

Story lines: *New freedoms, new and creative self-expression, breakup of old, predictable patterns, new and exciting opportunities.*

If you've been living your life in a routine, predictable fashion, then the conjunction will be a shock. You'll suddenly find yourself in the midst of chaos, with parts of your life collapsing around you. It really isn't as bad as it sounds. This is just the universe's way of clearing your life of relationships and situations that restrict your freedom. If you can go with the flow, you'll discover that new opportunities and interests come your way, that your creativity is soaring, and that a new and exciting chapter is opening up in your life.

The sextile and the trine feel lucky. But in both cases, whatever you gain is what you have earned. Embrace the new opportunities that come your way. Rejoice in the new you that is evolving.

Challenging Uranus/Sun Contacts

Story lines: A test. Disruptions that challenge your path. Breaking away from restrictions. The new, unexpected, sudden change that can be drastic and disturbing. Heightened creativity.

These transits test your commitment to the path you have chosen. If that path, professional or personal, is the right path for you, then the events and situations Uranus tosses your way won't be any big deal. But if you're uncertain about the path you're on or if you aren't entirely committed to it, these transits show you why and force you to make necessary changes.

The health risks with these challenging transits are most likely to come about when you resist change and may affect your heart or nervous system.

NEPTUNE TRANSITS

Story lines: Confusion, heightened intuitive and psychic ability, deeper compassion. Idealism, addictions. Dissolving of barriers between ego and higher self.

Movies/fiction: Castaway, Titanic, A Beautiful Mind, Brainstorm; The Bell Jar *by Sylvia Plath,* Passages *by Connie Willis,* "Dream of a Ridiculous Man" *by Doestoevsky*

These transits take a long time, so their impact is more a process of unfolding than a sudden shock. The confusion stems from the nature of Neptune, which blurs the border between illusion and reality, ego and higher self. Neptune's energy is a kind of fog that descends over an area of life where we must develop compassion and an awareness of a higher power. Idealism and addictions are also associated with these transits.

People born under the sign of Pisces should keep close tabs on Neptune's transits, since this planet rules their sign.

Positive Neptune/Sun Contacts

Story lines: *Compassion, victim or savior, sensitivity to the needs of others, selflessness, confusion about personal and professional goals. Escapism.*

Even the positive contacts may cause you to feel disassociated from yourself and confused about your goals. Meditation and any kind of physical discipline like yoga or tai chi help to mitigate the confusion of these transits by increasing your awareness of higher powers. Many people become involved in spiritual and charitable work during these transits, a perfect way to navigate any Neptune transit. However you deal with these transits, you will end up asking yourself the big questions: Is there a higher power? What's the ultimate meaning of life?

Challenging Neptune/Sun Contacts

Story lines: *Disappointments, confusion, unstable sense of reality. Don't give in to apparent defeat. Escapism. Another test.*

Thanks to the disorientation of the square and opposition, one of the possible side effects is escapism through drugs, alcohol, sex, food, or any kind of addiction. It's as if addiction becomes a place to hide from a reality you don't want to acknowledge. But it only makes things worse. You're better off looking for spiritual answers for whatever is happening. Use the "test" part of this square to develop and nurture your intuitive ability.

The opposition demands that you communicate clearly and precisely so that you aren't misunderstood and that you present yourself as you are. In other words, be as genuine as you possibly can. There can be trouble with bosses, authoritarian parents, or other authority figures.

PLUTO TRANSITS

Story lines: *Profound transformation. Death of the old, power struggles, control issues, reconstructions, rebirth and resurrection. Ambition. Rewards.*

Movies/fiction: The Stand *by Stephen King,* Alas, Babylon *by Pat Frank,* War and Peace *by Leo Tolstoy*

Pluto transits aren't brief or shallow. When they cause change, the changes are permanent and necessary. A significant relationship may fall apart, you may lose a job, change career, get married or divorced, have a child, lose a parent. At the other end of the transit, you are no longer the person you were.

Positive Pluto/Sun Contacts

Story lines: *Excellent energy, high ambitions, collapse of the old, sweeping and creative change.*

Even though the effects of these transits unfold over time due to the slowness with which Pluto moves, circumstances create tremendous change in your life. A Pluto transit can end relationships that no longer serve a purpose in your life or that are holding you back in some way. It can also usher people into your life who are tremendously helpful and supportive of your ambitions. Your creativity may deepen, your grasp of life certainly broadens, and you begin to realize there are some things you will never control.

Your experience of these transits will depend on how you use your own power. If you abuse it, you pay the price, and it's likely to be very steep. Your conscious awareness of Pluto's energies will allow you to draw on that energy to improve your life and the lives of the people you love.

Challenging Pluto/Sun Contacts

Story lines: A test. Power struggles. Make the unconscious conscious. Great achievements, ambition, drive, and energy. Health risks.

The Pluto square is about power—how you use it, how others use it with you, your relationship with power, your comfort zone with your own power. Power issues concerning sex and money can enter the picture, as can power struggles with authorities. However, the bottom line is your ability and willingness to stand up for yourself and for what you believe to be true and right.

The opposition is also about power, but here you're attempting to harness your own power without causing resentment or resistance in other people. This is part of why personal and professional relationships can be strained during an opposition. If you don't use your power to control others, you should be able to achieve a great deal.

OTHER POINTS

The Moon's Nodes

Story lines: Destiny. Prenatal agreements. Opportunities to evolve and to release the habits and attitudes that hold us back.
Movies/fiction: Dead Again, *Emma Thompson;* The End of the Affair *by Graham Greene*

Sometimes the nodes supplement the story line. Other times, they *are* the story line. They symbolize opportunities for spiritual advancement, anticipating trends, tuning into past life memories, achieving a goal or dream. With both positive and challenging aspects, they attract the people, events, and situations that we need most. Quite often, they are involved when we achieve recognition or fame or experience life events: births, deaths, marriages, moves, a major passage.

PART TWO

THE SUN SIGNS

7

ϒ

SUN IN ARIES: WARRIOR AND PIONEER

March 21–April 19

In the chapters in Part Two, you'll discover the primary storyline for your sun sign, for the planet that rules your sign, and what happens when that ruling planet forms various angles (transits) to your sign. You may want to refer back to the definitions of aspects in Part One as you read through this section.

WARRIOR

When you want something badly enough, you're willing to fight for it. You dismiss the naysayers who tell you it can't be done or there isn't enough money or who can make a living doing *that?* If there are obstacles, you ram your way through them. If there are problems, you don't just solve them, you mow them down. Obliterate them.

You do whatever has to be done to achieve or obtain whatever it is that you want.

Your raw nerve, bottomless courage, and fortitude are part of Mars's legacy as your ruling planet. Throughout your life, you'll have a choice where this warrior part of your personality is concerned. If you use it to your advantage and to benefit the people you love, then you will be in control of the warrior. Otherwise, the warrior will control you. And the ways the warrior will use you aren't pretty.

The warrior will make you confrontational, argumentative, and unpleasant to be around. It will drive away the people you love and the people who might love you. It will cause you to be reckless rather than impulsive. It will be make you accident prone and will stress you physically. But because this is the energy that makes you a survivor, once you learn how to direct it, you can achieve anything.

To learn to channel all your warrior energy constructively, you need to call upon the power of your second archetype, the pioneer.

PIONEER

You're a spinning vortex of energy, a whirlwind of passions. This powerful mix fuels your entrepreneurial and adventurous spirit and puts you at the forefront of anything you take on. Most of the time, you're exploding with ideas and putting them into action. When something incites your passion, there's no stopping you. When your passion wanes, you walk away without apologies or regrets. Other people may resent it, but you can't worry about what they think. You've never worried about what people think of you. They either like you and accept you the way you are, or they aren't part of your world.

You're a risk taker and extremely competitive. Only an Aries would scale a mountain because it's there—or because someone dared him or her to do it. This characteristic probably showed up pretty early in your life—and made your parents gray before their time. You were the kid who eagerly hopped on the highest and fastest roller coaster, rode the fastest skateboard, and played sports like there was no tomorrow. Your independence and enthusiasm also showed up early on. You were the kid whom everyone else followed.

As a cardinal fire sign ruled by Mars, you venture where other people don't. Outer space or inner worlds, the highest mountains or the fastest cars—it's all fair game for you. You're the proverbial kid in a candy store, sampling this and that, looking for what excites you, constantly restless, moving. The words *relax* and *patience* are foreign to you. No one can ever accuse you of being a couch potato. Even when you're at home on a weekend, you're *doing* things: yard work, cleaning out the attic, fixing leaky pipes.

Your intuition and creativity are highly developed, but you usually don't think about concepts like this. You're too busy *living* the concepts. Introspection isn't your strong suit; leave that to the earth signs. You're here to sample everything, to absorb as much experience as you can take in.

YOUR PLOTS AND MARS

How have the plots in your story line developed over the years? Have you constantly forged ahead in some area of your life? Have your challenges or triumphs occurred primarily in your relationships, your career, your creativity? Use the checklist below to identify some of the major events that have occurred in your life in the last thirteen years. After an event, jot down the month and year it occurred, if you remember them. Yes, this is also a memory exercise! If you don't recall the exact date, give a time frame. The idea here is that we're looking for patterns.

Remember that Mars represents physical and sexual energy, as well as your capacity for aggression. As the planet that rules Aries, its transits to your sun are triggers for change.

Compare the dates you've noted with the time frames for when Mars was in Aries, listed below. There should be some matches.

ARIES/MARS CHECKLIST

___ I got involved in a significant relationship. _____

___ I got a major promotion. _____

___ I got a raise in pay. _____

___ I got married. _____

___ I got divorced. _____

___ I had a child. _____

___ I moved. _____

___ I changed jobs. _____

___ I entered or won a competition. _____

___ I got an important contract. _____

___ I inherited money. _____

___ I was in a car accident. _____

___ I was injured or ill. _____

___ I had surgery. _____

___ I sold my home or a piece of
real estate. _____

___ I took a major trip. _____

___ My parents or someone in my family got ill
or died. _____

___ I got fired from a job. _____

___ I got a better job. _____

___ I started my own business. _____

___ I suffered financial losses. _____

___ I went deeply into debt. _____

___ I moved into my dream house. _____

___ My spiritual beliefs changed dramatically. _____

___ I got pregnant. _____

___ I had a major career breakthrough. _____

___ I found my creative niche. _____

___ I fell in love. _____

___ I met my significant other. _____

___ My life changed dramatically (how?). _____

___ Any other dramatic change. _____

DATES: MARS IN ARIES, 1990–2002

5/31/90 – 7/12/90
5/5/92 – 6/14/92
4/14/94 – 5/23/94
3/24/96 – 5/2/96
3/4/98 – 4/12/98
2/11/00 – 3/22/00
1/18/02 – 3/1/02

In addition to conjunctions, you're looking for oppositions (Mars in Libra), squares (Mars in Cancer or Capricorn), sextiles (Mars in Gemini or Aquarius), and trines (Mars in Leo and Sagittarius). Note the dates, aspect, and the possible story lines below. You can do this with any planet, but start with Mars, as the planet that rules your sun sign. If you know what your natal ascendant is, also do this activity with the planet that rules that sign.

Important Dates for Mars, 2003–2007

DATE	SIGN	ASPECT	STORY LINES

SHARON'S STORY

Sharon, an Aries in her late thirties, lost her husband on July 16, 1999. He had a massive heart attack in bed. Although he'd had heart bypass surgery some years before, his death was unexpected.

The most significant transits at the time of her husband's death were Mars in Scorpio, Uranus and Neptune in Aquarius, Pluto in Sagittarius. Mars had recently separated from an opposition to her sun. If you put her Aries sun on the ascendant, this puts Scorpio on the cusp of her eighth house. Depending on the degree of her Aries sun, Mars fell in either her seventh house of marriage and partnerships or her eighth house of transformations. The eighth house also represents our support systems and resources that we share with others. If you're married, this house represents your spouse's resources.

Uranus and Neptune fall in the eleventh house of the solar chart we just set up, forming sextiles to Sharon's Sun. Wishes and dreams go in this house. The simplest story line is a *sudden change* (Uranus) in her wishes and dreams (eleventh house) that impacts her eighth house (shared resources, Mars) through a change she didn't anticipate (Neptune). Pluto was in Sagittarius, which falls into her ninth house: a profound transformation in her worldview and spiritual beliefs. Pluto was trine her sun. The sextiles and trines generally indicate ease, but trines are sometimes involved in sudden deaths, perhaps indicating that the spirit of the deceased left without the pain, for example, or a prolonged illness.

Transiting Mars in Scorpio in either the seventh or eighth house may evolve through any number of possible story lines. But for Sharon, the story line spelled deep and painful transformation through the death of her husband.

Astrologers use many different techniques in predictions, looking for confirmation of one particular pattern. The transit pattern showed up using other techniques as well. Even so, death is a difficult thing to see in a chart before the fact because no one knows exactly how the energy of a transit will manifest itself, and only a fool would make such a prediction. But the value of the pattern, especially that Mars in Scorpio, is real. From now on, Sharon will know that when Mars is in Scorpio or just leaving an opposition with her sun, she should take steps beforehand to protect the resources that she shares with others.

For practice, use a blank chart and set up a horoscope with Aries on the ascendant and the transits in the appropriate houses.

THE OUTER PLANETS: THEMES

The transits of the inner, faster-moving planets are your best gauge for story lines that are evolving daily, weekly, or even monthly. The movement of the outer, slower-moving planets holds the deeper themes and layers of your evolving story line. But these planets move so slowly that you won't experience every aspect of the transiting outer planets to your sun unless you're exceptionally long-lived.

For Uranus, you'll experience the sextile in Aquarius, but only through early 2003 and then again for about three and a half months at the end of 2003, when Uranus is moving retrograde. The sextile brings new and exciting opportunities as well as the ability to work with groups in some capacity. It's a good time to advance professionally and creatively. The Uranus conjunction that begins in 2010 brings sudden, unexpected changes in your life. The underlying theme of this transit is that the things you experience refine your individuality and your creative voice. You may move, change jobs or careers, have a child, or send a child off to college. Your creative voice strengthens. Relationships begin and end abruptly. Whatever limits and restricts you will be eliminated from your life. You find your path as an individual.

The theme of this particular transit will be supported and triggered by the movement of the other planets. For example, about the same time that Uranus goes into Aries, Jupiter also will be going into Aries; Saturn will be in the final degrees of Virgo and moving toward Libra to oppose your sun; and Pluto in Capricorn will be squaring your sun. Neptune will be in Aquarius and then moving into Pisces. The Jupiter conjunction brings expansion and luck; Saturn brings confrontation or culmination, as well as delays and restrictions; the Pluto square brings friction surrounding power issues; and Neptune in Aquarius (sextile) heightens your friendships and deepens your compassion.

These influences work at various levels to create a kind of living hologram. The specific events, situations, and people you encounter during these transits always depend on where you are in your life path, what you've been doing with your potential up to this point, and what your soul needs to evolve in this lifetime.

TIMING AND TRANSITS

Timing is everything. When you work with transits, the truth of this simple adage becomes glaringly apparent. Whether you're planning a vacation or a wedding, the launch of a new product or a move, a knowledge of transits can help you stack the odds in your favor.

If you're planning to get married, for example, you would look for a time frame in which Venus and the moon are making positive contacts with your sun. If you're planning to launch a new product or project at work, Mars contacts with your sun would be important. If the product or project is artistic in some way, both Mars and Venus contacts would play important roles. To choose a propitious time for a business trip would involve Mercury contacts with your sun, or even Saturn contacts, for the structure and discipline that Saturn brings. For the timing of events in your daily life, look to the faster-moving planets first, then take into account the underlying themes of the slower-moving planets.

Once you understand the symbolic meanings of the planets, aspects, and houses, selecting the right time for anything becomes almost second nature.

The list below provides common situations in which timing can be crucial to your success, along with what planets and aspects are the best to ensure your success in these situations. But, please, don't spend so much time planning the events in your life according to the stars that you don't have time to live. If love is calling, don't wait around for Venus to be in a fire or an air sign or for the Moon to move into your seventh house. Just get married! The information below is merely a guideline.

For easy reference: A conjunction is a planet in Aries; a sextile is a planet in Gemini or Aquarius; a square is a planet in Capricorn or Cancer; a trine is a planet in Leo or Sagittarius; an opposition is a planet in Libra.

- ✦ **Move:** Mars conjunction. Mercury sextile or trine, moving direct. Sun or moon in Leo or Sagittarius. Jupiter conjunct, sextile, or trine. Moon transiting natal fourth house.
- ✦ **Wedding:** Venus in Aries or another fire sign or in an air sign. Moon in the natal seventh house. Positive Jupiter/sun contacts.
- ✦ **Honeymoon:** Venus in Aries or another fire sign. Mercury moving direct. Positive Jupiter/sun contacts.
- ✦ **Divorce:** Mercury direct. Positive Jupiter/sun contacts.
- ✦ **Job change:** Positive Jupiter/sun contacts. Venus sextile or trine. Moon in a compatible element.
- ✦ **Workshop/seminar:** Mercury conjunct, sextile, or trine and moving direct. If the workshop is spiritually or creatively oriented, then look for positive Venus and Neptune/sun contacts.
- ✦ **Return to school:** Mercury conjunct, sextile, trine, and moving direct. Even the Mercury squares and oppositions are good for learning.
- ✦ **Launch a project:** Mars in a fire sign. Jupiter or Venus conjunct, sextile, or trine.
- ✦ **Start a creative project:** Venus in a fire sign. New moon in a fire sign. Venus sextile or trine. Jupiter conjunct, sextile, or trine.
- ✦ **Interview for a job:** Venus conjunct, sextile, or trine. Saturn sextile or trine. Moon in a compatible element.
- ✦ **Business trip:** Mercury moving direct. Saturn sextile or trine.
- ✦ **Vacation:** Venus or Jupiter conjunct, sextile, or trine. Mercury moving direct.

- **Sign a contract:** Mercury moving direct. Jupiter conjunction, sextile, or trine. Saturn sextile or trine.
- **Hire an employee:** Mercury moving direct. Any positive Jupiter contact.
- **Fire an employee:** Mars conjunct. Positive Venus contacts. This gives you the strength to fire the person, but to do it without confrontation.
- **Revisions, rewrites:** Mercury moving retrograde.
- **Spiritual pursuits:** Look for contacts from Uranus, Neptune, and Pluto. Venus or Jupiter conjunct, sextile, or trine.
- **Schedule surgery:** Mercury moving direct. Mars sextile or trine. Jupiter or Venus conjunct, sextile, or trine.
- **Start a diet:** New Moon in a fire or earth sign. Mars in a fire sign.
- **Getting pregnant:** Moon in Cancer or in the sign on the cusp of the natal fifth house, Venus conjunct, sextile, or trine. Mars conjunct.

MANIFESTATION: "MAKE IT SO"

In one of the incarnations of *Star Trek*, Captain Picard had a saying that always caught my attention: "Make it so." It's the verbal equivalence of waving a magical wand to manifest something, and always has struck me as a very Aries kind of thing. State your wish, wave your wand, and—*voilà!*—your wish is right there in front of you, yours for the taking.

In the next activity, you're going to use *your* magical wand to manifest something that you want. It can be anything—a better job, the perfect mate, more money, the sale of a creative project, a vacation, a new car, a spiritual mentor, good health. Whatever it is, you must be able to condense it into a single, positive statement, in the present tense. Instead of saying, *I want to get rid of my debt*, you might phrase it as, *Financial abundance flows into my life.*

In the New Moon ephemeris (page 254), find the date for the next New Moon. On that date, write out your wish and back it with your deepest belief that what you want is within your grasp. Don't worry about how the wish will come about. Simply trust that it will. As you're writing your statement, say Picard's line: *Make it so.* Then post your statement where you'll see it often. If you have your natal chart, do this when the New Moon is in the sign that's on the cusp of whatever it is you're trying to manifest in your life.

During the next month, be open to impulses, intuitions, and any information that comes to you through unconventional sources—dreams, odd synchronicities, even things that strangers say to you. It's crucial that you maintain your trust and belief that your wish is possible. If you want to ritualize the whole thing, plant seeds in a ceramic pot and state your wish aloud as you're planting the seeds. The idea here is symbolic: as the seeds begin to sprout, your wish is being realized.

8

♉

SUN IN TAURUS:
REALIST AND SENSUALIST

April 20–May 20

REALIST

Your senses are so highly attuned to physical life that they define what you believe to be real. When your eyes tell you the sky is blue or your ears tell you that the music you're listening to is beautiful, no argument in the world can convince you otherwise. For you, the adage, *What you see is what you get* can be expanded to, *What you see, taste, touch, hear, and smell is true and real.* And anything else must be scrutinized beneath the lens of your perception before you decide one way or another.

Physicality is such a strong component of who you are that it's one of the primary forces in your life. Many Tauruses maintain regular exercise routines—yoga, workouts at the gym, running. If you don't fall into that category, then chances are you have a beautiful garden that you created or you enjoy hiking in the woods, camping, kayaking, some activity that gets you outside where there are trees, water, vast vistas of land. In either instance, you're deeply conscious of your body as a vehicle for transformation.

This part of your personality has more to do with the earth component than it does with the Venus rulership of your sign. In fact, some astrologers argue that Taurus is actually ruled by Earth. This makes a lot of sense, and yet, since none of us is composed of just one quality, it may be too simple. I think of Taurus as embodying qualities of both a Venus and an Earth rulership, the two archetypal energies working seamlessly together.

When it comes to how you handle money, both archetypes may be at work. The Venus part of you loves anything that appeals to the senses—art, good foods, music—and yet the Earth part of you demands that the beautiful thing must have practical applications.

Some Tauruses have an uncanny sense about which stocks to buy, which IRA to invest in, or how to make a buck go a very long way. When my Taurus husband was younger, he took off with about a thousand bucks in his pocket and spent six months traveling in South America. I had about the same amount of money when I took off for Europe one summer, and it got me through only six weeks.

Taurus is a cultivator. If you look up the definition of *cultivate,* it invariably talks about growing and harvesting crops. If you apply this metaphor to your own life, you'll realize that one of your great strengths is the ability to cultivate anything—an idea, money, a garden, your creativity, a particular talent, spirituality. You possess the realism and the relentlessness to achieve whatever you want.

SENSUALIST

This part of you definitely falls under the Venus rulership. It's the other side of your finely hewn physical senses, the aesthetic side that enjoys sensuous sex, romance, and beauty, and not necessarily in that order.

As a sensualist, you're a wonderful lover and are often able to communicate through touch some of the emotions you can't verbalize. You may also be a gourmet cook who raises the simple act of preparing food to an art form. Even if you don't cook, your palate is especially sensitive and you enjoy tasteful food prepared with sauces or herbs. You're an adventurous eater, willing to try nearly anything once.

This side of you allows you to walk into nature with your senses wide open. You instantly capture the smell of the earth, the bird-songs and the whisper of wind through the leaves, the very taste of the air itself. All of it transports you. You become a kind of time traveler, able to feel what Longfellow felt when he wrote about the forest primeval. A walk on the beach, where warm water washes over your feet and the hot sun burns against the soles, brings you up close and personal with William Blake's writings about the world con-tained within a grain of sand.

Through your senses, your knowing is direct and immediate. It is your most personal connection to the divine. This connection, in fact, is what launches a spiritual search for some Tauruses. Despite your here and now grounding, there is a part of you that seeks deeper meaning, that may be attracted to the mystical and the mythological, to the transcendent.

YOUR PLOTS AND VENUS

The influence of the planet that rules your sun sign is readily appar-ent if you study its transits over time. The checklist below is going to help you do that for the last thirteen years.

In addition to romance and love, Venus rules your creative thrust, significant women in your life, social contacts and friend-ships, your aesthetic senses and capacity for appreciating the arts, femininity and adornment, jewelry, the neck, throat, and small of the back. Its transits are beneficial for financial matters, too.

With all that in mind, think about the major events that have happened to you in the last thirteen years—marriage, the birth of a child, a major promotion, a move, the sale of a creative project or any other important event—and jot down the dates. Then go through the checklist and find the statements that pertain to you and your life in the last thirteen years. Scribble notes next to them if you need to. Try to remember dates. They don't have to be specific, but if they are, great. Then compare your dates with those in the Venus in Taurus list that follows. There should be some matches.

TAURUS/VENUS CHECKLIST

___ I fell in love. _____

___ I had a child. _____

___ I won a prize. _____

___ I got a big promotion or raise. _____

___ I got married. _____

___ I changed jobs. _____

___ I inherited money. _____

___ I lost a parent, sibling, or close friend. _____

___ I lost a spouse or significant other. _____

___ I got ill. _____

___ I injured my neck. _____

___ I recovered from an illness or
     from surgery. _____

___ I got an important contract. _____

___ My spiritual beliefs changed dramatically. _____

___ I met my significant other. _____

___ I met my mentor. _____

___ I moved into my dream house. _____

___ I made significant social or
     professional contacts. _____

___ I got pregnant. _____

___ My life changed dramatically (how?). _____

___ I found my creative niche. _____

___ I sold my first screenplay, book, etc. _____

___ I had a major career breakthrough. _____

___ I went into debt. _____

___ Any other event (describe). _____

Venus moves quickly, circling the sun in about 255 days. It spends three and a half weeks in a sign when it's moving direct, and when it's going retrograde, it can stay in a sign for as long as four months. You'll feel its influence most strongly when it goes into Taurus and as it approaches and then makes a direct hit on your sun.

Let's say you were born on May 16, at the tail end of the Taurus cycle. In the Venus dates section below, notice that on May 16, 1995, Venus went into Taurus and stayed there until June 9, 1995. Did something significant happen to you during that time period? If so, did it occur before or after your birthday? Make note of it.

DATES: VENUS IN TAURUS, 1990–2002

5/30/90–6/24/90
3/19/91–4/13/91
5/2/92–5/25/92
6/6/93–7/5/93
4/1/94–4/26/94
5/16/95–6/9/95
3/5/96–4/2/96
4/16/97–5/9/97
5/29/98–6/23/98
3/18/99–4/11/99
4/30/00–5/24/00
6/6/01–7/4/01
4/1/02–4/24/02

REPETITIVE PATTERNS

Patterns are the heart of astrological research and are particularly important when you're learning to make predictions for yourself. If, for example, you know that you experienced important events between mid-May and early June of 1995 and between April 30 and May 24, 2000, then you have the beginning of a *pattern* concerning your sensitivity to Venus conjunctions to your Sun.

Just as important, however, are patterns that involve other aspects—sextiles, squares, trines, and oppositions between Venus and your sun. Look in the Venus ephemeris for these aspects and when they're going to occur. Later in the chapter, we'll practice creating story lines for aspects from other planets. For easy reference: a conjunction is any planet in Taurus; a sextile is a planet in Cancer or Pisces; a square is a planet in Leo or Aquarius; a trine is a planet in Virgo or Capricorn; and an opposition is a planet in Scorpio.

Important Dates for Venus, 2003–2007

DATE	SIGN	ASPECT	STORY LINES

ROB'S STORY

On February 28, 1999, my double-Taurus husband was out windsurfing on a lake near where we live. As he came in to shore, he jumped down from the board and his left foot landed on what he suspects was a broken bottle partially buried in the sand. He ended up in the ER, where he learned that his foot had been cut to within a quarter inch of the bone. If the bone had been hit, he would have needed surgery. As it was, he needed eighteen stitches on a deep cut that was also oddly shaped, curving over the side of his foot. His doctor, a female resident in podiatry, was a Scorpio (yes, I asked) and was fascinated by the shape of the injury and expressed concern about whether there was enough skin on the side of his foot for the stitches to hold.

He was on crutches for a month, the total bill came to about

$3,000, and he now is very careful about where he windsurfs. I knew what time the accident had happened and ran the transits to his natal chart. Astrologically, the symbolic language for the accident was all there. Even though we're using solar rather than natal charts in this book, this is a good example because he has Taurus rising in his natal horoscope.

(If you wish, take a moment to tear out one of the blank charts in the back of the book so you can follow along. Put Taurus on the ascendant, representing his natal sun sign, Gemini on the cusp of the second house, and continue around the wheel until you have Aries on the cusp of the twelfth house.)

At the time, Mercury was in Pisces; Venus, Jupiter, and Saturn were in Aries; Mars was in Scorpio; Uranus and Neptune were in Aquarius; and Pluto was in Sagittarius. Now place the planets in their appropriate houses. Visually, one detail should be immediately obvious: Mars in the seventh house was opposed to his natal sun. Since the injury was accidental and involved a sharp instrument—a broken bottle—Mars, opposite his sun, is especially important. Oppositions spell confrontation and culmination—in this instance, confrontations with hospitals, which are ruled by the twelfth house.

In the twelfth house of the wheel we just set up, he has three planets in fiery Aries. Of these, Saturn indicates a confrontation with authority (doctors, the medical establishment), while Venus and Jupiter, as planets whose energies are basically harmonious, confer some element of protection—namely, that the injury didn't hit the bone, which would have meant surgery. Neptune in Aquarius in the tenth house, trine to those planets in the twelfth, is revealing; he wasn't paying attention to where he stepped (didn't see the broken bottle) and it had an impact on his work (tenth house). Neptune also rules the feet.

What's especially interesting about Mars in the seventh (coruler of Scorpio) is that it literally represents the Scorpio resident who worked on his foot! Surgeons fall under the rule of Mars.

The tricky part about transits is that the story is usually abundantly clear in retrospect. But I couldn't have foreseen the specifics of the event based solely on the symbolic language. If I had looked at his chart for that day, I probably would have noticed the opposition from Mars and the planets in the twelfth house and cautioned him to be careful about windsurfing. Maybe that would have been enough to prevent the accident. At any rate, Rob is now more aware of astrological patterns and exercises greater caution when he windsurfs!

THE OUTER PLANETS: THEMES

Daily, weekly, or monthly, the positions and signs of the faster-moving planets hold the key to your evolving story lines. But you should always watch the signs and positions of the slower-moving planets. They suggest the underlying themes and layers of the story lines that unfold over a period of years—seven years for Uranus, fourteen years for Neptune, and from twelve to thirty years for Pluto. These outer planets move so slowly that you won't experience every aspect of their transits to your sun in your lifetime.

The only Uranus aspect to your sun that you'll experience in the immediate future is the sextile in Pisces, which begins on December 30, 2003, and lasts until the end of May 2010.

During this period, the underlying themes of your story lines will involve changes that free you and support your individuality and creativity. Opportunities will fall in your lap and new, exciting people will enter your life. You may delve inward, seeking spiritual answers, and some type of involvement with groups is a possibility. These groups will support your spiritual beliefs or creative interests and will applaud your individuality.

The sextile's theme will be supported and challenged by transits from the other planets. About the same time that Uranus is forming a sextile to your sun, Neptune will be in Aquarius, where it has been since late November 1998. At some point during its lengthy transit through Aquarius, it will form a square to your sun. The Neptune square will highlight your spirituality and intuition and bring a degree of confusion and unreality into your life. It's as if the things that have been so important to you in life now take the backseat to your search for spiritual answers. This won't happen all at once, but will unfold over time.

Pluto will be in Sagittarius until late January 2008, when it begins its long transit in Capricorn. At some point during its journey, it will trine your sun. The trine highlights your personal power and ambition, and signals a time of deepening creativity and professional achievement.

The ways these influences combine and find expression in your life depends on where you are in your life, what you've been doing, and what your soul needs to evolve in this lifetime.

TIMING AND TRANSITS

The beauty of working with transits is that you're better able to stack the deck in your favor. Whether you're starting a novel or planning a vacation, launching a new product or changing careers, *timing is everything*. What planets and aspects are most propitious? What aspects and signs present the best windows of opportunity?

When I first started working with transits, I got a bit obsessive. *Oops, Mercury is retrograde; I can't take that trip*. Or, *Mars is opposed my sun today; I'd better not drive the interstate*. I eventually realized that I was avoiding certain situations rather than using the transits to increase my awareness of potentials and possibilities. So, please, use the information below only as a guideline, to heighten your potential for success.

For easy reference: A conjunction is a planet in Taurus; a sextile is a planet in Pisces or Cancer; a square is a planet in Leo or Aquarius; a trine is a planet in Virgo or Capricorn; an opposition is a planet in Scorpio.

✦ **Move:** Mars conjunction. Mercury sextile or trine, moving direct. Sun or moon in Cancer or in an element compatible with Taurus. Avoid moving when Mars is in Scorpio (opposed your sun).

- **Wedding:** Venus in Taurus or in an earth or water sign. Moon in the seventh house. Avoid Venus squares and oppositions. Jupiter conjunct, sextile, or trine.
- **Honeymoon:** Venus in Taurus or another fire earth sign. Mercury moving direct. Positive Jupiter/sun contacts.
- **Divorce:** Mercury direct. Positive Jupiter/sun contacts.
- **Job/career change:** Positive Jupiter/sun contacts. Venus sextile or trine. Moon in a compatible element.
- **List home for sale:** Moon in Cancer. Mars in Taurus or another earth sign. Positive Jupiter/sun contacts. Mercury direct and conjunct, sextile, or trine.
- **Buy a home:** Moon in Cancer or Taurus. Positive Venus or Jupiter/sun contacts. Mercury direct.
- **Workshop or seminar:** Mercury conjunct, sextile, or trine and moving direct. If spirituality or creativity is involved, look for positive Venus and Neptune/sun contacts.
- **Return to school:** Mercury conjunct, sextile, or trine. Mercury squares and oppositions allow you to learn easily.
- **Launch a project:** Mars in an earth sign. Jupiter or Venus conjunct, sextile, or trine.
- **Start a creative project:** Venus in Taurus or another earth sign. New moon in Taurus or another earth sign. Venus or Jupiter conjunct, sextile, or trine. Mars conjunct.
- **Begin a new job:** Mercury sextile or trine. Venus or Jupiter conjunct, sextile, or trine. Mars conjunct.
- **Interview for a job:** Venus conjunct, sextile, or trine. Moon in Taurus or another earth sign.
- **Business trip:** Mercury direct. Saturn sextile or trine.
- **Vacation:** Mercury direct. Venus or Jupiter conjunct, sextile, or trine.
- **Sign a contract:** Mercury direct. Jupiter conjunction, sextile, or trine.
- **Restructure your business:** Saturn conjunct. Jupiter conjunct, sextile, or trine.
- **Start a diet:** New moon in an earth sign. Moon in Virgo.

+ **Getting pregnant:** Moon in Cancer or in the sign on the cusp of the fifth house in a natal chart. Venus conjunct, sextile, or trine.
+ **Spiritual pursuits:** Positive contacts from Uranus, Neptune, and Pluto. Venus or Jupiter conjunct, sextile, or trine.

MANIFESTATION: PRACTICAL MAGIC

Each of us possesses a special kind of magic that makes things happen in our lives. For you, Taurus, part of that magic entails a relentless persistence in pursuing what you want. But magic is more than persistence. It's also your belief in yourself, your intent, and your capacity to imagine the seemingly impossible. Without those qualities, persistence is nothing more than a fight against some tremendous force, like gravity.

In the next activity, you're going to call upon belief, intent, and imagination to manifest something you really want. It can be a new job, a raise or promotion, an agent to sell your novel or screenplay, spiritual insight. Whatever it is, though, you must be able to distill your wish into a single positive statement, in the present tense. Instead of saying, *I want out of my job,* you might phrase your statement as, *I want a new job that pays me at least . . .* and put in the minimum salary you would like.

In the new moon ephemeris page 254, find the date for the next new moon. On that date, write out your wish and back it with all of the emotion, intent, belief, and imagination that you can muster. Trust that whatever you want will come about. It helps to ritualize this type of visualization in whatever way feels most comfortable to you—lighting a candle or a stick of incense, putting on your favorite music, meditating.

As a Taurus, you're good at working with your hands, particularly when it comes to gardening, so consider selecting seeds for a favorite plant or flower and plant the seeds as part of your ritual. If so, use a ceramic pot and state your wish aloud as you're planting the seeds. When the seeds begin to sprout, your wish is beginning to manifest itself in your life.

9

SUN IN GEMINI: COMMUNICATOR AND NETWORKER

May 21–June 20

COMMUNICATOR

See that symbol up there for Gemini? It stands for "the twins." It means there are at least two of you inhabiting the same body, two entities with their own moods, thoughts, beliefs, opinions, needs, and desires. No, it isn't schizophrenia—although people who live with you might disagree—it's just that there are two clearly defined aspects to your personality.

At least one of your twins is a communicator. Whether her preference is the written or the spoken word, her need to communicate is as necessary to her survival as breathing air. She can talk to anyone about anything, and even if her knowledge of a particular subject isn't deep, her gift of gab keeps the conversation moving.

The shadow side of this archetype is the person who never shuts up, who talks on and on about her grandparents, her third cousins, and simply assumes this is of great interest to you. Or there's Gemini the gossip, on the phone or in an E-mail loop spreading rumors and stories about other people. But when this archetype functions correctly, Gemini learns and absorbs information quickly and then communicates what she knows.

You're undoubtedly familiar with a secondary facet of your archetype—the chameleon. This quality enables you to walk into a room filled with people and to adjust your personality and presence so that you immediately blend in. It helps you to communicate with strangers in a way that makes them feel as if they have known you for years. It can also make you so malleable that you adjust your opinions and beliefs to fit someone else's. If you do that long enough, you eventually lose your hold on your own beliefs and your worldview becomes a game of trivia.

The communicator part of you is a voracious reader or moviegoer (or both), enjoys learning, and collects facts as if they are priceless pieces of art. The types of facts vary from one Gemini to another. Some gather statistics on everything from who is prone to cancer to the kinds of books that most women read. Others gather facts on stocks or best-sellers, politicians or movie stars. And then you use these facts to back up your opinions and beliefs. This, too, has a shadow side—the Gemini who spouts statistics to impress others.

It may seem that you're being picked on, what with all this talk about the shadow side. But for you, the twins, there are always two sides to everything. Your logic, for instance, can be so impeccable that you can convince yourself that nearly anything is true—at least for that moment. But another part of you acts on instinct and intuition, which is just as finely honed as your logic. You are two sides of a coin, and your challenge is to accept that both sides are equally valid.

NETWORKER

As the other twin, you're also a communicator, but your main interest is people. In a sense, you collect people the way the first twin collects facts, and your network is usually vast and intricate.

Imagine a spiderweb, a delicate construct of gossamer filaments that stretches from one coast to another or from one continent to another. Now imagine raindrops shimmering against those threads. Each drop is one of your contacts. You know each contact well enough to have some idea of his or her interests, areas of expertise. Perhaps one contact is a UFO buff and another claims to have been abducted by aliens. You don't pass judgment; you merely connect the two people. *Hey, you need to talk to so and so. Here's his E-mail address.* Usually, it's just that innocent, that spontaneous.

Of the two twins, you, the networker, are actually more social, more personable. The communicator needs an audience, but she doesn't have to know that audience personally. You, though, thrive on personal contact. Even if you meet someone over the Internet and get to know that person through E-mail and phone calls, you usually reach a point where you have to meet the person face-to-face. Even if that personal contact happens only a few times in your life, it makes the difference between acquaintance and friend.

One of the subtypes of the networker archetype is the messenger, a direct link to your ruling planet, Mercury, also known as Hermes in mythology. When you network with people, you *are* the messenger.

YOUR PLOTS AND MERCURY

Your sensitivity to your ruling planet depends to a large extent on your natal chart—how the planets line up in the houses, the aspects the planets make to each other, the whole tone and texture of the horoscope. However, since the sun symbolizes your primal energy, the aspects that Mercury—and the other planets—make to your sun sign reveals patterns that provide insight into the unfolding of your life.

The checklist below is intended to help you hone in on some of the broad patterns that repeat themselves over time. First glance at pages 38–39 and review the areas that Mercury rules. In a broad sense, it rules all types of communication. This includes writing, speaking, phone calls, faxes, E-mail and snail mail, and any other form of communication that you can think of. It symbolizes your intellect and your rational mind, your left brain as opposed to your right brain. It represents contracts and sales, travel and transportation, school and learning, books and manuscripts, teaching and teachers. Your siblings, relatives, and neighbors fall under Mercury's domain. In terms of the physical body, it rules what comes in pairs: hands, fingers, shoulders. It also rules your eyes.

The list for every planet's rulership is long. But for our purposes, the areas just mentioned should be enough for you to get some sense of how story lines might evolve when Mercury makes aspects to your sun. Using the checklist that follows, think about events that have happened to you since 1990 that involve the areas Mercury rules. Check off the events that apply and try to remember dates. Granted, some events connected with Mercury are so inconsequential that you probably won't recall dates. But since we're after patterns, fill in as many details about the time frame as you remember.

Then, in the list that follows, take a look at the time frames in the last thirteen years when Mercury was in Gemini. You should find some matches between the events you've pinpointed and those dates.

GEMINI/MERCURY CHECKLIST

___ I sold or bought a house.   _____

___ I sold a book or screenplay.   _____

___ I took a trip that was significant in
    some way.   _____

___ I had a falling out with a brother or sister.   _____

___ I had a significant disagreement
    with a relative or neighbor.   _____

___ I injured my hands or shoulders.   _____

___ I came down with a respiratory
    ailment.   _____

___ I recovered from an illness or injury.   _____

___ I was in car accident.   _____

___ I read a book that changed my life.   _____

___ My brother or sister was born.   _____

___ I got or lost an important contact
    or client.   _____

___ I lost a relative or neighbor who
    meant a lot to me.   _____

___ I made an important social or
    professional contact.   _____

___ I took a workshop or seminar that
    changed me in some way.   _____

___ I resumed my education.   _____

___ I changed schools.   _____

___ I went to college.   _____

___ I began a career in communication.   _____

___ I won a prize or award.   _____

___ I had a terrific vacation.   _____

___ My vacation went down the tubes.   _____

___ My eyesight changed.   _____

___ I had a child.   _____

___ I adopted a child.   _____

___ Any other significant event (describe).   _____

Now take a look at the dates below. Do any of your dates match these?

DATES: MERCURY IN GEMINI, 1990–2002

6/11/90–6/26/90
6/4/91–9/18/91
5/26/92–6/9/92
5/18/93–5/31/93
5/9/94–5/27/94
5/2/95–7/9/95
6/13/96–7/1/96
6/8/97–6/22/97
6/1/98–6/14/98
5/23/99–6/5/99
5/14/00–5/28/00
5/5/01–7/11/01
4/30/02–7/6/02

THE SCOOP ON MERCURY RETROGRADES

This planet moves quickly, racing through a single sign in fewer than three weeks, unless it's moving retrograde. Then it spends eight to ten weeks in a sign. You may feel its influence most strongly when it changes signs from Taurus to Gemini and as it approaches a direct hit on your sun.

The impact of Mercury retrograde is something all of us feel to varying degrees. Among my astrologers friends, whether they are Geminis or some other sign, there is usually a collective groan as the retrograde period approaches. Vicki, a Leo and a librarian—Mercury rules books, remember?—often jokes that at work, entire months feel like Mercury is retrograde—even when it isn't. *The computers at work went berserk today,* she reports. Or, *Our power went down for thirty minutes.*

As a Gemini, I pay attention to Mercury retrogrades in that I'm aware of them. But I don't plan my life around them. I figure I got along just fine for years without being aware of Mercury retrogrades at all, so just how terrible can they be?

As a writer, a field ruled by Mercury, I try to use the energy of a Mercury retrograde to my advantage—to revise, go over what I've written, or even to clean out my office. I'm aware that if I sign a contract when Mercury is retrograde, I may have to revisit the contract in some way, or there may be a delay involved. Yet if a contract lands in my mailbox during a Mercury retro, I can't justify setting it aside for three or four weeks. That only delays my check. Besides, how would I explain this to people who may not know anything about astrology, much less a Mercury retrograde? *Oh, sorry. I can't do this right now. Mercury is going backward.* But I do read the fine print to make sure I understand all the legalese.

Astrologers generally advise that travel under a Mercury retrograde isn't a good idea. And if you do travel you should expect delays, snafus, miscommunications. Yet there is something too fatalistic about this kind of thinking. *We* create our realities. If you expect delays and snafus, then that's probably what you'll encounter. But if you approach travel under a Mercury retro with a sense of adventure, who knows what incredible things might happen? Under one Mercury retro, for example, my family and I went to California. The trip out there was fine, the plane food was actually edible, no flights were delayed. On the way back, the flight was overbooked and free tickets were offered to people who gave up their seats. We went home with three free tickets, good for a year.

So when you begin to explore Mercury transits to your sun and run into retrogrades, look for the silver lining. You can usually find one.

In the ephemeris on pages 257–271 the Mercury retrograde periods between 2003 and 2007 are indicated by Rx. You may want to note these periods under "Important Dates."

REPETITIVE PATTERNS

If, in brainstorming your past, you recall important events that happened during at least two periods when Mercury was in Gemini, then you have the beginning of a pattern. It's just as likely that similar patterns have developed over the years when Mercury was making aspects to your sun other than the conjunction. In the Mercury ephemeris, look for the dates in the next five years when Mercury is going to be in Sagittarius (opposition), Aries or Leo (sextile), Virgo or Pisces (square), or Libra and Aquarius (trine). Create possible story lines for these aspects.

Important Dates for Mercury, 2003–2007

DATE	SIGN	ASPECT	STORY LINES

GENIUS AND MADNESS

Gemini. The twins. Two faces, two minds, two personalities inhabiting one body. At its darkest and most extreme, Gemini is schizophrenic. This propensity is brilliantly depicted in the biography and the movie *A Beautiful Mind,* the story of mathematician John Nash, a professor at Princeton University who suffered from schizophrenia for thirty years and went on to win the Nobel Prize in physics in 1994. Nash is a Gemini, born on June 13, 1928, putting his Gemini sun at 22 degrees.

After I saw the movie, I suspected that Nash was a Gemini but wasn't sure until I read the prologue of Sylvia Nasar's biography. "Nash's faith in rationality and the power of pure thought was extreme. . . . Einstein once chided him for wishing to amend relativity theory without studying physics," Nasar wrote. And yet, for all

his rationality, Nash worked at a deep intuitive level more often associated with music and art. "Nash saw the vision first, constructing
the laborious proofs long afterward."

In another part of the prologue, Nasar talks about Nash's solitary
nature and his apparent inability to form close emotional bonds. She
mentions that he had a secret life (the other twin's life?) that included
a mistress, an illegitimate son, and a profound ambivalence toward
his wife. And beneath all of this was "a haunting fear of failure."

Nasar doesn't give the exact time of Nash's birth, but for the day
he was born, his ruling planet, Mercury, was in the nurturing sign of
Cancer, suggesting a highly intuitive mind. Mercury was conjunct a
fixed star called Sirius. Astrologer Bernadette Brady, writing in her
landmark book *Fixed Stars*, calls Sirius "a marker of great deeds . . .
The individual, however, may be sacrificed to this collective expression or may gain fame and glory." It seems that Nash experienced
both sides of this fixed star.

On October 12, 1994, Nash learned that he'd won the Nobel.
(You may want to follow along using a blank chart, with Gemini on
the Ascendant.) On that day, Mercury (6 degrees), Jupiter (17
degrees), Venus (17 degrees), and Pluto (26 degrees) were all in
Scorpio; Neptune (10 degrees), Uranus (22 degrees), and the Moon
were in Capricorn; Mars was in Leo at 4 degrees; Saturn was in
Pisces at 6 degrees, and the Sun was in Libra at about 18 degrees.
Use one of the blank horoscope wheels and put Gemini on the
Ascendant, Cancer on the cusp of the second house, and move counterclockwise around the wheel, placing each of the subsequent signs
on the appropriate cusps. Then put the planets in their respective
houses. Mars falls into the second house, the transiting Sun into the
fourth, the Scorpio cluster into the sixth, the Moon and Neptune
into the seventh and Uranus on the cusp of the eighth.

Even the simplest story lines are revealing. On this day, the transiting Sun was making a trine to his natal Sun, giving him an ease
and facility with groups. His inner and outer selves were in harmony
and balance, the very things that had eluded Nash for three decades.
Uranus was forming an exact quincunx to his Sun, indicating that an
adjustment in his health had made this event possible. The cluster of

planets in his sixth house are directly related to his health and work. Mercury indicates news about health or work-related issues; Venus promises help from women as well as recognition; Jupiter is about luck, expansion, and creativity; and Pluto promises a profound transformation that could signal personal and professional triumph. For Nash, this grouping in transformative Scorpio spelled Nobel.

At 20 degrees, Neptune in Capricorn makes a two-degree quincunx to his Sun. This suggests there was some confusion among the powerful people in the Nobel academy and that they had to make an adjustment in their thinking. Nasar explains this as a division in the academy about awarding the prize to Nash because of his illness. The Moon in Capricorn transiting the seventh house indicates that the Nobel struck at the emotional heart of who Nash really is and recognized his professional achievements.

THE OUTER PLANETS: THEMES

The transits of the faster-moving planets are instrumental in figuring out your story lines on a daily, weekly, or monthly. But keep an eye on what the outer planets are doing, too. They provide the underlying themes, the deeper layers of the story lines that unfold over a period of years.

Uranus, Neptune, and Pluto move so slowly that you won't experience every aspect to your sun unless the length of your life defies present longevity statistics. In the immediate future, the only Uranus transits to your sun that you'll experience are the trine from Uranus in Aquarius, which has been happening since 1996, and the square from Uranus in Pisces, which begins in 2003.

The trine is all about liberation, heightened creativity, and the breakdown of anything in your life that restricts or limits your individuality. You can expect sudden and unexpected change in the areas where your life has become predictable. In real life, this can translate into a variety of experiences. Some are painful when they're happening, but they invariably open new vistas in your life. Your spiritual beliefs deepen, your work habits change, your creative interests burgeon. You begin to realize there are some things over which you have no control. But all of the events that lead to these realizations break up the parts of you that are stuck in routine and predictability. And the end results prepare you for the Uranus square in Pisces.

The square is a test of your individuality and the path you've chosen. It's the equivalent of a little devil whispering in your ear, tempting you to do something that goes against what you believe. If you resist the temptations, then the structures you've built and the path you've carved are definitely right for you.

Neptune has been in Aquarius since 1998, so you've been experiencing a double trine to your sun. The Neptune trine will continue until March 2011, then Neptune goes into Pisces and you get hit with a Neptune square. Neptune transits create confusion, deepening spirituality, a tenuous hold on reality, and sharpened intuition. There's a selflessness and compassion that goes along with these transits, too, that can sometimes border on martyrdom. Addiction or substance abuse also can be one of the manifestations. The trine harmonizes your inner and outer selves, the square in Pisces clarifies who you are. If a relationship or situation doesn't mirror the genuine you, out it goes.

As for Pluto, it's been in opposition to your Sun since November 1995, when it went into Sagittarius, and that won't end until January 2008. Mostly, the opposition is about power and transformative experiences. During my experience so far of this opposition, I've changed agents and publishers, expanded my writing into astrology and the tarot (the Uranus trine helped that along, too), and started writing thrillers instead of mysteries. My mother died and my father was diagnosed with Parkinson's and lived with us for three years. And that's just for starters.

TIMING AND TRANSITS

Since you were very small, you probably have heard the adage *Timing is everything.* This is certainly true with transits.

The list below provides common situations in which timing is often crucial to your success. What planets and aspects are the best for these situations? The answers are given after the activity. If your answers don't match mine, it doesn't mean they're wrong.

Remember that when working with transits, *you* script your life; transits merely provide information that can make the business of living easier.

For easy reference: A conjunction is a planet in Gemini; a sextile is a planet in Aries or Leo; a square is planet in Virgo or Pisces; a trine is a planet in Aquarius or Libra; and an opposition is a planet in Sagittarius.

+ **Move:** Moon in Cancer or an element compatible with Gemini. Mars conjunction. Mercury sextile or trine, moving direct.
+ **Wedding:** Venus in Gemini or a fire sign. Moon in the natal seventh house. Jupiter conjunct, sextile, or trine.
+ **Honeymoon:** Venus in Gemini or another air sign. Moon in Sagittarius.
+ **Divorce:** Mercury direct. Positive Jupiter/sun contacts
+ **Submit a creative project:** Mercury direct in Gemini. Positive Venus/sun or Jupiter/sun contacts.
+ **Take a course or return to school:** Mercury direct, sextile, or trine Gemini.
+ **Buy a home:** Moon in Cancer or Gemini. Positive Venus/sun and Jupiter/sun contacts. Mercury direct.
+ **List a home for sale:** Moon in Cancer. Mars in Gemini. Mercury direct.
+ **Interview for a job:** Venus sextile or trine. Moon or Mercury in Gemini, Mercury direct.
+ **Business trip:** Mercury direct. Saturn sextile or trine.
+ **Take a cruise:** Moon in a water sign or in Sagittarius. Mercury direct.
+ **Sign a contract:** Mercury direct. Jupiter conjunct, sextile, or trine.
+ **Begin a creative project:** Mercury direct. Venus or Mars conjunct. Positive Jupiter contacts.
+ **Start a diet:** New moon in Gemini or in an earth sign.
+ **Travel overseas:** Mercury direct, preferably in Sagittarius or other fire sign. Positive Jupiter/sun contacts.

✦ **Get pregnant:** Moon in Cancer or in sign on the cusp of natal fifth house. Positive Venus/sun contacts.

✦ **Buy a computer:** Mercury conjunct. Uranus sextile or trine.

✦ **Throw a party/socialize:** Venus sextile or trine.

✦ **Buy a new car:** Mercury direct.

✦ **Spiritual pursuits:** Positive contacts from Uranus, Neptune, or Pluto. Venus or Jupiter conjunct, sextile, trine.

MANIFESTATION: WHAT DREAMS MAY COME

If you haven't seen the movie or read the book, *What Dreams May Come* by Richard Matheson, do one or the other. Better yet, do both. The setup is simple: A married man is killed in a car accident. When he comes to, he doesn't realize he's dead, and he attempts to communicate with his wife and kids. Eventually, a guide gives him a "tour" of the afterlife, in which thoughts and desires are instantly manifested.

Robin Williams, in the leading role, learns to negotiate a world that is visually stunning and where everything materializes the instant he thinks of it. Okay, so he's dead. But the idea that what we want might materialize as soon as the desire rises in our hearts is empowering. And, really, it can be almost that easy if we just remember *how* to do it.

In the new moon ephemeris, on page 254, find the date for the next new moon in Gemini or in Libra or Aquarius (trine) or in Aries or Leo (sextile). On that date, write out your wish and back it with intense emotion and *belief* that what you want will manifest itself. *Imagine* it. *Smell* it. *Taste* it. Engage all your senses. Trust that whatever you desire will come about and don't worry about *how*.

If you want to ritualize this visualization, great. Do whatever feels comfortable. Aries and Taurus are encouraged to plant seeds in a ceramic pot and state their wish aloud. You, Gemini, may want to open a file on your computer or make an entry in your journal about how the realization of this wish will change your life.

Believe what you write. See it happening. Then get out of the way and let the universe do its part.

♋

10

SUN IN CANCER: NURTURER AND INTUITIVE

June 21–July 22

NURTURER

If I were in the hospital or recovering from an illness, my first choice in caregivers would be a Cancer. No other sign is as nurturing, which helps explain why many Cancers are drawn to the healing professions.

You are the quintessential enigma, compassionate and nurturing and, yet, often emotionally elusive. Your emotions, in fact, can be as puzzling to you as they are to other people. Despite your kindness and compassion toward others, you aren't emotionally confrontational. If someone attempts to pin you down about what you feel, you dodge the issue, moving sideways, just like the crab that symbolizes your sign. This tendency is due, at least in part, to a fear of being trapped.

You need roots—a home, a piece of land, even a van or an RV will do as long as its *yours*. Once you have that, your nurturing finds its fullest expression. You can nurture anything—your plants, your animals, your children, your creativity. If you don't have children of your own, you may have a special relationship with a child or children of friends and relatives. Or perhaps you volunteer for a local Big Brother, Big Sister organization. Or for a pet rescue organization.

Your need to nurture finds expression in some facet of your life and fulfills who you are. But it doesn't do that without the help of your secondary archetype.

INTUITIVE

As a cardinal water sign ruled by the moon, you are one of the most intuitive individuals in the zodiac. Your intuition works most smoothly through your emotions—the sudden hunch, the inexplicable lift or drop in your mood, the impulse to contact someone you haven't seen in years. If nurtured, this intuitive ability can easily develop into full-blown clairvoyance.

You're a naturally introspective person and probably already listen to your intuitive guidance. If you meditate or do tai chi or yoga or some other kind of physical/spiritual discipline, then your intuition is exceptionally strong. Your intuition may work most powerfully in the area of your life where you are the most nurturing—your family and kids, animals, or your patients, if you work in the healing profession. Or, because security is important to you, your intuition may be especially powerful in the area that provides you your greatest sense of security. Maybe you buy and sell homes or property, a natural area for Cancers, or maybe stocks or antique jewelry are your thing. Whatever your passion, let your intuition guide you.

Your intuition is your greatest and most loyal ally. If you use it to understand the evolving story lines in your life, you probably won't ever have a flawed interpretation.

YOUR PLANETARY PLOTS

In the first three sun sign chapters, a major part of the material explores story lines that have evolved when the sign's ruling planet makes aspects to the sun. But since the moon changes signs every two to three days, remembering significant events related to the moon in a particular sign would be a difficult and maybe impossible task, even for someone whose memory is legendary. So we're going to do things somewhat differently in this chapter.

Below is a checklist of common events. Cover up the column on the right (my suggested planet). Put a ✓ next to the events that have happened to you at least twice, then use the table on pages 39–41 to determine the planet that rules the event. In some instances, there's more than one correct answer. Also, some of these events may have extenuating circumstances.

PLANETARY CHECKLIST

EVENT	RULING PLANET	
	Your suggestion	*My suggestion*
___ I sold or bought a home.		Moon, Mercury
___ I sold a book or screenplay.		Mercury
___ I took a foreign trip that was significant in some way.		Jupiter
___ I was in a car accident.		Mars, Mercury
___ I won or lost an important client.		Saturn, Mars, Moon

EVENT	RULING PLANET	
	Your suggestion	*My suggestion*
I changed schools.		Moon, Mercury, Jupiter
I read a book that brought about a dramatic change in my life.		Mercury, Pluto
I changed careers.		Saturn, Mars, Uranus
I took up music, art, or some other creative endeavor.		Venus, Neptune
I resumed my education.		Mercury, Jupiter
I got pregnant.		Moon, Venus
I got involved in volunteer work.		Neptune
I had surgery.		Mars, moon
My intuition deepened significantly.		Uranus, Neptune
I found my path in life.		Jupiter
My spiritual beliefs changed dramatically.		Uranus, Neptune, Pluto, moon
I moved.		Moon, Mercury
I had elective surgery.		Mars, moon
A significant relationship abruptly began or ended.		Venus, Mars, moon, Uranus

EVENT	RULING PLANET	
	Your suggestion	*My suggestion*
___ I got fired from a job.		Mars, Saturn
___ I found my dream job.		Venus, Jupiter
___ I started my own business.		Saturn, Venus, Mars
___ I experienced a dramatic healing.		Pluto, Jupiter
___ Someone I loved deeply passed away.		Uranus, Neptune, Pluto
___ I fell in love.		Venus, Mars

A ✓ next to any of these events indicates that you may be sensitive to transits from the planets that rule that event. Find the planets with the most check marks, then use the ephemeris for each of those planets to find when it will be in Cancer (conjunction), Virgo and Taurus (sextile), Libra and Aries (square), Scorpio and Pisces (trine), and Capricorn (opposition). Jot the dates in the space below and create possible story lines.

Important Dates for 2003–2007

DATE	SIGN	ASPECT	STORY LINES

VIVIAN'S STORY

Vivian, a Cancer, is a psychiatric ER nurse in a large city hospital in Georgia. In most ways, she's a classic Cancer—nurturing and deeply intuitive. Her intuition works smoothly in both her professional and personal lives and is often uncanny when it comes to animals.

Like many Cancer individuals, Vivian has an exceptional memory. This comes from the moon's association with emotions and that we tend to remember people and situations with emotional connections. She can describe a scent from twenty years ago as though it were yesterday. But she is lousy with dates. When I asked her to give me the date of a significant event in her life that I could use as an example for this book, she hemmed and hawed. "For what kind of event?" she asked.

"Anything important. When you were married. When you bought your house . . ."

Silence. "You know, I'm not real good with dates. But, wait. How about this—the date of my eye surgery."

Two days earlier, Vivian had Laser surgery on her eyes to correct her vision so that she wouldn't have to wear glasses. I'd been hoping for something, well, more Cancerian, like the sale or purchase of a house or property. But I didn't have any eye surgery examples, so why not?

Before we get into the specifics, you may want to set up a horoscope wheel for a solar chart as we did in an earlier chapter. With a solar chart, the sun sign goes on the ascendant. Leo goes on the cusp of the second house, and on around the wheel so that Gemini ends up on the twelfth house cusp. Vivian was born on July 15, which puts her sun in Cancer at about 22 degrees. Put that degree on the cusp of each house, so that you have an equal-house solar chart, so we'll do this example more specifically than we have in the in the earlier charts.

The date of Vivian's surgery was February 11, 2002, and the lineup of the planets is given below. As you go through the list, place each planet in its appropriate house. Remember that the houses begin at 22 degrees. This means that Pluto at 17 degrees Sagittarius would go in the fifth house, not the sixth. Your wheel should look like this:

- ✦ Sun in Aquarius, 22 degrees
- ✦ Moon in Aquarius, 10 degrees
- ✦ Mercury in Capricorn, 28 degrees
- ✦ Venus in Aquarius, 28 degrees
- ✦ Mars in Aries, 16 degrees
- ✦ Jupiter in Cancer, 6 degrees, retrograde
- ✦ Saturn in Gemini, 8 degrees, retrograde
- ✦ Uranus in Aquarius, 24 degrees
- ✦ Neptune in Aquarius, 8 degrees
- ✦ Pluto in Sagittarius, 17 degrees

Let's look at the aspects first. Refer to page 58 to refresh your memory about aspects to Cancer. Or look at the section just above the important dates section.

The only possible opposition—and it's wide, 6 degrees, but not so wide as to be discounted—is Mercury in Capricorn at 28 degrees. Since Mercury rules the eyes, the opposition is important. The only square is Mars in Aries at 16 degrees (again, it's not exact, but it's not so wide as to disqualify it). Mars rules surgery, so this aspect is also significant. There aren't any sextiles or trines. What about all those planets in Aquarius? None of them is forming a major aspect to Vivian's sun. But there *is* a minor aspect: The transiting sun is forming an exact quincunx (150 degrees) with Vivian's natal sun. If we allow a 2-degree orb, then Uranus is also forming a quincunx to Vivian's natal sun. If you refer back to the descriptions of aspects in Chapter 5, you find that a quincunx usually means an adjustment of some kind that is often related to health.

In terms of the story line, the Mercury opposition represents Vivian's eyes, and the Mars square, the elective surgery on her eyes. This is something she wanted done primarily for cosmetic purposes, so that she wouldn't have to wear glasses anymore. In other words, this was an ego (sun) decision. The quincunxes from the transiting sun and from transiting Uranus symbolize adjustments in her health (in this case, her eyes). Quincunxes often represent situations that come about spontaneously, and this is certainly true in Vivian's case. She dances in her free time and had seen a video of a dance contest she was in and didn't like the way she looked in glasses. She'd heard about the ophthalmologist through a friend and decided to find out if she was a candidate for laser surgery and whether the price was right. The Uranus quincunx is especially interesting because Uranus represents cutting-edge technology like lasers.

Saturn in Gemini in the eleventh house represents a dream or goal that is realized through a structure of some kind. The structure was the doctor and medical science and the goal was to look better. However, the fact that Saturn is going retrograde could mean this surgery may not be the last. And actually, that's what happened. The cornea in one eye was torn slightly, and Vivian will have that eye redone in a couple of months. This didn't cause any impairment in her vision (Jupiter's protection in the twelfth house), but it's inconvenient. The retrograde Jupiter itself simply means that the planet's energies are turned inward. For Vivian, this means that she's looking at the experience as a metaphor, that she is prepared to "see" her life and her experiences differently.

Neptune and the moon in Aquarius don't form any aspects to Vivian's sun until February 12, when she made the emotional adjustment to the fact that the surgery on the other eye would have to be repeated. Those are the major points in the story line.

If we were working with Vivian's natal chart instead of the horoscope wheel we've set up, the aspects to her sun wouldn't change. But the placement of the transiting planets in the houses would change dramatically, another good reason to have your natal chart in front of you when you're doing predictive astrology. However, since we're working just with transits to your sun sign, the horoscope wheel gives you a fairly accurate picture of emerging story lines.

THE OUTER PLANETS: THEMES

The rapidly moving inner planets are key to understanding emerging story lines daily, weekly, and monthly. But the outer planets, because they move so slowly, provide underlying themes that unfold over time.

You won't experience every aspect from the outer planets to your sun during your lifetime. In the immediate future, you'll go through the Uranus trine in Pisces that begins in March 2003 and the square in Aries starting in May 2010.

In the list of the solar archetypes in the first chapter, Pisces is described as mystic and healer; the trine is about inner harmony and balance, and Uranus symbolizes sudden, unexpected events that highlight our individuality and creativity. Combine the meanings. You can expect the unexpected to present you with new opportunities that highlight your individuality and that both deepen and broaden your creativity. Relationships and structures that don't serve that underlying theme are eliminated from your life. Ultimately, the trine in Pisces takes you deeper into spiritual thought, and that new spirituality may be expressed somehow in your creative expression.

All of this prepares you for the square in Aries in 2010, a time of friction and challenges. People and situations will challenge your individuality and force you to stand up for yourself and what you believe. The Aries influence can bring disruption, wild impulses, recklessness, a hunger for adventure.

In the spring of 2011, Neptune in Pisces trine to your sun, considerably deepening your spiritual beliefs. You'll be confused about your goals and perhaps about your role in the world. Your sense of reality won't be as strong as it usually is. The best way to navigate this aspect is to have a spiritual discipline and belief system already in place.

In the summer of 2008, Pluto goes into Capricorn, forming an opposition to your sun. This aspect brings power struggles to the forefront of your life, along with various kinds of transformative experiences. The fact that part of the opposition will be happening with the Neptune trine can make this is a chaotic time. Find your grounding before either aspect approaches.

TIMING AND TRANSITS

The list below gives common situations in which timing is important to your success and tells what planets and aspects are best for these situations.

As you read through the list, please remember that transits don't make or break your life. All they do is provide information that empowers you and enables you to negotiate the business of living successfully and happily. If your answers differ from mine, don't worry about it. There are many aspects for various situations. Just be able to justify your answers in your own mind.

For easy reference: A conjunction is a planet in Cancer; a sextile is a planet in Virgo or Taurus; a square is a planet in Aries or Libra; a trine is a planet in Scorpio or Pisces; an opposition is a planet in Capricorn.

+ **Move:** Moon in Cancer or in another water sign or an earth sign. Mars conjunction. Mercury sextile or trine, moving direct.
+ **Wedding:** Venus in Cancer or an earth sign. Moon in the natal seventh house. Jupiter conjunct, sextile, or trine.
+ **Honeymoon:** Venus in Cancer or another water sign. Moon in an earth sign.
+ **Divorce:** Mercury direct. Positive Jupiter/sun contacts.
+ **Psychic/spiritual development:** Positive contacts from Jupiter, Uranus, or Neptune. Venus in Cancer or another water sign.
+ **Buy a home/property:** Moon in Cancer. Mercury direct. Positive contacts from Venus and Jupiter.
+ **List a home for sale:** Moon conjunct, sextile, or trine. Mercury direct. Mars sextile or trine.
+ **Interview for a job:** Venus sextile or trine. Moon in Cancer or another water sign. Mercury direct.

- **Begin a creative project:** Mercury direct. Venus conjunct. Mars sextile or trine. Jupiter conjunct, sextile, or trine.
- **Throw a huge party:** Venus sextile or trine. Jupiter conjunct, sextile, or trine.
- **Sign a contract:** Mercury direct. Jupiter conjunct, sextile, or trine.
- **Get pregnant:** Moon in Cancer or in sign on cusp of natal fifth house. Positive Venus contacts.
- **Get a new pet:** Moon in Cancer or Sagittarius. Venus in natal fifth house. Jupiter conjunct, sextile, or trine.
- **Schedule surgery:** Mars sextile or trine. Mercury direct. Positive Jupiter contacts.
- **Home projects:** Moon in Cancer, sextile, or trine. Mars conjunct.
- **Move your office:** Mercury direct. Jupiter conjunct, sextile, or trine.
- **House hunt:** Moon or Mars conjunct, sextile, or trine. Mercury direct.
- **Resign from a job (you hope to go to something better):** Jupiter conjunct, sextile, trine. Mercury direct.
- **Buy a new car:** Mercury direct in Cancer or sextile or trine.
- **Take a vacation:** Venus or Jupiter conjunct, sextile, or trine. Mercury direct. Transiting sun moving through natal fifth or ninth house.

MANIFESTATION: YOUR NORTH STAR

In the book *Finding Your Own North Star: Claiming the Life You Were Meant to Live,* Martha Beck makes a distinction between our "social selves" and our "essential selves." The first is the self that is composed of an accretion of negative beliefs about ourselves that we've learned from society. The second is our true self, which in many of us is a small, lost voice in a vast wilderness. By allowing our essential self to be heard, we find the life we were meant to live—our North Star.

In this activity, you're going to write out your deepest desire— your North Star—in a concise sentence. Maybe you wanted to play in a band when you were younger and gave up that dream because everyone around you told you it wasn't realistic. Or maybe you wanted to own your own company but relinquished that dream because your "social self" told you it was a stupid idea and you believed that.

On the next new moon, read your desire out loud. See yourself living your North Star. Taste it. Hear it. Experience it as fully as you can with all of your senses. Back the desire with emotion and intent. Make a gesture that symbolizes your desire. You might, for instance, create a poster board of photographs and drawings that represent your desire and post it where you'll see it often. Whatever your gesture is, make it genuine. Put the written version of your desire where you'll see it often and trust that by the next new moon, something about your desire will have manifested itself.

♌

11

SUN IN LEO:
ACTOR AND HERO

July 23–August 22

ACTOR

Face it: You love being the center of attention. The brighter the spot-
light, the happier you are, the bigger the audience, the greater your
acting ability. But you can assume a role anywhere, at any time, at a
moment's notice. You have an innate sense of the dramatic, the flamboyant, and life is always your stage.

Your magnetism and charisma are practically legendary in your
social circle. Even when you were very young, these qualities were
evident. In fact, if you ever doubt who you are, visit the lions at the
zoo. Watch how they stretch and preen and prowl, displaying their
sleek and incredible beauty, their rippling muscles, their breathtak-
ing power. Watch how they laze in the sun. And then notice the peo-

ple who watch the lions, their awe and amazement, their incredulity. *You* are the lion.

You're at your best when no one is telling you what to do, when you're completely in charge. Then you're the actor who owns the entire stage, who has a sixty-minute soliloquy to deliver and does it brilliantly. But beneath the bravado lies a small, insecure child who wants everyone to love her. This little kid figures that if she zips herself up inside the skin of some other person, if she becomes someone else, the object of her affection will love her back. Once you're an adult, this little kid is still crouched in the shadows, stirring up a storm. And this, Leo, is the source of your dilemma: Where do you drawn the line? Who is the *real* you? Where is the you separate from the public persona?

HERO

The hero always has a quest. Whether it's Han Solo saving the universe from Darth Vader or you going up against school bureaucracy for your seventh grader, the hero has an agenda that must be met. Many times, though, the hero doesn't even know he has an agenda. Indiana Jones usually started off looking for some ancient artifact and then suddenly found himself in the midst of a quest much larger than his personal search.

In one form or another, the hero's quest is your quest. Perhaps you're an animal rights activist. Or an advocate for literacy or abused children. Or maybe your quest is achieved through your creative endeavors. It may be that you don't even know you're a hero in your own life but at some point will be called upon to show your stuff. And then you rise magnificently to the occasion.

Quite often, the hero archetype works in subtle ways, its threads woven throughout your daily life. Your home may be where the neighborhood kids congregate after school because your door is always open and the welcome mat is always out. Or maybe the word has gotten out to every stray cat and dog that no hungry animal is ever turned away from your place.

The ways the hero archetype operate in a Leo's life vary from one individual to the other. But one thing is for sure: As a fixed fire sign ruled by the sun, your hero is alive and well and forever at your beck and call.

YOUR PLANETARY PLOTS

The activity you're going to do here differs somewhat from the activities for the first three signs because your ruling planet moves so quickly. Instead of exploring story lines that evolve when the transiting sun makes aspects to your natal sun, you're going to do a bit of brainstorming about your planetary plots in general.

The checklist below contains common situations and events. Put a ✓ next to the events that have happened to you at least twice, then use the table on pages 38–41 to determine the planet that rules the event. The idea here is that you may be especially sensitive to transits from a particular planet and, if you are, you know to pay attention to its transits. In many instances the sensitivity is to the planet that rules the ascendant in your natal chart. If you've got Aries rising in your natal chart, then you may have a strong sensitivity to Mars transits.

With some of the items in the checklist, there's more than one correct answer. Also, some of these situations have extenuating circumstances that change the planetary ruler of the event. Cover the column on the far right while you do the activity, then compare your answers with mine.

PLANETARY CHECKLIST

EVENT	RULING PLANET
Your suggestion	*My suggestion*
___ I won an audition.	Sun, Venus, Jupiter
___ I sold a book or screenplay.	Mercury
___ I moved.	Moon, Mercury
___ I met my significant other.	Venus, moon

EVENT	RULING PLANET	
	Your suggestion	*My suggestion*
__ I had elective surgery.		Mars, moon
__ I found my dream job.		Venus, Jupiter
__ I was in a car accident.		Mars, Mercury
__ I sold or bought a home.		Moon, Mercury
__ I took a foreign trip that was significant in some way.		Jupiter
__ I changed careers.		Moon, Mercury, Jupiter
__ My intuition deepened significantly.		Uranus, Neptune
__ I read a book that changed my life dramatically.		Mercury, Pluto
__ I found my creative path.		Jupiter, Venus
__ A significant relationship abruptly began or ended.		Venus, Mars, moon, Uranus
__ I started my own business.		Saturn, Mars
__ I fell in love.		Venus, Mars
__ I won an award that changed my life.		Sun, Venus, Jupiter
__ I got pregnant.		Moon, Venus

EVENT	RULING PLANET	
	Your suggestion	*My suggestion*
__ I found my spiritual path.		Neptune, Venus
__ A loved one passed away.		Uranus, Neptune, Pluto
__ I experienced a dramatic healing.		Pluto, Jupiter
__ I built my dream house.		Saturn, Jupiter
__ A parent moved in with us.		Saturn, sun or moon, Jupiter
__ I married or got involved with someone considerably older.		Saturn, Venus
__ I got an animal I love.		Sun

Count the planets with the most checks, then use each ephemeris to find out when each of those planets, during the next five years, will be in Leo (conjunction), Libra or Gemini (sextile), Scorpio or Taurus (square), Sagittarius or Aries (trine), and Aquarius (opposition).

Important Dates for 2003–2007

DATE	SIGN	ASPECT	STORY LINES

DATE	SIGN	ASPECT	STORY LINES

VICKI'S STORY

Vicki, a librarian, is a double Leo (sun and rising). Her story has the kind of drama often associated with Leos.

On February 6, 2000, Vicki had a "Nazi dream," as she calls it. She and a group of friends go to a Caribbean island for the weekend. They stay in a large mansion. They know that Nazis go to this island, too, but they never bother anyone. One day she's walking down a road and a small plane lands in a nearby field. A group of people get out and among them is a Nazi soldier. He's slim, handsome, elegant, and obviously the head guy, a high-ranking Nazi official.

The Nazi and his group take over the mansion where Vicki is staying. He is attracted to her, and she realizes that as long as that attraction persists, it's okay for her and her friends to stay there. Time passes, maybe days or weeks, and Vicki learns that the Nazi has at least two mistresses. He brings one of them to the island with him. The other visits when the first mistress isn't around.

On a subsequent trip to the island, Vicki brings her young son with her. They arrive by boat, as before, with friends, to stay in the mansion. While her son is inside the house playing, another boat docks at the pier. It's the Nazi officer again, with mistress #1. He doesn't realize that mistress #2 is also on the island and sees him arriving with the other woman. The Nazi is upset and surprised to see his waiting mistress. As Vicki watches this drama unfold, one woman is seized, a bag is put over her head, and she's dragged off toward the house. Both mistresses are shot.

Then the Nazi turns his attention on Vicki, and she realizes she's next. Terrified and unable to get to the house where her son is, Vicki throws herself off the pier and drowns.

When Vicki related the dream to me, the dominant theme seemed to be the forced separation from her child. We talked about it and wondered if it related, somehow, to the daughter Vicki had given up for adoption when she was twenty, which she had regretted over since. About a month later, she had a dream about her daughter's father and, several months after that, a second dream about him. She thought this odd, since she rarely dreams about him. As it turned out, all three dreams seemed to be directly related to events that began to occur in late August, around Vicki's birthday, and which culminated over the Labor Day weekend.

The events were metamorphic and involved the words *bowling*, a *blown electrical transformer*, and *adoption*. Vicki suspected that these events were significant, and as we started brainstorming, the pieces came together. We believed that something was approaching that would *bowl* her over and *transform* her life dramatically. We figured it involved the daughter she'd given up for *adoption*. On Friday of the Labor Day weekend, Vicki decided to go with the flow and started an Internet search for the daughter she hadn't seen in thirty years. She ended up on ancestry.com and typed in her maiden name. On the message board for that name was a request for information on a woman with Vicki's full name and birth date—off by a decade but the right day. The birthplace was wrong, but it was the city where Vicki had been living when she'd given up her infant daughter for adoption.

Vicki contacted the person who had left the message and, for several days, they traded E-mails. It turned out that the person who had left the E-mail was doing a favor for a friend—Vicki's long-lost daughter. On September 7, 2000, Vicki and the daughter she'd given up three decades earlier finally connected. *If* Vicki hadn't been keeping track of her dreams, *if* she hadn't been aware of the metaphors of the synchronicities that occurred, *if* she hadn't conducted her Internet search, would things have turned out differently? We'll never know. But the story line was there.

Vicki's story is so unusual that I've included her natal chart in Appendix C. The transits for the exact moment when the phone call started—when they first connected—are provided below. In this example, the moon's nodes play an important role. We haven't talked much about the nodes, the vertex, or the part of fortune, but all of these points play important roles in Vicki's story line. Just to refresh your memory, the natal north node symbolizes the direction in which we're supposed to move to evolve spiritually, and the natal south node indicates all that is familiar and routine, our comfort zone. All too often we get stuck in that comfort zone. In terms of transits, the north node suggest opportunities and contacts with people who help us evolve spiritually, in line with the nature of the planet that is transited. The transiting south node indicates what we should leave behind. The vertex symbolizes encounters that feel like destiny, and the part of fortune is like your astrological pot of gold.

The easiest way to see these transits is to place them on the outside of Vicki's natal chart, in their appropriate signs and houses.

The transits for September 7, 2000 at 3:10 P.M. EDT line up like this:

- ✦ Sun 15 degrees Virgo, second house
- ✦ Moon 9 degrees Capricorn, fifth house
- ✦ Mercury 29 degrees Virgo, second house
- ✦ Venus 9 degrees Libra, cusp of third house
- ✦ Mars 24 degrees Leo, first house
- ✦ Jupiter 10 degrees Gemini, tenth house
- ✦ Saturn 00 degrees Gemini, tenth house
- ✦ Uranus retrograde 17 degrees Aquarius, nearly at cusp of seventh house
- ✦ Neptune retrograde 4 degrees Aquarius, sixth house
- ✦ Pluto 10 degrees Sagittarius, fourth house
- ✦ North node 23 degrees Cancer, twelfth house
- ✦ South node 23 degrees Capricorn, sixth house
- ✦ Vertex 15 degrees Leo, twelfth house, close to ascendant
- ✦ Part of fortune 28 degrees Aries, ninth house

The most readily apparent aspects to Vicki's sun are the 4-degree Mars conjunction in the first house and the trine from the part of fortune. The first energizes the sun and gives her the willpower and fortitude to proceed on what is largely intuitive information. The part of fortune supports her efforts.

Even though this book is primarily about transits to the sun, let's look at the other transits in this story line. There are a number of them:

the transiting sun making a 4-degree conjunction with Mercury in the second house; transiting Mercury making a 2-degree conjunction with Venus in the second house; the transiting moon conjuncts her natal vertex to the degree in the 5th house; the conjunction between the transiting south node and natal Jupiter in the fifth house; the transiting Uranus opposition to her ascendant; and the 2-degree conjunction between the transiting north node and the moon in the twelfth house.

The transiting sun conjunct Mercury suggests news or conversations about something that is personally important to Vicki (second house). The transiting Mercury conjunct Venus in the same house reinforces the news/conversations. This conjunction can also bring about expressions of love and concern between the parties involved, something that certainly happened during Vicki's three-hour conversation with her daughter. The transiting moon conjunction to the natal vertex is particularly telling because it falls in the fifth house (of children): a destined encounter with your firstborn child. Unconscious memories surface. Emotions are high and profound.

With the exact conjunction between the transiting south node and Jupiter, Vicki challenged the mores and rules (Jupiter) that caused her to give up her daughter for adoption in the first place and expanded herself spiritually. With Uranus at a one-degree opposition to Vicki's Ascendant, the events that led to the contact were sudden, unexpected, and changed the way other people perceive her. She has a grown son and daughter who were overjoyed to find—and subsequently meet—their half-sister.

The transiting north node making a two-degree conjunction to Vicki's natal Moon is also revealing—an emotional confirmation that she did the right thing. The transiting Vertex conjunct her natal Pluto and making a three-degree conjunction to her Ascendant tells us that the encounter with her daughter resulted in a profound transformation in Vicki's life. She finally felt whole again.

THE OUTER PLANETS: THEMES

Where the inner planet transits provide emerging story lines daily, weekly, and monthly, the transits of the outer planets pinpoint broad underlying themes that unfold over time. Uranus, Neptune, and Pluto move so slowly that you won't experience every aspect from these planets to your sun.

In the immediate future, you'll continue to feel the Uranus square in Aquarius. That ends March 10, 2003, when Uranus slides into Pisces. In May 2010, Uranus goes into Aries, forming a trine to your sun. Its retrograde motion sends it back through Pisces until April 2011, when it moves into Aries again for a seven-year stay.

The square in Aquarius, which you've been experiencing since 1995, challenges your individuality. People, situations, and events all seem to be conspiring against you. All the square is doing, though, is testing your commitment to the path you're on.

The trine in Aries, the sign known as the warrior and the pioneer, brings opportunities that support and enhance your individuality and creativity. You're able to work effectively with groups to pioneer new concepts or products, or your consciousness is such that you have your finger on the pulse of public opinion and instinctively know how to target your product for the public market. Your inner and outer selves work together flawlessly to achieve your goals.

The only aspect from Neptune that you need to consider is the one you've been in since 1998, when the planet went into Aquarius, forming an opposition to your sun. It will be there until April 2011, when it goes into Pisces. Life can certainly feel pretty strange under a Neptune opposition in Aquarius, and by now you probably know exactly how strange. Aquarius gives you vision, but Neptune brings a lack of clarity to your thinking. Your strongest allies at this time are your intuition and the clarity of your self-expression. Your spirituality probably has deepened under this transit and will see you through challenges that lie ahead.

As for Pluto, it's been in Sagittarius since late 1995, forming a trine to your sun, and will be there until late January 2008. The trine brings achievements, rewards, and positive change in your life. On some level, you now have the power to effect change in other people's lives. If you lay the groundwork during the trine, the opposition that comes up in 2025 shouldn't be a problem.

TIMING AND TRANSITS

Below is a list of common situations in which timing can be vital to your success, along with the planets and aspects that are the most advantageous for these situations. As always, if your opinion differs from mine, don't worry about it. But be able to justify your answers in your own mind.

For easy reference: A conjunction is a planet in Leo; a sextile is a planet in Libra or Gemini; a square is a planet in Scorpio or Taurus; a trine is a planet in Aries or Sagittarius; an opposition is a planet in Aquarius.

+ **Move:** Moon in Cancer or in a fire sign. Mars conjunction. Mercury sextile or trine, moving direct.
+ **Wedding:** Venus in Leo or another fire sign. Moon transiting the natal seventh house. Jupiter conjunct, sextile, or trine.
+ **Honeymoon:** Venus in Leo or another fire sign. Moon in a fire sign.
+ **Divorce:** Mercury direct. Positive Jupiter/sun contacts.
+ **Audition/interview for a job:** Venus and/or Jupiter conjunct, sextile, or trine. Moon in Leo or another fire sign.
+ **Psychic/spiritual development:** Positive contacts from Jupiter, Uranus, or Neptune.
+ **Talk out problems with coworkers:** Mercury direct and sextile or trine. Mars and/or Jupiter conjunct.
+ **Talk out problems with a significant other:** Positive Jupiter and Venus contacts. Moon in Sagittarius or an air sign. Mercury direct.
+ **Sign a contract:** Mercury direct. Jupiter conjunct, sextile, or trine.
+ **Take a business trip:** Mercury direct. Mars sextile or trine.
+ **Buy a car:** Mercury direct in Sagittarius or an air sign.

✦ **Begin a creative project:** Mercury direct. Venus conjunct. Mars sextile or trine. Jupiter conjunct, sextile, or trine.

✦ **Start your own business:** Mercury direct. Mars conjunct.

✦ **Change professions:** Mars conjunct, sextile, or trine. Saturn sextile or trine.

✦ **House hunt:** Moon in Cancer or a fire sign.

✦ **Resign from a job (to move to something better):** Jupiter conjunct, sextile, or trine. Mercury direct.

✦ **Take a vacation:** Mercury direct. Venus or Jupiter conjunct, sextile, or trine. Transiting sun moving through natal fifth or ninth house.

✦ **Get pregnant:** Moon in Cancer or in sign on cusp of natal fifth house. Positive Venus contacts.

✦ **Move your office:** Mars conjunct. Saturn sextile or trine.

✦ **Get a new pet:** Moon in Leo or another fire sign. Venus in natal fifth house. Jupiter conjunct, sextile, or trine.

Manifestation: The Wizard of Oz

When Dorothy heads off to Oz with her three buddies to find the wizard, she embarks on the hero's quest. Initially, her goal is simple, to find the wizard so that he can send her home. But as her journey proceeds, the quest becomes something much larger than just Dorothy's desire to get home. The scarecrow hopes the wizard will give him a brain. The tin man wishes for a heart. And the lion wishes for courage. You're the lion, Leo.

It isn't that you lack courage. You, like the lion, simply *believe* that you lack courage. In fact, your desire to be appreciated and loved by everyone stems from a basic insecurity that you somehow don't measure up. What nonsense.

Think of two or three incidents in which you, like Vicki, acted with courage. Now look up the date for the next new moon. On that day, write out your deepest desire in a concise sentence, in the present tense. When you finish saying it aloud, add, *And I am now pursuing this desire with courage and the deepest belief that I can achieve this.* If you want, ritualize this visualization in some way—light a candle or a stick of incense, plant seeds of your favorite flowers or plant.

Post what you've written where you'll see it often. Don't check every few minutes to see if your wish is being realized; just trust that if you do your part, the universe will do the rest.

12

♍

SUN IN VIRGO: PERFECTIONIST AND ANALYST

August 23–September 22

PERFECTIONIST

You begin life with a series of questions perched on the tip of your tongue: what, where, when, how, and why? These questions form the foundation of your restless, discriminating intellect and allow you to delve deeply into whatever you take on. In this way, you are very different from Gemini, which is also ruled by Mercury. Where Gemini can be satisfied by answers that seem to fit the question, you must be absolutely sure the answers precisely fit the question before you accept them. This is all part and parcel of your eternal quest for perfection.

The perfectionist archetype is probably responsible for the bad rap that Virgos have gotten. They are often described as picky, compulsive people whose homes are so tidy they can withstand the white glove test from a judgmental mother-in-law. While there are probably Virgos who fit that description, I've never met one. Their perfectionist tendencies usually seem to be most obvious in one or two areas of their lives—their profession, their creativity, their money—rather than across the board. In the areas where they are perfectionists, their attention to details can be astonishing. They notice nuances that entirely elude the rest of us. This quality is especially valuable in creative work, unless you become so picky and obsessed with details that it blocks your ability to create.

You instinctively understand that nothing is thrust on you, that you're the creator of your reality. And yet, because one of your archetypes is the analyst, your left brain sometimes sabotages what the right brain knows.

ANALYST

You're a master analyst. You can easily break something down into smaller comprehensible parts and then put it back together again in a better, more efficient way. You can do this with anything you tackle, which is one of the reasons that Virgos make such fine writers and editors.

The problem is that you often turn this analysis on yourself, and it becomes an exercise in self-criticism and self-sabotage that is unparalleled in the zodiac. *I'm not good enough, smart enough, pretty enough, creative enough* . . . These litanies are prompted by that inner need for perfection, and to master them, you need to understand that what you actually are seeking is an *ideal*.

Whether you're seeking to perfect yourself or a creative project or just your life in general, you're doing it because you feel compelled to do so. You can't tolerate a diamond in the rough. You have to shape it, tumble it, shine it, cut at it until you release the utter brilliance of the gem.

Quite often, the ideal is found in what astrologers usually refer to as "service to others." Personally, I dislike the phrase. It makes Virgos sound like servants or victims. What the phrase really means is that you delight in using your talents to help others. In fact, the more often you do that, the less critical and judgmental you are of yourself. Do what makes you feel good, Virgo, and you'll never go wrong. Don't take my word for it, though. Get out there and try it yourself.

YOUR PLOTS AND MERCURY

Your ruling planet is what makes you such an effective communicator, and it doesn't matter whether that venue of communication is speaking, writing, acting. The fact is that you have the gift. Yeah, I know. Your inner critic has just risen up, shouting, *What? Me? Don't be absurd.* Silence the inner critic long enough to finish this chapter on Virgo, okay?

To explore Mercury's role in your life and your sensitivity to its transits, we're going to look for broad patterns that may have repeated themselves over time. The checklist below will help you pinpoint possible patterns. Before you start, though, take a look at pages 38–39 to review the areas that Mercury rules.

Now think about events that have happened to you since 1990 in the areas that Mercury rules. Check off the ones that apply. Jot notes next to the items on the checklist. Try to recall dates. Fill in as many details as you can remember.

Then look at the time frames since 1990 when Mercury was in Virgo, listed below. There should be some correlation between the events you've pinpointed and the Mercury in Virgo dates.

VIRGO/MERCURY CHECKLIST

___ I sold a creative project. _____

___ I sold or bought a house. _____

___ I went to/returned to college. _____

___ I won a prize or award. _____

___ I began a career in communication. _____

___ I read a book that changed
    me dramatically. _____

___ I injured my hands or shoulders. _____

___ I came down with a respiratory infection. _____

___ I received a vitally important
     E-mail, fax, letter. _____

___ My siblings were born. _____

___ I took a trip that impacted my life _____

___ I was in a car accident. _____

___ I was recognized for a professional
     achievement. _____

___ I moved. _____

___ I got married. _____

___ I had a child. _____

___ I adopted a child. _____

___ I went into sales. _____

___ I signed an important contract. _____

___ I broke a contract. _____

Now take a look at the dates below. Do any of your dates match these?

DATES: MERCURY IN GEMINI, 1990–2002

6/11/90–6/26/90
6/4/91–9/18/91
5/26/92–6/9/92
5/18/93–5/31/93
5/9/94–5/27/94
5/2/95–7/9/95
6/13/96–7/1/96
6/8/97–6/22/97
6/1/98–6/14/98
5/23/99–6/5/99
5/14/00–5/28/00
5/5/01–7/11/01
4/30/02–7/6/02

REPETITIVE PATTERNS

Patterns are the heart of any predictive system, whether it's the I Ching, tarot, or astrology. If, in brainstorming your past, you remembered events that happened during at least two periods when Mercury was in Virgo, then you have the beginning of a pattern. It's just as likely that certain patterns have evolved over the years when Mercury made other aspects to your Sun. In the Mercury ephemeris, look for the dates in the next five years when Mercury is going to be in Pisces (opposition); Scorpio or Cancer (sextile); Gemini or Sagittarius (square); or Capricorn or Taurus (trine). Create possible story lines for each of these aspects.

Important Dates for Mercury, 2003–2007

DATE	SIGN	ASPECT	STORY LINES

THE SCOOP ON MERCURY RETROGRADES

When Mercury turns retrograde, everyone feels it to one degree or another. This is especially true in the information age, when we rely on rapid communication and air travel. But Virgo and Gemini may be particularly sensitive to Mercury retrogrades because this planet rules their signs.

The crucial point in the retrograde period often begins the day before Mercury turns retrograde and continues for a day or so after the retrograde motion has started. The other sensitive time is at the end of the retrograde, as Mercury prepares to go direct and then turns direct.

Recently, I was planning to visit my sister and father in Georgia. The time frame when I could travel and when Delta was offering the least expensive tickets fell during a Mercury retrograde. I knew that Mercury was going direct on February 8, so I made my return flight for the 9th, figuring that Mercury would be stabilized in direct motion by then. The flight up there was uneventful. Midweek, my sister and I were supposed to visit a homeopath in South Carolina. But a few days before I left home, she called to say she couldn't get the time off work. Okay, I thought, Mercury is retro and this is typical. *Plans change. Remain flexible.* I planned to drive up there alone.

On the day I was supposed to leave for South Carolina, it snowed and sleeted in Georgia. It's been at least thirty years since I've driven in weather like that, so I canceled my appointment. I was disappointed, but hey, I did my best to remain flexible. On Friday, Mercury went direct and I was anxious to get home. I was sure the trip would be a breeze because Mercury would have been direct for an entire day. Saturday morning, I woke up with an intestinal bug and had to reschedule my flight for Sunday and pay a $100 fee.

My sister, who doesn't believe in astrology or Mercury retrogrades, just shakes her head when I blame the whole thing on Mercury. But the fact is, once you become aware of the potential for unexpected change during a Mercury retrograde, you learn to be flexible and patient, and to go ahead and travel when the spirit moves you!

In the ephemeris, the Mercury retrograde periods between 2003 and 2007 are indicated by Rx. You may want to note these periods in the section under important Mercury dates.

STEPHEN KING

I enjoy exploring Stephen King's chart. In *Creative Stars: Using Astrology to Tap Your Muse,* King was my Virgo example. I've been following his career since 1974, when one of my seventh-grade students gave me *The Shining* and told me it was the best book he'd ever read. I read the book over a weekend and was blown away. Here was a guy my age, writing the kind of fiction I loved to read, about the kinds of weirdness that fascinated me.

I went out and bought *Salem's Lot* and *Carrie* and have been hooked ever since—not just as a reader but also as a novelist. I studied how he constructed his stories, his characters, his plots. I studied his precision, his details. And I began to *get it*. I began to understand how a story is built, how characters leap to life, how plots unfold.

Now Stephen King is a cottage industry, with nearly thirty years of best-sellers, TV movies, movie movies, a new miniseries, and an entirely new generation of readers. He has survived alcoholism, cocaine addiction, and an accident that bore a spooky resemblance to some of his darker novels and nearly killed him. He recovered and came back to write about the craft of writing, about aliens and other things that go bump in the night. Good thing, too. I can't imagine walking into a bookstore without seeing a new novel by King.

On January 28, 2002, in a CNN Internet posting at 10:32 that morning, there it was, a headline: "Is Stephen King hanging it up?"

"You get to a point where you get to the edges of a room, and you can go back and go where you've been and basically recycle stuff," he said in the article. "You can either continue to go on, or say I left when I was still on top of my game. I left when I was still holding the ball, instead of it holding me."

What kind of void had King stumbled into that afternoon he was struck by a car and found himself brushing elbows with death? *He was hanging it up.* Really? To do what? Sit around in his mansion and twiddle his thumbs? Ride around Portland in Christine? Drive his wife crazy because he was retired and had time on his hands? If you give up who you are, you might as well stop breathing.

So I had the date and the time of his announcement about retiring and I had his natal chart in my database. I went to work. Here's what I found. (You may want to follow along with a blank chart. Put Virgo on the Ascendant.)

King, born September 21, 1947, in Portland, Maine, at 1:30

A.M., has a Virgo Sun at 27 degrees 24 minutes in his natal third house. His moon in Sagittarius is at 16 degrees 14 minutes in the fifth house. He has a Cancer ascendant at 29 degrees 52 minutes. His natal chart is in Appendix C. Place the transits around the outer circle of his horoscope in their appropriate houses. At the time his announcement was posted on the Internet, the planets lined up like this:

- Transiting sun in Aquarius 9 degrees, seventh house
- Moon in Leo 19 degrees, first house
- Mercury in Aquarius 5 degrees, seventh house
- Venus in Aquarius 13 degrees, seventh house
- Mars in Aries 7 degrees, ninth house
- Jupiter in Cancer retrograde 7 degrees, twelfth house
- Saturn in Gemini retrograde 8 degrees, eleventh house
- Uranus in Aquarius 23 degrees, eighth house
- Neptune in Aquarius 8 degrees, seventh house
- Pluto in Sagittarius 16 degrees, fifth house
- North node Gemini retrograde 26 degrees, eleventh house
- South node in Sagittarius 26 degrees, fifth house
- Part of fortune in Scorpio 17 degrees, fourth house
- Vertex in Libra 16 degrees Libra, fourth house

Let's see how the aspects support the story line—King announcing that he will retire.

Breakdown of King's Chart

The only significant transit to King's natal Virgo sun is a square from the moon's nodes and a sextile from transiting Mars. The north node in Gemini is in the eleventh house, the south node in Sagittarius is in the fifth house. This aspect suggests friction and challenge related to his ego (sun). He may feel obstructed by circumstances in his life or within society. This friction is related to his creativity (fifth house) and his wishes and dreams (eleventh house). The sextile from Mars indicates new opportunities for King, so it's possible this decision was made as a result of whatever these new opportunities are.

Transiting Mercury, the ruler of his sun sign and of his profession, is forming a 6-degree opposition to his ascendant, indicating conflict and tension. This decision certainly concerns his writing, his contractual business partnerships, and perhaps his marriage as well (seventh house). It impacts the way others perceive him (ascendant). King himself said he doesn't want to end up like Harold Robbins, who ended his career near the bottom of his game. The perception of others plays a big part in his decision.

Mercury (writing) is trine his natal Venus (the arts) in the third house: King feels comfortable about this decision.

The transiting moon in Leo makes a 1-degree conjunction with King's natal Saturn in the first house. Since he has a Cancer ascendant, the moon rules his chart. This aspects indicates that the decision wasn't made lightly (Saturn) and took a great deal of thought and consideration. Loneliness and depression and problems with women or in the domestic life sometimes accompany this transit. The transiting moon is also squaring King's natal Jupiter in Scorpio in the fourth house. This isn't a very difficult aspect, but it lends itself to philosophical musings.

Transiting Mars in Cancer makes a 5-degree conjunction to King's ascendant. This aspect seems to confirm King's concern over how others perceive him. It also make a 5-degree opposition to King's Venus, suggesting challenge or culmination related to his artistic endeavors. Or, simply put, quit while you're on top.

Transiting Pluto makes an exact conjunction with King's natal moon in Sagittarius. This is probably the most interesting aspect. Back at the beginning of King's career, when he learned that the paperback rights to Carrie had sold for $400,000, Pluto had recently separated from a conjunction with King's sun and was conjuncting his Venus in Libra. The Pluto transit reconstructed his external life (sun) and his art and finances (Venus). Now, Pluto's energy is bearing down on King's inner life, stirring up unsettled issues that may relate to his childhood and domestic life. This aspect can transform every dark corner of your emotional life.

Pluto is also making an exact conjunction on King's natal vertex, suggesting a destined quality to his decision. That doesn't mean the decision is cast in stone, only that when he made the announcement, he meant it. This wasn't a marketing ploy. Pluto's transit through the house of creativity tells us that King's entire approach to his own creativity is in the midst of deep flux and change. By the time Pluto nears the end of its transit through the fifth house, King will have reinvented himself as a writer.

Do the aspects support the story line? Yes. But it doesn't mean that the decision he made is forever. We can hope it isn't!

THE OUTER PLANETS: THEMES

Transits of the inner planets describe emerging story lines daily, weekly, and monthly. But beneath these story lines are the broad themes that are created and sustained by the transits of the outer planets. However, Uranus, Neptune, and Pluto move so slowly that you won't experience every aspects to your sun over the course of a single lifetime.

In the immediate future, the Uranus transits to your sun are an opposition in Pisces that begins in March 2003. The opposition in Pisces brings confrontation or culmination in terms of your individuality and creativity, your spiritual beliefs, and your personal unconscious. You're forced to stand up for who you are and, thanks to the Pisces part of the equation, the way this is expressed is likely to come from a very deep place. The types of story lines that emerge depend on where you are at this point in your life, the degree of awareness with which you have lived your life, and the degree to which your life has become routine and predictable.

The only aspect from Neptune that affects you in the next ten or twelve years is the opposition in Pisces that begins in February 2011. This aspect causes a lack of clarity about your goals and direction in life. It forces you to ask questions that don't have easy answers. But it also deepens your compassion and spiritual beliefs.

From Pluto, there are only two aspects to your sun coming up in the next dozen years. In 1995, Pluto went into Sagittarius, forming a square to your sun. By now you undoubtedly realize that this aspect brings about transformation in ways that can be unpleasant and painful. Power issues surface that create friction and conflict. There can be financial problems, professional problems, health problems. Usually, one particular area of your life will seem to be hit over and over again until you *get the message*. The good news is that this aspect ends in 2008, when Pluto goes into Capricorn and forms a trine to your sun.

Although the Pluto trine is easier, transformation at the deepest levels of your psyche still unfolds. You now have the personal power to achieve your goals and to bring about positive change. You evolve in new, exciting ways under this trine. Make the most of them.

TIMING AND TRANSITS

The next list is for quick, easy reference as well as practice. It provides common situations in which timing can be vital to your success. Think about what planets and aspects are the most advantageous for these situations. If your answers are different from mine, it doesn't mean they're wrong. Just be able to justify your answers in your own mind.

For easy reference: A conjunction is any planet in Virgo; a sextile is a planet in Scorpio or Cancer; a square is a planet in Gemini or Sagittarius; a trine is a planet in Capricorn or Taurus; an opposition is a planet in Pisces.

+ **Move:** Moon in Cancer or in an earth sign. Mars conjunction. Mercury sextile or trine, moving direct.
+ **Wedding:** Venus in Virgo or another earth sign. Moon transiting natal seventh house. Jupiter conjunct, sextile, or trine.
+ **Honeymoon:** Venus in Virgo or another earth sign. Moon in Scorpio.
+ **Divorce:** Mercury direct. Positive Jupiter/sun contacts. Saturn sextile or trine.

+ **Submit a manuscript or screenplay:** Mercury direct. Saturn sextile or trine. Venus or Jupiter conjunct, sextile, or trine.
+ **Sign a contract:** Mercury direct. Jupiter conjunct, sextile, or trine.
+ **Interview for a job:** Venus in Virgo. Venus sextile or trine. Mercury direct.
+ **Family discussion:** Moon in Cancer or transiting natal fourth house. Mercury direct.
+ **Romantic discussion:** Venus in Virgo. Mercury direct. Moon in Scorpio.
+ **Attend a professional workshop/seminar:** Mercury direct. Saturn sextile or trine. Jupiter conjunct, sextile, or trine.
+ **Change professions:** Mars conjunct, sextile, or trine. Saturn sextile or trine.
+ **Take a business trip:** Mercury direct. Saturn sextile or trine. Pluto sextile or trine.
+ **Buy a car:** Mercury direct in Virgo or another earth sign.
+ **List your home for sale:** Moon in Cancer or Virgo, Venus sextile or trine.
+ **Close on a home:** Mercury direct. Venus sextile or trine. Jupiter conjunct, sextile, or trine.
+ **Start a creative project:** Mercury direct. Venus conjunct. Mars sextile or trine. Jupiter conjunct, sextile, or trine.
+ **Take a vacation:** Mercury direct. Jupiter conjunct, sextile, or trine.
+ **Get pregnant:** Moon in Cancer or in sign on the cusp of natal fifth house, Positive Venus contacts.
+ **Publish your Web site:** Mercury direct. Uranus contacts.
+ **Start a new job:** Venus sextile or trine. Mercury direct.

MANIFESTATION: THE TALISMAN

Every Virgo needs a Talisman, some object imbued with personal meaning that you can carry with you, wear, or keep in a secure place at home or at work. The talisman is your personal power object and can be anything that you value or which holds positive personal memories.

Check your ephemeris for the next New Moon. On that date, set aside ten or fifteen minutes when you won't be interrupted. Write out your deepest desire in a single, powerful sentence, in present tense. As you're writing out your wish, back it with the full force of your emotions and use your senses to imagine this wish materializing in your life. Have your power object nearby as you're doing this visualization exercise and make sure that you touch it now and then, imbuing it with your intent and emotion.

Post the written statement where you'll see it frequently. Every time you concentrate on your power object or touch it, know that your intent to manifest this wish deepens every time. Then step aside and let the universe do its job.

13

≏

SUN IN LIBRA:
ARTIST AND MEDIATOR

September 23–October 22

ARTIST

Is every Libra an artist? Of course not. But every Libra has an innate appreciation for the arts and may have an artistic talent that begs to be nurtured and developed. If you aren't already involved in your creative niche, then your first and most important question, Libra, is what creative endeavor ignites your passion? Is it photography? Music? Art? Writing? Maybe you're a whiz with color and design or have a talent for invention. Perhaps your artistic leanings are best expressed with groups.

As one of the most social signs in the zodiac, the people whose company you enjoy may hold important clues about your particular artistic talents. Although you probably have friends from many walks of life, your closest friends are likely to reflect your artistic and creative passions. Sometimes, your artistic niche is whatever you enjoy doing most in your spare time. My Libra dad, for instance, never played a musical instrument but has a soul appreciation for music. It transports him.

Libras, as a cardinal air sign ruled by Venus, are usually physically attractive in some way. Look in the mirror. Are your eyes unusual? Is your face particularly striking? Is your body beautifully proportioned? When you speak in a natural tone, is your voice soft? You tend to radiate a kind of peace and calm even when you feel anything but. You dislike crudeness in any form and can't tolerate disharmony. You seek to balance your life and the lives of the people you love. All of these qualities are part of your "artist's package."

Your ability to see many sides of a given issue, to weigh everything, is why the scales symbolize your sign. You're a genius at comparisons, and it doesn't matter whether you're comparing clothes or books or pieces of music; you bring the same artistic discernment to each comparison. This can make you indecisive, however, because you sometimes take forever to weigh all the factors. In addition, you can't stand the thought of hurting anyone's feelings, so you procrastinate just a bit.

The thing to remember, Libra, is this: There are no right or wrong answers. There are *his* answers and *hers, yours* and *someone else's*. This is where your second archetype, the mediator, comes in.

MEDIATOR

It's been a hectic day, your nerves are frayed, you want nothing more than to put on some music and kick back with a book. But your teens are arguing and it's time to step in and do your second job: mediation.

When political figures mediate, the press is there. It makes the evening news. When *you* do it, it's you, the people for whom you are mediating, and their *issues*. But it always comes down to who's right and who's wrong. As the mediator, you can't take sides. As a Libra, you're able to see both sides, to experience each person's stance so clearly it's as if you slip into one person's skin and then the other. You know there's no right or wrong. There's only raw, undiluted perception. And your gift is being able to mediate a solution that is acceptable to everyone.

Both the artist and the mediator archetypes come into play in your relationships and are especially important in matters of the heart. The artist seeks a companion whose aesthetic interests are similar, and the mediator seeks to embrace whatever interests your significant other. The shadow side of the mediator archetype is that there's a tendency to idealize the partner, and even though that idealization may develop holes over the years, it's always there, somewhere, influencing your decisions.

You and Taurus have Venus rulership in common, and this link explains why you may have an attraction to Tauruses. The combination isn't especially good in the long run—air and earth use energy much differently. But if one of you has the moon, Venus, or ascendant in the other's sun sign, the combination can be quite surprising.

The most apparent difference between you and Taurus is that the bull is earthy and sensual and your heart reaches for the divine, seeking to embrace the spiritual dimension of your most significant relationships. In fact, if that spiritual dimension is lacking for you, the relationship won't last regardless of how much mediation you attempt or employ. You want nothing less than your true soul mate, a lover and best friend with whom you can share your life.

And, as your mother probably said, why settle for anything else?

YOUR VENUS PLOTS

One of the ways that astrologers determine story lines is through searching for patterns. In this instance, you're going to do some research on your own patterns.

First, use page 39 to review the areas that Venus rules. Then read through the checklist below and put a ✓ next to each event that happened to you between 1990 and 2002. If you recall the date, jot it down next to the event. Yes, this may take some fancy footwork in the memory department, but it's worth the effort. Next, glance through the dates for when Venus was in Libra, listed below. Some of your dates should match those.

LIBRA / VENUS CHECKLIST

___ I started a creative project. _____

___ I sold a creative project. _____

___ I began studying art. _____

___ I started piano lessons. _____

___ I had my first piano recital. _____

___ I got into an art/music school. _____

___ I injured my lower back. _____

___ My siblings were born. _____

___ I got married. _____

___ I had my first child. _____

___ I fell in love for the first time. _____

___ I won an award. _____

___ I joined a spiritual study group. _____

___ I met my closest friend. _____

___ I joined a music group/orchestra. _____

___ I found my creative niche. _____

___ I signed an important contract. _____

___ I met someone I knew in a past life. _____

___ I was recognized for a professional/
    artistic achievement. _____

Now take a look at the dates below. Do any of your dates match these?

DATES: VENUS IN LIBRA, 1990–2002

10/1/90–10/24/90
11/9/91–12/5/91
8/31/92–9/23/92
10/15/93–8/7/94
9/16/95–10/9/95

10/29/96–11/21/96
8/17/97–9/11/97
9/30/98–10/23/98
11/8/99–12/04/99
8/30/00–9/23/00
10/15/02–11/07/01
8/7/02–9/7/02

REPETITIVE PATTERNS

Granted, it may be difficult to recall specific dates for some of the events. On the other hand, when something is emotionally important to us, we tend to remember not just the date but the time as well. *I met the love of my life at exactly 8:52 on January 3, 1992.* Like that. So let's say that in your Venus checklist, you recalled that you got into art school sometime around your birthday in 1990 and that you got married (let's hope you remember *that* date) on October 20, 2002. Two events that happened when Venus was in Libra is the beginning of a pattern.

It's just as likely, however, that certain patterns have evolved over the years when Venus made other aspects to your sun. In the Venus ephemeris, look for dates in the next five years when Venus is going to be in Aries (opposition), Sagittarius and Leo (sextile), Capricorn and Cancer (square), and Aquarius and Gemini (trine). Create possible story lines for each of these aspects.

Important Dates for Venus, 2003–2007

DATE	SIGN	ASPECT	STORY LINES

DATE	SIGN	ASPECT	STORY LINES

CAROL BOWMAN

Author and past-life researcher Carol Bowman has written two books on the past lives of children: *Children's Past Lives* and *Return from Heaven*, about reincarnation within the same family. I mentioned her briefly in my book, *Creative Stars*, as an example of a Libra who stumbled upon her creative niche because of a personal dilemma.

When her son Chase was about four, he developed a terror of loud noises. It began on a July 4 weekend and quickly escalated for the next several months. In her first book, Bowman recounts the episodes of abject terror that Chase experienced and her efforts to allay his fears. She finally took him to a friend who was a professional hypnotist, and within moments, Chase described himself as a black soldier. From the description of his weapon, Carol realized that he was in the Civil War. He'd been wounded on the wrist, guns were exploding around him, and he was utterly terrified.

Sometime after the session, the recurring eczema that had plagued Chase for most of his young life suddenly disappeared. This convinced Carol that they were onto something and launched her investigation into children's past lives. She began talking with other mothers that she knew and slowly collected stories. A pattern began to emerge.

At some point in her research, a friend wrote to Oprah and told her about Carol's work. A year later, Oprah called and asked Carol to appear on her show with Chase and with Sara, Carol's daughter, who had experienced spontaneous recall of her own past lives. At the time, Carol hadn't written any books. She was simply a mother whose son's trauma had sent her searching in unconventional directions for answers. All she had was an unshakeable belief in the veracity of her research and in her children's experiences.

When I asked Carol if I could use her story as an example, she said she wasn't sure of the exact date of the taping, somewhere between February 20 and 22, 1994. The show aired on March 1, 1994. That's the date I've used. The transits are listed below. To visualize these transits, use one of the blank horoscope wheels. Put 8 degrees Libra on the Ascendant, Carol's actual rising, and then move counterclockwise around the wheel, placing 8 degrees Scorpio on the cusp of the second, 8 degrees Sagittarius on the third and on around to 8 degrees Virgo on the cusp of the twelfth. Put her natal Libra sun at 20 degrees in the first house. You're setting up a solar chart. The transits for March 1, 1994, were:

- ✦ Sun: 10 degrees Pisces, sixth house
- ✦ Moon: 1 degree Scorpio, first house
- ✦ Mercury: 23 degrees Aquarius, fifth house
- ✦ Venus: 21 degrees Pisces, sixth house
- ✦ Mars: 25 degrees Aquarius, fifth house
- ✦ Jupiter: 14 degrees Scorpio, second house
- ✦ Saturn: 3 degrees Pisces, fifth house
- ✦ Uranus: 24 degrees Capricorn, fourth house
- ✦ Neptune: 22 degrees Capricorn, fourth house
- ✦ Pluto: 28 degrees Scorpio, second house
- ✦ North node: 26 degrees Scorpio, second house

In the table below, the aspects are broken down so you can spot them easily. I've allowed orbs up to five degrees. You fill in the possible story lines.

Aspect Analysis

TRANSITING PLANET	ASPECT TO SUN	STORY LINE
☉	no	
☽	no	
☿	trine	
♀	quincunx	
♂	trine	
♃	no	
♄	no	
♅	square	
♆	square	
♀	no	
☊	no	

Interestingly, Carol's ruling planet, Venus, makes a quincunx to her sun, an aspect that signals an adjustment of some kind, usually in the area of health. This may relate to her son's health—the trauma that led her into her research. It also suggests that her daily work will undergo an adjustment of some sort, possibly related to the arts, and it could be financially lucrative (Venus). At the time, Carol hadn't thought much about writing a book, but this aspect seemed to predict it.

The Aquarius trine to her sun from both Mercury and Mars in the fifth house of creativity are perfect for a TV talk show about a topic as unusual and visionary (Aquarius) as reincarnation. The Mercury trine gives her the ability to express herself clearly and convincingly, to make her case. The Mars trine, though wider than the Mercury trine, infuses her with self-confidence and physical vitality that enable her to carry off the show without resistance from other people.

The Neptune square in Capricorn is usually a difficult transit. It requires that you remain true to yourself and your own vision. This is precisely what Carol did from the very beginning of Chase's trauma about loud noises. The entire experience also altered her beliefs at the deepest levels in her psyche (fourth house). The Uranus square, also in the fourth house, is typically as difficult as and more disruptive than the Neptune square. Chase's trauma was certainly disruptive and disturbing, yet it presented Carol with a unique opportunity to find her life's work and pursue it.

Even though we've been exploring aspects to the sun, there's another notable aspect in this picture that deserves mentioning. Carol's natal moon is in Sagittarius in the second house of personal values. On the day the show aired, her north node was making a 4-degree conjunction to her moon. This connection often has a destined feel to it and certainly pushed Carol in a direction that was personally important to her and that will help her to evolve spiritually in this lifetime.

THE OUTER PLANETS: THEMES

Uranus, Neptune, and Pluto move so slowly that you won't experience every aspect of these transits to your sun—not a bad thing, by any means. Some of these outer planet transits can be painful.

From Uranus, you've been experiencing the trine in Aquarius since April 1995. In March 2003, the trine ends and Uranus moves into Pisces. The opposition in Aries begins in March 2011. Any contact between Uranus and your natal sun brings disruptions, but the nature of the disruptions varies. The trine is positive, just remember that. Even if it brings about events that throw you for a loop, these same events ultimately free you creatively and spiritually.

In 2011, you're in for a wild, bumpy ride. Everything that happens to you during this opposition makes you feel as if you're zipping around on the highest, scariest roller coaster you've ever been on. At every step of the way, your individuality is challenged. If you've settled into a predictable routine, this transit will blow it to smithereens. If you've maintained a sense of adventure about your life and have embraced creative change, then you'll get through this one intact and much stronger.

Then there's Neptune. This planet's transit through a sign typically lasts about fourteen years, twice that of Uranus. Neptune has been in Aquarius, trine your natal sun, since 1998 and will be there until February 2011. Let's focus on that. Even the most positive aspects, like a trine, can be disturbing in the sense that you seem to detach from the physical world and move through inner worlds for which there is no guidebook. Yet if you allow your intuition its voice and listen to what it says, you'll navigate this transit with grace and wisdom. Your spiritual beliefs deepen and you realize there are some things over which you have no control.

Pluto. The heavy. He plays for keeps. Since 1995, when Pluto went into Sagittarius, you've been living out the sextile to your sun. Lucky you. The sextile in Sagittarius brings both change and opportunity. You begin to grasp the concept of power—how you are empowered and how you may have surrendered your power in the past. You feel comfortable with groups; serendipity is your middle name.

In late November 2008, Pluto goes into Capricorn, forming a square to your sun. This one can be difficult if you don't know who you are or where you're headed. Your ambition is a strong force in your life at this time, and you have the ability to achieve a great deal as long as use your personal power in a constructive and positive manner.

TIMING AND TRANSITS

Before you even do this activity, understand that some people seem to live out their sun signs and their natal charts so closely that it spooks me. Other people, though, take that raw potential of the sun sign and the natal chart and turn it into something that is either so extraordinary or so perverse that no astrologer could predict the result. I've met both types and realize they have one thing in common: They understand free will. They may not be able to articulate the concept, but deep inside, *they get it.*

That said, the next list is of common situations in which timing can be crucial to your success. What planets and aspects do you think are the best for these situations? If your answers are different than mine, that's fine. Just be able to justify them to yourself.

For easy reference: a conjunction is any planet in Libra; a sextile is a planet in Sagittarius or Leo; a square is a planet in Capricorn or Cancer; a trine is a planet in Aquarius or Gemini; an opposition is a planet in Aries.

+ **Move:** Moon in Aquarius or Gemini. Mars conjunction. Mercury sextile or trine, moving direct.
+ **Wedding:** Venus in Libra. Moon transiting natal seventh house. Jupiter conjunct, sextile, or trine.
+ **Honeymoon:** Venus in Libra, sextile or trine. Moon in Libra.
+ **Divorce:** Mercury direct. Jupiter conjunct, sextile, or trine.
+ **Submit a creative product:** Venus and/or Jupiter conjunct, sextile, or trine. Mercury direct. Venus transiting natal fifth house.
+ **Sign a contract:** Mercury direct. Jupiter conjunct, sextile, or trine.
+ **Attend a professional workshop/seminar:** Mercury direct. Saturn sextile or trine. Jupiter conjunct, sextile, or trine.
+ **Start/open your own business:** Mercury direct. Saturn sextile or trine. Jupiter and/or Mars conjunct.
+ **End a significant relationship:** Mercury direct. Jupiter conjunct, sextile, or trine. Mars conjunct.
+ **Change professions:** Mercury direct. Mars conjunct, sextile, or trine. Saturn sextile or trine.
+ **Return to college:** Mercury direct. Jupiter conjunct, sextile, or trine. Mars conjunct.
+ **Interview for a job:** Venus in Libra. Jupiter conjunct, sextile, or trine. Mercury direct.
+ **List a home for sale:** Moon in Libra or another air sign. Venus sextile or trine.
+ **Close on a home:** Mercury direct. Venus and/or Jupiter conjunct, sextile, or trine.
+ **Visit family:** Moon transiting natal fourth house. Moon sextile or trine. Mercury direct.

+ **Start a new job:** Mercury direct. Venus sextile or trine. Mars conjunct, sextile, or trine.
+ **Resign from a job:** Mercury direct. Venus and/or Jupiter conjunct, sextile, or trine.
+ **Romantic heart-to-heart:** Mercury direct. Venus conjunct, sextile, or trine.
+ **Schedule a party:** Moon or Venus sextile or trine.
+ **Buy a computer or other electronic device:** Mercury direct. Uranus sextile or trine.

MANIFESTATION: THE SIXTH SENSE

I chose this activity because Libra has a strong sixth sense—not for seeing ghosts, but in terms of intuition. But because you tend to weigh and ponder every issue before making decisions, your inner voice sometimes gets drowned out. In this activity, you're going to define exactly what it is that you want—your heart's desire—and then take steps to bring this wish into physical reality.

In the New Moon ephemeris, look up the date of the next New Moon. On that day, write your desire in a single sentence, in present tense. As you're doing this, imagine that what you desire is already yours. Use your sense to back up this visualization. If, for instance, you want a new computer, then see the computer in every detail. Find a picture of it and post it where you'll see it often. If you want to make your living doing what you love, then imagine that you are already doing that. Engage your senses and back your desire with the force of your willpower and intent.

Post your wish where you'll see it daily, but don't fret about it. Don't allow your left brain to fill you with doubts. Just trust that the wish is manifesting itself.

14

SUN IN SCORPIO: ALCHEMIST AND DETECTIVE

October 23–November 21

ALCHEMIST

In medieval times, alchemists claimed that they were privy to the secrets that enabled them to turn base metals into gold. For you, the alchemy refers to your ability to transform your life at the deepest levels.

As a fixed water sign ruled by Pluto, your natural element is the depths of the unconscious and the world of emotions. You read people well and have a finely honed intuition that enables you to quickly grasp other people's motives and issues. Intuition, in fact, is one of your greatest strengths and your most powerful ally as an alchemist. As long as you listen to that inner voice and follow its guidance, you rarely go wrong.

You're at home with intense experiences, and the more intense the experience, the more fulfilled you are. You constantly seek the absolute bottom line, the ultimate answer. The greater the riddle, the more intensely you probe. Your own secrecy about your life and feelings is very in line with the world of alchemists, where the answers to the greatest riddles are hidden away. It isn't so much that you try to shroud your life in secrecy, it just happens. However, once someone has earned your trust and proven himself worthy of your friendship, your penchant for secrecy loosens. You bring that person into the fold.

See that little arrow at the tail of the Scorpio glyph? That's the scorpion's stinger, and you don't hesitate to use it if you've been crossed. You don't get back; you get even, and you never forget the slight.

The challenge is to turn your intensity, your need for absolutes, to the larger world, where the alchemist can really make a difference. Find a cause that feeds your passions and pursue it. Volunteer for an organization that stands for something you believe in. Study for a profession or career in an area that's aligned with your beliefs. Scorpios excel at investigation, research, strategy. They make excellent physicians and psychologists, psychics, actors, artists, spies. Scorpios are often multitalented. If you fall into that category, your dilemma may be finding one true passion and then committing to it.

You rarely do anything without preparation, and committing to a particular path is no exception. Wrap your intuition around one endeavor and see how it feels. By learning to follow your inner promptings, your second archetype comes into play.

DETECTIVE

This archetype could be called investigator. Or researcher. Or spy. But at the heart of any of those terms lies the detective, relentless in her pursuit of the myriad details that lead to the source of whatever she's seeking.

Your perceptions are so keen that little escapes you. You walk into a crowded party and immediately feel the tone and texture of the crowd. Your son comes home from school and you sense what everyone else misses, that his color is off, that his voice is too soft, and you know that someone or something has shaken his self-confidence. Whether it's your home or your workplace, the detective in you tirelessly follows every lead, every clue.

For both the detective and the alchemist, power is a central issue. In real life, this means that power will always be one of the focal points around which your energy revolves. Sometimes, other people will hold power over you. And other times, you'll hold the power. Be sure that when you've got the power, you use it fairly, without thinking of personal gain or vendettas. Only then will other people's power over you cease to be a problem in your life.

You were born with tremendous self-confidence. When it's working smoothly and efficiently, it can move mountains. It can turn metal into gold, find the source of whatever you're seeking, and help you achieve whatever you desire. But when it malfunctions, it becomes arrogant and petty and all of your marvelous energy and focus is wasted on the mundane. For you, there should be nothing less than making the ordinary sacred. To do that, you may have to release your need to control others and put your trust in a higher power, whatever you perceive that to be.

YOUR PLANETARY PLOTS

It's ironic that a planet revolving at the very edge of our solar system has such enormous power in the astrological scheme of things. Death and rebirth. Regeneration. Destiny. Transcendence and redemption. Atomic power. The afterlife. Good and evil. Friend or enemy. *Black or white*. Pluto knows no gray areas. He's the zodiac heavy.

Since it takes Pluto 248 years to circle the zodiac, it would be fruitless to figure out how your story lines have evolved under Pluto transits. Day to day, month to month, even year to year, Pluto's position doesn't change much. But because Pluto rules your sun sign, its underlying theme is always at work in your life and can be heightened by the transits of other planets. So what we're going to do differs somewhat from other sun sign chapters. You're going to do some brainstorming about your planetary plots in general.

The list below contains situations and events that are transformative, profound, very Scorpio. Put a ✓ next to any event that has happened at least twice, then use the table on pages 38–41 to determine the planet that rules the event. The idea is that you may be especially sensitive to transits from a particular planet, and if you've got at least two check marks, you have the beginning of a *pattern*. Since your sign's coruler is Mars, pay attention to any event ruled by that planet. While you're doing this activity, cover up the right-hand column that has my suggestions and record your answers in the middle column. Then compare the two.

PLANETARY CHECKLIST

EVENT	RULING PLANET	
	Your suggestion	*My suggestion*
___ My brother or sister died.		Pluto
___ I got married.		Venus, Mars, Jupiter
___ I had a child.		Venus, Mars
___ I developed a serious physical problem.		Uranus, Neptune, Pluto
___ I had a serious accident.		Mars, Pluto
___ My career underwent dramatic change.		Mars, Saturn, Pluto
___ I got divorced.		Mars, Uranus, Neptune, Pluto

EVENT	RULING PLANET
Your suggestion	*My suggestion*
___ My religious/ spiritual beliefs changed dramatically.	Jupiter, Uranus, Neptune, Pluto
___ A parent betrayed me.	Moon, Venus, Saturn, Pluto
___ A parent saved me.	Moon, Venus, Saturn, Pluto
___ I changed careers.	Moon, Mercury, Jupiter
___ I fell madly and blindly in love.	Venus, Mars, Neptune
___ I had the greatest sex ever.	Pluto, Venus, Mars
___ I inherited a lot of money.	Pluto, Venus, Jupiter
___ A close friend/ relative died unexpectedly.	Uranus, Mercury, Pluto
___ I had a spiritual epiphany.	Jupiter, Uranus, Neptune, Pluto
___ I declared bankruptcy.	Pluto, Jupiter, Neptune
___ My home was destroyed.	Moon, Mars, Uranus, Pluto
___ I moved into my dream home.	Moon, Mars, Venus, Jupiter
___ I found my life's path.	Pluto and planet that rules natal chart

Count the planets with the most checks and use each planet's ephemeris to find out when it will be in Scorpio (conjunction), in Capricorn and Virgo (sextile); in Aquarius and Leo (square), in Pisces and Cancer (trine), and in Taurus (opposition). You should pay special attention to Mars, as the coruler of Scorpio.

Important Dates for 2003–2007

DATE	SIGN	ASPECT	STORY LINES

MIRA MORALES

Mira is a psychic who owns a New Age bookstore in south Florida. She's an early Scorpio, born on October 27, 1962, which puts her sun at 3 degrees. Given her profession, it isn't surprising that she has a crowded eighth house—sun, moon, Mercury, and Neptune. This house is Pluto's natural home and rules everything metaphysical as well as death and rebirth, the affairs of the dead, taxes and insurance, resources we share with others, and our support systems.

On the evening of April 11, 1992, Mira, her daughter, and her husband stopped at a convenience store. Tom went inside while Mira waited in the car with her daughter. For several years, Mira had had a repetitive dream in which her husband walked into a store where he was gunned down. Even though the details of her dream differed sufficiently from the setting in real life, she became distinctly uneasy as she waited in the car for him. By the time she realized that the dream and real life were coinciding, it was already too late.

When she rushed into the store, she saw her husband lying in a pool of blood on the floor. Despite countless attempts, she was never able to pick up anything psychic on the masked assailant who killed her husband, and the police never found the man.

Five years later, she dreamed of a murder in such exacting detail that she called the police to report the information. She was reluctant to make the call because police tended to be skeptical of psychic information. This time, though, a cop came out to speak to her. It turned out that a prominent psychiatrist had been murdered at about the same time of Mira's dream. She was completely perplexed about why she would dream of the murder of a man she'd never met, but as the police investigation proceeded, it became increasingly obvious that the man who killed the psychiatrist was the same man who had killed her husband.

Fortunately, Mira isn't a real person. She's the protagonist in *The Hanged Man,* and the background you just read is the back story and setup for the book. When I was creating Mira, I decided she would be a Scorpio because of the nature of her work. I picked the birth date at random, then played around with her time of birth until I found the chart that seemed to fit the way I imagined her. Her birth chart is in Appendix C.

She's a double water sign—Scorpio sun and Pisces rising. Her Libra moon is in the balsamic phase, the most karmic phase, indicating a lifetime in which loose ends are tied up. For balsamic moon people, many of their most intimate relationships have past-life connections. Pluto, the ruler of her sun sign, is sitting on the cusp of the seventh house of marriages and partnerships, indicating that her greatest transformations in life occur through partnerships. Mars, the coruler of her sun sign, falls in the fifth house. This suggests that a lot of her energy goes into her daughter and her creativity. We take a look at the transits that were going on the day her husband was shot and place them in the outer ring of her natal chart. Here's how the planets lined up for that day:

- ✦ Sun ☉: 22 degrees Aries
- ✦ Moon ☽: 13 degrees Leo
- ✦ Mercury ☿: 29 degrees Pisces
- ✦ Venus ♀: 5 degrees Aries
- ✦ Mars ♂: 11 degrees Pisces (smack on her ascendant)
- ✦ Jupiter ♃: 5 degrees Virgo
- ✦ Saturn ♄: 16 degrees Aquarius
- ✦ Uranus ♅: 17 degrees Capricorn
- ✦ Neptune ♆: 17 degrees Capricorn
- ✦ Pluto ♇: 22 degrees Scorpio
- ✦ North node ☊: Capricorn

Let's start with aspects to Mira's natal sun, then take in the whole chart and look at the other aspects as well. The planets that are most important in the overall picture are her natal sun, both natal and transiting Pluto, as the ruler of her sun sign; Mars as the coruler of her sun sign; and Neptune, which rules her ascendant. The planet that rules the ascendant rules the whole chart. Let's start with those aspects, move on to the others, and use orbs up to 5 degrees. Stick to the major aspects: conjunction, sextile, square, trine, and opposition.

These are the major aspects involving her natal sun and transiting Pluto, Mars, and Neptune. It's immediately apparent that transiting Mars is strategic in this picture, especially because Mars can represent a woman's husband. In the transits, Mars *opposes* her natal Pluto, *trines* her Neptune, *conjuncts* her ascendant. The opposition is by far the most dangerous. Under extreme conditions, it indicates violence by other people. In this instance, violence to Mira's husband.

The Pluto conjunction to Mira's Venus is also revealing. Pluto transforms and Venus represents love: Pluto took away the love of

Aspects to Mira's Chart for April 11, 1992

NATAL	TRANSITING	ASPECT
☉	♃	sextile
☉	☊	square
♀	♂	opposition (exact)
♂	☽	conjunction
♅	♂	trine
♅	♄	square
☿	♆	square
♀	♀	conjunction
ascendant	♂	conjunction (exact)

her life. Although Neptune rules her birth chart, its transits on the day her husband was killed seem to suggest deepening spirituality and intuitive ability—as a result of all the Mars activity.

There are other aspects in the chart that tell us more about the story line. Both transiting Neptune and Uranus square Mira's Mercury in the eighth house. Although I didn't realize it at the time I erected the charts, this aspect describes an experience Mira had when she ran into the store and saw her husband dead on the floor. *"She'd known immediately that he was dead because his phantom self, his soul, his spirit, whatever you wanted to call it, had hovered just over the body, visible to her, as transparent as glass.*

"She'd screamed and Tom's phantom self had looked up, eyes stricken with astonishment, shock. And then he had started to rise up like a balloon and she'd waited until he vanished through the ceiling."

The two squares sharpened her innate psychic ability to the point where she could see her husband's spirit as it left his physical body.

If Mira were a real person and I had seen these transits coming up in her chart, I would not have predicted the death of her husband. But I would have warned the two of them to exercise greater caution during the length of the Mars transit. In terms of storytelling, however, it's all there. And as a fiction writer, this is one of the most creative uses for astrology that I've found. By casting charts for my characters, I have deeper insight into who they are and what makes them tick, and a clearer idea of where their story lines may take me—and them.

When the life is your own and the story lines are what you hope will happen, you can use each planet's ephemeris to plan events on certain days to stack the deck in your favor.

THE OUTER PLANETS: THEMES

Daily, weekly, and monthly, the transits of the inner planets are invaluable in describing emerging story lines. The transits of the outer planets have a somewhat different function; they provide the underlying themes that unfold over time. When they coincide with inner transits, the story lines are heightened. But Uranus, Neptune, and Pluto move so slowly that you won't experience every transit to your sun within your lifetime.

In the immediate future, the only aspect from Uranus that should concern you is the one that's happening now. Since the mid-nineties, Uranus has been in Aquarius and will be there until 2003, when it goes into Pisces, forming a trine to your sun. The trine is about as good as it gets with Uranus. By now, you're ready to embrace change and new opportunities. With Uranus in a compatible water sign, many of the changes you experience come through emotions, intuition, and your spiritual beliefs.

Neptune went into Aquarius in 1998, squaring your sun, and will stay there until it goes into Pisces, forming a trine to your sun in 2011. The square is often confusing. Your external life and goals become less clear and seem unimportant compared to what's going on inside of you. You may become disoriented about your direction in life, and this often is reflected in professional disappointments. Trust issues may surface. However, your inner life blossoms. Your spirituality and intuition deepen and you begin to understand that what affects one affects all.

The Neptune trine changes your perspective on the larger world. You become more concerned about other people, your compassion and spirituality deepen, and you realize that we are all part of the family of man. Your intuition also becomes heightened, your dreams more vivid. This is the time when your contact with the ephemeral and the esoteric is profound.

That brings us to your ruling planet, Pluto. It goes into Capricorn in 2008, forming a sextile to your sun. During this fifteen-year transit, you have a tremendous opportunity to instigate change, to achieve your ambitions, and to make a difference in the world. Do it during this transit because when Pluto goes into Aquarius in 2023, it forms a square to your sun. And that's when you encounter friction and challenges related to the path you have chosen.

TIMING AND TRANSITS

This activity helps sharpen your skills for timing events in a way that support your success. Look at the events in the list below. Which planets and aspects do you think are the most advantageous for each situation? I've pinpointed the planets that are most propitious for each event. If your answers differ, that's fine, as long as you can justify them. There are many possible aspects for each event.

For easy reference: A conjunction is a planet in Scorpio; a sextile is a planet in Capricorn or Virgo; a square is a planet in Aquarius or Leo; a trine is a planet in Pisces or Cancer; an opposition is a planet in Taurus.

- ✦ **Move:** Moon in Cancer or an earth sign. Mars conjunction. Mercury sextile or trine, moving direct.
- ✦ **Wedding:** Venus in Scorpio or another water sign. Moon transiting natal seventh house. Jupiter conjunct, sextile, or trine.

+ **Honeymoon:** Venus in Scorpio or another water sign. Moon in sun sign of significant other.
+ **Divorce:** Mercury direct. Jupiter conjunct, sextile, or trine. Saturn sextile or trine.
+ **Change professions:** Mars conjunct, sextile, or trine. Saturn sextile or trine.
+ **Sign a contract:** Mercury direct. Jupiter conjunct, sextile or trine.
+ **Take a vacation:** Jupiter conjunct, sextile, or trine. Moon in Sagittarius. Mercury direct.
+ **Start a new job:** Venus sextile or trine. Mercury direct.
+ **Investigate spiritual issues:** Pluto in natal ninth house. Mars conjunct, sextile, or trine. Jupiter conjunct, sextile, or trine. Moon in Scorpio.
+ **Learn to play an instrument:** Venus conjunct, sextile, or trine. Jupiter conjunct. Neptune sextile or trine.
+ **Schedule elective surgery:** Mercury and Mars direct. Mars sextile or trine. Jupiter conjunct, sextile, or trine.
+ **Submit a manuscript or screenplay:** Mercury direct and sextile or trine. Venus or Jupiter conjunct, sextile, or trine.
+ **Launch your own business:** Mercury direct. Saturn sextile or trine. Mars conjunct, sextile, or trine.
+ **Buy a home:** Moon in Cancer. Mercury direct and conjunct. Venus conjunct.
+ **Buy a car:** Mercury direct and conjunct, sextile, or trine. Mars conjunct.
+ **Get pregnant:** Moon in Cancer or in sign on cusp of natal fifth house. Positive Venus contacts.
+ **Hire an employee:** Mercury direct and conjunct, sextile, or trine. Saturn sextile or trine.
+ **Fire an employee:** Mars conjunct, sextile, or trine. Mercury direct.
+ **Get your hair cut!** Moon in Libra or a water sign.
+ **Study healing/medicine:** Mars conjunct. Jupiter conjunct, sextile, or trine.

MANIFESTATION: PASSAGES

For a Scorpio, life is about passages—your passage from childhood to adulthood, from being single to being married, from amateur to professional. While it's true that all of us go through passages of one kind or another, your experience of each passage entails a degree of intensity that may be overpowering at times.

The most constructive way to channel all that intensity is to put it to use to attact what you want in life. Think of one wish that you have. Write it out in the present tense, in a clear, concise sentence. Look in the new moon ephemeris for the next new moon and, on that date, state your wish out loud and post what you've written where you'll see it frequently. It helps to ritualize this visualization in some way: Light a candle, a stick of incense, whatever suits you. When you write and say the wish out loud, use every sense to make it feel real. Back it with the full power and intent of your emotion. Then step back and let it unfold

15

SUN IN SAGITTARIUS: TRAVELER AND TRUTH SEEKER

November 22–December 21

TRAVELER

There are other archetypical themes for Sagittarius: preacher, creator, athlete, missionary, humanitarian. But at the core of your being, you are a traveler and a truth seeker.

Traveling doesn't necessarily mean that you're a globe-trotter, although you may be. You may also travel in other senses—mentally, emotionally, psychically, or through your imagination. Author and medical intuitive Carolyn Myss *(Anatomy of the Spirit, Sacred Contracts)* describes herself as a quadruple Sagittarian, which would mean she has the sun, moon, ascendant, and another prominent planet in that sign. Ever a triple Sag would take these archetypes and run with them, traveling through virgin jungle to spread the word about her truth. Myss certainly does that. What makes her unique, though, is that she holds a Ph.D. in theology and has worked as a medical intuitive with Harvard-educated physician Norman Sheahy. Even if you don't agree with her concepts, it's difficult to dismiss her credentials.

As a Sag, you have a your own vision about the world. You believe in what you're doing and you believe in your beliefs. When you travel—whether it's physical or otherwise—you soak up the atmosphere and are always on the lookout for the big picture. Whatever you learn is stored in that steel-trap mind of yours, where it connects with others bits of information you have tucked away over the years. Then, through a process like alchemy, all of this information— your base metal—is slowly integrated into a worldview that becomes your personal gold mine, your particular path.

You're a mutable fire sign ruled by expansive Jupiter, and this gives you a kind of Midas touch. Wherever you turn your focus— your creativity, your work, your personal life—you experience expansiveness, luck, and serendipitous events. Jupiter, which rules your worldview, the ninth house of the horoscope wheel, always attempts to expand who you are and the concepts you embrace. This is at the heart of your hunger for experience.

TRUTH SEEKER

When you travel, truth is what you're seeking. You may not think of it in those terms, but that's what it is. Imagine. You're in a city or country where you've never been before. You're moving around constantly, savoring the sights, the culture, the people, the foods, the shops. You feel *alive*. And under this feeling lies something else, a consciousness that fills with *experience* and swells like a hot-air balloon. You're soaring. You finally *get it*. What you understand may not be readily apparent for months or even years, but it's part of the Sagittarian process, connecting the dots until the big picture is right there in front of you.

Part of your search entails finding your passion and acting on it. For some Sagittarians, this passion may involve humanitarian ideals, a creative pursuit, or playing a particular sport. Your passions, in some way, define your truth.

Recently, a Sagittarian musician asked me to do his chart. He was torn between his need for freedom, specifically to go on the road to pursue his music, and his obligations to his family. This is a fairly common dilemma for Sagittarians. Although the particulars vary from one individual to another, you experience a tug of war between your need for freedom and something else in your life that you feel is tying you down. Maybe you want to earn your living doing what you love, but the job that you don't especially enjoy pays you so well that you're afraid to leave it.

Fear can be a major component in this dilemma, and the best way to resolve it is to deal with it. One Sagittarian friend was an insurance adjuster for years. He didn't like the job or the work and wanted to be independent to pursue his own truth. Instead of allowing fear to keep him a slave to a job he didn't like, he took steps to remedy it. He began saving his money and investing it. He retired in his late forties and is now living exactly as he wants, answering to no one, free to travel and seek *his* truth.

Once you define what it is you want and embrace the notion that it may entail risk, the journey becomes the truth or the truth becomes the journey. The two archetypes become so intimately intertwined you can no longer separate them.

The shadow side of this is the know-it-all who has been everywhere, seen everything, and has decided *his* truth is the only truth so help you God, amen. Or it's the misanthrope with three kids and a mortgage who splits for the hills so that he or she can write the great American novel and, well, too bad if the bank forecloses on the house. These are extreme examples, but illustrate the essential dilemma that you and all Sagittarians face: how to be free without compromise and yet fulfill whatever responsibilities you have.

YOUR PLOTS AND JUPITER

Lucky you, having Jupiter as the planet that rules your sun sign. It certainly gives you an edge in life. Just as a means of comparison, consider Capricorn, ruled by Mr. Heavy Responsibility himself (Saturn), or even Scorpio, shouldering the burden of a Pluto rulership. But before you stand up and cheer for yourself, keep in mind that too much of a good thing can result in excess, laziness, and such a laid-back approach to life that opportunities whiz past you at the speed of light. Balance is often the key to Sagittarius's success.

Jupiter spends about a year in each sign and takes twelve years to circle the zodiac. To explore Jupiter's impact on your life and your sensitivity to its transits, we're going to look for broad patterns that may have repeated themselves over time. The checklist that follows will help you pinpoint possible patterns. Before you start, though, glance at pages 39–40 to refresh your memory about the areas that Jupiter rules. Then think about events that have happened to you since 1990 in the areas that Jupiter rules. Jot notes next to the items on the checklist. Try to recall dates.

In the dates section following the checklist, compare the dates you've jotted with the time frames for when Jupiter was in Sagittarius (conjunct), in Aquarius or Libra (sextile), in Pisces or Virgo (square), and in Gemini (opposed). There should be some correlation. You may want to review the meanings for the various aspects on page 30.

SAGITTARIUS/JUPITER CHECKLIST

___ I finished a creative project. _____

___ I found my creative niche. _____

___ I started a job in publishing. _____

___ I moved. _____

___ I took an overseas trip that
expanded my horizons. _____

___ My spiritual beliefs changed
dramatically. _____

___ I got married. _____

___ My siblings were born. _____

___ I had trouble with my hips. _____

___ I had liver problems. _____

___ I was recognized for a professional
achievement. _____

___ I had a child. _____

___ I entered college/pursued an
advanced degree. _____

___ I won a prize/contest. _____

___ I became a preacher, reverend,
priest, nun. _____

___ I competed professionally in a sport. _____

___ I bought a home/property. _____

___ I started my own business. _____

___ I took a leap of faith. _____

___ I went to court. _____

Now take a look at the dates below. Do any of these dates match yours?

DATES: JUPITER ASPECTS, 1990–2002

8/18/90–9/11/91: Leo (trine)
9/12/91 10/9/92: Virgo (square)
10/10/92–11/9/93: Libra (sextile)
12/9/94–1/2/96: Sagittarius (conjunct)
1/21/97–2/3/98: Aquarius (sextile)
2/4/98–2/11/99: Pisces (square)
2/12/99–6/27/99: Aries (trine)
6/30/00–7/11/02: Gemini (opposition)
8/1/02–8/27/03: Leo (trine)

REPETITIVE PATTERNS

In any predictive system, patterns are the key to interpretation. If, in brainstorming about your past, you remembered two key events that happened during a particular time frame, you have the beginning of a pattern. Perhaps during a Jupiter sextile or trine you moved to a larger home and had a child. So you know that when Jupiter enters Leo or Aries, Aquarius or Libra, you have an opportunity for personal expansion.

Now look through the Jupiter ephemeris on pages 298–311 and, below, jot down the dates when Jupiter will be making aspects to your sun and the possible story lines that may emerge.

Important Dates for Jupiter, 2003–2007

_____

_____

_____

_____

_____

_____

_____

_____

_____

JAY HALDEMAN

Science fiction writer. Biologist. Computer genius. Racing enthusiast. Book lover. Animal lover. Husband, father, brother. Jay Haldeman, like many Sagittarians, played numerous roles in his life and embodied the traveler and truth seeker archetypes in unique ways.

I first met Jay in the early eighties, when he lived in Ormond Beach, Florida. My husband, who had known him since the seventies, raved about Jay as a person and a writer, and suggested we drive up the coast and spend the day with Jay and his brother, science fiction writer Joe Haldeman. What I remember most clearly about that day was my first sight of Jay, a tall man, rail thin, with thick, long hair that fell almost to the middle of his back. I remember talking about books, about writers and writing, and I remember being fascinated by Jay's stories about working in Alaska as a biologist.

By 1990, Jay and his family had moved to a farm outside of Gainesville, Florida, which they shared with numerous dogs, cats, cows, a couple of pigs, and some chickens. Rob and I and our daughter, a toddler at the time, spent several long weekends at the farm. This was paradise for a little kid who loves animals and got to collect eggs from the henhouse and run free with the Australian shepherds that kept herding her away from the lake. Jay loved kids and always treated Megan as though she were an adult who just happened to be small.

The farm was a writer's little Walden. At night, you could hear the crickets singing and watch stars exploding against an obsidian sky. There was an old Wurlitzer jukebox on the porch, all sorts of family heirlooms, and, of course, thousands of books. They were stacked neatly on bookshelves, on windowsills, in the kitchen and the living room and the bedrooms. Jay had read most of them. I was so taken with the farm that I used it as a setting for a novel called *Spree*.

After Jay's divorce, he sold the farm and moved into Gainesville. At least once a year, he passed through south Florida for a science fiction convention and always stayed with us. He would tinker with our computers, fixing glitches we didn't understand, and we always talked books and writing and exchanged stories about travels we had taken. Given his scientific background, I don't think Jay was interested in astrology. I don't think he was interested in UFOs, ghosts, or some of the other things that fascinate Rob and me. But he was never judgmental. He listened, he absorbed, and he had that rare gift of being fully present when you talked with him.

As far as I could tell, he didn't ever fall into Sagittarius's shadow. I never heard him describe "his truth" or even his spiritual beliefs. He personified the Sagittarian ideal, constantly learning, observing, traveling through new countries of the mind. In 1992, he met Barb, a Leo, a Canadian, and an aspiring writer, at a science fiction convention. They got married in the summer of 1995, but only after the complex green card process, which enabled Barb to move to the United States. I'd never seen Jay as content as he was during those six and a half years.

We stayed with them frequently during those years, blowing in with our dog and Megan and one of her friends. When we were looking at homes in the Gainesville area, they put us up and steered us toward the right realtor. On New Year's day 2002, Jay passed away from a brain tumor. He was sixty years old. The transits we're going to look at are those on the day he met Barb.

Jay was a double Sag: sun and moon exactly conjunct at 26 degrees Sagittarius. He was born under the new moon phase, which accentuated his pioneering spirit. He had Scorpio rising at 25 degrees. Instead of putting his sun sign on the ascendant of the horoscope wheel, put the sign and degree of his actual rising and place the natal sun and moon together in the second house. Label them each with an *N* to distinguish them from the transiting planets. Now you'll be able to see exactly where the planets fell on the day he met Barb.

Place the planets in the appropriate houses. Pay special attention to Pluto, the ruler of the chart, and to Jupiter, the ruler of his Sun sign.

- ✦ Sun 15 degrees Virgo
- ✦ Moon 26 degrees Capricorn
- ✦ Mercury 8 degrees Virgo
- ✦ Venus 8 degrees Libra
- ✦ Mars 27 degrees Gemini
- ✦ Jupiter 22 degrees Virgo
- ✦ Saturn 12 degrees Aquarius
- ✦ Uranus 14 degrees Capricorn, retrograde
- ✦ Neptune 16 degrees Capricorn, retrograde
- ✦ Pluto 20 degrees Scorpio
- ✦ North node 27 degrees Sagittarius

On the lines below, list the aspects that you see to Jay's sun. Do the story lines seem to support marriage?

Aspects to Jay's Sun

_____

_____

_____

_____

_____

_____

_____

_____

   Jupiter in the tenth house of profession and careers makes a 4-degree square to Jay's sun and moon in the second. Jupiter squares aren't as challenging as squares from Saturn and the outer planets and usually bring opportunities that expand your life in some way. In this instance, the opportunity came through a foreign-born person, an area that Jupiter rules and that also fits Barb. Mars in Gemini in the eighth house is opposed to Jay's sun and moon. Mars oppositions to the sun can be difficult, and this one affects money (second house) and shared resources (eighth). This aspect seems to be addressing the financial challenges of Jay's divorce. The north node conjunction to Jay's natal sun and moon is a very strong indicator of a karmic relationship. This pattern is repeated (but not shown on your horoscope wheel) with the transiting sun's conjunction with Jay's natal north node.

   Now take a look at Pluto's position. It's approaching a conjunction with Jay's ascendant. Any time this happens by transit or in any other predictive branch of astrology, it indicates profound change overall in your life and in how others view you. Venus transiting his eleventh house of wishes and dreams suggests that a woman will play a vital role in Jay's realization of his dreams.

   The story line for the day Jay met Barb certainly seems to support a close and unified relationship.

THE OUTER PLANETS: THEMES

Uranus, Neptune, and Pluto crawl along like molasses, so you won't experience every aspect of these planets to your sun. In some instances, that's good news. Of course, these planets will be making aspects to other planets and points in your chart, and if you decide to explore this area, you'll find that transits to your natal moon and ascendant can be as important as transits to your sun.

In the immediate future, there are two aspects from Uranus to your sun that you should know about. In March 2003, Uranus goes into Pisces, forming a square to your sun. In 2011, it goes into Aries, trining your sun.

Uranus aspects invariably challenge your individuality. The squares, though, test that individuality every inch of the way. You may move, change jobs or careers, go back to school or graduate from school, get married or divorced, have a child or send your child off to college. Whatever the event, it's disruptive, unexpected, and challenges the path you have been on. The trine can also be disruptive, but you embrace it. You're ready for change and find it exciting. Opportunities come out of nowhere. Your creativity accelerates and encompasses new ideas and techniques.

Since 1998, you've been experiencing Neptune in Aquarius, sextile to your sun, and that will continue until 2011, when it goes into Pisces, squaring your sun. This means that for a period of several months in 2011, you'll have the Uranus trine in Aries going on *and* the Neptune square. Then Neptune goes retrograde for a while, moving back into Aquarius, so the tension lets up. But by 2012 it's moving direct again, and you may end up feeling like Bridget Jones but without the humor. Your energy is driven inward. Your spiritual beliefs and intuitive ability expand and deepen. Neptune in Pisces also deepens your compassion and empathy, and your life may take strange turns that somehow satisfy your need to help others.

This brings us to Pluto. Since 1995, Pluto in Sagittarius has been conjuncting your sun and will continue to do so until 2008.

You've already gotten enough of a taste of this aspect to know that it brings up power issues—how you deal with personal power, how other people wield power over you. The conjunction eliminates dead wood from your life, whether it's a relationship, a job, a career, attitudes, or habits. Think of the phoenix, rising from the ashes: that's the Pluto conjunction.

TIMING AND TRANSITS

Free will is key to any predictive technique. Just because a certain pattern depicts a challenge, it doesn't mean the upcoming event or situation is already a done deal. Or if a certain pattern indicates that you have wonderful opportunities coming up in the near future, it doesn't mean you can kick back and do nothing. In both instances, what you do with the pattern is entirely up to you. To be empowered, you act on what you know.

That said, the list that follows is of common situations in which timing is important to your success. What planets and aspects are the best for these situations? If your answers are different from mine, that's okay. Just be able to justify them to yourself.

ANSWERS TO THE TIMING ACTIVITY

For easy reference: a conjunction is a planet in Sagittarius; a sextile in a planet in Aquarius or Libra; a square is a planet in Virgo or Pisces; a trine is a planet in Leo or Aries; and an opposition is a planet in Gemini.

+ **Move:** Moon in Aries or Leo. Mars conjunction. Mercury sextile or trine, moving direct.
+ **Wedding:** Venus in Sagittarius, Leo, or Libra, Moon transiting natal seventh house. Jupiter conjunct, sextile, or trine.
+ **Honeymoon:** Venus in Sagittarius, sextile or trine. Moon in Sagittarius, Mercury direct.
+ **Divorce:** direct. Jupiter conjunct, sextile, or trine.

+ **A spiritually oriented trip:** Moon or Jupiter in Sagittarius. Jupiter transitting natal ninth house. Jupiter sextile or trine.
+ **Sign a contract:** Mercury direct. Jupiter conjunct, sextile, or trine.
+ **Attend a professional workshop/seminar:** Mercury direct. Saturn sextile or trine. Jupiter conjunct, sextile, or trine.
+ **Submit a creative project:** Jupiter transiting natal fifth house. Venus and/or Jupiter conjunct, sextile, or trine. Mercury direct.
+ **End a significant relationship/friendship:** Mercury direct. Jupiter conjunct, sextile, or trine. Mars conjunct.
+ **Start/open your own business:** Mercury direct. Saturn sextile or trine. Jupiter and/or Mars conjunct.
+ **Volunteer for a pet rescue:** Jupiter and/or Venus conjunct, sextile, or trine. Positive Neptune/sun aspects.
+ **Return to college:** mercury direct. Jupiter conjunct, sextile, or trine. Mercury conjunct.
+ **Visit family:** Moon transiting natal fourth house. Moon sextile or trine. Mercury direct.
+ **Start a new job:** Mercury direct. Venus sextile or trine. Mars conjunct, sextile, or trine.
+ **Change professions:** Mercury direct. Mars conjunct, sextile, or trine. Saturn sextile or trine. Jupiter transiting natal tenth house or MC.
+ **Resign from a job:** Mercury direct. Venus and/or Jupiter conjunct, sextile, or trine.
+ **Buy a home/land:** Moon in Sagittarius, Leo, or Aries. Moon transiting natal fourth house. Mercury direct. Jupiter conjunct, sextile, or trine.
+ **Romantic heart-to-heart:** Mercury direct. Venus conjunct, sextile, or trine.
+ **Buy a new pet:** Jupiter conjunct, sextile, or trine. Jupiter transiting natal fifth house. Mercury direct. Venus conjunct, sextile, or trine.
+ **Buy a computer or other electronic device:** Mercury direct. Uranus sextile or trine.

MANIFESTATION: PROPERTIES OF LIGHT

In *Properties of Light,* by Rebecca Goldstein, three physicists wrestle with one of the greatest mysteries of science—the truth about the properties of light. And in their struggle, they also struggle with the mysteries of the heart. Either pursuit is a risk that entails the passionate need to understand. In your search for truth, in your passionate need to understand, you must remember to hold on to your dreams, to reach for them. This activity is designed to help you do that.

In the New Moon ephemeris (page 254), look up the date for the next New Moon. On that evening, in the magical period of dusk when the light is like a soft velvet, write out a desire that you have. Keep it to one sentence, written in present tense. Your phrasing is important. Instead of saying, *I want to get rid of my debt,* a more positive statement might be *Abundance flows into my life.* The act of writing out the desire imprints it on your unconscious mind. Repeat the statement aloud several times.

If you want, you can ritualize this in some way. I suggest lighting a fragrant candle or a stick of incense or even planting seeds in a ceramic pot. The idea here is that by the next New Moon, the seeds will have begun to sprout; your wish is being answered.

16

SUN IN CAPRICORN: ACHIEVER AND STRATEGIST

December 22–January 19

ACHIEVER

When I was trying to decide on the archetypes for each sign, Capricorn gave me trouble. I didn't want to repeat the themes I had used in *Creative Stars,* but the more I thought about it, the more I realized that achiever fits Capricorn as it does no other sign. In some form or another, your life is geared toward achieving something concrete and tangible.

You're a goal-oriented person. When you have a task to do, you do it. When you have responsibilities to fulfill, you fulfill them. You do whatever has to be done to fulfill your obligations and to achieve the goal. In constantly achieving a series of small goals, however, you may get bogged down too easily in the minutiae of daily living so that you lose sight of the larger picture of your life and your larger goals. What's your dream, Capricorn? Define it, then seek to achieve it with the same thorough patience that you exhibit in every other area of your life.

You're a builder. You delight in taking the raw material of anything and creating something out of it that you can touch, see, taste, feel, and hear. Whether it's building a solid foundation for yourself and your family or building a career and a business or building an imaginary universe, it's one of the things you do best. This is right in line with Saturn, the planet that rules your sun sign and the planet that gives structure and reality to the physical universe. Without Saturn, civilizations can't begin.

As a cardinal earth sign, your energy is highly focused. You tend to move in a single direction, like a horse wearing blinders. When something occurs that blocks that forward movement, you're forced to remove your blinders and look around for a way around the obstacle, a new path. But it never deters you from your goal. Like the goat that symbolizes Capricorn, you move forward and upward on rocky mountain slopes, your footing so certain that you rarely falter. As an earth sign, you specialize in making the intangible tangible. You can bring the loftiest concepts right down to earth.

One of the ways you do this is through strategy.

STRATEGIST

When I hear the word *strategist* I automatically think of military strategies. But strategy is what we use to attain many things in life. Whether it's a job promotion and a raise or getting into the college of our choice, we lay down a plan, a *strategy,* for achieving it. With Saturn's full power and force behind you, nothing is out of your reach, Capricorn. No other planet can bring such huge rewards and recognition. When you do *your* part in the scheme of things, Saturn rewards your efforts by doing *his* part. By the same token, when you fail to do your part, the repercussions can be severe.

On the shadow side of things, there can be a kind of gross materialism. For many Capricorns, the almighty buck is a god worthy of worship. It may start as a small thing, a need to have the best and most expensive toy, then the best and most expensive clothing, then the best and most expensive cars, homes, jewelry. And suddenly, it all becomes flat-out greed.

When my Capricorn sister got divorced and was faced with the prospect of raising three kids on her own on a single salary, she was working for an assisted-living facility. She laid out a strategy for what she would need, where she might live, and how she might advance in her profession, and today she is the wellness director of an assisted-living facility in Georgia. Through her enormous will, she *made things happen.* When you want something to happen, want it so badly that you feel it in your very bones, then Saturn comes to your aid and helps you manifest that desire.

The achiever needs the strategist, and vice versa. They balance each other; they should be inseparable. When one archetype isn't functioning correctly, the result is naked ambition or a control freak. Or the result may be someone whose mind is closed off to possibility and imagination. Due to the Saturn rulership of this sign, it's a good idea to know the sign of your natal moon. This tells you a great deal about how to put your Capricorn energy to work for you without compromising your sense of play, imagination, or creativity.

A Leo moon, for example, boosts your imagination, your passions, and your love of animals, and makes you shine inwardly. A Virgo moon reinforces the practical side of your nature and adds a precision for details to the strategist archetype. Once you find out your natal moon, simply combine the archetypes for that sign, apply them to your emotions, then create a description.

YOUR PLOTS AND SATURN

Saturn spends about two and a half years in a sign and takes nearly thirty years to circle the zodiac. With such a lengthy transit through a single sign, you have to be at least thirty or older to have any sense at all of Saturn's impact on your life as it makes various aspects to your sun. So in the next activity, we're going to expand the time frame used in the other sections. Instead of covering just the thirteen years between 1990 and 2002, we'll add ten years and take it back to 1980.

The next checklist is intended to help you brainstorm your past in search of repeating patterns. Put a next to any statement that applies to your life since 1980 (yes, this is also a memory test!) and, if you can recall the date, jot it down. In the dates section afterward, compare the dates you've noted with the time frames for when Saturn was in Capricorn (conjunct), in Scorpio or Pisces (sextile), in Aries or Libra (square), and in Virgo or Pisces (trine). There should be some correlation. You also may want to review the meanings for the various aspects on page 58.

CAPRICORN/SATURN CHECKLIST

___ I got a significant promotion. _____

___ I started college. _____

___ I got a big raise. _____

___ I found the ideal job. _____

___ I moved. _____

___ One of my parents or an older
    relative passed away. _____

___ I got married. _____

___ I got divorced. _____

___ My siblings were born. _____

___ I had trouble with my knees (Capricorn rulership) or with my
    bones, joints, skin, or teeth (Saturn). _____

___ I bought a home/property. _____

___ I won recognition for my
    professional efforts. _____

___ My spiritual beliefs changed
    dramatically. _____

___ I won a prize/contest. _____

___ I achieved a dream. _____

___ I had a financial setback. _____

___ I was sued or was involved with
    the courts. _____

___ One of my parents got seriously ill. _____

___ A parent moved in with me. _____

___ I shouldered a lot of responsibility. _____

___ I sold a creative project. _____

___ I began an exercise regime that
continues to the present. _____

___ I started my own business. _____

___ I had a child. _____

___ I met the love of my life. _____

Now take a look at the dates below. Do any of these match your dates?

DATES: SATURN ASPECTS, 1980–2002

1/1/80–9/20/80: Virgo (trine)
9/21/80–11/28/82: Libra (square)
11/29/82–11/15/85: Scorpio (sextile)
2/13/88–2/5/91: Capricorn (conjunct)
5/20/93–4/6/96: Pisces (sextile)
4/7/96–6/8/98: Aries (square)

The next aspect to your sun from Saturn is the opposition in Cancer, beginning in June 2003. Refer to Saturn ephemeris in Appendix A.

REPETITIVE PATTERNS

If, in brainstorming your past in this way, you discovered correlations between your dates and the dates when Saturn was aspecting your sun, you have the beginning of a pattern. Now look through the Saturn ephemeris and, on the lines below, make note of the time frames when Saturn will be making aspects to your sun and create possible story lines, based on what has happened to you in the past.

Important Dates for Saturn, 2003–2007

JANIS

She was born in Port Arthur, Texas, on January 19, 1943, at the tail end of Capricorn. She helped define the sixties. Her name was Janis Joplin and regardless of what anyone thought of her music then or now, she was a complete original. (Her natal chart is in Appendix C.)

According to the biography on her official Web site, maintained by her estate, "she led a triumphant and tumultuous life blessed by an innate talent to convey powerful emotion through heart-stomping rock-and-roll singing." That hardly conveys it. You had to see her perform live to feel the energy that she radiated, the total immersion in the music, the singing, the *performance*. But this wasn't performance in the way that Madonna, for example, performs. No ornate sets, no outlandish costumes, no MTV. This was from the gut, as genuine as her ruddy complexion, her frizzy hair, and her bottle of Southern Comfort. Crowds loved her for that energy. She transported them.

Her breakthrough came with Big Brother and the Holding Company, when they performed at the Monterrey International Pop Festival in the summer of 1967. As a result of that festival, Albert Grossman, one of the most powerful entertainment managers at the time, took them on and, through his representation, they eventually signed a three-record contract with Columbia Records. In August

1968, they released their *Cheap Thrills* album, which features two of Joplin's best-known songs: "Piece of My Heart" and "Summertime." The record went gold not long after it was released. Joplin had made the big time.

With the big time came money, and with the money came expensive drugs. Joplin's alcoholism and heroin abuse were well known. During the concert I saw before she and Big Brother broke up, she constantly gulped from a bottle of Southern Comfort. The drunker she got, the rowdier the audience got. The microphones were finally cut, nearly causing a riot in the crowd.

After the breakup with Big Brother in Christmas 1968, Janis formed two other bands. Before she formed the third, Full Tilt Boogie Band, she tried to clean up her addictions. While recording her album *Pearl* with the newly formed third band, Janis slipped back into the seduction of heroin and overdosed in an LA motel room on October 4, 1970, at the age of twenty-seven. The album, which contained two of her best songs, "Me and Bobby McGee" and "Mercedes Benz," was released posthumously.

Her albums have gone gold, platinum, and triple platinum.

What's fascinating about Joplin, as least from an astrological viewpoint, is that she didn't act like a Capricorn. But she had the ruddy complexion that some Capricorns have, she was ambitious, a relentless worker, she achieved acclaim, and according to some accounts I have read, she felt inferior to other musicians and performers. Saturn often squashes your optimism as though it's no more significant than an ant.

Joplin had a Cancer moon in the fifth house of creativity, which explains the emotional depths and energy she brought to her music and her performances. Her Aquarian ascendant made her a creative visionary and explains the electric quality of her performances. In her natal chart, Uranus, the ruler of her chart, is found in the fourth house, which describes, among other things, the ending of your life—sudden, unexpected.

For her addictions, we look to Neptune. In her natal chart, Neptune in Libra falls into her eighth house: support systems, death and rebirth, metaphysics. Quite often, this house describes the circumstances surrounding a person's death. She died of a heroin overdose. Neptune is square her sun in the natal chart, an aspect that can bring contact with higher spiritual dimensions or with addictions.

The other house we look at in terms of death is the twelfth. Janis had the sun, Mercury, and Venus in this house. That's a loaded twelfth house and points to unresolved issues about her father, men in life, her intellect, her siblings, and women and the arts. She also had the south node of the moon conjunct her ascendant. The nodes often play a part in the major events of our lives, of which death is the final event.

But what does the story line look like for the day she died? You may want to turn to Joplin's natal chart in the appendix and put the transiting planets in the outer wheel. On October 4, 1970, here's how the transiting planets lined up:

- ✦ Sun in Libra, 11 degrees
- ✦ Moon in Scorpio, 28 degrees
- ✦ Mercury in Virgo, 25 degrees
- ✦ Venus in Scorpio, 20 degrees
- ✦ Mars in Virgo, 20 degrees
- ✦ Jupiter in Scorpio, 8 degrees
- ✦ Saturn in Taurus, 21 degrees
- ✦ Uranus in Libra, 9 degrees
- ✦ Neptune in Scorpio, 28 degrees
- ✦ Pluto in Virgo, 27 degrees
- ✦ North node in Pisces, 2 degrees

Up there in the tenth house, you should have the transiting moon and Neptune at 28 degrees, forming an exact sextile to her natal sun. Transiting Jupiter and Venus are here, too. Neither planet forms an aspect with her sun. Transiting Pluto in Virgo in the eighth house is forming a nearly exact trine to her sun. Transiting Mercury in Virgo is forming a 3-degree trine to her sun and an exact quincunx to her ascendant. Based strictly on the aspects to her sun, it's doubtful that she suffered. She simply went to sleep and died. The Neptune and moon sextile to her sun suggests a drug overdose. The quincunx from Mercury to her ascendant indicates that she desperately needed an adjustment in her thinking (Mercury) about her public image (ascendant). It's likely that she was deeply depressed at the time she died.

The transits from other planets are less revealing. Transiting Saturn in the fourth house is forming a 4-degree square to her ascendant and her nodes. Saturn, Mr. Heavy, was sitting on her public image like a ton of bricks. She was depressed and alone, and felt like hell. But Saturn was forming a wide 7-degree trine to her sun. Jupiter was making an exact trine to her natal Cancer moon; that spells excess, and it's screaming, *Oh, God, make me feel good, make me feel mellow, make me feel loved.* Transiting Uranus is forming a 1-degree square to her moon. It's challenging her emotional individuality, forcing her to ask, *Am I any good? Have I peaked? Am I kidding myself?* The inner tension mounts, she needs release.

Overall, there are numerous aspects and possible story lines for the day that Joplin died. There are so many positive aspects that the story line could have gone in life-affirming directions and Joplin might still be with us today, a sixty-year-old broad still belting out the blues. But given her history with addictions, the hits from transiting Neptune, Uranus, and the Moon were tough hurdles to overcome. Unless you're psychic, death is difficult to see in a chart. Free will prevails even to the point of death.

When my Capricorn mother died, I spent hours poring over her chart, looking for the *pattern* using every technique I knew. If astrology worked, there had to be a pattern. I finally found it in the Arabic parts. This is an ancient facet of astrology based on geometric divisions of the natal chart. The only Arabic part Western astrologers use with any regularity is the part of fortune, your pot of gold. But the Arabic parts also include the part of death, and at the time my mother died, Pluto, the transformer, was making an exact conjunction with my mother's part of death.

Sometimes, astrology is so literal that we overlook the obvious. Other times, you have to dig to find the pattern.

THE OUTER PLANETS: THEMES

Whereas the transits of the inner planets are the best indicators of emerging story lines daily, weekly, and monthly, the transits of the outer planets provide the underlying themes. Since these planets move so slowly, you won't experience all of their aspects to your sun. In some cases, that's good news. However, they'll be making transits to other planets and points in your chart. If you decide to explore this area, you'll find that transits to your ascendant and natal moon are often just as important as transits to your sun.

In the near future, the Uranus aspects to your sun are the Pisces sextile that begins in March 2003 and the Aries square to your sun that begins in 2011. The sextile ushers in new, exciting opportunities that support your creativity and individuality. Your spiritual values may be reflected somehow in your work, and you now have access to much deeper parts of your psyche. The square challenges your individuality by forcing you to question whether the path you're on is right for you. If it isn't right, Uranus corrects your course. You're forced to become more independent and to define what *you* believe. Both the square and the opposition shake up the areas of your life that have become routine and predictable. These aspects don't feel good while they're happening, but they ultimately encourage you to reach for your dreams and to define your uniqueness.

Neptune remains in Aquarius until 2011, when it goes into Pisces and forms a sextile to your sun. In 2025, Neptune goes into Aries, forming a square to your sun, and in 2038 it goes into Taurus and trines your sun. The Pisces sextile deepens your spiritual beliefs, compassion, and intuitive abilities. Your spiritual life and beliefs are of paramount importance.

In January 2008, Pluto enters Capricorn and stays there for fifteen years. This aspect is most powerful as it's approaching your sun and when its conjunction is exact. Your ambition soars and you're able to overcome any obstacles that get in your way. You have the opportunity now to achieve your wildest dreams and goals, but with one major caveat: The process isn't painless. Pluto, as the great transformer, first gets rid of everything in your life that has outlived its usefulness. Relationships, beliefs, habits, and attitudes—nothing is exempt from the purge. But then Pluto gives you the strength and the power and the sheer will to achieve your potential.

TIMING AND TRANSITS

Recently, I had a client who was very concerned about a detail in her natal chart. She felt this detail inhibited her creativity and prevented her from succeeding at what she wanted to do. This sort of negative thinking gets you nowhere. A chart, whether it's natal or transits or something else, is just potential. It neither guarantees nor denies success, wealth, happiness, marriage, children, or a spot on *Oprah*. You activate the potential through your free will and beliefs.

When you see any aspect coming up, positive or challenging, don't think of it as a done deal. Use the information to your best advantage. That's true empowerment. If the aspect is a square or an opposition, be aware of the possible pitfalls and take steps to avoid them. If the aspect is a conjunction, sextile, or trine, create room in your life to embrace the opportunities they bring.

The list that follows is of common situations in which timing can be crucial to your success. What planets and aspects would give you the advantage? It's fine if your answers differ from mine as long as you can justify them to yourself.

+ **Move:** Moon in Virgo or Taurus. Mars conjunction. Mercury sextile or trine, moving direct.
+ **Wedding:** Venus in Capricorn, Scorpio, or Taurus. Moon transiting natal seventh house. Jupiter conjunct, sextile, or trine.
+ **Honeymoon:** Venus in Scorpio or Taurus. Moon sextile or trine. Mercury direct.
+ **Divorce:** Mercury direct. Jupiter conjunct, sextile, or trine.
+ **Request a raise or promotion:** Mars conjunct, sextile, or trine. Saturn sextile or trine. Jupiter conjunct, sextile, or trine.

+ **End a significant relationship:** Mars conjunct. Mercury direct. Jupiter conjunct, sextile, or trine.

+ **Start/open your own business:** Mercury direct. Saturn sextile or trine. Mars sextile or trine.

+ **Change careers:** Mercury direct. Saturn sextile or trine. Mars conjunct, sextile, or trine. Jupiter conjunct, sextile, or trine.

+ **House hunt:** Moon sextile or trine. Jupiter conjunct, sextile, or trine. Mercury direct.

+ **Buy a home/property:** Moon in Capricorn, Virgo, or Taurus. Moon transiting natal fourth house. Mercury direct.

+ **Obtain a bank loan:** Saturn sextile or trine. Jupiter and/or Venus conjunct, sextile, or trine.

+ **Buy a new pet:** Jupiter conjunct, sextile, or trine. Moon transiting natal fifth or sixth house. Mercury direct. Venus conjunct, sextile, or trine.

+ **Apply for a mortgage:** Saturn sextile or trine. Mercury direct. Jupiter and/or Venus sextile or trine.

+ **Start a 401k or other savings plan:** Saturn conjunct, sextile, or trine. Mars conjunct. Moon transiting natal fourth house.

+ **Buy stocks:** Saturn sextile or trine. Jupiter and/or Venus conjunct, sextile, or trine. Mercury direct.

+ **Buy a car:** Mercury direct, in Capricorn or sextile or trine. Saturn sextile or trine. Moon transiting natal third house.

+ **Romantic heart-to-heart:** Mercury direct. Venus conjunct, sextile, or trine. Jupiter conjunct, sextile, or trine. Moon and/or Venus transiting natal seventh house.

+ **Return to school/college:** Mercury direct. Jupiter conjunct, sextile, or trine.

+ **Submit a creative project:** Jupiter transiting natal fifth house. Venus and/or Jupiter conjunct, sextile, or trine. Mercury direct.

+ **Take a vacation:** Jupiter conjunct, sextile, or trine. Mercury direct.

≋

17

SUN IN AQUARIUS: INNOVATOR AND VISIONARY

January 20–February 18

INNOVATOR

As a fixed air sign ruled by Uranus, the mind is your kingdom. And what a kingdom it is! Your intellect makes connections that elude other people. You see opportunity where someone else might see an obstacle or an impossible challenge. You revel in the new, the untried, the cutting edge. You have always been an innovator, a paradigm buster, and now that your age has finally arrived, you should be feeling right at home.

Uranus, often referred to as the higher octave of Mercury, demands nothing less of you than to be at the forefront of innovation. Granted, we can't all be Thomas Edisons or Abe Lincolns (both

Aquarians), but in some area of your life, you're an innovator. Maybe you're the tinkering type who is always doing something around the house to improve your living conditions. Or perhaps your approach to parenting is unusual in some way. Maybe in your professional life, you're the one who comes up with unusual marketing plans or cutting-edge ideas.

You take your time in forming opinions and beliefs and can be as stubborn as Taurus in holding on to them. This is a definite asset when it comes to innovation. After all, if Abe Lincoln hadn't held onto his belief that slavery was wrong or if Charles Lindbergh had surrendered his belief to the consensus opinion about flight, we might be living in a very different world.

You place a high value on the individual—his or her talents and expertise, abilities, skills. To you, one individual can make a difference in the world. You also hold to an ideal that each individual is part of a collective and the collective has enormous power when it's united. You believe in the tribe called humanity. In your commitment to this tribe, to this larger family of man, you contribute to its betterment.

The innovator archetype doesn't stand alone; you have help from your second archetype, the visionary.

VISIONARY

When we speak of visionaries, we think of men and women whose contributions to the world drastically altered our concepts of what is possible and our quality of life. Thomas Edison, a seminal Aquarian, brought us out of the era of gaslights into electric power. Lincoln abolished slavery. Whenever I'm sitting on a jet that's hurtling at six hundred mph forty thousand feet above Earth, I think of Lindbergh, flying *The Spirit of St. Louis* through the darkness above the Atlantic all alone.

You are innovative precisely because you are visionary, and you are visionary precisely because you are innovative. The two are inseparable, two sides of the same coin. When these archetypes work smoothly together, you can accomplish anything you set your sights on. When the archetypes are at odds, when one insists on being head honcho, we encounter the Aquarian shadow, the individual who is merely eccentric, with a bundle of idiosyncratic behaviors and opinions, who rebels against the establishment just for the sake of rebellion.

In daily life, your visionary ability is always humming right along, nudging you in this direction or that, urging you to embrace the new and different, the untried and the unimagined. Sometimes, the urge comes through impulses, a sudden, inexplicable feeling that you should do something differently or try something new. If you follow the impulse, it often leads to opportunities you may not have considered before. On both a personal and collective basis, your job, Aquarius, is to envision what might be—and then help bring it about.

You need a lot of personal freedom to pursue the things that interest you. This can make intimate relationships difficult unless your significant other respects your need for space and exploration. There's a natural affinity between you and your fellow air signs, Gemini and Libra, who also need freedom and space, but for different reasons.

As a fixed sign, certain words don't exist in your vocabulary: *quit, surrender, give up, relinquish.* Like Taurus and Scorpio, the other fixed signs, you simply keep moving forward, trusting in your ability to achieve what you want.

YOUR PLOTS AND URANUS

In most of the previous chapters, this activity was intended to help the reader identify patterns related to the sign's ruler that have unfolded over a thirteen-year period, from 1990 to 2002. However, since Uranus, the first of the outer planets, takes seven years to move through a single sign and about eighty-four years to circle the zodiac, this time frame won't work. With Capricorn (Saturn), I extended the time frame back to 1980. With you, let's extend the time frame back even farther, to when Uranus entered Leo in November 1955. This gives us more to work with—Uranus in seven different signs.

Younger readers won't have as many years to work with, but there are other activities in this chapter that will help you understand the nature of Uranus.

Read through the items in the checklist below. Place a ✓ next to any statement that applies to you and try to recall the date. If specific dates are difficult to pinpoint, then give the month or even the season and the year. In the dates section afterward, compare the dates you've jotted down with the time frames for when Uranus was in Aquarius (conjunct), in Aries or Sagittarius (sextile), in Scorpio or Taurus (square), in Libra or Gemini (trine); in Leo (opposition).

AQUARIUS/URANUS CHECKLIST

___ I got married. _____

___ I got divorced. _____

___ I got a patent for an invention. _____

___ I started my own business. _____

___ I sold a creative project. _____

___ I found my creative path. _____

___ I had problems with my ankles. _____

___ My spiritual beliefs changed
    dramatically. _____

___ I won recognition for my innovative
    techniques. _____

___ I had problems with my legs/shins. _____

___ I had a child. _____

___ I met the love of my life. _____

___ I moved. _____

___ I found my dream job. _____

___ I took a trip that changed my life
    in some way. _____

___ I got a huge raise. _____

___ One of my parents passed away. _____

___ My siblings were born. _____

___ I bought a home/property. _____

___ I achieved a dream. _____

___ I took flying lessons. _____

___ My hobby became my profession. _____

___ I launched a Web site for my business. _____

___ I entered/returned to college. _____

___ I lived overseas. _____

___ I had problems with the courts/
judicial system. _____

Now take a look at the dates below. Do any of these match your dates?

DATES: URANUS ASPECTS, 1961–2002

Note: when a sign has several entries,
it means uranus went retrograde back into the previous sign.

8/25/55–11/1/61; 1/10/62–8/9/62: Leo (opposition)

8/10/62–9/28/68; 5/22/69–6/23/69: Virgo (no aspects)

9/29/68–5/21/69; 6/24/69–11/20/74; 5/2/75–9/7/75:
Libra (trine)

11/21/74–5/1/75; 9/8/75–2/16/81; 3/21/81–11/16/81:
Scorpio (square)

2/17/81–3/20/81; 11/17/81–2/13/88; 5/27/88–12/2/88:
Sagittarius (sextile)

2/14/88–5/26/88; 12/3/88–3/30/95; 6/10/95–1/11/96:
Capricorn (no aspects)

4/1/95–5/9/95; 1/2/96–3/10/03: Aquarius (conjunct)

REPETITIVE PATTERNS

What we're looking for here are patterns that repeat themselves over time. If, for example, you landed your dream job or fell in love during a Uranus sextile to your Sun, then you know that when Uranus goes into Aries in 2011, the underlying theme of that seven-year transit will be similar to the earlier transit. But on a daily, weekly, or monthly basis, the inner, faster-moving planets are the ones that you want to watch for approaching opportunities and challenges.

Take some time now to go through the ephemeris for Mercury, Venus, Mars, and Jupiter and in the date section below, note the dates when those planets will be making aspects to your Sun between 2003 and 2007. Create a brief story line for each one.

Important Transit Dates for 2003–2007

PLANET	SIGN	ASPECT	STORY LINES
Mercury			
Venus			
Mars			
Jupiter			

PHYLLIS'S STORY

I met Phyllis Vega in the early days of the Internet. We both contributed to a message board on Genie and found that we had shared many of the same interests. We also discovered some odd synchronicities in our lives. I had been born and raised in Venezuela; she had lived in Spain and her son-in-law was Venezuelan. I had a daughter the same age as her granddaughter. We had both practiced astrology and were interested in the tarot, myths, South America, the Incas, the Mayans.

At the time, Phyllis was living in New York and worked as a comptroller for an art gallery and various architects. But her grandchildren were in Florida and she wanted to move closer to them. The following year, she and her husband moved to Miami. We met for the first time at Ocean World in Fort Lauderdale and everyone hit it off. Within a year or so, Phyllis and I began working on a tarot book together (*Power Tarot, Fireside, 1998*).

She fits the Aquarian archetype so well that when it came to a story for the Aquarian chapter, I asked her for an event and a date, knowing that as an astrologer, she had an entire database of events and dates. The event she chose was the day she was hired to head up the accounting department for New Yorker Films, which was then the foremost distributor of foreign and independent films and art-house films.

Up until that day, Phyllis had been working as a bookkeeper in the garment district. She wanted to work in the arts, but was told by employment agencies that she'd better forget *that* idea; there weren't any jobs available in the arts. Phyllis refused to believe it (fixed sign). She knew what she wanted and wouldn't settle for anything else. Her desire was so intense, so focused, that an opportunity eventually manifested itself.

On November 19, 1979, Phyllis interviewed for a position at New Yorker Films and got it. When the transits are placed in a biwheel around Phyllis's birth chart, the story lines are compelling. Phyllis's birth chart is in Appendix C. Place the transits for that day, listed below, around the outside of the wheel. In this example, we'll use the whole chart and not just the aspects to the sun.

+ Sun ☉: 27 Scorpio
+ Moon ☽: 26 Scorpio
+ Mercury ☿: 27 Scorpio
+ Venus ♀: 19 Sagittarius

- Mars ♂: 29 Leo
- Jupiter ♃: 8 Virgo
- Saturn ♄: 25 Virgo
- Uranus ♅: 21 Scorpio
- Neptune ♆: 19 Sagittarius
- Pluto ♀: 28 Cancer
- North node ☊: 2 Virgo

In the space below, jot down the aspects that you see to Phyllis's sun and then aspects to any of the other planets. Feel free to practice with a phrase or two that describes the story line you see.

Aspects in Phyllis's Chart

ASPECTS TO THE NATAL SUN FROM TRANSITING	STORY LINE
☉	
☽	
☿	
♀	
♂	
♃	
♄	
♅	
♆	
♀	
♅	

The transiting sun, moon, and Mercury make 1- and 2-degree squares to Phyllis's natal Aquarian sun in the seventh house. This brings the house of partnerships—a business partnership—into the limelight. Her primal force (sun), emotions (moon), and Mercury (intellect) are represented in the fourth house, the foundation of her psyche, of her essential self. This reflects her determination to find a job in the arts; her desire resulted in friction and challenge but got results. *The squares created events.*

Transiting Venus and Neptune in 19 degrees Sagittarius, also in the fourth house, are approaching sextiles with her sun. Venus symbolizes the arts and women, and Neptune, in this instance, represents movies, glamour, the illusions that films create. The sextile suggests an ease with groups, perhaps a specific group that is like family, which is how Phyllis felt about the people with whom she worked for the next five years. The fourth house is obviously the focus of the transiting planets, indicating that Phyllis's deepest needs were changing. She wanted a job that was emotionally, intellectually, creatively, and spiritually satisfying. Quite often, profound life changes are reflected in the planets transiting the fourth house.

Transiting Saturn forms a perfect quincunx to Phyllis's sun. Some astrologers consider this a minor aspect, others look at it as major. It often means that an adjustment is necessary in the health area. But for Phyllis it seemed to suggest an adjustment she would have to make concerning her life path. Up to this point, she had been a practicing astrologer in her private life, but now film would become her life. She went to school to study film and actually attended college with her oldest daughter, who was also studying film. Astrology was left in the dust.

The transiting sun, moon, and Mercury are forming trines at 1 and 2 degrees with Phyllis's natal Pluto in the twelfth house, a certain indicator that her ego, emotional self, and intellect would undergo profound change as a result of this job.

Would an astrologer have been able to see the specifics before the fact? Probably not. That is, the astrologer wouldn't be able to say, *Hey, there's a job at New Yorker Films that's got your name on it.* But he or she would spot a major opportunity coming up in the arts that would profoundly change Phyllis's perspective on life.

When you're looking for story lines in your own life, follow this rule of thumb: Look for the big picture first, *for the prevalent pattern.* What's the ruling planet doing? What are the inner planets doing? What are the underlying themes of the outer planets? Are there any transits where both an inner and outer planet are bearing down on your natal sun or another natal planet? Any combination like the transiting Venus and Neptune in Sagittarius, an inner and an outer planet in the same degree and forming a sextile to the natal sun, should grab your attention. Any cluster of planets demands deeper scrutiny. If there's a coruler to your sun sign, check its position. Are there transiting planets making hits on the angles—the ascendant and the cusps of the fourth, seventh, and tenth houses?

Reading your story in the stars is both a science and an art. Do the science first, then let your intuition guide you.

THE OUTER PLANETS: THEMES

Daily, weekly, and monthly, the transits of the inner planets are indicative of emerging story lines. The transits of the outer planets, however, depict the underlying themes, the texture of the story lines, the stuff that's going on beneath the surface. Since these planets move so slowly, you won't experience every aspect they make to your sun.

Let's look at Uranus, your ruling planet. In 1995, it went into Aquarius, conjunct your sun, then went retrograde and moved back into Capricorn until January 1996. It will stay there until 2003, when it goes into Pisces. The conjunction shakes up your life. Whatever you take for granted, whatever has become routine and predictable in your life, is disrupted and changed. Ultimately, this is a good thing, even though it won't feel that way when it's happening. The conjunction makes room in your life for new and exciting experiences. That's its purpose. So any story lines connected to the inner planets will somehow enhance and work with this underlying theme.

In 2010, Uranus goes into Aries, sextile to your sun. This aspect heightens your creativity, independence, and individuality. The universe supports the path you've chosen. You may move—or perhaps have moved already—or change jobs or professions, return to or graduate from school. The manifestations of this aspect depend on where you are in your life right now.

The only Neptune aspect to your sun that you'll experience in the next twenty-five years is the sextile in Aries. Your compassion toward friends deepens and your friendships assume greater importance in your life. You may become part of a spiritual group or do work with a spiritually oriented group. Your deeper philosophy about life is changed.

Pluto in Sagittarius has been sextile to your sun since late 1995. With this aspect, Pluto is on your side, the best place to have this planet. Opportunities come to you for professional advancement and recognition. You're the one in power now, and if you use your power with integrity, this aspect is great. Pluto doesn't make any other aspects to your sun until the conjunction in 2023. And that's too far ahead to even worry about!

TIMING AND TRANSITS

In the film *The Graduate,* we all remember the line, "Plastics. The future is in plastics." With transits or any other type of astrology, what you have to remember is, *Potential. It's just potential.* Just because a square or opposition to your sun is coming up on a particular date doesn't spell disaster. On the day that Phyllis landed her dream job, most of the aspects were squares. If you see a window of opportunity approaching, reach out and seize it, don't just sit back and wait for it to come to you.

With that in mind, glance through the following list of situations in which timing can be everything. What planets and aspects would give you the advantage in these situations? If your answers are different from mine, fine. Just be able to justify them in your own mind.

For easy reference: A conjunction is a planet in Aquarius; a sextile is a planet in Aries or Sagittarius; a square is a planet in Scorpio or Taurus; a trine is a planet in Libra or Gemini; an opposition is a planet in Leo.

- **Move:** Moon in Aries or Sagittarius. Mercury sextile or trine, moving direct.
- **Wedding:** Venus in Aquarius, Libra, or Gemini. Mercury sextile or trine. Mercury direct. Jupiter conjunct, sextile, or trine.

+ **Honeymoon:** Venus in Aries or Sagittarius. Venus in Taurus. Moon sextile or trine. Mercury direct.
+ **Divorce:** Mercury direct. Jupiter conjunct, sextile, or trine.
+ **Take a professional workshop:** Mercury direct. Mercury sextile or trine.
+ **Take a spiritual workshop:** Uranus conjunct, sextile, or trine. Jupiter sextile or trine. Neptune sextile or trine.
+ **Buy a car:** Mercury direct. Mercury conjunct.
+ **Buy a computer:** Mercury direct. Uranus sextile or trine.
+ **Run for public office:** Mercury direct. Uranus and/or Saturn sextile or trine.
+ **Take a trip overseas:** Mercury direct. Moon and/or Jupiter in Sagittarius. Jupiter transiting natal ninth house.
+ **Change professions:** Mercury direct. Saturn sextile or trine. Mars conjunct, sextile, or trine. Jupiter conjunct, sextile, or trine.
+ **Quit a job:** Mars conjunct. Uranus sextile or trine. Jupiter conjunct, sextile, or trine.
+ **Start a job:** Jupiter sextile or trine. Mars conjunct. Mercury direct.
+ **Look for your dream job:** Venus and/or Jupiter conjunct, sextile, or trine. Mars conjunct. Saturn sextile or trine.
+ **Start a book/screenplay:** Venus and/or Jupiter conjunct. Mercury direct. Moon transiting natal fifth house.
+ **Exhibit your art:** Venus conjunct, sextile, or trine. Jupiter sextile or trine.
+ **Apply for a mortgage/loan:** Saturn sextile or trine. Mercury direct. Jupiter and/or Venus sextile or trine.
+ **Buy tech stocks:** Uranus sextile or trine. Saturn sextile or trine.
+ **Start your own business:** Saturn sextile or trine. Mercury direct. Mars sextile or trine.
+ **Request a raise or promotion:** Mars conjunct, sextile, or trine. Saturn sextile or trine. Jupiter conjunct, sextile, or trine.

MANIFESTATION: SPIRITWALKER

Hank Wasselman is an anthropologist, that breed of scientist that studies cultures. In *Spiritwalker,* his spiritual autobiography, he recounts a series of experiences that seemed to begin as intense, vivid dreams but ultimately convinced him that he'd been propelled five thousand years into the future. In this culture, he met shape-shifters and spirit helpers, and his consciousness seemed to merge with that of a kahuna mystic. They are initiated into nonordinary levels of reality and their adventures read like the best suspense novels.

You, too, are a spiritwalker, Aquarius, equipped for this journey into nonordinary states of consciousness and reality as no other sign can be. In the other chapters, readers looked up the next new moon and engaged in a manifestation activity. But you probably already do that or something like it. So your assignment (should you decide to accept) is to select two books about altered states of consciousness. They can be fiction or nonfiction, it doesn't matter.

Once you've read the books, absorbed them, incorporated them into your your being, look up the date of the next new moon. On that date, write the highlights of the life you would like to live. The insights will astonish you.

18

Ⅻ

SUN IN PISCES:
MYSTIC AND HEALER

February 18–March 20

MYSTIC

It's likely that people describe you as dreamy and mellow. While this description is undoubtedly true, it's not the full picture. As a mutable water sign ruled by Neptune, parts of you remain unknown to others, even to the people you love the most. You aren't secretive by nature, like your water brother, Scorpio, it's just that you often travel in realms that language can't describe.

You, like the other water signs, experience the world primarily through your emotions. But your emotions run as deep as an underground river and through them you touch what shamans refer to as nonordinary levels of reality. You're a mystic in disguise, spiritual to your core. Whether that spirituality finds expression through organized religion or nontraditional belief systems depends on what you're seeking. In the course of your life, you may swing back and forth between the two or may eventually incorporate elements of one into the other.

Piscean Albert Einstein was a scientist, and yet he embraced the mystical and the beauty of the unknown in all things. For some Pisces, their mystical bent finds expression through some creative passion. I have a Pisces friend who is a devout Catholic and her deep compassion is satisfied through volunteer work for various types of charities. But her mystic finds its clearest expression through her art.

Creative expression is important to you, and it's likely that you have exceptional talents. Thanks to Neptune, your creativity allows you to "shape-shift." Whether you're acting or writing fiction, you can easily fit into the skin of the character, becoming that character. You're deeply intuitive and often downright psychic. Thank your empathic ability for that. You may be the kind of Pisces who can touch someone and immediately feel what that person feels. It's as if a current connects you to the other person and you are instantly privy to all kinds of information about that person's life. Pisces individuals usually have talent at psychometry, the ability to touch an object and pick up specific information about it—how old it is, who has owned it, its origins.

This same ability is at work in your second archetype.

HEALER

The healer needs the mystic every bit as much as the mystic needs the healer. They are two sides of the same coin, their intrinsic qualities so interwoven in who you are that they are inseparable.

Your compassion and empathy allow you to intuit things that elude the rest of us, and part of what you understand is that we all need healing at one time or another in our lives. This is why so many Pisces individuals end up in the healing professions as physicians and nurses, massage therapists and chiropractors, and even in non-traditional healing practices such as Reiki.

Since Pisces rules the twelfth house in a horoscope, the house that symbolizes institutions, it isn't surprising to find these individuals working as caretakers in nursing homes, Alzheimer's units, assisted-living facilities, and hospices. Your healing archetype is at work when you do volunteer and charity work. Piscean Liz Taylor is as well known as a fund-raiser for AIDS research as she is as an actress.

This duality is prevalent among Pisces people. You and Gemini are the only signs whose symbols feature a pair. For Gemini, it's the twins, and for you, it's two fish, swimming in opposite directions. The fact that the fish aren't moving in the same direction represents the inner struggle you sometimes experience, when your heart wants to go one way and your head demands to go in another direction. The happiest Pisces is the one who is able to convince head and heart to work in unison.

This is easier said than done, and for many Pisceans, it's a life-long journey. But perhaps you can satisfy your head in your professional career while your heart finds satisfaction in creativity, volunteer work, or some other venue. However you do it, allow your sensitivity to guide you. Jupiter, your coruler, seeks to expand your inner world, so sometimes you simply have to get out of the way and let things happen and unfold.

You seem to have an innate understanding of patterns, so looking for patterns in your own life shouldn't be any big deal. You are always able to grasp the whole; it's the details that may slip past you. So the activities in this chapter are structured somewhat differently than they are for the other sun signs. Read on, Pisces.

YOUR PLANETARY PLOTS

Due to the length of time that Neptune is in a single sign, it would be counterproductive to try to pinpoint particular dates in your life when Neptune triggered an event. Its themes unfold over the course of the fourteen years it spends in each sign, and its effects are primarily internal. However, when a Neptune transit to your sun coincides with that of another, faster-moving planet, the effects can be dramatic and in some way always supports Neptune's themes.

Right now, Neptune is in Aquarius, where it will remain until

2011, when it goes into Pisces, conjuncting your sun. The theme of that conjunction—confusion about personal goals, a deepening compassion for other people, and concern about spiritual and metaphysical issues—will run beneath the surface of your life for the next fourteen years, changing you in subtle ways. But during that long transit, you'll also experience sextiles and squares and trines and oppositions to your sun from the faster-moving planets. One way or another, these transits will bring about events and experiences that support the Neptune theme.

The checklist below is intended to help you identify patterns that operated in your life between 1990 and 2002. We're going to peg the events to the transits of Jupiter, your coruler. Read through the checklist and put a ✓ next to any statement that pertains to you. Try to recall the specific date or at least a time frame. Then compare your dates to those listed below, when Jupiter was forming various aspects to your Sun and when the Neptune sextile to your sun ended.

PISCES/JUPITER AND NEPTUNE
CHECKLIST

___ I fell in love. _____

___ I got married. _____

___ I moved into my dream house. _____

___ I went/returned to college. _____

___ My spiritual beliefs changed dramatically. _____

___ I injured my feet. _____

___ I met my spiritual mentor. _____

___ I lost a spouse or significant other. _____

___ I got pregnant. _____

___ I changed professions/jobs. _____

___ I inherited money. _____

___ I took an overseas trip that had a
    dramatic effect on my life. _____

___ I got an important contract. _____

___ I got a promotion. _____

___ I began volunteering for charity.

___ I went to acting school.

___ I got my first acting part.

___ I sold a creative project.

___ I went into debt.

___ I consulted a nontraditional healer.

___ I became a healer.

___ I had a profound psychic/
spiritual experience.

___ I saw a spirit/ghost or experienced a
nonordinary state of reality.

___ I found my creative niche.

___ I got divorced.

___ Any other significant event (describe).

DATES: JUPITER IN ASPECT TO MY SUN; NEPTUNE CHANGES SIGNS

1/1/90–8/17/90: Jupiter in Cancer (trine)
1/90–1/28/98: Neptune in Capricorn (sextile)
8/18/90–9/11/91: Jupiter in Leo
9/12/91–10/9/92: Jupiter in Virgo (opposition)
10/10/92–11/9/93: Jupiter in Libra
11/10/93–12/8/94: Jupiter in Scorpio (trine)
12/9/94–1/2/96: Jupiter in Sagittarius (square)
1/3/96–1/20/97: Jupiter in Capricorn (sextile)
1/21/97–2/3/98: Jupiter in Aquarius
1/29/98–2001: Neptune in Aquarius
2/4/98–2/11/99: Jupiter in Pisces (conjunction)
2/12/99–6/27/99: Jupiter in Aries
6/28/99–6/29/00: Jupiter in Taurus (sextile)
6/30/00–7/11/01: Jupiter in Gemini (square)
2/12/01–7/31/02: Jupiter in Cancer (trine)
8/1/02–8/26/03: Jupiter in Leo

Repetitive Patterns

The thirteen-year period covers every possible aspect that Jupiter could make to your sun. If you're able to match any of your dates in the checklist with any of the above dates, you have the beginning of a pattern. If, for instance, you got married or experienced some other joyous life event between early February 1998 and February 1999, when Jupiter was in Pisces, you know that you're sensitive to the Jupiter conjunction. Even though the challenging aspects of Jupiter aren't challenging in the same way that a Saturn square or opposition would be, it's worth your while to note your sensitivity to any of these aspects.

Now look through the Jupiter ephemeris on pages 298–311 for the dates when Jupiter will be in Pisces (conjunction), Virgo (opposition), Taurus and Capricorn (sextile), Gemini and Sagittarius (square), and Cancer and Scorpio (trine). Record these dates below.

Important Dates for Jupiter, 2003–2007

DATE	SIGN	ASPECT	STORY LINES

ELLEN'S STORY

Ellen is a private-duty nurse who works mostly with elderly people, taking care of them in their homes. The Pisces archetypes of mystic and healer are alive and well in Ellen, and she's aware of the patterns in her own life.

She was raised Catholic but left the church when she was in her teens. In the years since, she has sampled a variety of different spiritual belief systems and at the point in her life we're going to scrutinize, she wasn't affiliated with any organized religion. Her spiritual beliefs were a hodgepodge, what she describes as "a little of this, a little of that." She believed in an afterlife but had never had any sort of experience that confirmed or validated that belief.

On December 13, 2001, she had an experience that changed all that. She had worked a night shift and had gotten home around seven that morning. She was beat but showered and ate breakfast before she finally fell into bed about an hour later. Since she often works at night and sleeps during the day, she has heavy venetian blinds on her windows that cut down on the light. At exactly 9:34 A.M., according to the digital clock on her nightstand, something awakened her. She sat straight up in bed, trying to determine the source of whatever had yanked her awake. Her cat, which usually slept curled at the foot of her bed, was hunkered down at the far corner of the bed, hissing, all the hair standing up on her back.

"A light appeared about two feet from the end of my bed. And within that light, a form appeared. The form gained clarity and I realized it was my aunt, my mother's oldest sister. Even though she lived two thousand miles from me, we'd always been close.

"She extended her hands toward me, as if she were reaching for me, and I was so startled I jerked my legs up against my chest and stammered something to the effect of, 'What're you doing here?' She smiled and then she waved and vanished."

Ellen was so shaken by this experience that for moments she didn't do anything. She just sat there, huddled against the headboard.

Her cat leaped off the bed and ran into the closet. Ellen finally called her aunt in Texas, but no one answered. She called her mother, who lived in the same town as Ellen's aunt, and told her someone should go over to the house to see if the aunt was okay. An hour later, Ellen got a call from her mother, telling her that her aunt apparently fell on the way to the bathroom around 9:30 that morning and hit her head when she landed. The blow to her head killed her.

"I knew that at the moment I saw her, her spirit or soul or whatever you want to call it had left her body. She wanted to tell me good-bye."

Use one of the blank horoscope wheels in the back of the book and put Ellen's Pisces sun at 19 degrees on the ascendant. Move counterclockwise around the wheel and place each subsequent sign at 19 degrees, on the cusp of each house, so that you end up with 19 Aquarius on the cusp of the twelfth house. Then place the transiting planets in their appropriate houses. Here's how the planets line up for that day:

- ✦ Sun: 21 Sagittarius
- ✦ Moon: 6 Sagittarius
- ✦ Mercury: 26 Sagittarius
- ✦ Venus: 14 Sagittarius
- ✦ Mars: 3 Pisces
- ✦ Jupiter: 13 Cancer
- ✦ Saturn: 10 Gemini, Rx
- ✦ Uranus: 21 Aquarius
- ✦ Neptune: 6 Aquarius
- ✦ Pluto: 15 Sagittarius
- ✦ North node: 27 Gemini
- ✦ South node: 27 Sagittarius

What's immediately obvious about these transits is the number of planets in Sagittarius. Of these, the transiting sun, Venus, and Pluto are forming squares at 3 to 5 degrees to her sun. If we allow a 5-degree orb, we can count these squares. The Mercury square is wide—7 degrees—but for now, let's count that, too. The Moon's nodes also form a wide square to Ellen's sun. At the bottom of the chart, we have trines from both Saturn and Jupiter in Cancer.

The proliferation of squares seemed to have created an event, in much the same way they did for Phyllis in the example in the Aquarius chapter. The transformative event (Pluto) involved a woman (Venus) and communication (Mercury). With transiting Saturn and Jupiter in the same sign and degrees, we have an expansion (Jupiter) of physical reality (Saturn) that allows for an ease of communication (trine) with Ellen's aunt as she dies. Even though the nodal square is wide, it's just one more tension factor in the story line that helped bring about the experience. Interestingly, Jupiter, the coruler, figures prominently in the picture, but Neptune in Aquarius isn't making any aspects to Ellen's sun. And yet, seeing a spirit or a ghost is certainly in the realm of Neptune in visionary Aquarius.

THE OUTER PLANETS: THEMES

Since your sun sign is ruled by an outer planet, its transits always provide insight into the underlying themes that are unfolding in your life. These themes will be amplified by the transits of the inner, swifter-moving planets daily, weekly, and monthly.

So what can you expect from the outer planets over the next few years? Uranus goes into Pisces in 2003, a conjunction that is certain to bring abrupt and sudden changes in your life, particularly in the area where you have fallen into a predictable routine. Uranus's purpose is to shake up the status quo and, in doing so, help you find your individual voice and creative strengths. You may move, change professions or jobs, get married or divorced, or start a family. However the energy manifests itself, the events will be unexpected and initially disruptive. You don't have to worry about another Uranus aspect to your sun until 2018, when it forms a sextile in Taurus. This is a great period when your individuality is supported and opportunities are presented that allow you to express that individuality.

From Neptune, the conjunction in 2011 begins a fourteen-year stretch that we spoke of earlier, when your external goals become less clear and your attention is drawn inward. Spirituality, compassion, your natural empathy—all of these traits are highlighted.

From Pluto, the sextile that begins in 2008 brings into focus power issues—your power and the powers hold over you. Your ambition deepens and you have many opportunities to advance professionally and leave your mark. This transit lasts until 2023. For part of this time, you'll also be feeling the Neptune in Pisces conjunction. The two energies will feel at odds with each other until you learn to balance them.

TIMING AND TRANSITS

Finding your story lines in the stars can help you achieve whatever you want or need because you'll know how to use time to your advantage. Whether you're planning a trip to Tahiti or launching a new software program, you'll be able to do it *at the right time.*

Based on what you've learned so far, which planets and aspects would you look for in the situations listed below to maximize your success? I give my answers. If yours differ, be sure you're able to justify them.

The thing to remember here is that transits don't create your life. *You* create your life, *you* are the scriptwriter. Transits and timing simply give you the edge. So if you really want to take that trip to Greece and four planets are going retrograde during the only time period you can go, please don't just throw up your hands and wait for the stars to be on your side. Take the trip! But do it with a sense of adventure, because with four planets retrograde, your itinerary will change for sure.

Again, for easy reference: A conjunction is a planet in Pisces; a sextile is a planet in Taurus or Capricorn; a square, is a planet in Gemini or Sagittarius; a trine is a planet in Cancer or Scorpio; an opposition is a planet in Virgo.

+ **Move:** Mars conjunct. Mercury sextile or trine, moving direct. Sun or moon in Cancer. Jupiter conjunct, sextile, or trine. Moon transiting natal fourth house.
+ **Wedding:** Venus in Pisces or another water sign. Moon in natal seventh house. Positive Jupiter/sun contacts.

+ **Honeymoon:** Venus in Pisces or another water sign. Mercury direct. Positive Jupiter/sun contacts.
+ **Divorce:** Mercury direct. Positive Jupiter/sun contacts.
+ **Spiritual workshop/seminar:** Neptune sextile or trine. Jupiter and/or Venus conjunct, sextile, or trine.
+ **Work on dream recall:** Neptune, Pluto, and/or Jupiter conjunct, sextile, or trine. Moon in Pisces.
+ **Seek guidance through meditation:** Neptune conjunct, sextile, or trine. Moon conjunct, sextile, or trine. Mars conjunct. New moon phase.
+ **Submit a creative project:** Venus conjunct, sextile, or trine. Moon sextile or trine. Jupiter conjunct, sextile, or trine.
+ **Start a diet:** New moon in a water or an earth sign. Mars in a water sign.
+ **Change professions/careers:** Jupiter conjunct. Mars conjunct, sextile, or trine. Even squares from various planets work for this at times. Mercury direct.
+ **Take an overseas trip:** Moon and/or Jupiter transiting natal ninth house. Jupiter in Pisces, Taurus, or Capricorn.
+ **Interview for a job:** Venus conjunct, sextile, or trine. Saturn sextile or trine. Moon in a compatible element.
+ **Learn to play a musical instrument:** Venus or Neptune conjunct, sextile, or trine. Moon and/or Jupiter transiting natal fifth house.
+ **Apply to college:** Mercury direct. Jupiter conjunct, sextile, or trine. Jupiter transiting natal ninth house. Mars conjunct.
+ **Revisions, rewrites:** Mercury retrograde. Venus conjunct. Jupiter conjunct, sextile, or trine.
+ **Get pregnant:** Moon in the sign on cusp of natal fifth house. Venus conjunct, sextile, or trine. Mars conjunct.
+ **Join a spiritual group:** Neptune and/or Jupiter conjunct, sextile, or trine. Mars conjunct.
+ **Sign a contract:** Mercury direct. Jupiter conjunct, sextile, or trine. Saturn sextile or trine.
+ **Seek medical advice (other than an emergency):** Mercury direct. Jupiter conjunct or sextile. Mars conjunct.

+ **Start counseling:** Jupiter conjunct, sextile, or trine. Saturn sextile or trine. Squares will work here, too.

MANIFESTATION: RESURRECTION

In the movie *Resurrection,* Ellen Burstyn plays a woman whose life is turned upside down as the result of a car accident. She loses her husband and ends up in a wheelchair, crippled and unable to walk. Through sheer will, she begins to heal herself, drawing on the deepest reservoirs of an ability that was awakened when she went through a near-death experience after the car accident.

She eventually is able to walk again, with a cane, and becomes a healer herself, the kind of nontraditional, hands-on healer who channels her enormous power by taking on the disease or disability that her patients have and transmuting it. You, Pisces, have this ability in some form. In the manifestation activity, you're going to call on this ability and heal some facet of your life.

In the new moon ephemeris on page 254, look up the date of the next new moon. On that day, write out a single aspect of your life that you would like to heal. Maybe it's a psychological wound from the past or the need to forgive someone who has hurt you. Maybe it's simply a need to forgive yourself. Whatever it is, pour the full power of your imagination and intent into the idea of healing as you're writing out your statement. Trust that the healing will come about. Ritualize this act if that makes it more real for you. Plant seeds in a ceramic pot, collect stones or crystals and make a mosaic with them in your yard, or just light a stick of incense.

Then take steps in your daily life that reinforce your intent to heal and, like the character Burstyn plays, resurrect your life.

PART THREE

PARTING THOUGHTS

It either works or it doesn't.

—RENIE WILEY

19

WHAT'S NEXT?

*Story is born in that place where the
subjective and objective realms touch.*

—ROBERT MCKEE, *STORY*

Astrologer 1: Something weird is going on. Every Libra, Capricorn, Sag, and Gemini I know is going through heavy-duty stuff.

Astrologer 2: Like what kind of stuff?

Astrologer 1: My daughter had to have her youngest dog put down. My husband is going nuts. My neighbors are driving me crazy *(and launches into story about specifics)*.

Astrologer 2: It can't be Pluto. He's already at sixteen Gemini, way too far to affect your Sag sun. How about Uranus?

Astrologer 1: No. I've checked everything. Transits, progressions, directions, returns, eclipses, midpoints, Arabic parts, you name it, I've checked it. Nothing is common to all of them.

Silence.

Astrologer 2: There has to be something. Either astrology works or it doesn't.

Astrologer 1: I know. But I can't find it.

Silence.

This is the moment every astrologer dreads, the distinct possibility that the system will break down, that we just can't find the death, the marriage, the explosion of creativity, the birth of the child, the conflict, the attack, the whatever it is that should be in the chart. Some chart. Any chart. So we call our astrologer friends. And they call their friends, and pretty soon, you have a dozen different opinions. Or, worse, no opinions. The event happened but it doesn't show up.

Oops. So what's next?

It took me a long time to find my mother's death in her chart. There were aspects that suggested it in her chart and those of other family members, but nothing definitive. I called astrologer friends, asking if they could see it. Was her time of birth correct? Did I try this astrological technique or that one? Was her time of death correct? Yes, yes, yes. Then one night I was fiddling around with Arabic parts and there it was. At the time she died, Pluto was making an exact conjunction with her part of death.

Sometimes, the story line is the simplest thing. In retrospect, it always seems simpler.

If I had been studying my mother's chart more closely during the end of her life, I might have found that little detail sooner. But I wouldn't automatically have assumed that she was going to die. Plenty of people don't die when their parts of death are transited by planets. But if I had seen two or three other indicators in her chart that meant peril to her, I would have recognized the beginning of a pattern. Once I had a pattern, I would have a time frame. With a time frame, I could have warned her to be careful.

Of course, even if I had warned her to be careful during a certain time frame, it might not have changed the outcome. There are some things over which we have no control. Perhaps these are the agreements that we made before we were born, as part of whatever it is we're here to learn. Or maybe there's no cosmic design, no bigger picture. We're born. We live. We die. It's all random and chaotic, the luck of the draw.

Sometimes, that possibility haunts me. It haunts everyone. Most of us hunger for deeper meaning, a wider, grander purpose. We call it God, Buddha, Christ, Mohammed. Some of us don't have a name for It. We seek out systems and structures that explain these larger stories. Everyone wants a system that works, that explains everything, that lays out the specifics about life and death. But there are no guarantees—isn't that what free will means?

No predictive system is perfect. No psychic is 100 percent accurate. Death can't be predicted any more than marriage can be predicted. Patterns can be identified, but they only represent *potential*. It's up to us to act on the potential. That's the meaning of free will.

At the beginning of the year, a friend asked if I saw anything in her chart that indicated new professional opportunities. I ran transits and saw that in early March, Jupiter would be hitting her Midheaven, which represents professions and careers. The story line was simple: an opportunity for professional expansion and new opportunities. So for the next two months, she focused on finding a job that was in line with her interests. She networked with friends and made room emotionally in her life for a new job, but didn't place any rules or restrictions on what this should entail. *She trusted the process.*

In early March, she called to let me know she'd been offered a counseling job at a local hospice. This is how story lines are supposed to work. Once my friend knew that a window of opportunity would open in a few months, she took steps to make the opportunity a reality. If she'd sat back and done nothing, waiting for the opportunity to drop in her lap, it's possible that nothing would have happened. *When you see a potential story line that spells opportunity, you have to do your part to make it happen.*

PUTTING IT TOGETHER:
THE POWER OF CONJUNCTIONS

Finding Opportunities

When I'm looking for opportunities in a chart, I look for conjunctions first. During a conjunction, the energies of two or more planets are fused, which makes conjunctions the most powerful indicators of opportunity. In this section, conjunctions are used to pinpoint important dates in 2003 for each sign. I've used Mercury, Venus, Mars, Jupiter, and Saturn and, where appropriate, the three outer planets. I suggest that you study the moon ingress ephemeris on pages 248–254 for the dates when the moon goes into your sun sign and make note of the dates.

A brief story line is also provided.

Aries Conjunctions

3/21/03–4/4/03, Mercury/Aries: Yakety-yak. You're a talker, and everything you say is clear and firm, and leaves no doubt in anyone's mind about where you're coming from. Just be sure that you listen to other people's ideas and opinions, too. Sign on the dotted line with confidence. Good time for business and pleasure travel.

4/21/03–5/15/03, Venus/Aries: Plan ahead for this one. Get away with your significant other. Take a long weekend or the entire three weeks and head for someplace exotic and exciting.

12/16/03–2/1/04: Mars/Aries: High physical energy. You feel as if you can take on anything, do anything, achieve anything—and you undoubtedly can! But if you burn your candles at both ends, burnout is a distinct possibility. Balance yourself, meditate, take deep breaths, and count to ten before you blurt what you think.

Taurus Conjunctions

4/5/03–6/11/03: Mercury/Taurus: A retrograde period runs from April 25 to May 19. Don't sign contracts during this period, and if you have to travel, be aware that your plans may change. Otherwise, the retrograde is great for revising and rethinking plans and projects. The rest of the Mercury conjunction keeps you clearheaded (although stubborn about your opinions), and your self-expression is strong. If you have kids, now is the time to get out and have fun with them.

5/16/03–6/8/03, Venus/Taurus: Sensuality, the arts, and your particular artistic talents are highlighted. This is a good time to throw a party for friends and steal away with your significant other for a romantic weekend. If you have a creative project to submit, do it now. On a purely frivolous note, go shopping!

Gemini Conjunctions

6/9/03–7/4/03, Venus/Gemini: Refine a creative project, get together with friends, enjoy the simple beauties of life. Go to the beach and feel the warm sand under your feet. Make time to get away somewhere with your significant other.

6/12/03–6/28/03, Mercury/Gemini: You have dual conjunctions this month. Not only are you romantically inclined with Venus in your sun sign, but your mind hums along with extreme clarity and your communication skills are excellent. Your days are busy with E-mails, deadlines, and a lot of hustle and bustle. No time for boredom!

Cancer Conjunctions

6/3/02–7/16/05, Saturn/Cancer: This is an important time in your life, one of those cycles that comes around every twenty-nine to thirty years. Your responsibilities and obligations increase, there may be delays and restrictions that you haven't foreseen, and your frustration may get the best of you at times. However, on a positive note, you're able to channel your life constructively and may be promoted and win professional recognition. Older people, particularly a father or father figure, a boss, an older spouse, will play a vital roles in your life during this conjunction. Your capacity for achievement is great.

6/29/03–7/13/03, Mercury/Cancer: Your intuition is exceptional during this period. Use it to help you navigate the Saturn conjunction to your sun. Take a workshop that is spiritually oriented or head to a place where you feel a deep kinship with the earth.

7/4/03–7/28/03, Venus/Cancer: A romantic interlude is called for. You've got a lot going on this summer and must remember to express your love and appreciation for the people who love you and to also love and appreciate yourself. If there are people in your life who have hurt you, now is the time to forgive them and move on.

Leo Conjunctions

7/13/03–7/30/03, Mercury/Leo: Your self-expression is dramatic and charismatic. If you're in the acting profession, now is the time to audition. Your daily life may be crowded during this seventeen-day period, but if you plan well, you can accomplish everything on your list and then some.

7/28/03–8/21/03. Venus/Leo: A vacation. Head off for the beach with your significant other. If there isn't anyone special, then plan a long weekend with friends, something laid back and fun. This is an excellent time to start or complete a creative project.

Virgo Conjunctions

7/30/03–10/6/03, Mercury/Virgo: Mercury is retrograde from August 28 to September 19, so this is a good time for revising personal and professional projects. If you have to sign a contract, make sure you know every detail that's involved. It's best not to close on a home or piece of property when Mercury is retrograde. Otherwise, this is a productive period on many levels, especially with Jupiter entering your sign on August 27.

8/22/03–9/15/03, Venus/Virgo: A double conjunction, with Mercury in your sign, too. Mark these dates on your calendar and do something nice for yourself and the people you love. Take a vacation. Go to a spa. Head for Greece. If you have job interviews, now is the time to schedule them.

8/27/03–9/24/04, Jupiter/Virgo: This opportunity comes around once every twelve years. Opportunities come out of nowhere. You have the chance during this year to expand in every facet of your life. Your creativity takes off, your spirituality deepens, luck follows you. Plan for this one.

Libra Conjunctions

9/15/03–10/8/03, Venus/Libra: With your ruling planet in your court, it's time to hit the museums and libraries, to take a workshop or seminar that feeds your creative soul. Your artistic inclinations are at their peak right now and it's possible to do the impossible. You're feeling romantic, too, and it's important to get away with your significant other and to save time for your kids and pets, too.

10/6/03–10/23/03, Mercury/Libra: Your intellect and communication skills are especially sharp and clear. Start or finish creative projects. Pay attention to the flow of thoughts you have during the day. This flow will tell you whether you're on the right track in your life.

Scorpio Conjunctions

10/9/03–11/2/03, Venus/Scorpio: Romance and sexuality are highlighted. Plan a getaway with your significant other. This is also a great time for any creative endeavor that you're involved in. Bring your piercing intuition to bear against anything that puzzles or disturbs you and follow its guidance.

10/24/03–11/11/03, Mercury/Scorpio: Research and investigation are the focus during this transit. Your mind is as keen as it gets, able to penetrate what others might see as barriers or obstacles.

Sagittarius Conjunctions

1/7/03–2/4/03; 11/2/03–11/26/03, Venus/Sagittarius: Consider yourself lucky to have two Venus conjunctions this year. These periods bring romance, the arts, and your creative talents to the forefront. They are good times to plan dinner parties with close friends, to take in new art exhibits, or to attend workshops and seminars about topics that interest you. Oh, and if there's a significant other in your life, plan a getaway trip for two.

1/16/03–3/4/03, Mars/Sagittarius: You feel like a million bucks, physically invigorated and strong, able to do just about anything. Watch your temper and make sure you have a physical outlet for your aggressive feelings. Take an adventure trip—the Galápagos, a slow boat up the Amazon, something exotic and far away.

11/12/03–12/2/03, Mercury/Sagittarius: You're able to communicate your ideas with such clarity now that other people sit up and take notice. If you write, this is an excellent time to just let the ideas flow; worry about punctuation and spelling later.

Capricorn Conjunctions

2/4/03–3/2/03, Venus/Capricorn: This is one of those times when you can throw off the heavy weight and responsibility of your ruling planet, Saturn, and really dive into your feelings about love, romance, and your creative abilities. Treat yourself to something, whether it's new clothes or a piece of art that you've coveted. You may feel like spending more than you can afford right now, so don't go overboard. But don't cheat yourself, either. And if you can, get away with your significant other.

3/4/03–4/21/03, Mars/Capricorn: Physically you're in top shape now. Your energy is good. If you don't have a regular exercise routine, now is the time to start one. If you already have a routine, add something to it. You need to have an outlet for your aggression. Even though you feel like you can accomplish anything right now, maintain balance.

12/30/03–1/13/04, Mercury/Capricorn: Practicality is your middle name right now. Balance your checkbook, get organized, schedule appointments. Make your dreams concrete. If you've always wanted to write a novel, start one. If you've always wanted to paint, go buy your supplies. Take steps to realize your dreams. The retrograde period runs from 12/17/03 to 1/5/04 and during that time, Mercury slips back into Sagittarius. Use the retrograde period to revise and rethink your goals.

Aquarius Conjunctions

2/12/03–3/4/03, Mercury/Aquarius: Your head is buzzing with ideas and possibilities. Get them all down on paper so that you can use them later. Your days may be busier than usual, with a lot of running around, friends dropping in, errands to finish. Set aside some time each day that's just for you.

3/2/03–3/27/03; 12/21/03–1/14/04, Venus/Aquarius: You get two Venus conjunctions this year, a bonus. You know all those ideas you filed away during the Mercury conjunction? Well, now is the time to pull them out and implement them. Let your creativity shine. And while you're at it, plan a weekend away with the love of your life.

4/21/03–6/16/03, Mars/Aquarius: Now is the time to make things happen. On the creative front, start projects, make contacts, put things into motion. Physically, your energy is strong. Even though you may feel you can work all night, don't. Practice balance. Take daily walks. Slow down. Sounds like your mother talking, doesn't it?

Pisces Conjunctions

3/4/03–3/21/03, Mercury/Pisces: You have a lot going on this year and it starts this spring. Your intuition during this period is heightened. Your communication skills are strong, too, enabling you to articulate things that are usually difficult to express. This is a good time to take a workshop or seminar in whatever interests you and to worry about the cost later. You need to fill the creative well and there's no time like right now.

3/27/03–4/21/04, Venus/Pisces: You're in the mood for romance, in love with love, and why not take advantage of it? Head for someplace exotic, preferably near or on the water, with your significant other. Schedule a party with close friends, start that screenplay you've thought about for years. Now is the time to tap your muse, Pisces. She's at your beck and call.

3/10/03–9/14/03; 12/30/03–3/11/11, Uranus/Pisces: This is a big transit that brings disruption and unexpected events, and it seems that you're suddenly surrounded by chaos. It tends to be most intense as Uranus goes into a new sign and as it closes in on an exact conjunction with your natal sun. Mark this one on your calendar, Pisces, and be prepared to go with the flow. The more you resist the changes that are coming, the tougher this transit is.

You actually get hit twice with this one because Uranus goes retrograde, and on 14, 20 enters Aquarius again until the tail end of the year. If you navigate the first hit with grace and flexibility, the second hit won't be as intense.

CREATING YOUR STORY LINES

About once a month, I run transits to my family's charts just to see if there's anything coming up that we should know about. Sometimes I post the biwheels on the walls in my study, to remind me of the time frames. Other times I make a notation on my calendar. If I see multiple transits coming up to a particular planet, the date gets a star next to it.

With five years' worth of planetary positions in each planet's ephemeris, you can do something similar for yourself. Here's a summary of how to do it:

1. **Look for the conjunctions first.** Take special note of any conjunctions to your sun by its ruling planet. If you have your natal chart, note any conjunctions by the planet that rules your sun sign and your natal ascendant to any other planets in your chart. Conjunctions to your natal sun, moon, and ascendant are especially important in determining story lines.
2. **Look for squares and oppositions, then sextiles and trines** to the sun. If you have your natal chart, look for these aspects to other natal planets. Note the dates for multiple aspects to a single planet.

3. **Look for any cluster of transiting planets in a particular natal house.** The affairs of that house will be highlighted.
4. **Keep your story lines simple.**

If you have any questions or inquiries about the material in this book, contact me at *trmacgregor@worldnet.att.net*. I publish a monthly horoscope column on creativity at *www.booktalk.com*.

Happy story hunting!

APPENDIX A

PLANETARY POSITIONS,
2003–2007

THE EPHEMERES

These tables were generated for midnight Eastern Standard Time, using Winstar 2, a product of Matrix Software. If you live in a different time zone, there will be some fluctuations in the positions of the faster-moving planets, particularly of the moon. But for the purpose of this book, where we're dealing with approximations, these tables should suffice. "Rx" means a planet is retrograde.

Here are the keys for the abbreviations and symbols for the signs and planets:

SUN SIGNS

Aries	Ar	♈
Taurus	Ta	♉
Gemini	Ge	♊
Cancer	Ca	♋
Leo	Le	♌
Virgo	Vi	♍
Libra	Li	♎
Scorpio	Sc	♏
Sagittarius	Sa	♐
Capricorn	Cap	♑
Aquarius	Aq	♒
Pisces	Pi	♓

PLANETS

Sun	☉
Moon	☽

Mercury	☿
Venus	♀
Mars	♂
Jupiter	♃
Saturn	♄
Uranus	♅
Neptune	♆
Pluto	♇
North node	☊
South node	☋
Part of fortune	⊗
Vertex	Vx

☽

Moon Ingress Ephemeris
2003–2007

☽

2003

01-01-2003,Mo Cnj Cap
01-03-2003,Mo Cnj Aq
01-06-2003,Mo Cnj Pi
01-08-2003,Mo Cnj Ar
01-11-2003,Mo Cnj Ta
01-13-2003,Mo Cnj Ge
01-16-2003,Mo Cnj Ca
01-18-2003,Mo Cnj Le
01-20-2003,Mo Cnj Vi
01-22-2003,Mo Cnj Li
01-24-2003,Mo Cnj Sc
01-26-2003,Mo Cnj Sa
01-29-2003,Mo Cnj Cap
01-31-2003,Mo Cnj Aq
02-02-2003,Mo Cnj Pi
02-05-2003,Mo Cnj Ar
02-07-2003,Mo Cnj Ta
02-10-2003,Mo Cnj Ge
02-12-2003,Mo Cnj Ca
02-14-2003,Mo Cnj Le

02-16-2003,Mo Cnj Vi
02-18-2003,Mo Cnj Li
02-21-2003,Mo Cnj Sc
02-23-2003,Mo Cnj Sa
02-25-2003,Mo Cnj Cap
02-27-2003,Mo Cnj Aq
03-01-2003,Mo Cnj Pi
03-04-2003,Mo Cnj Ar
03-06-2003,Mo Cnj Ta
03-09-2003,Mo Cnj Ge
03-11-2003,Mo Cnj Ca
03-14-2003,Mo Cnj Le
03-16-2003,Mo Cnj Vi
03-18-2003,Mo Cnj Li
03-20-2003,Mo Cnj Sc
03-22-2003,Mo Cnj Sa
03-24-2003,Mo Cnj Cap
03-26-2003,Mo Cnj Aq
03-29-2003,Mo Cnj Pi
03-31-2003,Mo Cnj Ar
04-03-2003,Mo Cnj Ta
04-05-2003,Mo Cnj Ge
04-08-2003,Mo Cnj Ca
04-10-2003,Mo Cnj Le

04-12-2003,Mo Cnj Vi
04-14-2003,Mo Cnj Li
04-16-2003,Mo Cnj Sc
04-18-2003,Mo Cnj Sa
04-20-2003,Mo Cnj Cap
04-23-2003,Mo Cnj Aq
04-25-2003,Mo Cnj Pi
04-27-2003,Mo Cnj Ar
04-30-2003,Mo Cnj Ta
05-02-2003,Mo Cnj Ge
05-05-2003,Mo Cnj Ca
05-07-2003,Mo Cnj Le
05-10-2003,Mo Cnj Vi
05-12-2003,Mo Cnj Li
05-14-2003,Mo Cnj Sc
05-16-2003,Mo Cnj Sa
05-18-2003,Mo Cnj Cap
05-20-2003,Mo Cnj Aq
05-22-2003,Mo Cnj Pi
05-25-2003,Mo Cnj Ar
05-27-2003,Mo Cnj Ta
05-30-2003,Mo Cnj Ge
06-01-2003,Mo Cnj Ca
06-04-2003,Mo Cnj Le

06-06-2003,Mo Cnj Vi	09-16-2003,Mo Cnj Ge	12-27-2003,Mo Cnj Pi
06-08-2003,Mo Cnj Li	09-18-2003,Mo Cnj Ca	12-29-2003,Mo Cnj Ar
06-10-2003,Mo Cnj Sc	09-21-2003,Mo Cnj Le	
06-12-2003,Mo Cnj Sa	09-23-2003,Mo Cnj Vi	**2004**
06-14-2003,Mo Cnj Cap	09-25-2003,Mo Cnj Li	01-01-2004,Mo Cnj Ta
06-16-2003,Mo Cnj Aq	09-27-2003,Mo Cnj Sc	01-03-2004,Mo Cnj Ge
06-19-2003,Mo Cnj Pi	09-29-2003,Mo Cnj Sa	01-06-2004,Mo Cnj Ca
06-21-2003,Mo Cnj Ar	10-01-2003,Mo Cnj Cap	01-08-2004,Mo Cnj Le
06-23-2003,Mo Cnj Ta	10-04-2003,Mo Cnj Aq	01-10-2004,Mo Cnj Vi
06-26-2003,Mo Cnj Ge	10-06-2003,Mo Cnj Pi	01-13-2004,Mo Cnj Li
06-28-2003,Mo Cnj Ca	10-08-2003,Mo Cnj Ar	01-15-2004,Mo Cnj Sc
07-01-2003,Mo Cnj Le	10-11-2003,Mo Cnj Ta	01-17-2004,Mo Cnj Sa
07-03-2003,Mo Cnj Vi	10-13-2003,Mo Cnj Ge	01-19-2004,Mo Cnj Cap
07-05-2003,Mo Cnj Li	10-16-2003,Mo Cnj Ca	01-21-2004,Mo Cnj Aq
07-07-2003,Mo Cnj Sc	10-18-2003,Mo Cnj Le	01-23-2004,Mo Cnj Pi
07-10-2003,Mo Cnj Sa	10-21-2003,Mo Cnj Vi	01-25-2004,Mo Cnj Ar
07-12-2003,Mo Cnj Cap	10-23-2003,Mo Cnj Li	01-28-2004,Mo Cnj Ta
07-14-2003,Mo Cnj Aq	10-25-2003,Mo Cnj Sc	01-30-2004,Mo Cnj Ge
07-16-2003,Mo Cnj Pi	10-27-2003,Mo Cnj Sa	02-02-2004,Mo Cnj Ca
07-18-2003,Mo Cnj Ar	10-29-2003,Mo Cnj Cap	02-04-2004,Mo Cnj Le
07-21-2003,Mo Cnj Ta	10-31-2003,Mo Cnj Aq	02-07-2004,Mo Cnj Vi
07-23-2003,Mo Cnj Ge	11-02-2003,Mo Cnj Pi	02-09-2004,Mo Cnj Li
07-26-2003,Mo Cnj Ca	11-05-2003,Mo Cnj Ar	02-11-2004,Mo Cnj Sc
07-28-2003,Mo Cnj Le	11-07-2003,Mo Cnj Ta	02-13-2004,Mo Cnj Sa
07-30-2003,Mo Cnj Vi	11-10-2003,Mo Cnj Ge	02-15-2004,Mo Cnj Cap
08-02-2003,Mo Cnj Li	11-12-2003,Mo Cnj Ca	02-17-2004,Mo Cnj Aq
08-04-2003,Mo Cnj Sc	11-15-2003,Mo Cnj Le	02-20-2004,Mo Cnj Pi
08-06-2003,Mo Cnj Sa	11-17-2003,Mo Cnj Vi	02-22-2004,Mo Cnj Ar
08-08-2003,Mo Cnj Cap	11-19-2003,Mo Cnj Li	02-24-2004,Mo Cnj Ta
08-10-2003,Mo Cnj Aq	11-21-2003,Mo Cnj Sc	02-27-2004,Mo Cnj Ge
08-12-2003,Mo Cnj Pi	11-23-2003,Mo Cnj Sa	02-29-2004,Mo Cnj Ca
08-15-2003,Mo Cnj Ar	11-25-2003,Mo Cnj Cap	03-03-2004,Mo Cnj Le
08-17-2003,Mo Cnj Ta	11-27-2003,Mo Cnj Aq	03-05-2004,Mo Cnj Vi
08-20-2003,Mo Cnj Ge	11-29-2003,Mo Cnj Pi	03-07-2004,Mo Cnj Li
08-22-2003,Mo Cnj Ca	12-02-2003,Mo Cnj Ar	03-09-2004,Mo Cnj Sc
08-24-2003,Mo Cnj Le	12-04-2003,Mo Cnj Ta	03-11-2004,Mo Cnj Sa
08-27-2003,Mo Cnj Vi	12-07-2003,Mo Cnj Ge	03-14-2004,Mo Cnj Cap
08-29-2003,Mo Cnj Li	12-09-2003,Mo Cnj Ca	03-16-2004,Mo Cnj Aq
08-31-2003,Mo Cnj Sc	12-12-2003,Mo Cnj Le	03-18-2004,Mo Cnj Pi
09-02-2003,Mo Cnj Sa	12-14-2003,Mo Cnj Vi	03-20-2004,Mo Cnj Ar
09-04-2003,Mo Cnj Cap	12-16-2003,Mo Cnj Li	03-23-2004,Mo Cnj Ta
09-06-2003,Mo Cnj Aq	12-19-2003,Mo Cnj Sc	03-25-2004,Mo Cnj Ge
09-09-2003,Mo Cnj Pi	12-21-2003,Mo Cnj Sa	03-28-2004,Mo Cnj Ca
09-11-2003,Mo Cnj Ar	12-23-2003,Mo Cnj Cap	03-30-2004,Mo Cnj Le
09-13-2003,Mo Cnj Ta	12-25-2003,Mo Cnj Aq	04-01-2004,Mo Cnj Vi

04-04-2004,Mo Cnj Li	07-15-2004,Mo Cnj Ca	10-25-2004,Mo Cnj Ar
04-06-2004,Mo Cnj Sc	07-17-2004,Mo Cnj Le	10-27-2004,Mo Cnj Ta
04-08-2004,Mo Cnj Sa	07-20-2004,Mo Cnj Vi	10-29-2004,Mo Cnj Ge
04-10-2004,Mo Cnj Cap	07-22-2004,Mo Cnj Li	11-01-2004,Mo Cnj Ca
04-12-2004,Mo Cnj Aq	07-24-2004,Mo Cnj Sc	11-03-2004,Mo Cnj Le
04-14-2004,Mo Cnj Pi	07-26-2004,Mo Cnj Sa	11-06-2004,Mo Cnj Vi
04-16-2004,Mo Cnj Ar	07-28-2004,Mo Cnj Cap	11-08-2004,Mo Cnj Li
04-19-2004,Mo Cnj Ta	07-30-2004,Mo Cnj Aq	11-10-2004,Mo Cnj Sc
04-21-2004,Mo Cnj Ge	08-01-2004,Mo Cnj Pi	11-13-2004,Mo Cnj Sa
04-24-2004,Mo Cnj Ca	08-04-2004,Mo Cnj Ar	11-15-2004,Mo Cnj Cap
04-26-2004,Mo Cnj Le	08-06-2004,Mo Cnj Ta	11-17-2004,Mo Cnj Aq
04-29-2004,Mo Cnj Vi	08-08-2004,Mo Cnj Ge	11-19-2004,Mo Cnj Pi
05-01-2004,Mo Cnj Li	08-11-2004,Mo Cnj Ca	11-21-2004,Mo Cnj Ar
05-03-2004,Mo Cnj Sc	08-13-2004,Mo Cnj Le	11-23-2004,Mo Cnj Ta
05-05-2004,Mo Cnj Sa	08-16-2004,Mo Cnj Vi	11-26-2004,Mo Cnj Ge
05-07-2004,Mo Cnj Cap	08-18-2004,Mo Cnj Li	11-28-2004,Mo Cnj Ca
05-09-2004,Mo Cnj Aq	08-20-2004,Mo Cnj Sc	12-01-2004,Mo Cnj Le
05-11-2004,Mo Cnj Pi	08-23-2004,Mo Cnj Sa	12-03-2004,Mo Cnj Vi
05-14-2004,Mo Cnj Ar	08-25-2004,Mo Cnj Cap	12-06-2004,Mo Cnj Li
05-16-2004,Mo Cnj Ta	08-27-2004,Mo Cnj Aq	12-08-2004,Mo Cnj Sc
05-19-2004,Mo Cnj Ge	08-29-2004,Mo Cnj Pi	12-10-2004,Mo Cnj Sa
05-21-2004,Mo Cnj Ca	08-31-2004,Mo Cnj Ar	12-12-2004,Mo Cnj Cap
05-24-2004,Mo Cnj Le	09-02-2004,Mo Cnj Ta	12-14-2004,Mo Cnj Aq
05-26-2004,Mo Cnj Vi	09-05-2004,Mo Cnj Ge	12-16-2004,Mo Cnj Pi
05-28-2004,Mo Cnj Li	09-07-2004,Mo Cnj Ca	12-18-2004,Mo Cnj Ar
05-31-2004,Mo Cnj Sc	09-10-2004,Mo Cnj Le	12-21-2004,Mo Cnj Ta
06-02-2004,Mo Cnj Sa	09-12-2004,Mo Cnj Vi	12-23-2004,Mo Cnj Ge
06-04-2004,Mo Cnj Cap	09-14-2004,Mo Cnj Li	12-25-2004,Mo Cnj Ca
06-06-2004,Mo Cnj Aq	09-17-2004,Mo Cnj Sc	12-28-2004,Mo Cnj Le
06-08-2004,Mo Cnj Pi	09-19-2004,Mo Cnj Sa	12-31-2004,Mo Cnj Vi
06-10-2004,Mo Cnj Ar	09-21-2004,Mo Cnj Cap	
06-12-2004,Mo Cnj Ta	09-23-2004,Mo Cnj Aq	**2005**
06-15-2004,Mo Cnj Ge	09-25-2004,Mo Cnj Pi	01-02-2005,Mo Cnj Li
06-17-2004,Mo Cnj Ca	09-27-2004,Mo Cnj Ar	01-04-2005,Mo Cnj Sc
06-20-2004,Mo Cnj Le	09-30-2004,Mo Cnj Ta	01-06-2005,Mo Cnj Sa
06-22-2004,Mo Cnj Vi	10-02-2004,Mo Cnj Ge	01-08-2005,Mo Cnj Cap
06-25-2004,Mo Cnj Li	10-05-2004,Mo Cnj Ca	01-10-2005,Mo Cnj Aq
06-27-2004,Mo Cnj Sc	10-07-2004,Mo Cnj Le	01-12-2005,Mo Cnj Pi
06-29-2004,Mo Cnj Sa	10-10-2004,Mo Cnj Vi	01-15-2005,Mo Cnj Ar
07-01-2004,Mo Cnj Cap	10-12-2004,Mo Cnj Li	01-17-2005,Mo Cnj Ta
07-03-2004,Mo Cnj Aq	10-14-2004,Mo Cnj Sc	01-19-2005,Mo Cnj Ge
07-05-2004,Mo Cnj Pi	10-16-2004,Mo Cnj Sa	01-22-2005,Mo Cnj Ca
07-07-2004,Mo Cnj Ar	10-18-2004,Mo Cnj Cap	01-24-2005,Mo Cnj Le
07-10-2004,Mo Cnj Ta	10-20-2004,Mo Cnj Aq	01-27-2005,Mo Cnj Vi
07-12-2004,Mo Cnj Ge	10-23-2004,Mo Cnj Pi	01-29-2005,Mo Cnj Li

02-01-2005,Mo Cnj Sc
02-03-2005,Mo Cnj Sa
02-05-2005,Mo Cnj Cap
02-07-2005,Mo Cnj Aq
02-09-2005,Mo Cnj Pi
02-11-2005,Mo Cnj Ar
02-13-2005,Mo Cnj Ta
02-16-2005,Mo Cnj Ge
02-18-2005,Mo Cnj Ca
02-21-2005,Mo Cnj Le
02-23-2005,Mo Cnj Vi
02-25-2005,Mo Cnj Li
02-28-2005,Mo Cnj Sc
03-02-2005,Mo Cnj Sa
03-04-2005,Mo Cnj Cap
03-06-2005,Mo Cnj Aq
03-08-2005,Mo Cnj Pi
03-10-2005,Mo Cnj Ar
03-13-2005,Mo Cnj Ta
03-15-2005,Mo Cnj Ge
03-17-2005,Mo Cnj Ca
03-20-2005,Mo Cnj Le
03-22-2005,Mo Cnj Vi
03-25-2005,Mo Cnj Li
03-27-2005,Mo Cnj Sc
03-29-2005,Mo Cnj Sa
03-31-2005,Mo Cnj Cap
04-03-2005,Mo Cnj Aq
04-05-2005,Mo Cnj Pi
04-07-2005,Mo Cnj Ar
04-09-2005,Mo Cnj Ta
04-11-2005,Mo Cnj Ge
04-14-2005,Mo Cnj Ca
04-16-2005,Mo Cnj Le
04-19-2005,Mo Cnj Vi
04-21-2005,Mo Cnj Li
04-23-2005,Mo Cnj Sc
04-26-2005,Mo Cnj Sa
04-28-2005,Mo Cnj Cap
04-30-2005,Mo Cnj Aq
05-02-2005,Mo Cnj Pi
05-04-2005,Mo Cnj Ar
05-06-2005,Mo Cnj Ta
05-09-2005,Mo Cnj Ge
05-11-2005,Mo Cnj Ca

05-14-2005,Mo Cnj Le
05-16-2005,Mo Cnj Vi
05-18-2005,Mo Cnj Li
05-21-2005,Mo Cnj Sc
05-23-2005,Mo Cnj Sa
05-25-2005,Mo Cnj Cap
05-27-2005,Mo Cnj Aq
05-29-2005,Mo Cnj Pi
05-31-2005,Mo Cnj Ar
06-03-2005,Mo Cnj Ta
06-05-2005,Mo Cnj Ge
06-07-2005,Mo Cnj Ca
06-10-2005,Mo Cnj Le
06-12-2005,Mo Cnj Vi
06-15-2005,Mo Cnj Li
06-17-2005,Mo Cnj Sc
06-19-2005,Mo Cnj Sa
06-21-2005,Mo Cnj Cap
06-23-2005,Mo Cnj Aq
06-25-2005,Mo Cnj Pi
06-28-2005,Mo Cnj Ar
06-30-2005,Mo Cnj Ta
07-02-2005,Mo Cnj Ge
07-05-2005,Mo Cnj Ca
07-07-2005,Mo Cnj Le
07-10-2005,Mo Cnj Vi
07-12-2005,Mo Cnj Li
07-15-2005,Mo Cnj Sc
07-17-2005,Mo Cnj Sa
07-19-2005,Mo Cnj Cap
07-21-2005,Mo Cnj Aq
07-23-2005,Mo Cnj Pi
07-25-2005,Mo Cnj Ar
07-27-2005,Mo Cnj Ta
07-29-2005,Mo Cnj Ge
08-01-2005,Mo Cnj Ca
08-03-2005,Mo Cnj Le
08-06-2005,Mo Cnj Vi
08-08-2005,Mo Cnj Li
08-11-2005,Mo Cnj Sc
08-13-2005,Mo Cnj Sa
08-15-2005,Mo Cnj Cap
08-17-2005,Mo Cnj Aq
08-19-2005,Mo Cnj Pi
08-21-2005,Mo Cnj Ar

08-23-2005,Mo Cnj Ta
08-26-2005,Mo Cnj Ge
08-28-2005,Mo Cnj Ca
08-31-2005,Mo Cnj Le
09-02-2005,Mo Cnj Vi
09-05-2005,Mo Cnj Li
09-07-2005,Mo Cnj Sc
09-09-2005,Mo Cnj Sa
09-12-2005,Mo Cnj Cap
09-14-2005,Mo Cnj Aq
09-16-2005,Mo Cnj Pi
09-18-2005,Mo Cnj Ar
09-20-2005,Mo Cnj Ta
09-22-2005,Mo Cnj Ge
09-24-2005,Mo Cnj Ca
09-27-2005,Mo Cnj Le
09-29-2005,Mo Cnj Vi
10-02-2005,Mo Cnj Li
10-04-2005,Mo Cnj Sc
10-07-2005,Mo Cnj Sa
10-09-2005,Mo Cnj Cap
10-11-2005,Mo Cnj Aq
10-13-2005,Mo Cnj Pi
10-15-2005,Mo Cnj Ar
10-17-2005,Mo Cnj Ta
10-19-2005,Mo Cnj Ge
10-22-2005,Mo Cnj Ca
10-24-2005,Mo Cnj Le
10-27-2005,Mo Cnj Vi
10-29-2005,Mo Cnj Li
11-01-2005,Mo Cnj Sc
11-03-2005,Mo Cnj Sa
11-05-2005,Mo Cnj Cap
11-07-2005,Mo Cnj Aq
11-09-2005,Mo Cnj Pi
11-11-2005,Mo Cnj Ar
11-14-2005,Mo Cnj Ta
11-16-2005,Mo Cnj Ge
11-18-2005,Mo Cnj Ca
11-21-2005,Mo Cnj Le
11-23-2005,Mo Cnj Vi
11-26-2005,Mo Cnj Li
11-28-2005,Mo Cnj Sc
11-30-2005,Mo Cnj Sa
12-02-2005,Mo Cnj Cap

12-04-2005,Mo Cnj Aq
12-07-2005,Mo Cnj Pi
12-09-2005,Mo Cnj Ar
12-11-2005,Mo Cnj Ta
12-13-2005,Mo Cnj Ge
12-15-2005,Mo Cnj Ca
12-18-2005,Mo Cnj Le
12-20-2005,Mo Cnj Vi
12-23-2005,Mo Cnj Li
12-25-2005,Mo Cnj Sc
12-28-2005,Mo Cnj Sa
12-30-2005,Mo Cnj Cap

2006
01-01-2006,Mo Cnj Aq
01-03-2006,Mo Cnj Pi
01-05-2006,Mo Cnj Ar
01-07-2006,Mo Cnj Ta
01-09-2006,Mo Cnj Ge
01-12-2006,Mo Cnj Ca
01-14-2006,Mo Cnj Le
01-17-2006,Mo Cnj Vi
01-19-2006,Mo Cnj Li
01-22-2006,Mo Cnj Sc
01-24-2006,Mo Cnj Sa
01-26-2006,Mo Cnj Cap
01-28-2006,Mo Cnj Aq
01-30-2006,Mo Cnj Pi
02-01-2006,Mo Cnj Ar
02-03-2006,Mo Cnj Ta
02-06-2006,Mo Cnj Ge
02-08-2006,Mo Cnj Ca
02-10-2006,Mo Cnj Le
02-13-2006,Mo Cnj Vi
02-16-2006,Mo Cnj Li
02-18-2006,Mo Cnj Sc
02-20-2006,Mo Cnj Sa
02-23-2006,Mo Cnj Cap
02-25-2006,Mo Cnj Aq
02-27-2006,Mo Cnj Pi
03-01-2006,Mo Cnj Ar
03-03-2006,Mo Cnj Ta
03-05-2006,Mo Cnj Ge
03-07-2006,Mo Cnj Ca

03-10-2006,Mo Cnj Le
03-12-2006,Mo Cnj Vi
03-15-2006,Mo Cnj Li
03-17-2006,Mo Cnj Sc
03-20-2006,Mo Cnj Sa
03-22-2006,Mo Cnj Cap
03-24-2006,Mo Cnj Aq
03-26-2006,Mo Cnj Pi
03-28-2006,Mo Cnj Ar
03-30-2006,Mo Cnj Ta
04-01-2006,Mo Cnj Ge
04-04-2006,Mo Cnj Ca
04-06-2006,Mo Cnj Le
04-08-2006,Mo Cnj Vi
04-11-2006,Mo Cnj Li
04-14-2006,Mo Cnj Sc
04-16-2006,Mo Cnj Sa
04-18-2006,Mo Cnj Cap
04-20-2006,Mo Cnj Aq
04-22-2006,Mo Cnj Pi
04-25-2006,Mo Cnj Ar
04-27-2006,Mo Cnj Ta
04-29-2006,Mo Cnj Ge
05-01-2006,Mo Cnj Ca
05-03-2006,Mo Cnj Le
05-06-2006,Mo Cnj Vi
05-08-2006,Mo Cnj Li
05-11-2006,Mo Cnj Sc
05-13-2006,Mo Cnj Sa
05-15-2006,Mo Cnj Cap
05-18-2006,Mo Cnj Aq
05-20-2006,Mo Cnj Pi
05-22-2006,Mo Cnj Ar
05-24-2006,Mo Cnj Ta
05-26-2006,Mo Cnj Ge
05-28-2006,Mo Cnj Ca
05-31-2006,Mo Cnj Le
06-02-2006,Mo Cnj Vi
06-05-2006,Mo Cnj Li
06-07-2006,Mo Cnj Sc
06-10-2006,Mo Cnj Sa
06-12-2006,Mo Cnj Cap
06-14-2006,Mo Cnj Aq
06-16-2006,Mo Cnj Pi

06-18-2006,Mo Cnj Ar
06-20-2006,Mo Cnj Ta
06-22-2006,Mo Cnj Ge
06-25-2006,Mo Cnj Ca
06-27-2006,Mo Cnj Le
06-29-2006,Mo Cnj Vi
07-02-2006,Mo Cnj Li
07-05-2006,Mo Cnj Sc
07-07-2006,Mo Cnj Sa
07-09-2006,Mo Cnj Cap
07-11-2006,Mo Cnj Aq
07-13-2006,Mo Cnj Pi
07-15-2006,Mo Cnj Ar
07-17-2006,Mo Cnj Ta
07-20-2006,Mo Cnj Ge
07-22-2006,Mo Cnj Ca
07-24-2006,Mo Cnj Le
07-27-2006,Mo Cnj Vi
07-29-2006,Mo Cnj Li
08-01-2006,Mo Cnj Sc
08-03-2006,Mo Cnj Sa
08-06-2006,Mo Cnj Cap
08-08-2006,Mo Cnj Aq
08-10-2006,Mo Cnj Pi
08-12-2006,Mo Cnj Ar
08-14-2006,Mo Cnj Ta
08-16-2006,Mo Cnj Ge
08-18-2006,Mo Cnj Ca
08-21-2006,Mo Cnj Le
08-23-2006,Mo Cnj Vi
08-26-2006,Mo Cnj Li
08-28-2006,Mo Cnj Sc
08-31-2006,Mo Cnj Sa
09-02-2006,Mo Cnj Cap
09-04-2006,Mo Cnj Aq
09-06-2006,Mo Cnj Pi
09-08-2006,Mo Cnj Ar
09-10-2006,Mo Cnj Ta
09-12-2006,Mo Cnj Ge
09-14-2006,Mo Cnj Ca
09-17-2006,Mo Cnj Le
09-19-2006,Mo Cnj Vi
09-22-2006,Mo Cnj Li
09-24-2006,Mo Cnj Sc

09-27-2006,Mo Cnj Sa	**2007**	04-11-2007,Mo Cnj Aq
09-29-2006,Mo Cnj Cap	01-02-2007,Mo Cnj Ca	04-13-2007,Mo Cnj Pi
10-01-2006,Mo Cnj Aq	01-04-2007,Mo Cnj Le	04-15-2007,Mo Cnj Ar
10-04-2006,Mo Cnj Pi	01-07-2007,Mo Cnj Vi	04-17-2007,Mo Cnj Ta
10-06-2006,Mo Cnj Ar	01-09-2007,Mo Cnj Li	04-19-2007,Mo Cnj Ge
10-08-2006,Mo Cnj Ta	01-12-2007,Mo Cnj Sc	04-21-2007,Mo Cnj Ca
10-10-2006,Mo Cnj Ge	01-14-2007,Mo Cnj Sa	04-23-2007,Mo Cnj Le
10-12-2006,Mo Cnj Ca	01-16-2007,Mo Cnj Cap	04-26-2007,Mo Cnj Vi
10-14-2006,Mo Cnj Le	01-19-2007,Mo Cnj Aq	04-28-2007,Mo Cnj Li
10-17-2006,Mo Cnj Vi	01-21-2007,Mo Cnj Pi	05-01-2007,Mo Cnj Sc
10-19-2006,Mo Cnj Li	01-23-2007,Mo Cnj Ar	05-03-2007,Mo Cnj Sa
10-22-2006,Mo Cnj Sc	01-25-2007,Mo Cnj Ta	05-06-2007,Mo Cnj Cap
10-24-2006,Mo Cnj Sa	01-27-2007,Mo Cnj Ge	05-08-2007,Mo Cnj Aq
10-26-2006,Mo Cnj Cap	01-29-2007,Mo Cnj Ca	05-10-2007,Mo Cnj Pi
10-29-2006,Mo Cnj Aq	02-01-2007,Mo Cnj Le	05-12-2007,Mo Cnj Ar
10-31-2006,Mo Cnj Pi	02-03-2007,Mo Cnj Vi	05-14-2007,Mo Cnj Ta
11-02-2006,Mo Cnj Ar	02-05-2007,Mo Cnj Li	05-16-2007,Mo Cnj Ge
11-04-2006,Mo Cnj Ta	02-08-2007,Mo Cnj Sc	05-18-2007,Mo Cnj Ca
11-06-2006,Mo Cnj Ge	02-10-2007,Mo Cnj Sa	05-21-2007,Mo Cnj Le
11-08-2006,Mo Cnj Ca	02-13-2007,Mo Cnj Cap	05-23-2007,Mo Cnj Vi
11-10-2006,Mo Cnj Le	02-15-2007,Mo Cnj Aq	05-25-2007,Mo Cnj Li
11-13-2006,Mo Cnj Vi	02-17-2007,Mo Cnj Pi	05-28-2007,Mo Cnj Sc
11-15-2006,Mo Cnj Li	02-19-2007,Mo Cnj Ar	05-31-2007,Mo Cnj Sa
11-18-2006,Mo Cnj Sc	02-21-2007,Mo Cnj Ta	06-02-2007,Mo Cnj Cap
11-20-2006,Mo Cnj Sa	02-23-2007,Mo Cnj Ge	06-04-2007,Mo Cnj Aq
11-23-2006,Mo Cnj Cap	02-25-2007,Mo Cnj Ca	06-07-2007,Mo Cnj Pi
11-25-2006,Mo Cnj Aq	02-28-2007,Mo Cnj Le	06-09-2007,Mo Cnj Ar
11-27-2006,Mo Cnj Pi	03-02-2007,Mo Cnj Vi	06-11-2007,Mo Cnj Ta
11-29-2006,Mo Cnj Ar	03-05-2007,Mo Cnj Li	06-13-2007,Mo Cnj Ge
12-01-2006,Mo Cnj Ta	03-07-2007,Mo Cnj Sc	06-15-2007,Mo Cnj Ca
12-03-2006,Mo Cnj Ge	03-10-2007,Mo Cnj Sa	06-17-2007,Mo Cnj Le
12-06-2006,Mo Cnj Ca	03-12-2007,Mo Cnj Cap	06-19-2007,Mo Cnj Vi
12-08-2006,Mo Cnj Le	03-14-2007,Mo Cnj Aq	06-22-2007,Mo Cnj Li
12-10-2006,Mo Cnj Vi	03-17-2007,Mo Cnj Pi	06-24-2007,Mo Cnj Sc
12-13-2006,Mo Cnj Li	03-19-2007,Mo Cnj Ar	06-27-2007,Mo Cnj Sa
12-15-2006,Mo Cnj Sc	03-21-2007,Mo Cnj Ta	06-29-2007,Mo Cnj Cap
12-18-2006,Mo Cnj Sa	03-23-2007,Mo Cnj Ge	07-02-2007,Mo Cnj Aq
12-20-2006,Mo Cnj Cap	03-25-2007,Mo Cnj Ca	07-04-2007,Mo Cnj Pi
12-22-2006,Mo Cnj Aq	03-27-2007,Mo Cnj Le	07-06-2007,Mo Cnj Ar
12-24-2006,Mo Cnj Pi	03-29-2007,Mo Cnj Vi	07-08-2007,Mo Cnj Ta
12-27-2006,Mo Cnj Ar	04-01-2007,Mo Cnj Li	07-10-2007,Mo Cnj Ge
12-29-2006,Mo Cnj Ta	04-03-2007,Mo Cnj Sc	07-12-2007,Mo Cnj Ca
12-31-2006,Mo Cnj Ge	04-06-2007,Mo Cnj Sa	07-14-2007,Mo Cnj Le
	04-08-2007,Mo Cnj Cap	07-17-2007,Mo Cnj Vi

07-19-2007,Mo Cnj Li	09-14-2007,Mo Cnj Sc	11-10-2007,Mo Cnj Sa
07-22-2007,Mo Cnj Sc	09-17-2007,Mo Cnj Sa	11-13-2007,Mo Cnj Cap
07-24-2007,Mo Cnj Sa	09-19-2007,Mo Cnj Cap	11-15-2007,Mo Cnj Aq
07-27-2007,Mo Cnj Cap	09-22-2007,Mo Cnj Aq	11-18-2007,Mo Cnj Pi
07-29-2007,Mo Cnj Aq	09-24-2007,Mo Cnj Pi	11-20-2007,Mo Cnj Ar
07-31-2007,Mo Cnj Pi	09-26-2007,Mo Cnj Ar	11-22-2007,Mo Cnj Ta
08-02-2007,Mo Cnj Ar	09-28-2007,Mo Cnj Ta	11-24-2007,Mo Cnj Ge
08-04-2007,Mo Cnj Ta	09-30-2007,Mo Cnj Ge	11-26-2007,Mo Cnj Ca
08-06-2007,Mo Cnj Ge	10-02-2007,Mo Cnj Ca	11-28-2007,Mo Cnj Le
08-09-2007,Mo Cnj Ca	10-04-2007,Mo Cnj Le	11-30-2007,Mo Cnj Vi
08-11-2007,Mo Cnj Le	10-07-2007,Mo Cnj Vi	12-03-2007,Mo Cnj Li
08-13-2007,Mo Cnj Vi	10-09-2007,Mo Cnj Li	12-05-2007,Mo Cnj Sc
08-15-2007,Mo Cnj Li	10-12-2007,Mo Cnj Sc	12-08-2007,Mo Cnj Sa
08-18-2007,Mo Cnj Sc	10-14-2007,Mo Cnj Sa	12-10-2007,Mo Cnj Cap
08-20-2007,Mo Cnj Sa	10-17-2007,Mo Cnj Cap	12-13-2007,Mo Cnj Aq
08-23-2007,Mo Cnj Cap	10-19-2007,Mo Cnj Aq	12-15-2007,Mo Cnj Pi
08-25-2007,Mo Cnj Aq	10-21-2007,Mo Cnj Pi	12-17-2007,Mo Cnj Ar
08-27-2007,Mo Cnj Pi	10-23-2007,Mo Cnj Ar	12-19-2007,Mo Cnj Ta
08-29-2007,Mo Cnj Ar	10-25-2007,Mo Cnj Ta	12-21-2007,Mo Cnj Ge
09-01-2007,Mo Cnj Ta	10-27-2007,Mo Cnj Ge	12-23-2007,Mo Cnj Ca
09-03-2007,Mo Cnj Ge	10-29-2007,Mo Cnj Ca	12-25-2007,Mo Cnj Le
09-05-2007,Mo Cnj Ca	10-31-2007,Mo Cnj Le	12-27-2007,Mo Cnj Vi
09-07-2007,Mo Cnj Le	11-03-2007,Mo Cnj Vi	12-30-2007,Mo Cnj Li
09-09-2007,Mo Cnj Vi	11-05-2007,Mo Cnj Li	
09-12-2007,Mo Cnj Li	11-08-2007,Mo Cnj Sc	

☽

New Moon Ephemeris

2003–2007

The full moon follows the new moon two weeks later in the opposite sign.

2003	10/25 1Sc41	7/17 25Ca13
1/2 12 Cap 01	11/23 1Sa14	8/16 23Le31
2/1 12Aq09	12/23 1Cap08	9/14 22Vi06
3/1 12Pi06		10/14 21Li06
4/1 11Ar39	**2004**	11/12 20Sc33
5/1 10Ta43	1/21 1Aq10	12/12 20Sa22
5/31 9Ge20	2/20 1Pi04	
6/29 7Ca37	3/20 0Ar39	**2005**
7/29 5Le46	4/19 29Ar49	1/10 20Cap21
8/27 4Vi02	5/19 28Ta33	2/8 20Aq16
9/26 2Li38	6/17 26Ge57	3/10 19Pi54

4/8 19Ar06	3/29 8Ar35	3/19 28Pi07
5/8 17Ta52	4/27 7Ta24	4/17 27Ar05
6/6 16Ge16	5/27 5Ge48	5/16 25Ta33
7/6 14Ca31	6/25 3Ca58	6/15 23Ge41
8/5 12Le48	7/25 2Le07	7/14 21Ca41
9/3 11Vi21	8/23 0Vi31	8/12 19Le51
10/3 10Li19	9/22 29Vi20	9/11 18Vi25
11/2 9Sc43	10/22 28Li40	10/11 17Li30
12/1 9Sa31	11/20 28Sc27	11/9 17Sc10
12/31 9Cap32	12/20 28Sa32	12/9 17Sa16

2006

1/29 9Aq32
2/28 9Pi16

2007

1/19 28Cap41
2/17 28Aq37

☊ North Node
☋ South Node

Moon's Nodes Ephemeris

2003–2007

North node listings once a week; south node in opposite sign.

2003
01-01-2003,07°GeRx
01-08-2003,06°GeRx
01-15-2003,06°GeRx
01-22-2003,05°GeRx
01-29-2003,05°GeRx
02-05-2003,05°GeRx
02-12-2003,04°GeRx
02-19-2003,04°GeRx
02-26-2003,04°GeRx
03-05-2003,03°GeRx
03-12-2003,03°GeRx
03-19-2003,02°GeRx
03-26-2003,02°GeRx
04-02-2003,02°GeRx
04-09-2003,01°GeRx
04-16-2003,01°GeRx
04-23-2003,01°GeRx
04-30-2003,00°GeRx
05-07-2003,00°GeRx
05-14-2003,29°TaRx

05-21-2003,29°TaRx
05-28-2003,29°TaRx
06-04-2003,28°TaRx
06-11-2003,28°TaRx
06-18-2003,28°TaRx
06-25-2003,27°TaRx
07-02-2003,27°TaRx
07-09-2003,27°TaRx
07-16-2003,26°TaRx
07-23-2003,26°TaRx
07-30-2003,25°TaRx
08-06-2003,25°TaRx
08-13-2003,25°TaRx
08-20-2003,24°TaRx
08-27-2003,24°TaRx
09-03-2003,24°TaRx
09-10-2003,23°TaRx
09-17-2003,23°TaRx
09-24-2003,22°TaRx
10-01-2003,22°TaRx
10-08-2003,22°TaRx

10-15-2003,21°TaRx
10-22-2003,21°TaRx
10-29-2003,21°TaRx
11-05-2003,20°TaRx
11-12-2003,20°TaRx
11-19-2003,19°TaRx
11-26-2003,19°TaRx
12-03-2003,19°TaRx
12-10-2003,18°TaRx
12-17-2003,18°TaRx
12-24-2003,18°TaRx
12-31-2003,17°TaRx

2004
01-07-2004,17°TaRx
01-14-2004,17°TaRx
01-21-2004,16°TaRx
01-28-2004,16°TaRx
02-04-2004,15°TaRx
02-11-2004,15°TaRx
02-18-2004,15°TaRx

02-25-2004,14°TaRx
03-03-2004,14°TaRx
03-10-2004,14°TaRx
03-17-2004,13°TaRx
03-24-2004,13°TaRx
03-31-2004,12°TaRx
04-07-2004,12°TaRx
04-14-2004,12°TaRx
04-21-2004,11°TaRx
04-28-2004,11°TaRx
05-05-2004,11°TaRx
05-12-2004,10°TaRx
05-19-2004,10°TaRx
05-26-2004,09°TaRx
06-02-2004,09°TaRx
06-09-2004,09°TaRx
06-16-2004,08°TaRx
06-23-2004,08°TaRx
06-30-2004,08°TaRx
07-07-2004,07°TaRx
07-14-2004,07°TaRx
07-21-2004,07°TaRx
07-28-2004,06°TaRx
08-04-2004,06°TaRx
08-11-2004,05°TaRx
08-18-2004,05°TaRx
08-25-2004,05°TaRx
09-01-2004,04°TaRx
09-08-2004,04°TaRx
09-15-2004,04°TaRx
09-22-2004,03°TaRx
09-29-2004,03°TaRx
10-06-2004,02°TaRx
10-13-2004,02°TaRx
10-20-2004,02°TaRx
10-27-2004,01°TaRx
11-03-2004,01°TaRx
11-10-2004,01°TaRx
11-17-2004,00°TaRx
11-24-2004,00°TaRx
12-01-2004,29°ArRx
12-08-2004,29°ArRx
12-15-2004,29°ArRx
12-22-2004,28°ArRx
12-29-2004,28°ArRx

2005
01-05-2005,28°ArRx
01-12-2005,27°ArRx
01-19-2005,27°ArRx
01-26-2005,26°ArRx
02-02-2005,26°ArRx
02-09-2005,26°ArRx
02-16-2005,25°ArRx
02-23-2005,25°ArRx
03-02-2005,25°ArRx
03-09-2005,24°ArRx
03-16-2005,24°ArRx
03-23-2005,24°ArRx
03-30-2005,23°ArRx
04-06-2005,23°ArRx
04-13-2005,22°ArRx
04-20-2005,22°ArRx
04-27-2005,22°ArRx
05-04-2005,21°ArRx
05-11-2005,21°ArRx
05-18-2005,21°ArRx
05-25-2005,20°ArRx
06-01-2005,20°ArRx
06-08-2005,19°ArRx
06-15-2005,19°ArRx
06-22-2005,19°ArRx
06-29-2005,18°ArRx
07-06-2005,18°ArRx
07-13-2005,18°ArRx
07-20-2005,17°ArRx
07-27-2005,17°ArRx
08-03-2005,16°ArRx
08-10-2005,16°ArRx
08-17-2005,16°ArRx
08-24-2005,15°ArRx
08-31-2005,15°ArRx
09-07-2005,15°ArRx
09-14-2005,14°ArRx
09-21-2005,14°ArRx
09-28-2005,14°ArRx
10-05-2005,13°ArRx
10-12-2005,13°ArRx
10-19-2005,12°ArRx
10-26-2005,12°ArRx
11-02-2005,12°ArRx

11-09-2005,11°ArRx
11-16-2005,11°ArRx
11-23-2005,11°ArRx
11-30-2005,10°ArRx
12-07-2005,10°ArRx
12-14-2005,09°ArRx
12-21-2005,09°ArRx
12-28-2005,09°ArRx

2006
01-04-2006,08°ArRx
01-11-2006,08°ArRx
01-18-2006,08°ArRx
01-25-2006,07°ArRx
02-01-2006,07°ArRx
02-08-2006,06°ArRx
02-15-2006,06°ArRx
02-22-2006,06°ArRx
03-01-2006,05°ArRx
03-08-2006,05°ArRx
03-15-2006,05°ArRx
03-22-2006,04°ArRx
03-29-2006,04°ArRx
04-05-2006,04°ArRx
04-12-2006,03°ArRx
04-19-2006,03°ArRx
04-26-2006,02°ArRx
05-03-2006,02°ArRx
05-10-2006,02°ArRx
05-17-2006,01°ArRx
05-24-2006,01°ArRx
05-31-2006,01°ArRx
06-07-2006,00°ArRx
06-14-2006,00°ArRx
06-21-2006,29°PiRx
06-28-2006,29°PiRx
07-05-2006,29°PiRx
07-12-2006,28°PiRx
07-19-2006,28°PiRx
07-26-2006,28°PiRx
08-02-2006,27°PiRx
08-09-2006,27°PiRx
08-16-2006,26°PiRx
08-23-2006,26°PiRx
08-30-2006,26°PiRx

09-06-2006,25°PiRx	02-07-2007,17°PiRx	07-25-2007,08°PiRx
09-13-2006,25°PiRx	02-14-2007,17°PiRx	08-01-2007,08°PiRx
09-20-2006,25°PiRx	02-21-2007,16°PiRx	08-08-2007,08°PiRx
09-27-2006,24°PiRx	02-28-2007,16°PiRx	08-15-2007,07°PiRx
10-04-2006,24°PiRx	03-07-2007,16°PiRx	08-22-2007,07°PiRx
10-11-2006,24°PiRx	03-14-2007,15°PiRx	08-29-2007,06°PiRx
10-18-2006,23°PiRx	03-21-2007,15°PiRx	09-05-2007,06°PiRx
10-25-2006,23°PiRx	03-28-2007,15°PiRx	09-12-2007,06°PiRx
11-01-2006,22°PiRx	04-04-2007,14°PiRx	09-19-2007,05°PiRx
11-08-2006,22°PiRx	04-11-2007,14°PiRx	09-26-2007,05°PiRx
11-15-2006,22°PiRx	04-18-2007,13°PiRx	10-03-2007,05°PiRx
11-22-2006,21°PiRx	04-25-2007,13°PiRx	10-10-2007,04°PiRx
11-29-2006,21°PiRx	05-02-2007,13°PiRx	10-17-2007,04°PiRx
12-06-2006,21°PiRx	05-09-2007,12°PiRx	10-24-2007,03°PiRx
12-13-2006,20°PiRx	05-16-2007,12°PiRx	10-31-2007,03°PiRx
12-20-2006,20°PiRx	05-23-2007,12°PiRx	11-07-2007,03°PiRx
12-27-2006,19°PiRx	05-30-2007,11°PiRx	11-14-2007,02°PiRx
	06-06-2007,11°PiRx	11-21-2007,02°PiRx
2007	06-13-2007,11°PiRx	11-28-2007,02°PiRx
01-03-2007,19°PiRx	06-20-2007,10°PiRx	12-05-2007,01°PiRx
01-10-2007,19°PiRx	06-27-2007,10°PiRx	12-12-2007,01°PiRx
01-17-2007,18°PiRx	07-04-2007,09°PiRx	12-19-2007,01°PiRx
01-24-2007,18°PiRx	07-11-2007,09°PiRx	12-26-2007,00°PiRx
01-31-2007,18°PiRx	07-18-2007,09°PiRx	

☿

Mercury Ephemeris

2003–2007

2003	01-14-2003,18°CapRx	01-28-2003,13°Cap
01-01-2003,28°Cap	01-15-2003,16°CapRx	01-29-2003,14°Cap
01-02-2003,28°Cap	01-16-2003,15°CapRx	01-30-2003,15°Cap
01-03-2003,28°CapRx	01-17-2003,14°CapRx	01-31-2003,15°Cap
01-04-2003,28°CapRx	01-18-2003,14°CapRx	02-01-2003,16°Cap
01-05-2003,27°CapRx	01-19-2003,13°CapRx	02-02-2003,17°Cap
01-06-2003,27°CapRx	01-20-2003,12°CapRx	02-03-2003,18°Cap
01-07-2003,26°CapRx	01-21-2003,12°CapRx	02-04-2003,19°Cap
01-08-2003,25°CapRx	01-22-2003,12°CapRx	02-05-2003,20°Cap
01-09-2003,24°CapRx	01-23-2003,12°Cap	02-06-2003,21°Cap
01-10-2003,23°CapRx	01-24-2003,12°Cap	02-07-2003,22°Cap
01-11-2003,22°CapRx	01-25-2003,12°Cap	02-08-2003,24°Cap
01-12-2003,20°CapRx	01-26-2003,12°Cap	02-09-2003,25°Cap
01-13-2003,19°CapRx	01-27-2003,13°Cap	02-10-2003,26°Cap

02-11-2003,27°Cap	03-28-2003,13°Ar	05-12-2003,13°TaRx
02-12-2003,28°Cap	03-29-2003,15°Ar	05-13-2003,12°TaRx
02-13-2003,00°Aq	03-30-2003,17°Ar	05-14-2003,12°TaRx
02-14-2003,01°Aq	03-31-2003,19°Ar	05-15-2003,12°TaRx
02-15-2003,02°Aq	04-01-2003,21°Ar	05-16-2003,11°TaRx
02-16-2003,04°Aq	04-02-2003,23°Ar	05-17-2003,11°TaRx
02-17-2003,05°Aq	04-03-2003,25°Ar	05-18-2003,11°TaRx
02-18-2003,07°Aq	04-04-2003,27°Ar	05-19-2003,11°TaRx
02-19-2003,08°Aq	04-05-2003,29°Ar	05-20-2003,11°TaRx
02-20-2003,09°Aq	04-06-2003,01°Ta	05-21-2003,11°Ta
02-21-2003,11°Aq	04-07-2003,02°Ta	05-22-2003,11°Ta
02-22-2003,12°Aq	04-08-2003,04°Ta	05-23-2003,11°Ta
02-23-2003,14°Aq	04-09-2003,06°Ta	05-24-2003,11°Ta
02-24-2003,15°Aq	04-10-2003,07°Ta	05-25-2003,12°Ta
02-25-2003,17°Aq	04-11-2003,09°Ta	05-26-2003,12°Ta
02-26-2003,18°Aq	04-12-2003,10°Ta	05-27-2003,12°Ta
02-27-2003,20°Aq	04-13-2003,11°Ta	05-28-2003,13°Ta
02-28-2003,22°Aq	04-14-2003,13°Ta	05-29-2003,14°Ta
03-01-2003,23°Aq	04-15-2003,14°Ta	05-30-2003,14°Ta
03-02-2003,25°Aq	04-16-2003,15°Ta	05-31-2003,15°Ta
03-03-2003,26°Aq	04-17-2003,16°Ta	06-01-2003,16°Ta
03-04-2003,28°Aq	04-18-2003,17°Ta	06-02-2003,17°Ta
03-05-2003,00°Pi	04-19-2003,17°Ta	06-03-2003,18°Ta
03-06-2003,01°Pi	04-20-2003,18°Ta	06-04-2003,19°Ta
03-07-2003,03°Pi	04-21-2003,19°Ta	06-05-2003,20°Ta
03-08-2003,05°Pi	04-22-2003,19°Ta	06-06-2003,21°Ta
03-09-2003,07°Pi	04-23-2003,20°Ta	06-07-2003,22°Ta
03-10-2003,08°Pi	04-24-2003,20°Ta	06-08-2003,23°Ta
03-11-2003,10°Pi	04-25-2003,20°Ta	06-09-2003,24°Ta
03-12-2003,12°Pi	04-26-2003,20°Ta	06-10-2003,26°Ta
03-13-2003,14°Pi	04-27-2003,20°TaRx	06-11-2003,27°Ta
03-14-2003,16°Pi	04-28-2003,20°TaRx	06-12-2003,28°Ta
03-15-2003,17°Pi	04-29-2003,20°TaRx	06-13-2003,00°Ge
03-16-2003,19°Pi	04-30-2003,19°TaRx	06-14-2003,01°Ge
03-17-2003,21°Pi	05-01-2003,19°TaRx	06-15-2003,03°Ge
03-18-2003,23°Pi	05-02-2003,19°TaRx	06-16-2003,04°Ge
03-19-2003,25°Pi	05-03-2003,18°TaRx	06-17-2003,06°Ge
03-20-2003,27°Pi	05-04-2003,18°TaRx	06-18-2003,08°Ge
03-21-2003,29°Pi	05-05-2003,17°TaRx	06-19-2003,09°Ge
03-22-2003,01°Ar	05-06-2003,17°TaRx	06-20-2003,11°Ge
03-23-2003,03°Ar	05-07-2003,16°TaRx	06-21-2003,13°Ge
03-24-2003,05°Ar	05-08-2003,15°TaRx	06-22-2003,15°Ge
03-25-2003,07°Ar	05-09-2003,15°TaRx	06-23-2003,17°Ge
03-26-2003,09°Ar	05-10-2003,14°TaRx	06-24-2003,19°Ge
03-27-2003,11°Ar	05-11-2003,13°TaRx	06-25-2003,21°Ge

06-26-2003,23°Ge	08-10-2003,14°Vi	09-24-2003,13°Vi
06-27-2003,25°Ge	08-11-2003,15°Vi	09-25-2003,14°Vi
06-28-2003,27°Ge	08-12-2003,16°Vi	09-26-2003,14°Vi
06-29-2003,29°Ge	08-13-2003,17°Vi	09-27-2003,15°Vi
06-30-2003,01°Ca	08-14-2003,18°Vi	09-28-2003,16°Vi
07-01-2003,03°Ca	08-15-2003,19°Vi	09-29-2003,18°Vi
07-02-2003,06°Ca	08-16-2003,20°Vi	09-30-2003,19°Vi
07-03-2003,08°Ca	08-17-2003,21°Vi	10-01-2003,20°Vi
07-04-2003,10°Ca	08-18-2003,21°Vi	10-02-2003,22°Vi
07-05-2003,12°Ca	08-19-2003,22°Vi	10-03-2003,23°Vi
07-06-2003,14°Ca	08-20-2003,23°Vi	10-04-2003,25°Vi
07-07-2003,16°Ca	08-21-2003,23°Vi	10-05-2003,26°Vi
07-08-2003,18°Ca	08-22-2003,24°Vi	10-06-2003,28°Vi
07-09-2003,21°Ca	08-23-2003,25°Vi	10-07-2003,00°Li
07-10-2003,23°Ca	08-24-2003,25°Vi	10-08-2003,01°Li
07-11-2003,25°Ca	08-25-2003,25°Vi	10-09-2003,03°Li
07-12-2003,27°Ca	08-26-2003,26°Vi	10-10-2003,05°Li
07-13-2003,29°Ca	08-27-2003,26°Vi	10-11-2003,07°Li
07-14-2003,01°Le	08-28-2003,26°Vi	10-12-2003,08°Li
07-15-2003,03°Le	08-29-2003,26°ViRx	10-13-2003,10°Li
07-16-2003,05°Le	08-30-2003,26°ViRx	10-14-2003,12°Li
07-17-2003,07°Le	08-31-2003,25°ViRx	10-15-2003,14°Li
07-18-2003,09°Le	09-01-2003,25°ViRx	10-16-2003,15°Li
07-19-2003,10°Le	09-02-2003,25°ViRx	10-17-2003,17°Li
07-20-2003,12°Le	09-03-2003,24°ViRx	10-18-2003,19°Li
07-21-2003,14°Le	09-04-2003,24°ViRx	10-19-2003,21°Li
07-22-2003,16°Le	09-05-2003,23°ViRx	10-20-2003,22°Li
07-23-2003,18°Le	09-06-2003,22°ViRx	10-21-2003,24°Li
07-24-2003,19°Le	09-07-2003,21°ViRx	10-22-2003,26°Li
07-25-2003,21°Le	09-08-2003,20°ViRx	10-23-2003,27°Li
07-26-2003,23°Le	09-09-2003,19°ViRx	10-24-2003,29°Li
07-27-2003,24°Le	09-10-2003,18°ViRx	10-25-2003,01°Sc
07-28-2003,26°Le	09-11-2003,17°ViRx	10-26-2003,02°Sc
07-29-2003,27°Le	09-12-2003,16°ViRx	10-27-2003,04°Sc
07-30-2003,29°Le	09-13-2003,15°ViRx	10-28-2003,06°Sc
07-31-2003,00°Vi	09-14-2003,15°ViRx	10-29-2003,07°Sc
08-01-2003,02°Vi	09-15-2003,14°ViRx	10-30-2003,09°Sc
08-02-2003,03°Vi	09-16-2003,13°ViRx	10-31-2003,11°Sc
08-03-2003,05°Vi	09-17-2003,12°ViRx	11-01-2003,12°Sc
08-04-2003,06°Vi	09-18-2003,12°ViRx	11-02-2003,14°Sc
08-05-2003,07°Vi	09-19-2003,12°ViRx	11-03-2003,15°Sc
08-06-2003,09°Vi	09-20-2003,12°ViRx	11-04-2003,17°Sc
08-07-2003,10°Vi	09-21-2003,12°Vi	11-05-2003,19°Sc
08-08-2003,11°Vi	09-22-2003,12°Vi	11-06-2003,20°Sc
08-09-2003,12°Vi	09-23-2003,12°Vi	11-07-2003,22°Sc

11-08-2003,23°Sc
11-09-2003,25°Sc
11-10-2003,26°Sc
11-11-2003,28°Sc
11-12-2003,29°Sc
11-13-2003,01°Sg
11-14-2003,02°Sg
11-15-2003,04°Sg
11-16-2003,05°Sg
11-17-2003,07°Sg
11-18-2003,08°Sg
11-19-2003,10°Sg
11-20-2003,11°Sg
11-21-2003,13°Sg
11-22-2003,14°Sg
11-23-2003,16°Sg
11-24-2003,17°Sg
11-25-2003,19°Sg
11-26-2003,20°Sg
11-27-2003,22°Sg
11-28-2003,23°Sg
11-29-2003,24°Sg
11-30-2003,26°Sg
12-01-2003,27°Sg
12-02-2003,29°Sg
12-03-2003,00°Cap
12-04-2003,01°Cap
12-05-2003,02°Cap
12-06-2003,04°Cap
12-07-2003,05°Cap
12-08-2003,06°Cap
12-09-2003,07°Cap
12-10-2003,08°Cap
12-11-2003,09°Cap
12-12-2003,10°Cap
12-13-2003,10°Cap
12-14-2003,11°Cap
12-15-2003,12°Cap
12-16-2003,12°Cap
12-17-2003,12°Cap
12-18-2003,12°CapRx
12-19-2003,12°CapRx
12-20-2003,11°CapRx
12-21-2003,11°CapRx
12-22-2003,10°CapRx

12-23-2003,09°CapRx
12-24-2003,08°CapRx
12-25-2003,07°CapRx
12-26-2003,06°CapRx
12-27-2003,04°CapRx
12-28-2003,03°CapRx
12-29-2003,01°CapRx
12-30-2003,00°CapRx
12-31-2003,29°SgRx

2004
01-01-2004,28°SgRx
01-02-2004,27°SgRx
01-03-2004,27°SgRx
01-04-2004,26°SgRx
01-05-2004,26°SgRx
01-06-2004,26°SgRx
01-07-2004,26°Sg
01-08-2004,26°Sg
01-09-2004,26°Sg
01-10-2004,27°Sg
01-11-2004,27°Sg
01-12-2004,28°Sg
01-13-2004,29°Sg
01-14-2004,29°Sg
01-15-2004,00°Cap
01-16-2004,01°Cap
01-17-2004,02°Cap
01-18-2004,03°Cap
01-19-2004,04°Cap
01-20-2004,05°Cap
01-21-2004,06°Cap
01-22-2004,08°Cap
01-23-2004,09°Cap
01-24-2004,10°Cap
01-25-2004,11°Cap
01-26-2004,13°Cap
01-27-2004,14°Cap
01-28-2004,15°Cap
01-29-2004,17°Cap
01-30-2004,18°Cap
01-31-2004,19°Cap
02-01-2004,21°Cap
02-02-2004,22°Cap
02-03-2004,24°Cap

02-04-2004,25°Cap
02-05-2004,27°Cap
02-06-2004,28°Cap
02-07-2004,00°Aq
02-08-2004,01°Aq
02-09-2004,03°Aq
02-10-2004,04°Aq
02-11-2004,06°Aq
02-12-2004,07°Aq
02-13-2004,09°Aq
02-14-2004,10°Aq
02-15-2004,12°Aq
02-16-2004,14°Aq
02-17-2004,15°Aq
02-18-2004,17°Aq
02-19-2004,19°Aq
02-20-2004,20°Aq
02-21-2004,22°Aq
02-22-2004,24°Aq
02-23-2004,25°Aq
02-24-2004,27°Aq
02-25-2004,29°Aq
02-26-2004,01°Pi
02-27-2004,02°Pi
02-28-2004,04°Pi
02-29-2004,06°Pi
03-01-2004,08°Pi
03-02-2004,10°Pi
03-03-2004,12°Pi
03-04-2004,14°Pi
03-05-2004,15°Pi
03-06-2004,17°Pi
03-07-2004,19°Pi
03-08-2004,21°Pi
03-09-2004,23°Pi
03-10-2004,25°Pi
03-11-2004,27°Pi
03-12-2004,29°Pi
03-13-2004,01°Ar
03-14-2004,03°Ar
03-15-2004,05°Ar
03-16-2004,07°Ar
03-17-2004,09°Ar
03-18-2004,11°Ar
03-19-2004,12°Ar

03-20-2004,14°Ar	05-04-2004,21°Ar	06-18-2004,26°Ge
03-21-2004,16°Ar	05-05-2004,21°Ar	06-19-2004,28°Ge
03-22-2004,18°Ar	05-06-2004,22°Ar	06-20-2004,00°Ca
03-23-2004,19°Ar	05-07-2004,22°Ar	06-21-2004,03°Ca
03-24-2004,21°Ar	05-08-2004,23°Ar	06-22-2004,05°Ca
03-25-2004,22°Ar	05-09-2004,24°Ar	06-23-2004,07°Ca
03-26-2004,24°Ar	05-10-2004,24°Ar	06-24-2004,09°Ca
03-27-2004,25°Ar	05-11-2004,25°Ar	06-25-2004,11°Ca
03-28-2004,26°Ar	05-12-2004,26°Ar	06-26-2004,13°Ca
03-29-2004,27°Ar	05-13-2004,27°Ar	06-27-2004,15°Ca
03-30-2004,28°Ar	05-14-2004,27°Ar	06-28-2004,17°Ca
03-31-2004,29°Ar	05-15-2004,28°Ar	06-29-2004,19°Ca
04-01-2004,00°Ta	05-16-2004,29°Ar	06-30-2004,21°Ca
04-02-2004,00°Ta	05-17-2004,00°Ta	07-01-2004,23°Ca
04-03-2004,01°Ta	05-18-2004,02°Ta	07-02-2004,25°Ca
04-04-2004,01°Ta	05-19-2004,03°Ta	07-03-2004,27°Ca
04-05-2004,01°Ta	05-20-2004,04°Ta	07-04-2004,29°Ca
04-06-2004,01°Ta	05-21-2004,05°Ta	07-05-2004,01°Le
04-07-2004,01°TaRx	05-22-2004,06°Ta	07-06-2004,02°Le
04-08-2004,01°TaRx	05-23-2004,08°Ta	07-07-2004,04°Le
04-09-2004,01°TaRx	05-24-2004,09°Ta	07-08-2004,06°Le
04-10-2004,01°TaRx	05-25-2004,11°Ta	07-09-2004,07°Le
04-11-2004,00°TaRx	05-26-2004,12°Ta	07-10-2004,09°Le
04-12-2004,00°TaRx	05-27-2004,14°Ta	07-11-2004,11°Le
04-13-2004,29°ArRx	05-28-2004,15°Ta	07-12-2004,12°Le
04-14-2004,29°ArRx	05-29-2004,17°Ta	07-13-2004,14°Le
04-15-2004,28°ArRx	05-30-2004,18°Ta	07-14-2004,15°Le
04-16-2004,27°ArRx	05-31-2004,20°Ta	07-15-2004,17°Le
04-17-2004,27°ArRx	06-01-2004,22°Ta	07-16-2004,18°Le
04-18-2004,26°ArRx	06-02-2004,23°Ta	07-17-2004,19°Le
04-19-2004,25°ArRx	06-03-2004,25°Ta	07-18-2004,21°Le
04-20-2004,25°ArRx	06-04-2004,27°Ta	07-19-2004,22°Le
04-21-2004,24°ArRx	06-05-2004,29°Ta	07-20-2004,23°Le
04-22-2004,23°ArRx	06-06-2004,01°Ge	07-21-2004,25°Le
04-23-2004,23°ArRx	06-07-2004,03°Ge	07-22-2004,26°Le
04-24-2004,22°ArRx	06-08-2004,05°Ge	07-23-2004,27°Le
04-25-2004,22°ArRx	06-09-2004,07°Ge	07-24-2004,28°Le
04-26-2004,21°ArRx	06-10-2004,09°Ge	07-25-2004,29°Le
04-27-2004,21°ArRx	06-11-2004,11°Ge	07-26-2004,00°Vi
04-28-2004,21°ArRx	06-12-2004,13°Ge	07-27-2004,01°Vi
04-29-2004,21°ArRx	06-13-2004,15°Ge	07-28-2004,02°Vi
04-30-2004,21°ArRx	06-14-2004,17°Ge	07-29-2004,03°Vi
05-01-2004,21°Ar	06-15-2004,19°Ge	07-30-2004,04°Vi
05-02-2004,21°Ar	06-16-2004,22°Ge	07-31-2004,04°Vi
05-03-2004,21°Ar	06-17-2004,24°Ge	08-01-2004,05°Vi

08-02-2004,06°Vi	09-16-2004,07°Vi	10-31-2004,23°Sc
08-03-2004,06°Vi	09-17-2004,09°Vi	11-01-2004,25°Sc
08-04-2004,07°Vi	09-18-2004,11°Vi	11-02-2004,26°Sc
08-05-2004,07°Vi	09-19-2004,12°Vi	11-03-2004,27°Sc
08-06-2004,08°Vi	09-20-2004,14°Vi	11-04-2004,29°Sc
08-07-2004,08°Vi	09-21-2004,16°Vi	11-05-2004,00°Sg
08-08-2004,08°Vi	09-22-2004,18°Vi	11-06-2004,02°Sg
08-09-2004,08°Vi	09-23-2004,20°Vi	11-07-2004,03°Sg
08-10-2004,08°ViRx	09-24-2004,21°Vi	11-08-2004,05°Sg
08-11-2004,08°ViRx	09-25-2004,23°Vi	11-09-2004,06°Sg
08-12-2004,08°ViRx	09-26-2004,25°Vi	11-10-2004,07°Sg
08-13-2004,08°ViRx	09-27-2004,27°Vi	11-11-2004,09°Sg
08-14-2004,07°ViRx	09-28-2004,29°Vi	11-12-2004,10°Sg
08-15-2004,07°ViRx	09-29-2004,01°Li	11-13-2004,11°Sg
08-16-2004,07°ViRx	09-30-2004,02°Li	11-14-2004,13°Sg
08-17-2004,06°ViRx	10-01-2004,04°Li	11-15-2004,14°Sg
08-18-2004,05°ViRx	10-02-2004,06°Li	11-16-2004,15°Sg
08-19-2004,05°ViRx	10-03-2004,08°Li	11-17-2004,16°Sg
08-20-2004,04°ViRx	10-04-2004,10°Li	11-18-2004,18°Sg
08-21-2004,03°ViRx	10-05-2004,11°Li	11-19-2004,19°Sg
08-22-2004,02°ViRx	10-06-2004,13°Li	11-20-2004,20°Sg
08-23-2004,01°ViRx	10-07-2004,15°Li	11-21-2004,21°Sg
08-24-2004,00°ViRx	10-08-2004,17°Li	11-22-2004,22°Sg
08-25-2004,29°LeRx	10-09-2004,18°Li	11-23-2004,23°Sg
08-26-2004,29°LeRx	10-10-2004,20°Li	11-24-2004,23°Sg
08-27-2004,28°LeRx	10-11-2004,22°Li	11-25-2004,24°Sg
08-28-2004,27°LeRx	10-12-2004,23°Li	11-26-2004,25°Sg
08-29-2004,26°LeRx	10-13-2004,25°Li	11-27-2004,25°Sg
08-30-2004,26°LeRx	10-14-2004,27°Li	11-28-2004,26°Sg
08-31-2004,26°LeRx	10-15-2004,28°Li	11-29-2004,26°Sg
09-01-2004,25°LeRx	10-16-2004,00°Sc	11-30-2004,26°Sg
09-02-2004,25°LeRx	10-17-2004,02°Sc	12-01-2004,26°SgRx
09-03-2004,25°Le	10-18-2004,03°Sc	12-02-2004,26°SgRx
09-04-2004,25°Le	10-19-2004,05°Sc	12-03-2004,26°SgRx
09-05-2004,26°Le	10-20-2004,06°Sc	12-04-2004,25°SgRx
09-06-2004,26°Le	10-21-2004,08°Sc	12-05-2004,24°SgRx
09-07-2004,27°Le	10-22-2004,09°Sc	12-06-2004,23°SgRx
09-08-2004,28°Le	10-23-2004,11°Sc	12-07-2004,22°SgRx
09-09-2004,28°Le	10-24-2004,13°Sc	12-08-2004,21°SgRx
09-10-2004,29°Le	10-25-2004,14°Sc	12-09-2004,20°SgRx
09-11-2004,00°Vi	10-26-2004,16°Sc	12-10-2004,18°SgRx
09-12-2004,02°Vi	10-27-2004,17°Sc	12-11-2004,17°SgRx
09-13-2004,03°Vi	10-28-2004,19°Sc	12-12-2004,16°SgRx
09-14-2004,04°Vi	10-29-2004,20°Sc	12-13-2004,14°SgRx
09-15-2004,06°Vi	10-30-2004,22°Sc	12-14-2004,13°SgRx

12-15-2004,12°SgRx	01-26-2005,23°Cap	03-12-2005,09°Ar
12-16-2004,11°SgRx	01-27-2005,25°Cap	03-13-2005,10°Ar
12-17-2004,11°SgRx	01-28-2005,26°Cap	03-14-2005,11°Ar
12-18-2004,10°SgRx	01-29-2005,28°Cap	03-15-2005,12°Ar
12-19-2004,10°SgRx	01-30-2005,29°Cap	03-16-2005,13°Ar
12-20-2004,10°SgRx	01-31-2005,01°Aq	03-17-2005,13°Ar
12-21-2004,10°Sg	02-01-2005,03°Aq	03-18-2005,13°Ar
12-22-2004,10°Sg	02-02-2005,04°Aq	03-19-2005,14°Ar
12-23-2004,11°Sg	02-03-2005,06°Aq	03-20-2005,14°ArRx
12-24-2004,11°Sg	02-04-2005,08°Aq	03-21-2005,14°ArRx
12-25-2004,12°Sg	02-05-2005,09°Aq	03-22-2005,13°ArRx
12-26-2004,12°Sg	02-06-2005,11°Aq	03-23-2005,13°ArRx
12-27-2004,13°Sg	02-07-2005,13°Aq	03-24-2005,12°ArRx
12-28-2004,14°Sg	02-08-2005,14°Aq	03-25-2005,12°ArRx
12-29-2004,15°Sg	02-09-2005,16°Aq	03-26-2005,11°ArRx
12-30-2004,16°Sg	02-10-2005,18°Aq	03-27-2005,11°ArRx
12-31-2004,17°Sg	02-11-2005,20°Aq	03-28-2005,10°ArRx
	02-12-2005,21°Aq	03-29-2005,09°ArRx
2005	02-13-2005,23°Aq	03-30-2005,08°ArRx
01-01-2005,18°Sg	02-14-2005,25°Aq	03-31-2005,07°ArRx
01-01-2005,18°Sg	02-15-2005,27°Aq	04-01-2005,06°ArRx
01-02-2005,19°Sg	02-16-2005,29°Aq	04-02-2005,06°ArRx
01-03-2005,20°Sg	02-17-2005,00°Pi	04-03-2005,05°ArRx
01-04-2005,22°Sg	02-18-2005,02°Pi	04-04-2005,04°ArRx
01-05-2005,23°Sg	02-19-2005,04°Pi	04-05-2005,03°ArRx
01-06-2005,24°Sg	02-20-2005,06°Pi	04-06-2005,03°ArRx
01-07-2005,26°Sg	02-21-2005,08°Pi	04-07-2005,02°ArRx
01-08-2005,27°Sg	02-22-2005,10°Pi	04-08-2005,02°ArRx
01-09-2005,28°Sg	02-23-2005,12°Pi	04-09-2005,02°ArRx
01-10-2005,00°Cap	02-24-2005,13°Pi	04-10-2005,01°ArRx
01-11-2005,01°Cap	02-25-2005,15°Pi	04-11-2005,01°ArRx
01-12-2005,02°Cap	02-26-2005,17°Pi	04-12-2005,01°ArRx
01-13-2005,04°Cap	02-27-2005,19°Pi	04-13-2005,01°Ar
01-14-2005,05°Cap	02-28-2005,21°Pi	04-14-2005,01°Ar
01-15-2005,07°Cap	03-01-2005,23°Pi	04-15-2005,02°Ar
01-16-2005,08°Cap	03-02-2005,25°Pi	04-16-2005,02°Ar
01-17-2005,10°Cap	03-03-2005,26°Pi	04-17-2005,02°Ar
01-18-2005,11°Cap	03-04-2005,28°Pi	04-18-2005,03°Ar
01-19-2005,12°Cap	03-05-2005,00°Ar	04-19-2005,03°Ar
01-20-2005,14°Cap	03-06-2005,01°Ar	04-20-2005,04°Ar
01-21-2005,15°Cap	03-07-2005,03°Ar	04-21-2005,04°Ar
01-22-2005,17°Cap	03-08-2005,04°Ar	04-22-2005,05°Ar
01-23-2005,19°Cap	03-09-2005,06°Ar	04-23-2005,06°Ar
01-24-2005,20°Cap	03-10-2005,07°Ar	04-24-2005,07°Ar
01-25-2005,22°Cap	03-11-2005,08°Ar	04-25-2005,08°Ar

04-26-2005,09°Ar	06-10-2005,27°Ge	07-25-2005,20°LeRx
04-27-2005,10°Ar	06-11-2005,29°Ge	07-26-2005,20°LeRx
04-28-2005,11°Ar	06-12-2005,01°Ca	07-27-2005,19°LeRx
04-29-2005,12°Ar	06-13-2005,03°Ca	07-28-2005,19°LeRx
04-30-2005,13°Ar	06-14-2005,05°Ca	07-29-2005,18°LeRx
05-01-2005,14°Ar	06-15-2005,07°Ca	07-30-2005,18°LeRx
05-02-2005,15°Ar	06-16-2005,09°Ca	07-31-2005,17°LeRx
05-03-2005,16°Ar	06-17-2005,11°Ca	08-01-2005,17°LeRx
05-04-2005,18°Ar	06-18-2005,13°Ca	08-02-2005,16°LeRx
05-05-2005,19°Ar	06-19-2005,15°Ca	08-03-2005,15°LeRx
05-06-2005,20°Ar	06-20-2005,17°Ca	08-04-2005,15°LeRx
05-07-2005,22°Ar	06-21-2005,18°Ca	08-05-2005,14°LeRx
05-08-2005,23°Ar	06-22-2005,20°Ca	08-06-2005,13°LeRx
05-09-2005,25°Ar	06-23-2005,22°Ca	08-07-2005,12°LeRx
05-10-2005,26°Ar	06-24-2005,23°Ca	08-08-2005,11°LeRx
05-11-2005,28°Ar	06-25-2005,25°Ca	08-09-2005,11°LeRx
05-12-2005,29°Ar	06-26-2005,27°Ca	08-10-2005,10°LeRx
05-13-2005,01°Ta	06-27-2005,28°Ca	08-11-2005,10°LeRx
05-14-2005,02°Ta	06-28-2005,00°Le	08-12-2005,09°LeRx
05-15-2005,04°Ta	06-29-2005,01°Le	08-13-2005,09°LeRx
05-16-2005,06°Ta	06-30-2005,02°Le	08-14-2005,08°LeRx
05-17-2005,08°Ta	07-01-2005,04°Le	08-15-2005,08°LeRx
05-18-2005,09°Ta	07-02-2005,05°Le	08-16-2005,08°Le
05-19-2005,11°Ta	07-03-2005,06°Le	08-17-2005,08°Le
05-20-2005,13°Ta	07-04-2005,07°Le	08-18-2005,09°Le
05-21-2005,15°Ta	07-05-2005,09°Le	08-19-2005,09°Le
05-22-2005,17°Ta	07-06-2005,10°Le	08-20-2005,09°Le
05-23-2005,19°Ta	07-07-2005,11°Le	08-21-2005,10°Le
05-24-2005,21°Ta	07-08-2005,12°Le	08-22-2005,11°Le
05-25-2005,23°Ta	07-09-2005,13°Le	08-23-2005,11°Le
05-26-2005,25°Ta	07-10-2005,14°Le	08-24-2005,12°Le
05-27-2005,27°Ta	07-11-2005,15°Le	08-25-2005,13°Le
05-28-2005,29°Ta	07-12-2005,15°Le	08-26-2005,14°Le
05-29-2005,01°Ge	07-13-2005,16°Le	08-27-2005,16°Le
05-30-2005,03°Ge	07-14-2005,17°Le	08-28-2005,17°Le
05-31-2005,05°Ge	07-15-2005,18°Le	08-29-2005,18°Le
06-01-2005,08°Ge	07-16-2005,18°Le	08-30-2005,20°Le
06-02-2005,10°Ge	07-17-2005,19°Le	08-31-2005,22°Le
06-03-2005,12°Ge	07-18-2005,19°Le	09-01-2005,23°Le
06-04-2005,14°Ge	07-19-2005,19°Le	09-02-2005,25°Le
06-05-2005,16°Ge	07-20-2005,20°Le	09-03-2005,27°Le
06-06-2005,19°Ge	07-21-2005,20°Le	09-04-2005,29°Le
06-07-2005,21°Ge	07-22-2005,20°Le	09-05-2005,00°Vi
06-08-2005,23°Ge	07-23-2005,20°LeRx	09-06-2005,02°Vi
06-09-2005,25°Ge	07-24-2005,20°LeRx	09-07-2005,04°Vi

09-08-2005,06°Vi
09-09-2005,08°Vi
09-10-2005,10°Vi
09-11-2005,12°Vi
09-12-2005,14°Vi
09-13-2005,16°Vi
09-14-2005,17°Vi
09-15-2005,19°Vi
09-16-2005,21°Vi
09-17-2005,23°Vi
09-18-2005,25°Vi
09-19-2005,27°Vi
09-20-2005,29°Vi
09-21-2005,00°Li
09-22-2005,02°Li
09-23-2005,04°Li
09-24-2005,06°Li
09-25-2005,07°Li
09-26-2005,09°Li
09-27-2005,11°Li
09-28-2005,13°Li
09-29-2005,14°Li
09-30-2005,16°Li
10-01-2005,18°Li
10-02-2005,19°Li
10-03-2005,21°Li
10-04-2005,22°Li
10-05-2005,24°Li
10-06-2005,26°Li
10-07-2005,27°Li
10-08-2005,29°Li
10-09-2005,00°Sc
10-10-2005,02°Sc
10-11-2005,03°Sc
10-12-2005,05°Sc
10-13-2005,06°Sc
10-14-2005,08°Sc
10-15-2005,09°Sc
10-16-2005,11°Sc
10-17-2005,12°Sc
10-18-2005,14°Sc
10-19-2005,15°Sc
10-20-2005,16°Sc
10-21-2005,18°Sc
10-22-2005,19°Sc

10-23-2005,20°Sc
10-24-2005,22°Sc
10-25-2005,23°Sc
10-26-2005,24°Sc
10-27-2005,26°Sc
10-28-2005,27°Sc
10-29-2005,28°Sc
10-30-2005,29°Sc
10-31-2005,00°Sg
11-01-2005,02°Sg
11-02-2005,03°Sg
11-03-2005,04°Sg
11-04-2005,05°Sg
11-05-2005,06°Sg
11-06-2005,07°Sg
11-07-2005,07°Sg
11-08-2005,08°Sg
11-09-2005,09°Sg
11-10-2005,09°Sg
11-11-2005,10°Sg
11-12-2005,10°Sg
11-13-2005,10°Sg
11-14-2005,10°Sg
11-15-2005,10°SgRx
11-16-2005,10°SgRx
11-17-2005,10°SgRx
11-18-2005,09°SgRx
11-19-2005,08°SgRx
11-20-2005,07°SgRx
11-21-2005,06°SgRx
11-22-2005,05°SgRx
11-23-2005,04°SgRx
11-24-2005,03°SgRx
11-25-2005,01°SgRx
11-26-2005,00°SgRx
11-27-2005,29°ScRx
11-28-2005,27°ScRx
11-29-2005,26°ScRx
11-30-2005,26°ScRx
12-01-2005,25°ScRx
12-02-2005,25°ScRx
12-03-2005,24°ScRx
12-04-2005,24°Sc
12-05-2005,24°Sc
12-06-2005,25°Sc

12-07-2005,25°Sc
12-08-2005,26°Sc
12-09-2005,26°Sc
12-10-2005,27°Sc
12-11-2005,28°Sc
12-12-2005,29°Sc
12-13-2005,00°Sg
12-14-2005,01°Sg
12-15-2005,02°Sg
12-16-2005,03°Sg
12-17-2005,04°Sg
12-18-2005,06°Sg
12-19-2005,07°Sg
12-20-2005,08°Sg
12-21-2005,10°Sg
12-22-2005,11°Sg
12-23-2005,12°Sg
12-24-2005,14°Sg
12-25-2005,15°Sg
12-26-2005,17°Sg
12-27-2005,18°Sg
12-28-2005,20°Sg
12-29-2005,21°Sg
12-30-2005,23°Sg
12-31-2005,24°Sg

2006
01-01-2006,25°Sg
01-02-2006,27°Sg
01-03-2006,28°Sg
01-04-2006,00°Cap
01-05-2006,02°Cap
01-06-2006,03°Cap
01-07-2006,05°Cap
01-08-2006,06°Cap
01-09-2006,08°Cap
01-10-2006,09°Cap
01-11-2006,11°Cap
01-12-2006,12°Cap
01-13-2006,14°Cap
01-14-2006,15°Cap
01-15-2006,17°Cap
01-16-2006,19°Cap
01-17-2006,20°Cap
01-18-2006,22°Cap

01-19-2006,23°Cap	03-05-2006,26°PiRx	04-19-2006,03°Ar
01-20-2006,25°Cap	03-06-2006,26°PiRx	04-20-2006,05°Ar
01-21-2006,27°Cap	03-07-2006,25°PiRx	04-21-2006,06°Ar
01-22-2006,28°Cap	03-08-2006,24°PiRx	04-22-2006,07°Ar
01-23-2006,00°Aq	03-09-2006,24°PiRx	04-23-2006,09°Ar
01-24-2006,02°Aq	03-10-2006,23°PiRx	04-24-2006,10°Ar
01-25-2006,03°Aq	03-11-2006,22°PiRx	04-25-2006,12°Ar
01-26-2006,05°Aq	03-12-2006,21°PiRx	04-26-2006,14°Ar
01-27-2006,07°Aq	03-13-2006,20°PiRx	04-27-2006,15°Ar
01-28-2006,09°Aq	03-14-2006,19°PiRx	04-28-2006,17°Ar
01-29-2006,10°Aq	03-15-2006,18°PiRx	04-29-2006,19°Ar
01-30-2006,12°Aq	03-16-2006,17°PiRx	04-30-2006,20°Ar
01-31-2006,14°Aq	03-17-2006,16°PiRx	05-01-2006,22°Ar
02-01-2006,15°Aq	03-18-2006,15°PiRx	05-02-2006,24°Ar
02-02-2006,17°Aq	03-19-2006,15°PiRx	05-03-2006,26°Ar
02-03-2006,19°Aq	03-20-2006,14°PiRx	05-04-2006,27°Ar
02-04-2006,21°Aq	03-21-2006,14°PiRx	05-05-2006,29°Ar
02-05-2006,23°Aq	03-22-2006,13°PiRx	05-06-2006,01°Ta
02-06-2006,24°Aq	03-23-2006,13°PiRx	05-07-2006,03°Ta
02-07-2006,26°Aq	03-24-2006,13°PiRx	05-08-2006,05°Ta
02-08-2006,28°Aq	03-25-2006,13°PiRx	05-09-2006,07°Ta
02-09-2006,00°Pi	03-26-2006,13°Pi	05-10-2006,09°Ta
02-10-2006,02°Pi	03-27-2006,13°Pi	05-11-2006,11°Ta
02-11-2006,03°Pi	03-28-2006,13°Pi	05-12-2006,13°Ta
02-12-2006,05°Pi	03-29-2006,13°Pi	05-13-2006,15°Ta
02-13-2006,07°Pi	03-30-2006,14°Pi	05-14-2006,17°Ta
02-14-2006,09°Pi	03-31-2006,14°Pi	05-15-2006,19°Ta
02-15-2006,10°Pi	04-01-2006,15°Pi	05-16-2006,22°Ta
02-16-2006,12°Pi	04-02-2006,15°Pi	05-17-2006,24°Ta
02-17-2006,14°Pi	04-03-2006,16°Pi	05-18-2006,26°Ta
02-18-2006,15°Pi	04-04-2006,17°Pi	05-19-2006,28°Ta
02-19-2006,17°Pi	04-05-2006,17°Pi	05-20-2006,00°Ge
02-20-2006,18°Pi	04-06-2006,18°Pi	05-21-2006,02°Ge
02-21-2006,20°Pi	04-07-2006,19°Pi	05-22-2006,05°Ge
02-22-2006,21°Pi	04-08-2006,20°Pi	05-23-2006,07°Ge
02-23-2006,22°Pi	04-09-2006,21°Pi	05-24-2006,09°Ge
02-24-2006,23°Pi	04-10-2006,22°Pi	05-25-2006,11°Ge
02-25-2006,24°Pi	04-11-2006,23°Pi	05-26-2006,13°Ge
02-26-2006,25°Pi	04-12-2006,24°Pi	05-27-2006,15°Ge
02-27-2006,25°Pi	04-13-2006,25°Pi	05-28-2006,17°Ge
02-28-2006,26°Pi	04-14-2006,27°Pi	05-29-2006,19°Ge
03-01-2006,26°Pi	04-15-2006,28°Pi	05-30-2006,21°Ge
03-02-2006,26°Pi	04-16-2006,29°Pi	05-31-2006,23°Ge
03-03-2006,26°PiRx	04-17-2006,00°Ar	06-01-2006,25°Ge
03-04-2006,26°PiRx	04-18-2006,02°Ar	06-02-2006,27°Ge

06-03-2006,29°Ge
06-04-2006,01°Ca
06-05-2006,03°Ca
06-06-2006,04°Ca
06-07-2006,06°Ca
06-08-2006,08°Ca
06-09-2006,09°Ca
06-10-2006,11°Ca
06-11-2006,12°Ca
06-12-2006,14°Ca
06-13-2006,15°Ca
06-14-2006,16°Ca
06-15-2006,18°Ca
06-16-2006,19°Ca
06-17-2006,20°Ca
06-18-2006,21°Ca
06-19-2006,22°Ca
06-20-2006,23°Ca
06-21-2006,24°Ca
06-22-2006,25°Ca
06-23-2006,26°Ca
06-24-2006,27°Ca
06-25-2006,27°Ca
06-26-2006,28°Ca
06-27-2006,29°Ca
06-28-2006,29°Ca
06-29-2006,00°Le
06-30-2006,00°Le
07-01-2006,00°Le
07-02-2006,01°Le
07-03-2006,01°Le
07-04-2006,01°Le
07-05-2006,01°LeRx
07-06-2006,01°LeRx
07-07-2006,01°LeRx
07-08-2006,00°LeRx
07-09-2006,00°LeRx
07-10-2006,00°LeRx
07-11-2006,29°CaRx
07-12-2006,29°CaRx
07-13-2006,28°CaRx
07-14-2006,28°CaRx
07-15-2006,27°CaRx
07-16-2006,26°CaRx
07-17-2006,26°CaRx

07-18-2006,25°CaRx
07-19-2006,24°CaRx
07-20-2006,24°CaRx
07-21-2006,23°CaRx
07-22-2006,23°CaRx
07-23-2006,22°CaRx
07-24-2006,22°CaRx
07-25-2006,21°CaRx
07-26-2006,21°CaRx
07-27-2006,21°CaRx
07-28-2006,21°CaRx
07-29-2006,21°Ca
07-30-2006,21°Ca
07-31-2006,21°Ca
08-01-2006,21°Ca
08-02-2006,21°Ca
08-03-2006,22°Ca
08-04-2006,23°Ca
08-05-2006,23°Ca
08-06-2006,24°Ca
08-07-2006,25°Ca
08-08-2006,26°Ca
08-09-2006,27°Ca
08-10-2006,28°Ca
08-11-2006,00°Le
08-12-2006,01°Le
08-13-2006,02°Le
08-14-2006,04°Le
08-15-2006,06°Le
08-16-2006,07°Le
08-17-2006,09°Le
08-18-2006,11°Le
08-19-2006,13°Le
08-20-2006,15°Le
08-21-2006,16°Le
08-22-2006,18°Le
08-23-2006,20°Le
08-24-2006,22°Le
08-25-2006,24°Le
08-26-2006,26°Le
08-27-2006,28°Le
08-28-2006,00°Vi
08-29-2006,02°Vi
08-30-2006,04°Vi
08-31-2006,06°Vi

09-01-2006,08°Vi
09-02-2006,10°Vi
09-03-2006,12°Vi
09-04-2006,14°Vi
09-05-2006,16°Vi
09-06-2006,18°Vi
09-07-2006,19°Vi
09-08-2006,21°Vi
09-09-2006,23°Vi
09-10-2006,25°Vi
09-11-2006,27°Vi
09-12-2006,28°Vi
09-13-2006,00°Li
09-14-2006,02°Li
09-15-2006,03°Li
09-16-2006,05°Li
09-17-2006,07°Li
09-18-2006,08°Li
09-19-2006,10°Li
09-20-2006,12°Li
09-21-2006,13°Li
09-22-2006,15°Li
09-23-2006,16°Li
09-24-2006,18°Li
09-25-2006,19°Li
09-26-2006,21°Li
09-27-2006,22°Li
09-28-2006,24°Li
09-29-2006,25°Li
09-30-2006,27°Li
10-01-2006,28°Li
10-02-2006,00°Sc
10-03-2006,01°Sc
10-04-2006,02°Sc
10-05-2006,04°Sc
10-06-2006,05°Sc
10-07-2006,06°Sc
10-08-2006,08°Sc
10-09-2006,09°Sc
10-10-2006,10°Sc
10-11-2006,11°Sc
10-12-2006,12°Sc
10-13-2006,14°Sc
10-14-2006,15°Sc
10-15-2006,16°Sc

10-16-2006,17°Sc	11-30-2006,18°Sc	01-12-2007,24°Cap
10-17-2006,18°Sc	12-01-2006,20°Sc	01-13-2007,26°Cap
10-18-2006,19°Sc	12-02-2006,21°Sc	01-14-2007,28°Cap
10-19-2006,20°Sc	12-03-2006,22°Sc	01-15-2007,29°Cap
10-20-2006,21°Sc	12-04-2006,24°Sc	01-16-2007,01°Aq
10-21-2006,21°Sc	12-05-2006,25°Sc	01-17-2007,03°Aq
10-22-2006,22°Sc	12-06-2006,27°Sc	01-18-2007,04°Aq
10-23-2006,23°Sc	12-07-2006,28°Sc	01-19-2007,06°Aq
10-24-2006,23°Sc	12-08-2006,29°Sc	01-20-2007,08°Aq
10-25-2006,24°Sc	12-09-2006,01°Sg	01-21-2007,09°Aq
10-26-2006,24°Sc	12-10-2006,02°Sg	01-22-2007,11°Aq
10-27-2006,24°Sc	12-11-2006,04°Sg	01-23-2007,13°Aq
10-28-2006,25°Sc	12-12-2006,05°Sg	01-24-2007,15°Aq
10-29-2006,25°ScRx	12-13-2006,07°Sg	01-25-2007,16°Aq
10-30-2006,24°ScRx	12-14-2006,08°Sg	01-26-2007,18°Aq
10-31-2006,24°ScRx	12-15-2006,10°Sg	01-27-2007,20°Aq
11-01-2006,24°ScRx	12-16-2006,11°Sg	01-28-2007,21°Aq
11-02-2006,23°ScRx	12-17-2006,13°Sg	01-29-2007,23°Aq
11-03-2006,22°ScRx	12-18-2006,15°Sg	01-30-2007,25°Aq
11-04-2006,22°ScRx	12-19-2006,16°Sg	01-31-2007,26°Aq
11-05-2006,20°ScRx	12-20-2006,18°Sg	02-01-2007,28°Aq
11-06-2006,19°ScRx	12-21-2006,19°Sg	02-02-2007,29°Aq
11-07-2006,18°ScRx	12-22-2006,21°Sg	02-03-2007,01°Pi
11-08-2006,17°ScRx	12-23-2006,22°Sg	02-04-2007,02°Pi
11-09-2006,15°ScRx	12-24-2006,24°Sg	02-05-2007,03°Pi
11-10-2006,14°ScRx	12-25-2006,25°Sg	02-06-2007,05°Pi
11-11-2006,13°ScRx	12-26-2006,27°Sg	02-07-2007,06°Pi
11-12-2006,12°ScRx	12-27-2006,28°Sg	02-08-2007,07°Pi
11-13-2006,11°ScRx	12-28-2006,00°Cp	02-09-2007,08°Pi
11-14-2006,10°ScRx	12-29-2006,02°Cp	02-10-2007,08°Pi
11-15-2006,09°ScRx	12-30-2006,03°Cp	02-11-2007,09°Pi
11-16-2006,09°ScRx	12-31-2006,05°Cp	02-12-2007,09°Pi
11-17-2006,09°ScRx		02-13-2007,10°Pi
11-18-2006,09°Sc	**2007**	02-14-2007,10°PiRx
11-19-2006,09°Sc	01-01-2007,06°Cap	02-15-2007,10°PiRx
11-20-2006,09°Sc	01-02-2007,08°Cap	02-16-2007,09°PiRx
11-21-2006,09°Sc	01-03-2007,10°Cap	02-17-2007,09°PiRx
11-22-2006,10°Sc	01-04-2007,11°Cap	02-18-2007,08°PiRx
11-23-2006,11°Sc	01-05-2007,13°Cap	02-19-2007,08°PiRx
11-24-2006,12°Sc	01-06-2007,14°Cap	02-20-2007,07°PiRx
11-25-2006,13°Sc	01-07-2007,16°Cap	02-21-2007,06°PiRx
11-26-2006,14°Sc	01-08-2007,18°Cap	02-22-2007,05°PiRx
11-27-2006,15°Sc	01-09-2007,19°Cap	02-23-2007,04°PiRx
11-28-2006,16°Sc	01-10-2007,21°Cap	02-24-2007,03°PiRx
11-29-2006,17°Sc	01-11-2007,23°Cap	02-25-2007,01°PiRx

02-26-2007,00°PiRx	04-12-2007,02°Ar	05-27-2007,27°Ge
02-27-2007,29°AqRx	04-13-2007,03°Ar	05-28-2007,28°Ge
02-28-2007,29°AqRx	04-14-2007,05°Ar	05-29-2007,00°Ca
03-01-2007,28°AqRx	04-15-2007,07°Ar	05-30-2007,01°Ca
03-02-2007,27°AqRx	04-16-2007,08°Ar	05-31-2007,02°Ca
03-03-2007,26°AqRx	04-17-2007,10°Ar	06-01-2007,03°Ca
03-04-2007,26°AqRx	04-18-2007,12°Ar	06-02-2007,04°Ca
03-05-2007,25°AqRx	04-19-2007,14°Ar	06-03-2007,05°Ca
03-06-2007,25°AqRx	04-20-2007,16°Ar	06-04-2007,06°Ca
03-07-2007,25°AqRx	04-21-2007,17°Ar	06-05-2007,07°Ca
03-08-2007,25°Aq	04-22-2007,19°Ar	06-06-2007,08°Ca
03-09-2007,25°Aq	04-23-2007,21°Ar	06-07-2007,08°Ca
03-10-2007,25°Aq	04-24-2007,23°Ar	06-08-2007,09°Ca
03-11-2007,25°Aq	04-25-2007,25°Ar	06-09-2007,09°Ca
03-12-2007,26°Aq	04-26-2007,27°Ar	06-10-2007,10°Ca
03-13-2007,26°Aq	04-27-2007,29°Ar	06-11-2007,10°Ca
03-14-2007,27°Aq	04-28-2007,01°Ta	06-12-2007,11°Ca
03-15-2007,27°Aq	04-29-2007,03°Ta	06-13-2007,11°Ca
03-16-2007,28°Aq	04-30-2007,06°Ta	06-14-2007,11°Ca
03-17-2007,29°Aq	05-01-2007,08°Ta	06-15-2007,11°Ca
03-18-2007,29°Aq	05-02-2007,10°Ta	06-16-2007,11°CaRx
03-19-2007,00°Pi	05-03-2007,12°Ta	06-17-2007,11°CaRx
03-20-2007,01°Pi	05-04-2007,14°Ta	06-18-2007,11°CaRx
03-21-2007,02°Pi	05-05-2007,16°Ta	06-19-2007,11°CaRx
03-22-2007,03°Pi	05-06-2007,18°Ta	06-20-2007,10°CaRx
03-23-2007,04°Pi	05-07-2007,21°Ta	06-21-2007,10°CaRx
03-24-2007,05°Pi	05-08-2007,23°Ta	06-22-2007,10°CaRx
03-25-2007,06°Pi	05-09-2007,25°Ta	06-23-2007,09°CaRx
03-26-2007,07°Pi	05-10-2007,27°Ta	06-24-2007,09°CaRx
03-27-2007,09°Pi	05-11-2007,29°Ta	06-25-2007,08°CaRx
03-28-2007,10°Pi	05-12-2007,01°Ge	06-26-2007,08°CaRx
03-29-2007,11°Pi	05-13-2007,03°Ge	06-27-2007,07°CaRx
03-30-2007,12°Pi	05-14-2007,05°Ge	06-28-2007,07°CaRx
03-31-2007,14°Pi	05-15-2007,07°Ge	06-29-2007,06°CaRx
04-01-2007,15°Pi	05-16-2007,09°Ge	06-30-2007,05°CaRx
04-02-2007,16°Pi	05-17-2007,11°Ge	07-01-2007,05°CaRx
04-03-2007,18°Pi	05-18-2007,13°Ge	07-02-2007,04°CaRx
04-04-2007,19°Pi	05-19-2007,15°Ge	07-03-2007,04°CaRx
04-05-2007,21°Pi	05-20-2007,16°Ge	07-04-2007,03°CaRx
04-06-2007,22°Pi	05-21-2007,18°Ge	07-05-2007,03°CaRx
04-07-2007,24°Pi	05-22-2007,20°Ge	07-06-2007,03°CaRx
04-08-2007,25°Pi	05-23-2007,21°Ge	07-07-2007,02°CaRx
04-09-2007,27°Pi	05-24-2007,23°Ge	07-08-2007,02°CaRx
04-10-2007,28°Pi	05-25-2007,24°Ge	07-09-2007,02°CaRx
04-11-2007,00°Ar	05-26-2007,26°Ge	07-10-2007,02°Ca

07-11-2007,02°Ca	08-25-2007,10°Vi	10-09-2007,08°Sc
07-12-2007,02°Ca	08-26-2007,12°Vi	10-10-2007,08°Sc
07-13-2007,02°Ca	08-27-2007,14°Vi	10-11-2007,09°Sc
07-14-2007,03°Ca	08-28-2007,16°Vi	10-12-2007,09°ScRx
07-15-2007,03°Ca	08-29-2007,17°Vi	10-13-2007,09°ScRx
07-16-2007,04°Ca	08-30-2007,19°Vi	10-14-2007,08°ScRx
07-17-2007,04°Ca	08-31-2007,21°Vi	10-15-2007,08°ScRx
07-18-2007,05°Ca	09-01-2007,22°Vi	10-16-2007,08°ScRx
07-19-2007,06°Ca	09-02-2007,24°Vi	10-17-2007,07°ScRx
07-20-2007,06°Ca	09-03-2007,26°Vi	10-18-2007,06°ScRx
07-21-2007,07°Ca	09-04-2007,27°Vi	10-19-2007,05°ScRx
07-22-2007,08°Ca	09-05-2007,29°Vi	10-20-2007,04°ScRx
07-23-2007,10°Ca	09-06-2007,01°Li	10-21-2007,03°ScRx
07-24-2007,11°Ca	09-07-2007,02°Li	10-22-2007,02°ScRx
07-25-2007,12°Ca	09-08-2007,04°Li	10-23-2007,01°ScRx
07-26-2007,13°Ca	09-09-2007,05°Li	10-24-2007,29°LiRx
07-27-2007,15°Ca	09-10-2007,07°Li	10-25-2007,28°LiRx
07-28-2007,16°Ca	09-11-2007,08°Li	10-26-2007,27°LiRx
07-29-2007,18°Ca	09-12-2007,10°Li	10-27-2007,26°LiRx
07-30-2007,19°Ca	09-13-2007,11°Li	10-28-2007,25°LiRx
07-31-2007,21°Ca	09-14-2007,13°Li	10-29-2007,24°LiRx
08-01-2007,23°Ca	09-15-2007,14°Li	10-30-2007,24°LiRx
08-02-2007,25°Ca	09-16-2007,15°Li	10-31-2007,23°LiRx
08-03-2007,27°Ca	09-17-2007,17°Li	11-01-2007,23°LiRx
08-04-2007,29°Ca	09-18-2007,18°Li	11-02-2007,23°Li
08-05-2007,00°Le	09-19-2007,19°Li	11-03-2007,23°Li
08-06-2007,02°Le	09-20-2007,21°Li	11-04-2007,23°Li
08-07-2007,04°Le	09-21-2007,22°Li	11-05-2007,24°Li
08-08-2007,06°Le	09-22-2007,23°Li	11-06-2007,24°Li
08-09-2007,09°Le	09-23-2007,24°Li	11-07-2007,25°Li
08-10-2007,11°Le	09-24-2007,26°Li	11-08-2007,26°Li
08-11-2007,13°Le	09-25-2007,27°Li	11-09-2007,27°Li
08-12-2007,15°Le	09-26-2007,28°Li	11-10-2007,28°Li
08-13-2007,17°Le	09-27-2007,29°Li	11-11-2007,29°Li
08-14-2007,19°Le	09-28-2007,00°Sc	11-12-2007,01°Sc
08-15-2007,21°Le	09-29-2007,01°Sc	11-13-2007,02°Sc
08-16-2007,23°Le	09-30-2007,02°Sc	11-14-2007,03°Sc
08-17-2007,25°Le	10-01-2007,03°Sc	11-15-2007,05°Sc
08-18-2007,27°Le	10-02-2007,04°Sc	11-16-2007,06°Sc
08-19-2007,29°Le	10-03-2007,05°Sc	11-17-2007,07°Sc
08-20-2007,01°Vi	10-04-2007,05°Sc	11-18-2007,09°Sc
08-21-2007,03°Vi	10-05-2007,06°Sc	11-19-2007,10°Sc
08-22-2007,05°Vi	10-06-2007,07°Sc	11-20-2007,12°Sc
08-23-2007,07°Vi	10-07-2007,07°Sc	11-21-2007,13°Sc
08-24-2007,08°Vi	10-08-2007,08°Sc	11-22-2007,15°Sc

11-23-2007,17°Sc
11-24-2007,18°Sc
11-25-2007,20°Sc
11-26-2007,21°Sc
11-27-2007,23°Sc
11-28-2007,24°Sc
11-29-2007,26°Sc
11-30-2007,27°Sc
12-01-2007,29°Sc
12-02-2007,01°Sg
12-03-2007,02°Sg
12-04-2007,04°Sg
12-05-2007,05°Sg

12-06-2007,07°Sg
12-07-2007,08°Sg
12-08-2007,10°Sg
12-09-2007,12°Sg
12-10-2007,13°Sg
12-11-2007,15°Sg
12-12-2007,16°Sg
12-13-2007,18°Sg
12-14-2007,19°Sg
12-15-2007,21°Sg
12-16-2007,23°Sg
12-17-2007,24°Sg
12-18-2007,26°Sg

12-19-2007,27°Sg
12-20-2007,29°Sg
12-21-2007,00°Cap
12-22-2007,02°Cap
12-23-2007,04°Cap
12-24-2007,05°Cap
12-25-2007,07°Cap
12-26-2007,08°Cap
12-27-2007,10°Cap
12-28-2007,12°Cap
12-29-2007,13°Cap
12-30-2007,15°Cap
12-31-2007,16°Cap

♀
Venus Ephemeris
2003–2007

2003
01-01-2003,23°Sc
01-02-2003,24°Sc
01-03-2003,25°Sc
01-04-2003,26°Sc
01-05-2003,27°Sc
01-06-2003,28°Sc
01-07-2003,29°Sc
01-08-2003,00°Sg
01-09-2003,01°Sg
01-10-2003,02°Sg
01-11-2003,03°Sg
01-12-2003,04°Sg
01-13-2003,05°Sg
01-14-2003,06°Sg
01-15-2003,07°Sg
01-16-2003,08°Sg
01-17-2003,09°Sg
01-18-2003,10°Sg
01-19-2003,12°Sg
01-20-2003,13°Sg
01-21-2003,14°Sg
01-22-2003,15°Sg
01-23-2003,16°Sg
01-24-2003,17°Sg

01-25-2003,18°Sg
01-26-2003,19°Sg
01-27-2003,20°Sg
01-28-2003,21°Sg
01-29-2003,22°Sg
01-30-2003,24°Sg
01-31-2003,25°Sg
02-01-2003,26°Sg
02-02-2003,27°Sg
02-03-2003,28°Sg
02-04-2003,29°Sg
02-05-2003,00°Cap
02-06-2003,01°Cap
02-07-2003,03°Cap
02-08-2003,04°Cap
02-09-2003,05°Cap
02-10-2003,06°Cap
02-11-2003,07°Cap
02-12-2003,08°Cap
02-13-2003,09°Cap
02-14-2003,10°Cap
02-15-2003,12°Cap
02-16-2003,13°Cap
02-17-2003,14°Cap
02-18-2003,15°Cap

02-19-2003,16°Cap
02-20-2003,17°Cap
02-21-2003,19°Cap
02-22-2003,20°Cap
02-23-2003,21°Cap
02-24-2003,22°Cap
02-25-2003,23°Cap
02-26-2003,24°Cap
02-27-2003,26°Cap
02-28-2003,27°Cap
03-01-2003,28°Cap
03-02-2003,29°Cap
03-03-2003,00°Aq
03-04-2003,01°Aq
03-05-2003,03°Aq
03-06-2003,04°Aq
03-07-2003,05°Aq
03-08-2003,06°Aq
03-09-2003,07°Aq
03-10-2003,09°Aq
03-11-2003,10°Aq
03-12-2003,11°Aq
03-13-2003,12°Aq
03-14-2003,13°Aq
03-15-2003,15°Aq

03-16-2003,16°Aq	04-30-2003,10°Ar	06-14-2003,04°Ge
03-17-2003,17°Aq	05-01-2003,11°Ar	06-15-2003,06°Ge
03-18-2003,18°Aq	05-02-2003,12°Ar	06-16-2003,07°Ge
03-19-2003,19°Aq	05-03-2003,13°Ar	06-17-2003,08°Ge
03-20-2003,20°Aq	05-04-2003,15°Ar	06-18-2003,09°Ge
03-21-2003,22°Aq	05-05-2003,16°Ar	06-19-2003,11°Ge
03-22-2003,23°Aq	05-06-2003,17°Ar	06-20-2003,12°Ge
03-23-2003,24°Aq	05-07-2003,18°Ar	06-21-2003,13°Ge
03-24-2003,25°Aq	05-08-2003,20°Ar	06-22-2003,14°Ge
03-25-2003,26°Aq	05-09-2003,21°Ar	06-23-2003,15°Ge
03-26-2003,28°Aq	05-10-2003,22°Ar	06-24-2003,17°Ge
03-27-2003,29°Aq	05-11-2003,23°Ar	06-25-2003,18°Ge
03-28-2003,00°Pi	05-12-2003,24°Ar	06-26-2003,19°Ge
03-29-2003,01°Pi	05-13-2003,26°Ar	06-27-2003,20°Ge
03-30-2003,02°Pi	05-14-2003,27°Ar	06-28-2003,22°Ge
03-31-2003,04°Pi	05-15-2003,28°Ar	06-29-2003,23°Ge
04-01-2003,05°Pi	05-16-2003,29°Ar	06-30-2003,24°Ge
04-02-2003,06°Pi	05-17-2003,00°Ta	07-01-2003,25°Ge
04-03-2003,07°Pi	05-18-2003,02°Ta	07-02-2003,26°Ge
04-04-2003,08°Pi	05-19-2003,03°Ta	07-03-2003,28°Ge
04-05-2003,10°Pi	05-20-2003,04°Ta	07-04-2003,29°Ge
04-06-2003,11°Pi	05-21-2003,05°Ta	07-05-2003,00°Ca
04-07-2003,12°Pi	05-22-2003,06°Ta	07-06-2003,01°Ca
04-08-2003,13°Pi	05-23-2003,08°Ta	07-07-2003,03°Ca
04-09-2003,14°Pi	05-24-2003,09°Ta	07-08-2003,04°Ca
04-10-2003,16°Pi	05-25-2003,10°Ta	07-09-2003,05°Ca
04-11-2003,17°Pi	05-26-2003,11°Ta	07-10-2003,06°Ca
04-12-2003,18°Pi	05-27-2003,13°Ta	07-11-2003,07°Ca
04-13-2003,19°Pi	05-28-2003,14°Ta	07-12-2003,09°Ca
04-14-2003,20°Pi	05-29-2003,15°Ta	07-13-2003,10°Ca
04-15-2003,22°Pi	05-30-2003,16°Ta	07-14-2003,11°Ca
04-16-2003,23°Pi	05-31-2003,17°Ta	07-15-2003,12°Ca
04-17-2003,24°Pi	06-01-2003,19°Ta	07-16-2003,14°Ca
04-18-2003,25°Pi	06-02-2003,20°Ta	07-17-2003,15°Ca
04-19-2003,27°Pi	06-03-2003,21°Ta	07-18-2003,16°Ca
04-20-2003,28°Pi	06-04-2003,22°Ta	07-19-2003,17°Ca
04-21-2003,29°Pi	06-05-2003,23°Ta	07-20-2003,18°Ca
04-22-2003,00°Ar	06-06-2003,25°Ta	07-21-2003,20°Ca
04-23-2003,01°Ar	06-07-2003,26°Ta	07-22-2003,21°Ca
04-24-2003,03°Ar	06-08-2003,27°Ta	07-23-2003,22°Ca
04-25-2003,04°Ar	06-09-2003,28°Ta	07-24-2003,23°Ca
04-26-2003,05°Ar	06-10-2003,00°Ge	07-25-2003,25°Ca
04-27-2003,06°Ar	06-11-2003,01°Ge	07-26-2003,26°Ca
04-28-2003,07°Ar	06-12-2003,02°Ge	07-27-2003,27°Ca
04-29-2003,09°Ar	06-13-2003,03°Ge	07-28-2003,28°Ca

07-29-2003,00°Le	09-12-2003,25°Vi	10-27-2003,21°Sc
07-30-2003,01°Le	09-13-2003,26°Vi	10-28-2003,22°Sc
07-31-2003,02°Le	09-14-2003,28°Vi	10-29-2003,24°Sc
08-01-2003,03°Le	09-15-2003,29°Vi	10-30-2003,25°Sc
08-02-2003,04°Le	09-16-2003,00°Li	10-31-2003,26°Sc
08-03-2003,06°Le	09-17-2003,01°Li	11-01-2003,27°Sc
08-04-2003,07°Le	09-18-2003,03°Li	11-02-2003,29°Sc
08-05-2003,08°Le	09-19-2003,04°Li	11-03-2003,00°Sg
08-06-2003,09°Le	09-20-2003,05°Li	11-04-2003,01°Sg
08-07-2003,11°Le	09-21-2003,06°Li	11-05-2003,02°Sg
08-08-2003,12°Le	09-22-2003,08°Li	11-06-2003,04°Sg
08-09-2003,13°Le	09-23-2003,09°Li	11-07-2003,05°Sg
08-10-2003,14°Le	09-24-2003,10°Li	11-08-2003,06°Sg
08-11-2003,16°Le	09-25-2003,11°Li	11-09-2003,07°Sg
08-12-2003,17°Le	09-26-2003,13°Li	11-10-2003,09°Sg
08-13-2003,18°Le	09-27-2003,14°Li	11-11-2003,10°Sg
08-14-2003,19°Le	09-28-2003,15°Li	11-12-2003,11°Sg
08-15-2003,21°Le	09-29-2003,16°Li	11-13-2003,12°Sg
08-16-2003,22°Le	09-30-2003,18°Li	11-14-2003,14°Sg
08-17-2003,23°Le	10-01-2003,19°Li	11-15-2003,15°Sg
08-18-2003,24°Le	10-02-2003,20°Li	11-16-2003,16°Sg
08-19-2003,25°Le	10-03-2003,21°Li	11-17-2003,17°Sg
08-20-2003,27°Le	10-04-2003,23°Li	11-18-2003,19°Sg
08-21-2003,28°Le	10-05-2003,24°Li	11-19-2003,20°Sg
08-22-2003,29°Le	10-06-2003,25°Li	11-20-2003,21°Sg
08-23-2003,00°Vi	10-07-2003,26°Li	11-21-2003,22°Sg
08-24-2003,02°Vi	10-08-2003,28°Li	11-22-2003,23°Sg
08-25-2003,03°Vi	10-09-2003,29°Li	11-23-2003,25°Sg
08-26-2003,04°Vi	10-10-2003,00°Sc	11-24-2003,26°Sg
08-27-2003,05°Vi	10-11-2003,01°Sc	11-25-2003,27°Sg
08-28-2003,07°Vi	10-12-2003,03°Sc	11-26-2003,28°Sg
08-29-2003,08°Vi	10-13-2003,04°Sc	11-27-2003,00°Cap
08-30-2003,09°Vi	10-14-2003,05°Sc	11-28-2003,01°Cap
08-31-2003,10°Vi	10-15-2003,06°Sc	11-29-2003,02°Cap
09-01-2003,12°Vi	10-16-2003,07°Sc	11-30-2003,03°Cap
09-02-2003,13°Vi	10-17-2003,09°Sc	12-01-2003,05°Cap
09-03-2003,14°Vi	10-18-2003,10°Sc	12-02-2003,06°Cap
09-04-2003,15°Vi	10-19-2003,11°Sc	12-03-2003,07°Cap
09-05-2003,17°Vi	10-20-2003,12°Sc	12-04-2003,08°Cap
09-06-2003,18°Vi	10-21-2003,14°Sc	12-05-2003,10°Cap
09-07-2003,19°Vi	10-22-2003,15°Sc	12-06-2003,11°Cap
09-08-2003,20°Vi	10-23-2003,16°Sc	12-07-2003,12°Cap
09-09-2003,21°Vi	10-24-2003,17°Sc	12-08-2003,13°Cap
09-10-2003,23°Vi	10-25-2003,19°Sc	12-09-2003,15°Cap
09-11-2003,24°Vi	10-26-2003,20°Sc	12-10-2003,16°Cap

12-11-2003,17°Cap	01-23-2004,10°Pi	03-08-2004,02°Ta
12-12-2003,18°Cap	01-24-2004,11°Pi	03-09-2004,03°Ta
12-13-2003,20°Cap	01-25-2004,12°Pi	03-10-2004,04°Ta
12-14-2003,21°Cap	01-26-2004,13°Pi	03-11-2004,06°Ta
12-15-2003,22°Cap	01-27-2004,15°Pi	03-12-2004,07°Ta
12-16-2003,23°Cap	01-28-2004,16°Pi	03-13-2004,08°Ta
12-17-2003,24°Cap	01-29-2004,17°Pi	03-14-2004,09°Ta
12-18-2003,26°Cap	01-30-2004,18°Pi	03-15-2004,10°Ta
12-19-2003,27°Cap	01-31-2004,19°Pi	03-16-2004,11°Ta
12-20-2003,28°Cap	02-01-2004,21°Pi	03-17-2004,12°Ta
12-21-2003,29°Cap	02-02-2004,22°Pi	03-18-2004,13°Ta
12-22-2003,01°Aq	02-03-2004,23°Pi	03-19-2004,14°Ta
12-23-2003,02°Aq	02-04-2004,24°Pi	03-20-2004,15°Ta
12-24-2003,03°Aq	02-05-2004,25°Pi	03-21-2004,16°Ta
12-25-2003,04°Aq	02-06-2004,27°Pi	03-22-2004,17°Ta
12-26-2003,06°Aq	02-07-2004,28°Pi	03-23-2004,18°Ta
12-27-2003,07°Aq	02-08-2004,29°Pi	03-24-2004,19°Ta
12-28-2003,08°Aq	02-09-2004,00°Ar	03-25-2004,20°Ta
12-29-2003,09°Aq	02-10-2004,01°Ar	03-26-2004,21°Ta
12-30-2003,11°Aq	02-11-2004,02°Ar	03-27-2004,22°Ta
12-31-2003,12°Aq	02-12-2004,04°Ar	03-28-2004,23°Ta
	02-13-2004,05°Ar	03-29-2004,24°Ta
2004	02-14-2004,06°Ar	03-30-2004,25°Ta
01-01-2004,13°Aq	02-15-2004,07°Ar	03-31-2004,26°Ta
01-02-2004,14°Aq	02-16-2004,08°Ar	04-01-2004,27°Ta
01-03-2004,15°Aq	02-17-2004,10°Ar	04-02-2004,28°Ta
01-04-2004,17°Aq	02-18-2004,11°Ar	04-03-2004,29°Ta
01-05-2004,18°Aq	02-19-2004,12°Ar	04-04-2004,00°Ge
01-06-2004,19°Aq	02-20-2004,13°Ar	04-05-2004,01°Ge
01-07-2004,20°Aq	02-21-2004,14°Ar	04-06-2004,02°Ge
01-08-2004,22°Aq	02-22-2004,15°Ar	04-07-2004,03°Ge
01-09-2004,23°Aq	02-23-2004,16°Ar	04-08-2004,04°Ge
01-10-2004,24°Aq	02-24-2004,18°Ar	04-09-2004,05°Ge
01-11-2004,25°Aq	02-25-2004,19°Ar	04-10-2004,06°Ge
01-12-2004,26°Aq	02-26-2004,20°Ar	04-11-2004,06°Ge
01-13-2004,28°Aq	02-27-2004,21°Ar	04-12-2004,07°Ge
01-14-2004,29°Aq	02-28-2004,22°Ar	04-13-2004,08°Ge
01-15-2004,00°Pi	02-29-2004,23°Ar	04-14-2004,09°Ge
01-16-2004,01°Pi	03-01-2004,24°Ar	04-15-2004,10°Ge
01-17-2004,03°Pi	03-02-2004,26°Ar	04-16-2004,11°Ge
01-18-2004,04°Pi	03-03-2004,27°Ar	04-17-2004,11°Ge
01-19-2004,05°Pi	03-04-2004,28°Ar	04-18-2004,12°Ge
01-20-2004,06°Pi	03-05-2004,29°Ar	04-19-2004,13°Ge
01-21-2004,07°Pi	03-06-2004,00°Ta	04-20-2004,14°Ge
01-22-2004,09°Pi	03-07-2004,01°Ta	04-21-2004,14°Ge

04-22-2004,15°Ge	06-06-2004,19°GeRx	07-21-2004,16°Ge
04-23-2004,16°Ge	06-07-2004,18°GeRx	07-22-2004,17°Ge
04-24-2004,17°Ge	06-08-2004,17°GeRx	07-23-2004,18°Ge
04-25-2004,17°Ge	06-09-2004,17°GeRx	07-24-2004,18°Ge
04-26-2004,18°Ge	06-10-2004,16°GeRx	07-25-2004,19°Ge
04-27-2004,19°Ge	06-11-2004,16°GeRx	07-26-2004,20°Ge
04-28-2004,19°Ge	06-12-2004,15°GeRx	07-27-2004,21°Ge
04-29-2004,20°Ge	06-13-2004,14°GeRx	07-28-2004,21°Ge
04-30-2004,20°Ge	06-14-2004,14°GeRx	07-29-2004,22°Ge
05-01-2004,21°Ge	06-15-2004,13°GeRx	07-30-2004,23°Ge
05-02-2004,21°Ge	06-16-2004,13°GeRx	07-31-2004,24°Ge
05-03-2004,22°Ge	06-17-2004,12°GeRx	08-01-2004,24°Ge
05-04-2004,22°Ge	06-18-2004,12°GeRx	08-02-2004,25°Ge
05-05-2004,23°Ge	06-19-2004,11°GeRx	08-03-2004,26°Ge
05-06-2004,23°Ge	06-20-2004,11°GeRx	08-04-2004,27°Ge
05-07-2004,24°Ge	06-21-2004,11°GeRx	08-05-2004,28°Ge
05-08-2004,24°Ge	06-22-2004,10°GeRx	08-06-2004,28°Ge
05-09-2004,24°Ge	06-23-2004,10°GeRx	08-07-2004,29°Ge
05-10-2004,25°Ge	06-24-2004,10°GeRx	08-08-2004,00°Ca
05-11-2004,25°Ge	06-25-2004,10°GeRx	08-09-2004,01°Ca
05-12-2004,25°Ge	06-26-2004,09°GeRx	08-10-2004,02°Ca
05-13-2004,25°Ge	06-27-2004,09°GeRx	08-11-2004,03°Ca
05-14-2004,25°Ge	06-28-2004,09°GeRx	08-12-2004,04°Ca
05-15-2004,26°Ge	06-29-2004,09°GeRx	08-13-2004,05°Ca
05-16-2004,26°Ge	06-30-2004,09°Ge	08-14-2004,06°Ca
05-17-2004,26°Ge	07-01-2004,09°Ge	08-15-2004,07°Ca
05-18-2004,26°GeRx	07-02-2004,09°Ge	08-16-2004,07°Ca
05-19-2004,26°GeRx	07-03-2004,09°Ge	08-17-2004,08°Ca
05-20-2004,26°GeRx	07-04-2004,09°Ge	08-18-2004,09°Ca
05-21-2004,25°GeRx	07-05-2004,10°Ge	08-19-2004,10°Ca
05-22-2004,25°GeRx	07-06-2004,10°Ge	08-20-2004,11°Ca
05-23-2004,25°GeRx	07-07-2004,10°Ge	08-21-2004,12°Ca
05-24-2004,25°GeRx	07-08-2004,10°Ge	08-22-2004,13°Ca
05-25-2004,25°GeRx	07-09-2004,11°Ge	08-23-2004,14°Ca
05-26-2004,24°GeRx	07-10-2004,11°Ge	08-24-2004,15°Ca
05-27-2004,24°GeRx	07-11-2004,11°Ge	08-25-2004,16°Ca
05-28-2004,24°GeRx	07-12-2004,12°Ge	08-26-2004,17°Ca
05-29-2004,23°GeRx	07-13-2004,12°Ge	08-27-2004,18°Ca
05-30-2004,23°GeRx	07-14-2004,13°Ge	08-28-2004,19°Ca
05-31-2004,22°GeRx	07-15-2004,13°Ge	08-29-2004,20°Ca
06-01-2004,22°GeRx	07-16-2004,14°Ge	08-30-2004,21°Ca
06-02-2004,21°GeRx	07-17-2004,14°Ge	08-31-2004,22°Ca
06-03-2004,21°GeRx	07-18-2004,15°Ge	09-01-2004,23°Ca
06-04-2004,20°GeRx	07-19-2004,15°Ge	09-02-2004,24°Ca
06-05-2004,19°GeRx	07-20-2004,16°Ge	09-03-2004,26°Ca

09-04-2004,27°Ca	10-19-2004,18°Vi	12-03-2004,13°Sc
09-05-2004,28°Ca	10-20-2004,19°Vi	12-04-2004,14°Sc
09-06-2004,29°Ca	10-21-2004,20°Vi	12-05-2004,15°Sc
09-07-2004,00°Le	10-22-2004,21°Vi	12-06-2004,16°Sc
09-08-2004,01°Le	10-23-2004,23°Vi	12-07-2004,18°Sc
09-09-2004,02°Le	10-24-2004,24°Vi	12-08-2004,19°Sc
09-10-2004,03°Le	10-25-2004,25°Vi	12-09-2004,20°Sc
09-11-2004,04°Le	10-26-2004,26°Vi	12-10-2004,21°Sc
09-12-2004,05°Le	10-27-2004,27°Vi	12-11-2004,23°Sc
09-13-2004,06°Le	10-28-2004,29°Vi	12-12-2004,24°Sc
09-14-2004,07°Le	10-29-2004,00°Li	12-13-2004,25°Sc
09-15-2004,09°Le	10-30-2004,01°Li	12-14-2004,26°Sc
09-16-2004,10°Le	10-31-2004,02°Li	12-15-2004,28°Sc
09-17-2004,11°Le	11-01-2004,03°Li	12-16-2004,29°Sc
09-18-2004,12°Le	11-02-2004,05°Li	12-17-2004,00°Sg
09-19-2004,13°Le	11-03-2004,06°Li	12-18-2004,01°Sg
09-20-2004,14°Le	11-04-2004,07°Li	12-19-2004,03°Sg
09-21-2004,15°Le	11-05-2004,08°Li	12-20-2004,04°Sg
09-22-2004,16°Le	11-06-2004,09°Li	12-21-2004,05°Sg
09-23-2004,17°Le	11-07-2004,11°Li	12-22-2004,06°Sg
09-24-2004,19°Le	11-08-2004,12°Li	12-23-2004,08°Sg
09-25-2004,20°Le	11-09-2004,13°Li	12-24-2004,09°Sg
09-26-2004,21°Le	11-10-2004,14°Li	12-25-2004,10°Sg
09-27-2004,22°Le	11-11-2004,16°Li	12-26-2004,11°Sg
09-28-2004,23°Le	11-12-2004,17°Li	12-27-2004,13°Sg
09-29-2004,24°Le	11-13-2004,18°Li	12-28-2004,14°Sg
09-30-2004,25°Le	11-14-2004,19°Li	12-29-2004,15°Sg
10-01-2004,27°Le	11-15-2004,20°Li	12-30-2004,16°Sg
10-02-2004,28°Le	11-16-2004,22°Li	12-31-2004,18°Sg
10-03-2004,29°Le	11-17-2004,23°Li	
10-04-2004,00°Vi	11-18-2004,24°Li	**2005**
10-05-2004,01°Vi	11-19-2004,25°Li	01-01-2005,19°Sg
10-06-2004,02°Vi	11-20-2004,27°Li	01-02-2005,20°Sg
10-07-2004,04°Vi	11-21-2004,28°Li	01-03-2005,21°Sg
10-08-2004,05°Vi	11-22-2004,29°Li	01-04-2005,23°Sg
10-09-2004,06°Vi	11-23-2004,00°Sc	01-05-2005,24°Sg
10-10-2004,07°Vi	11-24-2004,02°Sc	01-06-2005,25°Sg
10-11-2004,08°Vi	11-25-2004,03°Sc	01-07-2005,26°Sg
10-12-2004,09°Vi	11-26-2004,04°Sc	01-08-2005,28°Sg
10-13-2004,11°Vi	11-27-2004,05°Sc	01-09-2005,29°Sg
10-14-2004,12°Vi	11-28-2004,06°Sc	01-10-2005,00°Cap
10-15-2004,13°Vi	11-29-2004,08°Sc	01-11-2005,01°Cap
10-16-2004,14°Vi	11-30-2004,09°Sc	01-12-2005,03°Cap
10-17-2004,15°Vi	12-01-2004,10°Sc	01-13-2005,04°Cap
10-18-2004,17°Vi	12-02-2004,11°Sc	01-14-2005,05°Cap

01-15-2005,06°Cap	03-01-2005,03°Pi	04-15-2005,29°Ar
01-16-2005,08°Cap	03-02-2005,04°Pi	04-16-2005,00°Ta
01-17-2005,09°Cap	03-03-2005,05°Pi	04-17-2005,01°Ta
01-18-2005,10°Cap	03-04-2005,06°Pi	04-18-2005,02°Ta
01-19-2005,11°Cap	03-05-2005,08°Pi	04-19-2005,04°Ta
01-20-2005,13°Cap	03-06-2005,09°Pi	04-20-2005,05°Ta
01-21-2005,14°Cap	03-07-2005,10°Pi	04-21-2005,06°Ta
01-22-2005,15°Cap	03-08-2005,11°Pi	04-22-2005,07°Ta
01-23-2005,16°Cap	03-09-2005,13°Pi	04-23-2005,09°Ta
01-24-2005,18°Cap	03-10-2005,14°Pi	04-24-2005,10°Ta
01-25-2005,19°Cap	03-11-2005,15°Pi	04-25-2005,11°Ta
01-26-2005,20°Cap	03-12-2005,16°Pi	04-26-2005,12°Ta
01-27-2005,21°Cap	03-13-2005,18°Pi	04-27-2005,14°Ta
01-28-2005,23°Cap	03-14-2005,19°Pi	04-28-2005,15°Ta
01-29-2005,24°Cap	03-15-2005,20°Pi	04-29-2005,16°Ta
01-30-2005,25°Cap	03-16-2005,21°Pi	04-30-2005,17°Ta
01-31-2005,26°Cap	03-17-2005,23°Pi	05-01-2005,18°Ta
02-01-2005,28°Cap	03-18-2005,24°Pi	05-02-2005,20°Ta
02-02-2005,29°Cap	03-19-2005,25°Pi	05-03-2005,21°Ta
02-03-2005,00°Aq	03-20-2005,26°Pi	05-04-2005,22°Ta
02-04-2005,01°Aq	03-21-2005,28°Pi	05-05-2005,23°Ta
02-05-2005,03°Aq	03-22-2005,29°Pi	05-06-2005,25°Ta
02-06-2005,04°Aq	03-23-2005,00°Ar	05-07-2005,26°Ta
02-07-2005,05°Aq	03-24-2005,01°Ar	05-08-2005,27°Ta
02-08-2005,06°Aq	03-25-2005,03°Ar	05-09-2005,28°Ta
02-09-2005,08°Aq	03-26-2005,04°Ar	05-10-2005,00°Ge
02-10-2005,09°Aq	03-27-2005,05°Ar	05-11-2005,01°Ge
02-11-2005,10°Aq	03-28-2005,06°Ar	05-12-2005,02°Ge
02-12-2005,11°Aq	03-29-2005,08°Ar	05-13-2005,03°Ge
02-13-2005,13°Aq	03-30-2005,09°Ar	05-14-2005,04°Ge
02-14-2005,14°Aq	03-31-2005,10°Ar	05-15-2005,06°Ge
02-15-2005,15°Aq	04-01-2005,11°Ar	05-16-2005,07°Ge
02-16-2005,16°Aq	04-02-2005,13°Ar	05-17-2005,08°Ge
02-17-2005,18°Aq	04-03-2005,14°Ar	05-18-2005,09°Ge
02-18-2005,19°Aq	04-04-2005,15°Ar	05-19-2005,11°Ge
02-19-2005,20°Aq	04-05-2005,16°Ar	05-20-2005,12°Ge
02-20-2005,21°Aq	04-06-2005,18°Ar	05-21-2005,13°Ge
02-21-2005,23°Aq	04-07-2005,19°Ar	05-22-2005,14°Ge
02-22-2005,24°Aq	04-08-2005,20°Ar	05-23-2005,16°Ge
02-23-2005,25°Aq	04-09-2005,21°Ar	05-24-2005,17°Ge
02-24-2005,26°Aq	04-10-2005,23°Ar	05-25-2005,18°Ge
02-25-2005,28°Aq	04-11-2005,24°Ar	05-26-2005,19°Ge
02-26-2005,29°Aq	04-12-2005,25°Ar	05-27-2005,20°Ge
02-27-2005,00°Pi	04-13-2005,26°Ar	05-28-2005,22°Ge
02-28-2005,01°Pi	04-14-2005,27°Ar	05-29-2005,23°Ge

05-30-2005,24°Ge	07-14-2005,19°Le	08-28-2005,13°Li
05-31-2005,25°Ge	07-15-2005,20°Le	08-29-2005,14°Li
06-01-2005,27°Ge	07-16-2005,21°Le	08-30-2005,15°Li
06-02-2005,28°Ge	07-17-2005,22°Le	08-31-2005,16°Li
06-03-2005,29°Ge	07-18-2005,24°Le	09-01-2005,17°Li
06-04-2005,00°Ca	07-19-2005,25°Le	09-02-2005,18°Li
06-05-2005,01°Ca	07-20-2005,26°Le	09-03-2005,20°Li
06-06-2005,03°Ca	07-21-2005,27°Le	09-04-2005,21°Li
06-07-2005,04°Ca	07-22-2005,29°Le	09-05-2005,22°Li
06-08-2005,05°Ca	07-23-2005,00°Vi	09-06-2005,23°Li
06-09-2005,06°Ca	07-24-2005,01°Vi	09-07-2005,24°Li
06-10-2005,08°Ca	07-25-2005,02°Vi	09-08-2005,25°Li
06-11-2005,09°Ca	07-26-2005,03°Vi	09-09-2005,27°Li
06-12-2005,10°Ca	07-27-2005,05°Vi	09-10-2005,28°Li
06-13-2005,11°Ca	07-28-2005,06°Vi	09-11-2005,29°Li
06-14-2005,12°Ca	07-29-2005,07°Vi	09-12-2005,00°Sc
06-15-2005,14°Ca	07-30-2005,08°Vi	09-13-2005,01°Sc
06-16-2005,15°Ca	07-31-2005,09°Vi	09-14-2005,02°Sc
06-17-2005,16°Ca	08-01-2005,11°Vi	09-15-2005,04°Sc
06-18-2005,17°Ca	08-02-2005,12°Vi	09-16-2005,05°Sc
06-19-2005,19°Ca	08-03-2005,13°Vi	09-17-2005,06°Sc
06-20-2005,20°Ca	08-04-2005,14°Vi	09-18-2005,07°Sc
06-21-2005,21°Ca	08-05-2005,15°Vi	09-19-2005,08°Sc
06-22-2005,22°Ca	08-06-2005,17°Vi	09-20-2005,09°Sc
06-23-2005,23°Ca	08-07-2005,18°Vi	09-21-2005,10°Sc
06-24-2005,25°Ca	08-08-2005,19°Vi	09-22-2005,12°Sc
06-25-2005,26°Ca	08-09-2005,20°Vi	09-23-2005,13°Sc
06-26-2005,27°Ca	08-10-2005,21°Vi	09-24-2005,14°Sc
06-27-2005,28°Ca	08-11-2005,22°Vi	09-25-2005,15°Sc
06-28-2005,29°Ca	08-12-2005,24°Vi	09-26-2005,16°Sc
06-29-2005,01°Le	08-13-2005,25°Vi	09-27-2005,17°Sc
06-30-2005,02°Le	08-14-2005,26°Vi	09-28-2005,18°Sc
07-01-2005,03°Le	08-15-2005,27°Vi	09-29-2005,20°Sc
07-02-2005,04°Le	08-16-2005,28°Vi	09-30-2005,21°Sc
07-03-2005,06°Le	08-17-2005,00°Li	10-01-2005,22°Sc
07-04-2005,07°Le	08-18-2005,01°Li	10-02-2005,23°Sc
07-05-2005,08°Le	08-19-2005,02°Li	10-03-2005,24°Sc
07-06-2005,09°Le	08-20-2005,03°Li	10-04-2005,25°Sc
07-07-2005,10°Le	08-21-2005,04°Li	10-05-2005,26°Sc
07-08-2005,12°Le	08-22-2005,06°Li	10-06-2005,27°Sc
07-09-2005,13°Le	08-23-2005,07°Li	10-07-2005,29°Sc
07-10-2005,14°Le	08-24-2005,08°Li	10-08-2005,00°Sg
07-11-2005,15°Le	08-25-2005,09°Li	10-09-2005,01°Sg
07-12-2005,16°Le	08-26-2005,10°Li	10-10-2005,02°Sg
07-13-2005,18°Le	08-27-2005,11°Li	10-11-2005,03°Sg

10-12-2005,04°Sg
10-13-2005,05°Sg
10-14-2005,06°Sg
10-15-2005,07°Sg
10-16-2005,08°Sg
10-17-2005,10°Sg
10-18-2005,11°Sg
10-19-2005,12°Sg
10-20-2005,13°Sg
10-21-2005,14°Sg
10-22-2005,15°Sg
10-23-2005,16°Sg
10-24-2005,17°Sg
10-25-2005,18°Sg
10-26-2005,19°Sg
10-27-2005,20°Sg
10-28-2005,21°Sg
10-29-2005,22°Sg
10-30-2005,23°Sg
10-31-2005,24°Sg
11-01-2005,25°Sg
11-02-2005,26°Sg
11-03-2005,27°Sg
11-04-2005,28°Sg
11-05-2005,29°Sg
11-06-2005,00°Cap
11-07-2005,01°Cap
11-08-2005,02°Cap
11-09-2005,03°Cap
11-10-2005,04°Cap
11-11-2005,05°Cap
11-12-2005,06°Cap
11-13-2005,07°Cap
11-14-2005,08°Cap
11-15-2005,09°Cap
11-16-2005,10°Cap
11-17-2005,11°Cap
11-18-2005,12°Cap
11-19-2005,12°Cap
11-20-2005,13°Cap
11-21-2005,14°Cap
11-22-2005,15°Cap
11-23-2005,16°Cap
11-24-2005,17°Cap
11-25-2005,17°Cap

11-26-2005,18°Cap
11-27-2005,19°Cap
11-28-2005,20°Cap
11-29-2005,20°Cap
11-30-2005,21°Cap
12-01-2005,22°Cap
12-02-2005,23°Cap
12-03-2005,23°Cap
12-04-2005,24°Cap
12-05-2005,25°Cap
12-06-2005,25°Cap
12-07-2005,26°Cap
12-08-2005,26°Cap
12-09-2005,27°Cap
12-10-2005,27°Cap
12-11-2005,28°Cap
12-12-2005,28°Cap
12-13-2005,29°Cap
12-14-2005,29°Cap
12-15-2005,29°Cap
12-16-2005,00°Aq
12-17-2005,00°Aq
12-18-2005,00°Aq
12-19-2005,00°Aq
12-20-2005,01°Aq
12-21-2005,01°Aq
12-22-2005,01°Aq
12-23-2005,01°Aq
12-24-2005,01°Aq
12-25-2005,01°AqRx
12-26-2005,01°AqRx
12-27-2005,01°AqRx
12-28-2005,01°AqRx
12-29-2005,00°AqRx
12-30-2005,00°AqRx
12-31-2005,00°AqRx

2006
01-01-2006,00°AqRx
01-02-2006,29°CapRx
01-03-2006,29°CapRx
01-04-2006,29°CapRx
01-05-2006,28°CapRx
01-06-2006,28°CapRx
01-07-2006,27°CapRx

01-08-2006,27°CapRx
01-09-2006,26°CapRx
01-10-2006,25°CapRx
01-11-2006,25°CapRx
01-12-2006,24°CapRx
01-13-2006,24°CapRx
01-14-2006,23°CapRx
01-15-2006,22°CapRx
01-16-2006,22°CapRx
01-17-2006,21°CapRx
01-18-2006,21°CapRx
01-19-2006,20°CapRx
01-20-2006,20°CapRx
01-21-2006,19°CapRx
01-22-2006,19°CapRx
01-23-2006,18°CapRx
01-24-2006,18°CapRx
01-25-2006,17°CapRx
01-26-2006,17°CapRx
01-27-2006,17°CapRx
01-28-2006,16°CapRx
01-29-2006,16°CapRx
01-30-2006,16°CapRx
01-31-2006,16°CapRx
02-01-2006,16°CapRx
02-02-2006,16°CapRx
02-03-2006,16°CapRx
02-04-2006,16°Cap
02-05-2006,16°Cap
02-06-2006,16°Cap
02-07-2006,16°Cap
02-08-2006,16°Cap
02-09-2006,16°Cap
02-10-2006,16°Cap
02-11-2006,17°Cap
02-12-2006,17°Cap
02-13-2006,17°Cap
02-14-2006,18°Cap
02-15-2006,18°Cap
02-16-2006,19°Cap
02-17-2006,19°Cap
02-18-2006,19°Cap
02-19-2006,20°Cap
02-20-2006,21°Cap
02-21-2006,21°Cap

02-22-2006,22°Cap	04-07-2006,01°Pi	05-21-2006,20°Ar
02-23-2006,22°Cap	04-08-2006,02°Pi	05-22-2006,21°Ar
02-24-2006,23°Cap	04-09-2006,03°Pi	05-23-2006,22°Ar
02-25-2006,24°Cap	04-10-2006,04°Pi	05-24-2006,23°Ar
02-26-2006,24°Cap	04-11-2006,05°Pi	05-25-2006,24°Ar
02-27-2006,25°Cap	04-12-2006,06°Pi	05-26-2006,26°Ar
02-28-2006,26°Cap	04-13-2006,07°Pi	05-27-2006,27°Ar
03-01-2006,26°Cap	04-14-2006,08°Pi	05-28-2006,28°Ar
03-02-2006,27°Cap	04-15-2006,09°Pi	05-29-2006,29°Ar
03-03-2006,28°Cap	04-16-2006,10°Pi	05-30-2006,00°Ta
03-04-2006,29°Cap	04-17-2006,11°Pi	05-31-2006,01°Ta
03-05-2006,29°Cap	04-18-2006,13°Pi	06-01-2006,03°Ta
03-06-2006,00°Aq	04-19-2006,14°Pi	06-02-2006,04°Ta
03-07-2006,01°Aq	04-20-2006,15°Pi	06-03-2006,05°Ta
03-08-2006,02°Aq	04-21-2006,16°Pi	06-04-2006,06°Ta
03-09-2006,03°Aq	04-22-2006,17°Pi	06-05-2006,07°Ta
03-10-2006,04°Aq	04-23-2006,18°Pi	06-06-2006,08°Ta
03-11-2006,04°Aq	04-24-2006,19°Pi	06-07-2006,10°Ta
03-12-2006,05°Aq	04-25-2006,20°Pi	06-08-2006,11°Ta
03-13-2006,06°Aq	04-26-2006,21°Pi	06-09-2006,12°Ta
03-14-2006,07°Aq	04-27-2006,23°Pi	06-10-2006,13°Ta
03-15-2006,08°Aq	04-28-2006,24°Pi	06-11-2006,14°Ta
03-16-2006,09°Aq	04-29-2006,25°Pi	06-12-2006,16°Ta
03-17-2006,10°Aq	04-30-2006,26°Pi	06-13-2006,17°Ta
03-18-2006,11°Aq	05-01-2006,27°Pi	06-14-2006,18°Ta
03-19-2006,12°Aq	05-02-2006,28°Pi	06-15-2006,19°Ta
03-20-2006,13°Aq	05-03-2006,29°Pi	06-16-2006,20°Ta
03-21-2006,14°Aq	05-04-2006,00°Ar	06-17-2006,21°Ta
03-22-2006,14°Aq	05-05-2006,02°Ar	06-18-2006,23°Ta
03-23-2006,15°Aq	05-06-2006,03°Ar	06-19-2006,24°Ta
03-24-2006,16°Aq	05-07-2006,04°Ar	06-20-2006,25°Ta
03-25-2006,17°Aq	05-08-2006,05°Ar	06-21-2006,26°Ta
03-26-2006,18°Aq	05-09-2006,06°Ar	06-22-2006,27°Ta
03-27-2006,19°Aq	05-10-2006,07°Ar	06-23-2006,29°Ta
03-28-2006,20°Aq	05-11-2006,08°Ar	06-24-2006,00°Ge
03-29-2006,21°Aq	05-12-2006,09°Ar	06-25-2006,01°Ge
03-30-2006,22°Aq	05-13-2006,11°Ar	06-26-2006,02°Ge
03-31-2006,23°Aq	05-14-2006,12°Ar	06-27-2006,03°Ge
04-01-2006,24°Aq	05-15-2006,13°Ar	06-28-2006,04°Ge
04-02-2006,26°Aq	05-16-2006,14°Ar	06-29-2006,06°Ge
04-03-2006,27°Aq	05-17-2006,15°Ar	06-30-2006,07°Ge
04-04-2006,28°Aq	05-18-2006,16°Ar	07-01-2006,08°Ge
04-05-2006,29°Aq	05-19-2006,18°Ar	07-02-2006,09°Ge
04-06-2006,00°Pi	05-20-2006,19°Ar	07-03-2006,10°Ge

07-04-2006,12°Ge	08-17-2006,05°Le	09-30-2006,29°Vi
07-05-2006,13°Ge	08-18-2006,06°Le	10-01-2006,00°Li
07-06-2006,14°Ge	08-19-2006,07°Le	10-02-2006,02°Li
07-07-2006,15°Ge	08-20-2006,09°Le	10-03-2006,03°Li
07-08-2006,16°Ge	08-21-2006,10°Le	10-04-2006,04°Li
07-09-2006,18°Ge	08-22-2006,11°Le	10-05-2006,05°Li
07-10-2006,19°Ge	08-23-2006,12°Le	10-06-2006,07°Li
07-11-2006,20°Ge	08-24-2006,13°Le	10-07-2006,08°Li
07-12-2006,21°Ge	08-25-2006,15°Le	10-08-2006,09°Li
07-13-2006,22°Ge	08-26-2006,16°Le	10-09-2006,10°Li
07-14-2006,24°Ge	08-27-2006,17°Le	10-10-2006,12°Li
07-15-2006,25°Ge	08-28-2006,18°Le	10-11-2006,13°Li
07-16-2006,26°Ge	08-29-2006,20°Le	10-12-2006,14°Li
07-17-2006,27°Ge	08-30-2006,21°Le	10-13-2006,15°Li
07-18-2006,28°Ge	08-31-2006,22°Le	10-14-2006,17°Li
07-19-2006,00°Ca	09-01-2006,23°Le	10-15-2006,18°Li
07-20-2006,01°Ca	09-02-2006,25°Le	10-16-2006,19°Li
07-21-2006,02°Ca	09-03-2006,26°Le	10-17-2006,20°Li
07-22-2006,03°Ca	09-04-2006,27°Le	10-18-2006,22°Li
07-23-2006,04°Ca	09-05-2006,28°Le	10-19-2006,23°Li
07-24-2006,06°Ca	09-06-2006,29°Le	10-20-2006,24°Li
07-25-2006,07°Ca	09-07-2006,01°Vi	10-21-2006,25°Li
07-26-2006,08°Ca	09-08-2006,02°Vi	10-22-2006,27°Li
07-27-2006,09°Ca	09-09-2006,03°Vi	10-23-2006,28°Li
07-28-2006,10°Ca	09-10-2006,04°Vi	10-24-2006,29°Li
07-29-2006,12°Ca	09-11-2006,06°Vi	10-25-2006,01°Sc
07-30-2006,13°Ca	09-12-2006,07°Vi	10-26-2006,02°Sc
07-31-2006,14°Ca	09-13-2006,08°Vi	10-27-2006,03°Sc
08-01-2006,15°Ca	09-14-2006,09°Vi	10-28-2006,04°Sc
08-02-2006,17°Ca	09-15-2006,11°Vi	10-29-2006,06°Sc
08-03-2006,18°Ca	09-16-2006,12°Vi	10-30-2006,07°Sc
08-04-2006,19°Ca	09-17-2006,13°Vi	10-31-2006,08°Sc
08-05-2006,20°Ca	09-18-2006,14°Vi	11-01-2006,09°Sc
08-06-2006,21°Ca	09-19-2006,16°Vi	11-02-2006,11°Sc
08-07-2006,23°Ca	09-20-2006,17°Vi	11-03-2006,12°Sc
08-08-2006,24°Ca	09-21-2006,18°Vi	11-04-2006,13°Sc
08-09-2006,25°Ca	09-22-2006,19°Vi	11-05-2006,14°Sc
08-10-2006,26°Ca	09-23-2006,21°Vi	11-06-2006,16°Sc
08-11-2006,28°Ca	09-24-2006,22°Vi	11-07-2006,17°Sc
08-12-2006,29°Ca	09-25-2006,23°Vi	11-08-2006,18°Sc
08-13-2006,00°Le	09-26-2006,24°Vi	11-09-2006,19°Sc
08-14-2006,01°Le	09-27-2006,26°Vi	11-10-2006,21°Sc
08-15-2006,02°Le	09-28-2006,27°Vi	11-11-2006,22°Sc
08-16-2006,04°Le	09-29-2006,28°Vi	11-12-2006,23°Sc

11-13-2006,24°Sc	12-28-2006,21°Cap	02-09-2007,14°Pi
11-14-2006,26°Sc	12-29-2006,22°Cap	02-10-2007,16°Pi
11-15-2006,27°Sc	12-30-2006,23°Cap	02-11-2007,17°Pi
11-16-2006,28°Sc	12-31-2006,25°Cap	02-12-2007,18°Pi
11-17-2006,29°Sc		02-13-2007,19°Pi
11-18-2006,01°Sg	**2007**	02-14-2007,21°Pi
11-19-2006,02°Sg	01-01-2007,26°Cap	02-15-2007,22°Pi
11-20-2006,03°Sg	01-02-2007,27°Cap	02-16-2007,23°Pi
11-21-2006,04°Sg	01-03-2007,28°Cap	02-17-2007,24°Pi
11-22-2006,06°Sg	01-04-2007,00°Aq	02-18-2007,26°Pi
11-23-2006,07°Sg	01-05-2007,01°Aq	02-19-2007,27°Pi
11-24-2006,08°Sg	01-06-2007,02°Aq	02-20-2007,28°Pi
11-25-2006,09°Sg	01-07-2007,03°Aq	02-21-2007,29°Pi
11-26-2006,11°Sg	01-08-2007,05°Aq	02-22-2007,01°Ar
11-27-2006,12°Sg	01-09-2007,06°Aq	02-23-2007,02°Ar
11-28-2006,13°Sg	01-10-2007,07°Aq	02-24-2007,03°Ar
11-29-2006,14°Sg	01-11-2007,08°Aq	02-25-2007,04°Ar
11-30-2006,16°Sg	01-12-2007,10°Aq	02-26-2007,05°Ar
12-01-2006,17°Sg	01-13-2007,11°Aq	02-27-2007,07°Ar
12-02-2006,18°Sg	01-14-2007,12°Aq	02-28-2007,08°Ar
12-03-2006,19°Sg	01-15-2007,13°Aq	03-01-2007,09°Ar
12-04-2006,21°Sg	01-16-2007,15°Aq	03-02-2007,10°Ar
12-05-2006,22°Sg	01-17-2007,16°Aq	03-03-2007,12°Ar
12-06-2006,23°Sg	01-18-2007,17°Aq	03-04-2007,13°Ar
12-07-2006,24°Sg	01-19-2007,18°Aq	03-05-2007,14°Ar
12-08-2006,26°Sg	01-20-2007,20°Aq	03-06-2007,15°Ar
12-09-2006,27°Sg	01-21-2007,21°Aq	03-07-2007,17°Ar
12-10-2006,28°Sg	01-22-2007,22°Aq	03-08-2007,18°Ar
12-11-2006,29°Sg	01-23-2007,23°Aq	03-09-2007,19°Ar
12-12-2006,01°Cap	01-24-2007,25°Aq	03-10-2007,20°Ar
12-13-2006,02°Cap	01-25-2007,26°Aq	03-11-2007,21°Ar
12-14-2006,03°Cap	01-26-2007,27°Aq	03-12-2007,23°Ar
12-15-2006,04°Cap	01-27-2007,28°Aq	03-13-2007,24°Ar
12-16-2006,06°Cap	01-28-2007,00°Pi	03-14-2007,25°Ar
12-17-2006,07°Cap	01-29-2007,01°Pi	03-15-2007,26°Ar
12-18-2006,08°Cap	01-30-2007,02°Pi	03-16-2007,27°Ar
12-19-2006,10°Cap	01-31-2007,03°Pi	03-17-2007,29°Ar
12-20-2006,11°Cap	02-01-2007,05°Pi	03-18-2007,00°Ta
12-21-2006,12°Cap	02-02-2007,06°Pi	03-19-2007,01°Ta
12-22-2006,13°Cap	02-03-2007,07°Pi	03-20-2007,02°Ta
12-23-2006,15°Cap	02-04-2007,08°Pi	03-21-2007,03°Ta
12-24-2006,16°Cap	02-05-2007,10°Pi	03-22-2007,05°Ta
12-25-2006,17°Cap	02-06-2007,11°Pi	03-23-2007,06°Ta
12-26-2006,18°Cap	02-07-2007,12°Pi	03-24-2007,07°Ta
12-27-2006,20°Cap	02-08-2007,13°Pi	03-25-2007,08°Ta

03-26-2007,09°Ta
03-27-2007,11°Ta
03-28-2007,12°Ta
03-29-2007,13°Ta
03-30-2007,14°Ta
03-31-2007,15°Ta
04-01-2007,17°Ta
04-02-2007,18°Ta
04-03-2007,19°Ta
04-04-2007,20°Ta
04-05-2007,21°Ta
04-06-2007,23°Ta
04-07-2007,24°Ta
04-08-2007,25°Ta
04-09-2007,26°Ta
04-10-2007,27°Ta
04-11-2007,28°Ta
04-12-2007,00°Ge
04-13-2007,01°Ge
04-14-2007,02°Ge
04-15-2007,03°Ge
04-16-2007,04°Ge
04-17-2007,05°Ge
04-18-2007,07°Ge
04-19-2007,08°Ge
04-20-2007,09°Ge
04-21-2007,10°Ge
04-22-2007,11°Ge
04-23-2007,12°Ge
04-24-2007,14°Ge
04-25-2007,15°Ge
04-26-2007,16°Ge
04-27-2007,17°Ge
04-28-2007,18°Ge
04-29-2007,19°Ge
04-30-2007,20°Ge
05-01-2007,22°Ge
05-02-2007,23°Ge
05-03-2007,24°Ge
05-04-2007,25°Ge
05-05-2007,26°Ge
05-06-2007,27°Ge
05-07-2007,28°Ge
05-08-2007,29°Ge
05-09-2007,01°Ca

05-10-2007,02°Ca
05-11-2007,03°Ca
05-12-2007,04°Ca
05-13-2007,05°Ca
05-14-2007,06°Ca
05-15-2007,07°Ca
05-16-2007,08°Ca
05-17-2007,09°Ca
05-18-2007,10°Ca
05-19-2007,11°Ca
05-20-2007,12°Ca
05-21-2007,14°Ca
05-22-2007,15°Ca
05-23-2007,16°Ca
05-24-2007,17°Ca
05-25-2007,18°Ca
05-26-2007,19°Ca
05-27-2007,20°Ca
05-28-2007,21°Ca
05-29-2007,22°Ca
05-30-2007,23°Ca
05-31-2007,24°Ca
06-01-2007,25°Ca
06-02-2007,26°Ca
06-03-2007,27°Ca
06-04-2007,28°Ca
06-05-2007,29°Ca
06-06-2007,00°Le
06-07-2007,01°Le
06-08-2007,02°Le
06-09-2007,03°Le
06-10-2007,04°Le
06-11-2007,05°Le
06-12-2007,06°Le
06-13-2007,07°Le
06-14-2007,08°Le
06-15-2007,08°Le
06-16-2007,09°Le
06-17-2007,10°Le
06-18-2007,11°Le
06-19-2007,12°Le
06-20-2007,13°Le
06-21-2007,14°Le
06-22-2007,15°Le
06-23-2007,15°Le

06-24-2007,16°Le
06-25-2007,17°Le
06-26-2007,18°Le
06-27-2007,19°Le
06-28-2007,19°Le
06-29-2007,20°Le
06-30-2007,21°Le
07-01-2007,22°Le
07-02-2007,22°Le
07-03-2007,23°Le
07-04-2007,24°Le
07-05-2007,24°Le
07-06-2007,25°Le
07-07-2007,26°Le
07-08-2007,26°Le
07-09-2007,27°Le
07-10-2007,27°Le
07-11-2007,28°Le
07-12-2007,28°Le
07-13-2007,29°Le
07-14-2007,29°Le
07-15-2007,00°Vi
07-16-2007,00°Vi
07-17-2007,00°Vi
07-18-2007,01°Vi
07-19-2007,01°Vi
07-20-2007,01°Vi
07-21-2007,02°Vi
07-22-2007,02°Vi
07-23-2007,02°Vi
07-24-2007,02°Vi
07-25-2007,02°Vi
07-26-2007,02°Vi
07-27-2007,02°Vi
07-28-2007,02°ViRx
07-29-2007,02°ViRx
07-30-2007,02°ViRx
07-31-2007,02°ViRx
08-01-2007,02°ViRx
08-02-2007,02°ViRx
08-03-2007,02°ViRx
08-04-2007,01°ViRx
08-05-2007,01°ViRx
08-06-2007,01°ViRx
08-07-2007,00°ViRx

08-08-2007,00°ViRx	08-24-2007,21°LeRx	09-09-2007,16°Le
08-09-2007,29°LeRx	08-25-2007,20°LeRx	09-10-2007,16°Le
08-10-2007,29°LeRx	08-26-2007,20°LeRx	09-11-2007,16°Le
08-11-2007,28°LeRx	08-27-2007,19°LeRx	09-12-2007,16°Le
08-12-2007,28°LeRx	08-28-2007,19°LeRx	09-13-2007,16°Le
08-13-2007,27°LeRx	08-29-2007,18°LeRx	09-14-2007,17°Le
08-14-2007,27°LeRx	08-30-2007,18°LeRx	09-15-2007,17°Le
08-15-2007,26°LeRx	08-31-2007,18°LeRx	09-16-2007,17°Le
08-16-2007,26°LeRx	09-01-2007,17°LeRx	09-17-2007,17°Le
08-17-2007,25°LeRx	09-02-2007,17°LeRx	09-18-2007,18°Le
08-18-2007,24°LeRx	09-03-2007,17°LeRx	09-19-2007,18°Le
08-19-2007,24°LeRx	09-04-2007,16°LeRx	09-20-2007,18°Le
08-20-2007,23°LeRx	09-05-2007,16°LeRx	09-21-2007,19°Le
08-21-2007,22°LeRx	09-06-2007,16°LeRx	09-22-2007,19°Le
08-22-2007,22°LeRx	09-07-2007,16°LeRx	
08-23-2007,21°LeRx	09-08-2007,16°LeRx	

♂
Mars Ephemeris
2003–2007

2003	01-22-2003,03°Sg	02-13-2003,17°Sg
01-01-2003,19°Sc	01-23-2003,03°Sg	02-14-2003,18°Sg
01-02-2003,20°Sc	01-24-2003,04°Sg	02-15-2003,18°Sg
01-03-2003,21°Sc	01-25-2003,05°Sg	02-16-2003,19°Sg
01-04-2003,21°Sc	01-26-2003,05°Sg	02-17-2003,19°Sg
01-05-2003,22°Sc	01-27-2003,06°Sg	02-18-2003,20°Sg
01-06-2003,22°Sc	01-28-2003,07°Sg	02-19-2003,21°Sg
01-07-2003,23°Sc	01-29-2003,07°Sg	02-20-2003,21°Sg
01-08-2003,24°Sc	01-30-2003,08°Sg	02-21-2003,22°Sg
01-09-2003,24°Sc	01-31-2003,09°Sg	02-22-2003,23°Sg
01-10-2003,25°Sc	02-01-2003,09°Sg	02-23-2003,23°Sg
01-11-2003,26°Sc	02-02-2003,10°Sg	02-24-2003,24°Sg
01-12-2003,26°Sc	02-03-2003,10°Sg	02-25-2003,25°Sg
01-13-2003,27°Sc	02-04-2003,11°Sg	02-26-2003,25°Sg
01-14-2003,28°Sc	02-05-2003,12°Sg	02-27-2003,26°Sg
01-15-2003,28°Sc	02-06-2003,12°Sg	02-28-2003,27°Sg
01-16-2003,29°Sc	02-07-2003,13°Sg	03-01-2003,27°Sg
01-17-2003,00°Sg	02-08-2003,14°Sg	03-02-2003,28°Sg
01-18-2003,00°Sg	02-09-2003,14°Sg	03-03-2003,28°Sg
01-19-2003,01°Sg	02-10-2003,15°Sg	03-04-2003,29°Sg
01-20-2003,01°Sg	02-11-2003,16°Sg	03-05-2003,00°Cap
01-21-2003,02°Sg	02-12-2003,16°Sg	03-06-2003,00°Cap

03-07-2003,01°Cap	04-21-2003,29°Cap	06-05-2003,24°Aq
03-08-2003,02°Cap	04-22-2003,00°Aq	06-06-2003,25°Aq
03-09-2003,02°Cap	04-23-2003,00°Aq	06-07-2003,25°Aq
03-10-2003,03°Cap	04-24-2003,01°Aq	06-08-2003,26°Aq
03-11-2003,04°Cap	04-25-2003,01°Aq	06-09-2003,26°Aq
03-12-2003,04°Cap	04-26-2003,02°Aq	06-10-2003,26°Aq
03-13-2003,05°Cap	04-27-2003,03°Aq	06-11-2003,27°Aq
03-14-2003,05°Cap	04-28-2003,03°Aq	06-12-2003,27°Aq
03-15-2003,06°Cap	04-29-2003,04°Aq	06-13-2003,28°Aq
03-16-2003,07°Cap	04-30-2003,04°Aq	06-14-2003,28°Aq
03-17-2003,07°Cap	05-01-2003,05°Aq	06-15-2003,29°Aq
03-18-2003,08°Cap	05-02-2003,06°Aq	06-16-2003,29°Aq
03-19-2003,09°Cap	05-03-2003,06°Aq	06-17-2003,00°Pi
03-20-2003,09°Cap	05-04-2003,07°Aq	06-18-2003,00°Pi
03-21-2003,10°Cap	05-05-2003,07°Aq	06-19-2003,00°Pi
03-22-2003,10°Cap	05-06-2003,08°Aq	06-20-2003,01°Pi
03-23-2003,11°Cap	05-07-2003,08°Aq	06-21-2003,01°Pi
03-24-2003,12°Cap	05-08-2003,09°Aq	06-22-2003,02°Pi
03-25-2003,12°Cap	05-09-2003,10°Aq	06-23-2003,02°Pi
03-26-2003,13°Cap	05-10-2003,10°Aq	06-24-2003,02°Pi
03-27-2003,14°Cap	05-11-2003,11°Aq	06-25-2003,03°Pi
03-28-2003,14°Cap	05-12-2003,11°Aq	06-26-2003,03°Pi
03-29-2003,15°Cap	05-13-2003,12°Aq	06-27-2003,03°Pi
03-30-2003,16°Cap	05-14-2003,12°Aq	06-28-2003,04°Pi
03-31-2003,16°Cap	05-15-2003,13°Aq	06-29-2003,04°Pi
04-01-2003,17°Cap	05-16-2003,14°Aq	06-30-2003,04°Pi
04-02-2003,17°Cap	05-17-2003,14°Aq	07-01-2003,05°Pi
04-03-2003,18°Cap	05-18-2003,15°Aq	07-02-2003,05°Pi
04-04-2003,19°Cap	05-19-2003,15°Aq	07-03-2003,05°Pi
04-05-2003,19°Cap	05-20-2003,16°Aq	07-04-2003,06°Pi
04-06-2003,20°Cap	05-21-2003,16°Aq	07-05-2003,06°Pi
04-07-2003,20°Cap	05-22-2003,17°Aq	07-06-2003,06°Pi
04-08-2003,21°Cap	05-23-2003,17°Aq	07-07-2003,07°Pi
04-09-2003,22°Cap	05-24-2003,18°Aq	07-08-2003,07°Pi
04-10-2003,22°Cap	05-25-2003,18°Aq	07-09-2003,07°Pi
04-11-2003,23°Cap	05-26-2003,19°Aq	07-10-2003,07°Pi
04-12-2003,24°Cap	05-27-2003,20°Aq	07-11-2003,08°Pi
04-13-2003,24°Cap	05-28-2003,20°Aq	07-12-2003,08°Pi
04-14-2003,25°Cap	05-29-2003,21°Aq	07-13-2003,08°Pi
04-15-2003,25°Cap	05-30-2003,21°Aq	07-14-2003,08°Pi
04-16-2003,26°Cap	05-31-2003,22°Aq	07-15-2003,08°Pi
04-17-2003,27°Cap	06-01-2003,22°Aq	07-16-2003,09°Pi
04-18-2003,27°Cap	06-02-2003,23°Aq	07-17-2003,09°Pi
04-19-2003,28°Cap	06-03-2003,23°Aq	07-18-2003,09°Pi
04-20-2003,28°Cap	06-04-2003,24°Aq	07-19-2003,09°Pi

07-20-2003,09°Pi	09-03-2003,03°PiRx	10-18-2003,02°Pi
07-21-2003,09°Pi	09-04-2003,03°PiRx	10-19-2003,03°Pi
07-22-2003,09°Pi	09-05-2003,03°PiRx	10-20-2003,03°Pi
07-23-2003,09°Pi	09-06-2003,02°PiRx	10-21-2003,03°Pi
07-24-2003,09°Pi	09-07-2003,02°PiRx	10-22-2003,04°Pi
07-25-2003,10°Pi	09-08-2003,02°PiRx	10-23-2003,04°Pi
07-26-2003,10°Pi	09-09-2003,02°PiRx	10-24-2003,04°Pi
07-27-2003,10°Pi	09-10-2003,01°PiRx	10-25-2003,04°Pi
07-28-2003,10°Pi	09-11-2003,01°PiRx	10-26-2003,05°Pi
07-29-2003,10°Pi	09-12-2003,01°PiRx	10-27-2003,05°Pi
07-30-2003,10°PiRx	09-13-2003,01°PiRx	10-28-2003,05°Pi
07-31-2003,10°PiRx	09-14-2003,01°PiRx	10-29-2003,06°Pi
08-01-2003,10°PiRx	09-15-2003,01°PiRx	10-30-2003,06°Pi
08-02-2003,10°PiRx	09-16-2003,00°PiRx	10-31-2003,07°Pi
08-03-2003,09°PiRx	09-17-2003,00°PiRx	11-01-2003,07°Pi
08-04-2003,09°PiRx	09-18-2003,00°PiRx	11-02-2003,07°Pi
08-05-2003,09°PiRx	09-19-2003,00°PiRx	11-03-2003,08°Pi
08-06-2003,09°PiRx	09-20-2003,00°PiRx	11-04-2003,08°Pi
08-07-2003,09°PiRx	09-21-2003,00°PiRx	11-05-2003,08°Pi
08-08-2003,09°PiRx	09-22-2003,00°PiRx	11-06-2003,09°Pi
08-09-2003,09°PiRx	09-23-2003,00°PiRx	11-07-2003,09°Pi
08-10-2003,09°PiRx	09-24-2003,00°PiRx	11-08-2003,10°Pi
08-11-2003,09°PiRx	09-25-2003,00°PiRx	11-09-2003,10°Pi
08-12-2003,08°PiRx	09-26-2003,00°PiRx	11-10-2003,11°Pi
08-13-2003,08°PiRx	09-27-2003,00°PiRx	11-11-2003,11°Pi
08-14-2003,08°PiRx	09-28-2003,00°Pi	11-12-2003,11°Pi
08-15-2003,08°PiRx	09-29-2003,00°Pi	11-13-2003,12°Pi
08-16-2003,08°PiRx	09-30-2003,00°Pi	11-14-2003,12°Pi
08-17-2003,07°PiRx	10-01-2003,00°Pi	11-15-2003,13°Pi
08-18-2003,07°PiRx	10-02-2003,00°Pi	11-16-2003,13°Pi
08-19-2003,07°PiRx	10-03-2003,00°Pi	11-17-2003,14°Pi
08-20-2003,07°PiRx	10-04-2003,00°Pi	11-18-2003,14°Pi
08-21-2003,06°PiRx	10-05-2003,00°Pi	11-19-2003,15°Pi
08-22-2003,06°PiRx	10-06-2003,00°Pi	11-20-2003,15°Pi
08-23-2003,06°PiRx	10-07-2003,00°Pi	11-21-2003,16°Pi
08-24-2003,06°PiRx	10-08-2003,00°Pi	11-22-2003,16°Pi
08-25-2003,05°PiRx	10-09-2003,01°Pi	11-23-2003,17°Pi
08-26-2003,05°PiRx	10-10-2003,01°Pi	11-24-2003,17°Pi
08-27-2003,05°PiRx	10-11-2003,01°Pi	11-25-2003,18°Pi
08-28-2003,05°PiRx	10-12-2003,01°Pi	11-26-2003,18°Pi
08-29-2003,04°PiRx	10-13-2003,01°Pi	11-27-2003,19°Pi
08-30-2003,04°PiRx	10-14-2003,01°Pi	11-28-2003,19°Pi
08-31-2003,04°PiRx	10-15-2003,02°Pi	11-29-2003,20°Pi
09-01-2003,04°PiRx	10-16-2003,02°Pi	11-30-2003,20°Pi
09-02-2003,03°PiRx	10-17-2003,02°Pi	12-01-2003,21°Pi

12-02-2003,21°Pi

12-03-2003,22°Pi

12-04-2003,23°Pi

12-05-2003,23°Pi

12-06-2003,24°Pi

12-07-2003,24°Pi

12-08-2003,25°Pi

12-09-2003,25°Pi

12-10-2003,26°Pi

12-11-2003,26°Pi

12-12-2003,27°Pi

12-13-2003,28°Pi

12-14-2003,28°Pi

12-15-2003,29°Pi

12-16-2003,29°Pi

12-17-2003,00°Ar

12-18-2003,00°Ar

12-19-2003,01°Ar

12-20-2003,02°Ar

12-21-2003,02°Ar

12-22-2003,03°Ar

12-23-2003,03°Ar

12-24-2003,04°Ar

12-25-2003,05°Ar

12-26-2003,05°Ar

12-27-2003,06°Ar

12-28-2003,06°Ar

12-29-2003,07°Ar

12-30-2003,08°Ar

12-31-2003,08°Ar

2004

01-01-2004,09°Ar

01-02-2004,09°Ar

01-03-2004,10°Ar

01-04-2004,11°Ar

01-05-2004,11°Ar

01-06-2004,12°Ar

01-07-2004,12°Ar

01-08-2004,13°Ar

01-09-2004,14°Ar

01-10-2004,14°Ar

01-11-2004,15°Ar

01-12-2004,16°Ar

01-13-2004,16°Ar

01-14-2004,17°Ar

01-15-2004,17°Ar

01-16-2004,18°Ar

01-17-2004,19°Ar

01-18-2004,19°Ar

01-19-2004,20°Ar

01-20-2004,21°Ar

01-21-2004,21°Ar

01-22-2004,22°Ar

01-23-2004,22°Ar

01-24-2004,23°Ar

01-25-2004,24°Ar

01-26-2004,24°Ar

01-27-2004,25°Ar

01-28-2004,26°Ar

01-29-2004,26°Ar

01-30-2004,27°Ar

01-31-2004,27°Ar

02-01-2004,28°Ar

02-02-2004,29°Ar

02-03-2004,29°Ar

02-04-2004,00°Ta

02-05-2004,01°Ta

02-06-2004,01°Ta

02-07-2004,02°Ta

02-08-2004,03°Ta

02-09-2004,03°Ta

02-10-2004,04°Ta

02-11-2004,04°Ta

02-12-2004,05°Ta

02-13-2004,06°Ta

02-14-2004,06°Ta

02-15-2004,07°Ta

02-16-2004,08°Ta

02-17-2004,08°Ta

02-18-2004,09°Ta

02-19-2004,10°Ta

02-20-2004,10°Ta

02-21-2004,11°Ta

02-22-2004,11°Ta

02-23-2004,12°Ta

02-24-2004,13°Ta

02-25-2004,13°Ta

02-26-2004,14°Ta

02-27-2004,15°Ta

02-28-2004,15°Ta

02-29-2004,16°Ta

03-01-2004,17°Ta

03-02-2004,17°Ta

03-03-2004,18°Ta

03-04-2004,19°Ta

03-05-2004,19°Ta

03-06-2004,20°Ta

03-07-2004,20°Ta

03-08-2004,21°Ta

03-09-2004,22°Ta

03-10-2004,22°Ta

03-11-2004,23°Ta

03-12-2004,24°Ta

03-13-2004,24°Ta

03-14-2004,25°Ta

03-15-2004,26°Ta

03-16-2004,26°Ta

03-17-2004,27°Ta

03-18-2004,28°Ta

03-19-2004,28°Ta

03-20-2004,29°Ta

03-21-2004,29°Ta

03-22-2004,00°Ge

03-23-2004,01°Ge

03-24-2004,01°Ge

03-25-2004,02°Ge

03-26-2004,03°Ge

03-27-2004,03°Ge

03-28-2004,04°Ge

03-29-2004,05°Ge

03-30-2004,05°Ge

03-31-2004,06°Ge

04-01-2004,06°Ge

04-02-2004,07°Ge

04-03-2004,08°Ge

04-04-2004,08°Ge

04-05-2004,09°Ge

04-06-2004,10°Ge

04-07-2004,10°Ge

04-08-2004,11°Ge

04-09-2004,12°Ge

04-10-2004,12°Ge

04-11-2004,13°Ge

04-12-2004,14°Ge

04-13-2004,14°Ge	05-28-2004,13°Ca	07-12-2004,11°Le
04-14-2004,15°Ge	05-29-2004,13°Ca	07-13-2004,12°Le
04-15-2004,15°Ge	05-30-2004,14°Ca	07-14-2004,12°Le
04-16-2004,16°Ge	05-31-2004,15°Ca	07-15-2004,13°Le
04-17-2004,17°Ge	06-01-2004,15°Ca	07-16-2004,14°Le
04-18-2004,17°Ge	06-02-2004,16°Ca	07-17-2004,14°Le
04-19-2004,18°Ge	06-03-2004,16°Ca	07-18-2004,15°Le
04-20-2004,19°Ge	06-04-2004,17°Ca	07-19-2004,15°Le
04-21-2004,19°Ge	06-05-2004,18°Ca	07-20-2004,16°Le
04-22-2004,20°Ge	06-06-2004,18°Ca	07-21-2004,17°Le
04-23-2004,21°Ge	06-07-2004,19°Ca	07-22-2004,17°Le
04-24-2004,21°Ge	06-08-2004,20°Ca	07-23-2004,18°Le
04-25-2004,22°Ge	06-09-2004,20°Ca	07-24-2004,19°Le
04-26-2004,22°Ge	06-10-2004,21°Ca	07-25-2004,19°Le
04-27-2004,23°Ge	06-11-2004,22°Ca	07-26-2004,20°Le
04-28-2004,24°Ge	06-12-2004,22°Ca	07-27-2004,21°Le
04-29-2004,24°Ge	06-13-2004,23°Ca	07-28-2004,21°Le
04-30-2004,25°Ge	06-14-2004,23°Ca	07-29-2004,22°Le
05-01-2004,26°Ge	06-15-2004,24°Ca	07-30-2004,22°Le
05-02-2004,26°Ge	06-16-2004,25°Ca	07-31-2004,23°Le
05-03-2004,27°Ge	06-17-2004,25°Ca	08-01-2004,24°Le
05-04-2004,28°Ge	06-18-2004,26°Ca	08-02-2004,24°Le
05-05-2004,28°Ge	06-19-2004,27°Ca	08-03-2004,25°Le
05-06-2004,29°Ge	06-20-2004,27°Ca	08-04-2004,26°Le
05-07-2004,29°Ge	06-21-2004,28°Ca	08-05-2004,26°Le
05-08-2004,00°Ca	06-22-2004,28°Ca	08-06-2004,27°Le
05-09-2004,01°Ca	06-23-2004,29°Ca	08-07-2004,27°Le
05-10-2004,01°Ca	06-24-2004,00°Le	08-08-2004,28°Le
05-11-2004,02°Ca	06-25-2004,00°Le	08-09-2004,29°Le
05-12-2004,03°Ca	06-26-2004,01°Le	08-10-2004,29°Le
05-13-2004,03°Ca	06-27-2004,02°Le	08-11-2004,00°Vi
05-14-2004,04°Ca	06-28-2004,02°Le	08-12-2004,01°Vi
05-15-2004,04°Ca	06-29-2004,03°Le	08-13-2004,01°Vi
05-16-2004,05°Ca	06-30-2004,04°Le	08-14-2004,02°Vi
05-17-2004,06°Ca	07-01-2004,04°Le	08-15-2004,03°Vi
05-18-2004,06°Ca	07-02-2004,05°Le	08-16-2004,03°Vi
05-19-2004,07°Ca	07-03-2004,05°Le	08-17-2004,04°Vi
05-20-2004,08°Ca	07-04-2004,06°Le	08-18-2004,04°Vi
05-21-2004,08°Ca	07-05-2004,07°Le	08-19-2004,05°Vi
05-22-2004,09°Ca	07-06-2004,07°Le	08-20-2004,06°Vi
05-23-2004,10°Ca	07-07-2004,08°Le	08-21-2004,06°Vi
05-24-2004,10°Ca	07-08-2004,09°Le	08-22-2004,07°Vi
05-25-2004,11°Ca	07-09-2004,09°Le	08-23-2004,08°Vi
05-26-2004,11°Ca	07-10-2004,10°Le	08-24-2004,08°Vi
05-27-2004,12°Ca	07-11-2004,10°Le	08-25-2004,09°Vi

08-26-2004,10°Vi
08-27-2004,10°Vi
08-28-2004,11°Vi
08-29-2004,11°Vi
08-30-2004,12°Vi
08-31-2004,13°Vi
09-01-2004,13°Vi
09-02-2004,14°Vi
09-03-2004,15°Vi
09-04-2004,15°Vi
09-05-2004,16°Vi
09-06-2004,17°Vi
09-07-2004,17°Vi
09-08-2004,18°Vi
09-09-2004,18°Vi
09-10-2004,19°Vi
09-11-2004,20°Vi
09-12-2004,20°Vi
09-13-2004,21°Vi
09-14-2004,22°Vi
09-15-2004,22°Vi
09-16-2004,23°Vi
09-17-2004,24°Vi
09-18-2004,24°Vi
09-19-2004,25°Vi
09-20-2004,26°Vi
09-21-2004,26°Vi
09-22-2004,27°Vi
09-23-2004,27°Vi
09-24-2004,28°Vi
09-25-2004,29°Vi
09-26-2004,29°Vi
09-27-2004,00°Li
09-28-2004,01°Li
09-29-2004,01°Li
09-30-2004,02°Li
10-01-2004,03°Li
10-02-2004,03°Li
10-03-2004,04°Li
10-04-2004,05°Li
10-05-2004,05°Li
10-06-2004,06°Li
10-07-2004,07°Li
10-08-2004,07°Li
10-09-2004,08°Li

10-10-2004,08°Li
10-11-2004,09°Li
10-12-2004,10°Li
10-13-2004,10°Li
10-14-2004,11°Li
10-15-2004,12°Li
10-16-2004,12°Li
10-17-2004,13°Li
10-18-2004,14°Li
10-19-2004,14°Li
10-20-2004,15°Li
10-21-2004,16°Li
10-22-2004,16°Li
10-23-2004,17°Li
10-24-2004,18°Li
10-25-2004,18°Li
10-26-2004,19°Li
10-27-2004,20°Li
10-28-2004,20°Li
10-29-2004,21°Li
10-30-2004,22°Li
10-31-2004,22°Li
11-01-2004,23°Li
11-02-2004,24°Li
11-03-2004,24°Li
11-04-2004,25°Li
11-05-2004,26°Li
11-06-2004,26°Li
11-07-2004,27°Li
11-08-2004,28°Li
11-09-2004,28°Li
11-10-2004,29°Li
11-11-2004,30°Li
11-12-2004,00°Sc
11-13-2004,01°Sc
11-14-2004,01°Sc
11-15-2004,02°Sc
11-16-2004,03°Sc
11-17-2004,03°Sc
11-18-2004,04°Sc
11-19-2004,05°Sc
11-20-2004,06°Sc
11-21-2004,06°Sc
11-22-2004,07°Sc
11-23-2004,08°Sc

11-24-2004,08°Sc
11-25-2004,09°Sc
11-26-2004,10°Sc
11-27-2004,10°Sc
11-28-2004,11°Sc
11-29-2004,12°Sc
11-30-2004,12°Sc
12-01-2004,13°Sc
12-02-2004,14°Sc
12-03-2004,14°Sc
12-04-2004,15°Sc
12-05-2004,16°Sc
12-06-2004,16°Sc
12-07-2004,17°Sc
12-08-2004,18°Sc
12-09-2004,18°Sc
12-10-2004,19°Sc
12-11-2004,20°Sc
12-12-2004,20°Sc
12-13-2004,21°Sc
12-14-2004,22°Sc
12-15-2004,22°Sc
12-16-2004,23°Sc
12-17-2004,24°Sc
12-18-2004,24°Sc
12-19-2004,25°Sc
12-20-2004,26°Sc
12-21-2004,26°Sc
12-22-2004,27°Sc
12-23-2004,28°Sc
12-24-2004,29°Sc
12-25-2004,29°Sc
12-26-2004,00°Sg
12-27-2004,01°Sg
12-28-2004,01°Sg
12-29-2004,02°Sg
12-30-2004,03°Sg
12-31-2004,03°Sg

2005
01-01-2005,04°Sg
01-02-2005,05°Sg
01-03-2005,05°Sg
01-04-2005,06°Sg
01-05-2005,07°Sg

01-06-2005,07°Sg	02-20-2005,09°Cap	04-06-2005,11°Aq
01-07-2005,08°Sg	02-21-2005,10°Cap	04-07-2005,12°Aq
01-08-2005,09°Sg	02-22-2005,10°Cap	04-08-2005,13°Aq
01-09-2005,10°Sg	02-23-2005,11°Cap	04-09-2005,14°Aq
01-10-2005,10°Sg	02-24-2005,12°Cap	04-10-2005,14°Aq
01-11-2005,11°Sg	02-25-2005,13°Cap	04-11-2005,15°Aq
01-12-2005,12°Sg	02-26-2005,13°Cap	04-12-2005,16°Aq
01-13-2005,12°Sg	02-27-2005,14°Cap	04-13-2005,17°Aq
01-14-2005,13°Sg	02-28-2005,15°Cap	04-14-2005,17°Aq
01-15-2005,14°Sg	03-01-2005,15°Cap	04-15-2005,18°Aq
01-16-2005,14°Sg	03-02-2005,16°Cap	04-16-2005,19°Aq
01-17-2005,15°Sg	03-03-2005,17°Cap	04-17-2005,19°Aq
01-18-2005,16°Sg	03-04-2005,18°Cap	04-18-2005,20°Aq
01-19-2005,16°Sg	03-05-2005,18°Cap	04-19-2005,21°Aq
01-20-2005,17°Sg	03-06-2005,19°Cap	04-20-2005,22°Aq
01-21-2005,18°Sg	03-07-2005,20°Cap	04-21-2005,22°Aq
01-22-2005,19°Sg	03-08-2005,20°Cap	04-22-2005,23°Aq
01-23-2005,19°Sg	03-09-2005,21°Cap	04-23-2005,24°Aq
01-24-2005,20°Sg	03-10-2005,22°Cap	04-24-2005,24°Aq
01-25-2005,21°Sg	03-11-2005,23°Cap	04-25-2005,25°Aq
01-26-2005,21°Sg	03-12-2005,23°Cap	04-26-2005,26°Aq
01-27-2005,22°Sg	03-13-2005,24°Cap	04-27-2005,27°Aq
01-28-2005,23°Sg	03-14-2005,25°Cap	04-28-2005,27°Aq
01-29-2005,23°Sg	03-15-2005,26°Cap	04-29-2005,28°Aq
01-30-2005,24°Sg	03-16-2005,26°Cap	04-30-2005,29°Aq
01-31-2005,25°Sg	03-17-2005,27°Cap	05-01-2005,00°Pi
02-01-2005,26°Sg	03-18-2005,28°Cap	05-02-2005,00°Pi
02-02-2005,26°Sg	03-19-2005,28°Cap	05-03-2005,01°Pi
02-03-2005,27°Sg	03-20-2005,29°Cap	05-04-2005,02°Pi
02-04-2005,28°Sg	03-21-2005,00°Aq	05-05-2005,02°Pi
02-05-2005,28°Sg	03-22-2005,01°Aq	05-06-2005,03°Pi
02-06-2005,29°Sg	03-23-2005,01°Aq	05-07-2005,04°Pi
02-07-2005,00°Cap	03-24-2005,02°Aq	05-08-2005,05°Pi
02-08-2005,01°Cap	03-25-2005,03°Aq	05-09-2005,05°Pi
02-09-2005,01°Cap	03-26-2005,03°Aq	05-10-2005,06°Pi
02-10-2005,02°Cap	03-27-2005,04°Aq	05-11-2005,07°Pi
02-11-2005,03°Cap	03-28-2005,05°Aq	05-12-2005,08°Pi
02-12-2005,03°Cap	03-29-2005,06°Aq	05-13-2005,08°Pi
02-13-2005,04°Cap	03-30-2005,06°Aq	05-14-2005,09°Pi
02-14-2005,05°Cap	03-31-2005,07°Aq	05-15-2005,10°Pi
02-15-2005,05°Cap	04-01-2005,08°Aq	05-16-2005,10°Pi
02-16-2005,06°Cap	04-02-2005,09°Aq	05-17-2005,11°Pi
02-17-2005,07°Cap	04-03-2005,09°Aq	05-18-2005,12°Pi
02-18-2005,08°Cap	04-04-2005,10°Aq	05-19-2005,13°Pi
02-19-2005,08°Cap	04-05-2005,11°Aq	05-20-2005,13°Pi

05-21-2005,14°Pi	07-05-2005,15°Ar	08-19-2005,11°Ta
05-22-2005,15°Pi	07-06-2005,16°Ar	08-20-2005,12°Ta
05-23-2005,15°Pi	07-07-2005,16°Ar	08-21-2005,12°Ta
05-24-2005,16°Pi	07-08-2005,17°Ar	08-22-2005,13°Ta
05-25-2005,17°Pi	07-09-2005,18°Ar	08-23-2005,13°Ta
05-26-2005,18°Pi	07-10-2005,18°Ar	08-24-2005,13°Ta
05-27-2005,18°Pi	07-11-2005,19°Ar	08-25-2005,14°Ta
05-28-2005,19°Pi	07-12-2005,20°Ar	08-26-2005,14°Ta
05-29-2005,20°Pi	07-13-2005,20°Ar	08-27-2005,15°Ta
05-30-2005,20°Pi	07-14-2005,21°Ar	08-28-2005,15°Ta
05-31-2005,21°Pi	07-15-2005,22°Ar	08-29-2005,16°Ta
06-01-2005,22°Pi	07-16-2005,22°Ar	08-30-2005,16°Ta
06-02-2005,23°Pi	07-17-2005,23°Ar	08-31-2005,16°Ta
06-03-2005,23°Pi	07-18-2005,23°Ar	09-01-2005,17°Ta
06-04-2005,24°Pi	07-19-2005,24°Ar	09-02-2005,17°Ta
06-05-2005,25°Pi	07-20-2005,25°Ar	09-03-2005,17°Ta
06-06-2005,25°Pi	07-21-2005,25°Ar	09-04-2005,18°Ta
06-07-2005,26°Pi	07-22-2005,26°Ar	09-05-2005,18°Ta
06-08-2005,27°Pi	07-23-2005,27°Ar	09-06-2005,18°Ta
06-09-2005,27°Pi	07-24-2005,27°Ar	09-07-2005,19°Ta
06-10-2005,28°Pi	07-25-2005,28°Ar	09-08-2005,19°Ta
06-11-2005,29°Pi	07-26-2005,28°Ar	09-09-2005,19°Ta
06-12-2005,00°Ar	07-27-2005,29°Ar	09-10-2005,20°Ta
06-13-2005,00°Ar	07-28-2005,30°Ar	09-11-2005,20°Ta
06-14-2005,01°Ar	07-29-2005,00°Ta	09-12-2005,20°Ta
06-15-2005,02°Ar	07-30-2005,01°Ta	09-13-2005,20°Ta
06-16-2005,02°Ar	07-31-2005,01°Ta	09-14-2005,21°Ta
06-17-2005,03°Ar	08-01-2005,02°Ta	09-15-2005,21°Ta
06-18-2005,04°Ar	08-02-2005,02°Ta	09-16-2005,21°Ta
06-19-2005,04°Ar	08-03-2005,03°Ta	09-17-2005,21°Ta
06-20-2005,05°Ar	08-04-2005,03°Ta	09-18-2005,22°Ta
06-21-2005,06°Ar	08-05-2005,04°Ta	09-19-2005,22°Ta
06-22-2005,06°Ar	08-06-2005,05°Ta	09-20-2005,22°Ta
06-23-2005,07°Ar	08-07-2005,05°Ta	09-21-2005,22°Ta
06-24-2005,08°Ar	08-08-2005,06°Ta	09-22-2005,22°Ta
06-25-2005,09°Ar	08-09-2005,06°Ta	09-23-2005,22°Ta
06-26-2005,09°Ar	08-10-2005,07°Ta	09-24-2005,22°Ta
06-27-2005,10°Ar	08-11-2005,07°Ta	09-25-2005,23°Ta
06-28-2005,11°Ar	08-12-2005,08°Ta	09-26-2005,23°Ta
06-29-2005,11°Ar	08-13-2005,08°Ta	09-27-2005,23°Ta
06-30-2005,12°Ar	08-14-2005,09°Ta	09-28-2005,23°Ta
07-01-2005,13°Ar	08-15-2005,09°Ta	09-29-2005,23°Ta
07-02-2005,13°Ar	08-16-2005,10°Ta	09-30-2005,23°Ta
07-03-2005,14°Ar	08-17-2005,10°Ta	10-01-2005,23°Ta
07-04-2005,15°Ar	08-18-2005,11°Ta	10-02-2005,23°TaRx

10-03-2005,23°TaRx	11-17-2005,11°TaRx	**2006**
10-04-2005,23°TaRx	11-18-2005,11°TaRx	01-01-2006,11°Ta
10-05-2005,23°TaRx	11-19-2005,11°TaRx	01-02-2006,11°Ta
10-06-2005,23°TaRx	11-20-2005,10°TaRx	01-03-2006,11°Ta
10-07-2005,23°TaRx	11-21-2005,10°TaRx	01-04-2006,11°Ta
10-08-2005,23°TaRx	11-22-2005,10°TaRx	01-05-2006,12°Ta
10-09-2005,22°TaRx	11-23-2005,10°TaRx	01-06-2006,12°Ta
10-10-2005,22°TaRx	11-24-2005,09°TaRx	01-07-2006,12°Ta
10-11-2005,22°TaRx	11-25-2005,09°TaRx	01-08-2006,13°Ta
10-12-2005,22°TaRx	11-26-2005,09°TaRx	01-09-2006,13°Ta
10-13-2005,22°TaRx	11-27-2005,09°TaRx	01-10-2006,13°Ta
10-14-2005,22°TaRx	11-28-2005,09°TaRx	01-11-2006,14°Ta
10-15-2005,22°TaRx	11-29-2005,09°TaRx	01-12-2006,14°Ta
10-16-2005,21°TaRx	11-30-2005,08°TaRx	01-13-2006,14°Ta
10-17-2005,21°TaRx	12-01-2005,08°TaRx	01-14-2006,15°Ta
10-18-2005,21°TaRx	12-02-2005,08°TaRx	01-15-2006,15°Ta
10-19-2005,21°TaRx	12-03-2005,08°TaRx	01-16-2006,15°Ta
10-20-2005,20°TaRx	12-04-2005,08°TaRx	01-17-2006,16°Ta
10-21-2005,20°TaRx	12-05-2005,08°TaRx	01-18-2006,16°Ta
10-22-2005,20°TaRx	12-06-2005,08°TaRx	01-19-2006,16°Ta
10-23-2005,20°TaRx	12-07-2005,08°TaRx	01-20-2006,17°Ta
10-24-2005,19°TaRx	12-08-2005,08°TaRx	01-21-2006,17°Ta
10-25-2005,19°TaRx	12-09-2005,08°TaRx	01-22-2006,17°Ta
10-26-2005,19°TaRx	12-10-2005,08°Ta	01-23-2006,18°Ta
10-27-2005,18°TaRx	12-11-2005,08°Ta	01-24-2006,18°Ta
10-28-2005,18°TaRx	12-12-2005,08°Ta	01-25-2006,19°Ta
10-29-2005,18°TaRx	12-13-2005,08°Ta	01-26-2006,19°Ta
10-30-2005,17°TaRx	12-14-2005,08°Ta	01-27-2006,20°Ta
10-31-2005,17°TaRx	12-15-2005,08°Ta	01-28-2006,20°Ta
11-01-2005,17°TaRx	12-16-2005,08°Ta	01-29-2006,20°Ta
11-02-2005,16°TaRx	12-17-2005,08°Ta	01-30-2006,21°Ta
11-03-2005,16°TaRx	12-18-2005,08°Ta	01-31-2006,21°Ta
11-04-2005,16°TaRx	12-19-2005,08°Ta	02-01-2006,22°Ta
11-05-2005,15°TaRx	12-20-2005,08°Ta	02-02-2006,22°Ta
11-06-2005,15°TaRx	12-21-2005,09°Ta	02-03-2006,23°Ta
11-07-2005,15°TaRx	12-22-2005,09°Ta	02-04-2006,23°Ta
11-08-2005,14°TaRx	12-23-2005,09°Ta	02-05-2006,23°Ta
11-09-2005,14°TaRx	12-24-2005,09°Ta	02-06-2006,24°Ta
11-10-2005,14°TaRx	12-25-2005,09°Ta	02-07-2006,24°Ta
11-11-2005,13°TaRx	12-26-2005,09°Ta	02-08-2006,25°Ta
11-12-2005,13°TaRx	12-27-2005,10°Ta	02-09-2006,25°Ta
11-13-2005,13°TaRx	12-28-2005,10°Ta	02-10-2006,26°Ta
11-14-2005,12°TaRx	12-29-2005,10°Ta	02-11-2006,26°Ta
11-15-2005,12°TaRx	12-30-2005,10°Ta	02-12-2006,27°Ta
11-16-2005,12°TaRx	12-31-2005,10°Ta	02-13-2006,27°Ta

02-14-2006,28°Ta
02-15-2006,28°Ta
02-16-2006,29°Ta
02-17-2006,29°Ta
02-18-2006,00°Ge
02-19-2006,00°Ge
02-20-2006,01°Ge
02-21-2006,01°Ge
02-22-2006,02°Ge
02-23-2006,02°Ge
02-24-2006,03°Ge
02-25-2006,03°Ge
02-26-2006,04°Ge
02-27-2006,04°Ge
02-28-2006,05°Ge
03-01-2006,05°Ge
03-02-2006,06°Ge
03-03-2006,06°Ge
03-04-2006,07°Ge
03-05-2006,07°Ge
03-06-2006,08°Ge
03-07-2006,08°Ge
03-08-2006,09°Ge
03-09-2006,09°Ge
03-10-2006,10°Ge
03-11-2006,11°Ge
03-12-2006,11°Ge
03-13-2006,12°Ge
03-14-2006,12°Ge
03-15-2006,13°Ge
03-16-2006,13°Ge
03-17-2006,14°Ge
03-18-2006,14°Ge
03-19-2006,15°Ge
03-20-2006,15°Ge
03-21-2006,16°Ge
03-22-2006,17°Ge
03-23-2006,17°Ge
03-24-2006,18°Ge
03-25-2006,18°Ge
03-26-2006,19°Ge
03-27-2006,19°Ge
03-28-2006,20°Ge
03-29-2006,20°Ge
03-30-2006,21°Ge

03-31-2006,22°Ge
04-01-2006,22°Ge
04-02-2006,23°Ge
04-03-2006,23°Ge
04-04-2006,24°Ge
04-05-2006,24°Ge
04-06-2006,25°Ge
04-07-2006,26°Ge
04-08-2006,26°Ge
04-09-2006,27°Ge
04-10-2006,27°Ge
04-11-2006,28°Ge
04-12-2006,28°Ge
04-13-2006,29°Ge
04-14-2006,00°Ca
04-15-2006,00°Ca
04-16-2006,01°Ca
04-17-2006,01°Ca
04-18-2006,02°Ca
04-19-2006,02°Ca
04-20-2006,03°Ca
04-21-2006,04°Ca
04-22-2006,04°Ca
04-23-2006,05°Ca
04-24-2006,05°Ca
04-25-2006,06°Ca
04-26-2006,07°Ca
04-27-2006,07°Ca
04-28-2006,08°Ca
04-29-2006,08°Ca
04-30-2006,09°Ca
05-01-2006,10°Ca
05-02-2006,10°Ca
05-03-2006,11°Ca
05-04-2006,11°Ca
05-05-2006,12°Ca
05-06-2006,12°Ca
05-07-2006,13°Ca
05-08-2006,14°Ca
05-09-2006,14°Ca
05-10-2006,15°Ca
05-11-2006,15°Ca
05-12-2006,16°Ca
05-13-2006,17°Ca
05-14-2006,17°Ca

05-15-2006,18°Ca
05-16-2006,18°Ca
05-17-2006,19°Ca
05-18-2006,20°Ca
05-19-2006,20°Ca
05-20-2006,21°Ca
05-21-2006,21°Ca
05-22-2006,22°Ca
05-23-2006,23°Ca
05-24-2006,23°Ca
05-25-2006,24°Ca
05-26-2006,24°Ca
05-27-2006,25°Ca
05-28-2006,26°Ca
05-29-2006,26°Ca
05-30-2006,27°Ca
05-31-2006,27°Ca
06-01-2006,28°Ca
06-02-2006,29°Ca
06-03-2006,29°Ca
06-04-2006,00°Le
06-05-2006,00°Le
06-06-2006,01°Le
06-07-2006,02°Le
06-08-2006,02°Le
06-09-2006,03°Le
06-10-2006,03°Le
06-11-2006,04°Le
06-12-2006,05°Le
06-13-2006,05°Le
06-14-2006,06°Le
06-15-2006,06°Le
06-16-2006,07°Le
06-17-2006,08°Le
06-18-2006,08°Le
06-19-2006,09°Le
06-20-2006,09°Le
06-21-2006,10°Le
06-22-2006,11°Le
06-23-2006,11°Le
06-24-2006,12°Le
06-25-2006,13°Le
06-26-2006,13°Le
06-27-2006,14°Le
06-28-2006,14°Le

06-29-2006,15°Le	08-13-2006,13°Vi	09-27-2006,12°Li
06-30-2006,16°Le	08-14-2006,14°Vi	09-28-2006,13°Li
07-01-2006,16°Le	08-15-2006,14°Vi	09-29-2006,13°Li
07-02-2006,17°Le	08-16-2006,15°Vi	09-30-2006,14°Li
07-03-2006,17°Le	08-17-2006,15°Vi	10-01-2006,15°Li
07-04-2006,18°Le	08-18-2006,16°Vi	10-02-2006,15°Li
07-05-2006,19°Le	08-19-2006,17°Vi	10-03-2006,16°Li
07-06-2006,19°Le	08-20-2006,17°Vi	10-04-2006,17°Li
07-07-2006,20°Le	08-21-2006,18°Vi	10-05-2006,17°Li
07-08-2006,20°Le	08-22-2006,19°Vi	10-06-2006,18°Li
07-09-2006,21°Le	08-23-2006,19°Vi	10-07-2006,18°Li
07-10-2006,22°Le	08-24-2006,20°Vi	10-08-2006,19°Li
07-11-2006,22°Le	08-25-2006,21°Vi	10-09-2006,20°Li
07-12-2006,23°Le	08-26-2006,21°Vi	10-10-2006,20°Li
07-13-2006,24°Le	08-27-2006,22°Vi	10-11-2006,21°Li
07-14-2006,24°Le	08-28-2006,22°Vi	10-12-2006,22°Li
07-15-2006,25°Le	08-29-2006,23°Vi	10-13-2006,22°Li
07-16-2006,25°Le	08-30-2006,24°Vi	10-14-2006,23°Li
07-17-2006,26°Le	08-31-2006,24°Vi	10-15-2006,24°Li
07-18-2006,27°Le	09-01-2006,25°Vi	10-16-2006,24°Li
07-19-2006,27°Le	09-02-2006,26°Vi	10-17-2006,25°Li
07-20-2006,28°Le	09-03-2006,26°Vi	10-18-2006,26°Li
07-21-2006,29°Le	09-04-2006,27°Vi	10-19-2006,26°Li
07-22-2006,29°Le	09-05-2006,28°Vi	10-20-2006,27°Li
07-23-2006,00°Vi	09-06-2006,28°Vi	10-21-2006,28°Li
07-24-2006,00°Vi	09-07-2006,29°Vi	10-22-2006,29°Li
07-25-2006,01°Vi	09-08-2006,00°Li	10-23-2006,29°Li
07-26-2006,02°Vi	09-09-2006,00°Li	10-24-2006,00°Sc
07-27-2006,02°Vi	09-10-2006,01°Li	10-25-2006,01°Sc
07-28-2006,03°Vi	09-11-2006,01°Li	10-26-2006,01°Sc
07-29-2006,04°Vi	09-12-2006,02°Li	10-27-2006,02°Sc
07-30-2006,04°Vi	09-13-2006,03°Li	10-28-2006,03°Sc
07-31-2006,05°Vi	09-14-2006,03°Li	10-29-2006,03°Sc
08-01-2006,05°Vi	09-15-2006,04°Li	10-30-2006,04°Sc
08-02-2006,06°Vi	09-16-2006,05°Li	10-31-2006,05°Sc
08-03-2006,07°Vi	09-17-2006,05°Li	11-01-2006,05°Sc
08-04-2006,07°Vi	09-18-2006,06°Li	11-02-2006,06°Sc
08-05-2006,08°Vi	09-19-2006,07°Li	11-03-2006,07°Sc
08-06-2006,09°Vi	09-20-2006,07°Li	11-04-2006,07°Sc
08-07-2006,09°Vi	09-21-2006,08°Li	11-05-2006,08°Sc
08-08-2006,10°Vi	09-22-2006,09°Li	11-06-2006,09°Sc
08-09-2006,10°Vi	09-23-2006,09°Li	11-07-2006,09°Sc
08-10-2006,11°Vi	09-24-2006,10°Li	11-08-2006,10°Sc
08-11-2006,12°Vi	09-25-2006,11°Li	11-09-2006,11°Sc
08-12-2006,12°Vi	09-26-2006,11°Li	11-10-2006,11°Sc

11-11-2006,12°Sc
11-12-2006,13°Sc
11-13-2006,13°Sc
11-14-2006,14°Sc
11-15-2006,15°Sc
11-16-2006,16°Sc
11-17-2006,16°Sc
11-18-2006,17°Sc
11-19-2006,18°Sc
11-20-2006,18°Sc
11-21-2006,19°Sc
11-22-2006,20°Sc
11-23-2006,20°Sc
11-24-2006,21°Sc
11-25-2006,22°Sc
11-26-2006,22°Sc
11-27-2006,23°Sc
11-28-2006,24°Sc
11-29-2006,25°Sc
11-30-2006,25°Sc
12-01-2006,26°Sc
12-02-2006,27°Sc
12-03-2006,27°Sc
12-04-2006,28°Sc
12-05-2006,29°Sc
12-06-2006,00°Sg
12-07-2006,00°Sg
12-08-2006,01°Sg
12-09-2006,02°Sg
12-10-2006,02°Sg
12-11-2006,03°Sg
12-12-2006,04°Sg
12-13-2006,04°Sg
12-14-2006,05°Sg
12-15-2006,06°Sg
12-16-2006,07°Sg
12-17-2006,07°Sg
12-18-2006,08°Sg
12-19-2006,09°Sg
12-20-2006,09°Sg
12-21-2006,10°Sg
12-22-2006,11°Sg
12-23-2006,12°Sg
12-24-2006,12°Sg
12-25-2006,13°Sg

12-26-2006,14°Sg
12-27-2006,14°Sg
12-28-2006,15°Sg
12-29-2006,16°Sg
12-30-2006,17°Sg
12-31-2006,17°Sg

2007
01-01-2007,18°Sg
01-02-2007,19°Sg
01-03-2007,20°Sg
01-04-2007,20°Sg
01-05-2007,21°Sg
01-06-2007,22°Sg
01-07-2007,22°Sg
01-08-2007,23°Sg
01-09-2007,24°Sg
01-10-2007,25°Sg
01-11-2007,25°Sg
01-12-2007,26°Sg
01-13-2007,27°Sg
01-14-2007,28°Sg
01-15-2007,28°Sg
01-16-2007,29°Sg
01-17-2007,00°Cap
01-18-2007,00°Cap
01-19-2007,01°Cap
01-20-2007,02°Cap
01-21-2007,03°Cap
01-22-2007,03°Cap
01-23-2007,04°Cap
01-24-2007,05°Cap
01-25-2007,06°Cap
01-26-2007,06°Cap
01-27-2007,07°Cap
01-28-2007,08°Cap
01-29-2007,09°Cap
01-30-2007,09°Cap
01-31-2007,10°Cap
02-01-2007,11°Cap
02-02-2007,12°Cap
02-03-2007,12°Cap
02-04-2007,13°Cap
02-05-2007,14°Cap
02-06-2007,15°Cap

02-07-2007,15°Cap
02-08-2007,16°Cap
02-09-2007,17°Cap
02-10-2007,18°Cap
02-11-2007,18°Cap
02-12-2007,19°Cap
02-13-2007,20°Cap
02-14-2007,21°Cap
02-15-2007,21°Cap
02-16-2007,22°Cap
02-17-2007,23°Cap
02-18-2007,24°Cap
02-19-2007,24°Cap
02-20-2007,25°Cap
02-21-2007,26°Cap
02-22-2007,27°Cap
02-23-2007,27°Cap
02-24-2007,28°Cap
02-25-2007,29°Cap
02-26-2007,00°Aq
02-27-2007,00°Aq
02-28-2007,01°Aq
03-01-2007,02°Aq
03-02-2007,03°Aq
03-03-2007,03°Aq
03-04-2007,04°Aq
03-05-2007,05°Aq
03-06-2007,06°Aq
03-07-2007,06°Aq
03-08-2007,07°Aq
03-09-2007,08°Aq
03-10-2007,09°Aq
03-11-2007,09°Aq
03-12-2007,10°Aq
03-13-2007,11°Aq
03-14-2007,12°Aq
03-15-2007,13°Aq
03-16-2007,13°Aq
03-17-2007,14°Aq
03-18-2007,15°Aq
03-19-2007,16°Aq
03-20-2007,16°Aq
03-21-2007,17°Aq
03-22-2007,18°Aq
03-23-2007,19°Aq

03-24-2007,19°Aq	05-07-2007,23°Pi	06-20-2007,26°Ar
03-25-2007,20°Aq	05-08-2007,24°Pi	06-21-2007,27°Ar
03-26-2007,21°Aq	05-09-2007,25°Pi	06-22-2007,28°Ar
03-27-2007,22°Aq	05-10-2007,25°Pi	06-23-2007,28°Ar
03-28-2007,22°Aq	05-11-2007,26°Pi	06-24-2007,29°Ar
03-29-2007,23°Aq	05-12-2007,27°Pi	06-25-2007,00°Ta
03-30-2007,24°Aq	05-13-2007,28°Pi	06-26-2007,00°Ta
03-31-2007,25°Aq	05-14-2007,28°Pi	06-27-2007,01°Ta
04-01-2007,26°Aq	05-15-2007,29°Pi	06-28-2007,02°Ta
04-02-2007,26°Aq	05-16-2007,00°Ar	06-29-2007,03°Ta
04-03-2007,27°Aq	05-17-2007,01°Ar	06-30-2007,03°Ta
04-04-2007,28°Aq	05-18-2007,01°Ar	07-01-2007,04°Ta
04-05-2007,29°Aq	05-19-2007,02°Ar	07-02-2007,05°Ta
04-06-2007,29°Aq	05-20-2007,03°Ar	07-03-2007,05°Ta
04-07-2007,00°Pi	05-21-2007,04°Ar	07-04-2007,06°Ta
04-08-2007,01°Pi	05-22-2007,05°Ar	07-05-2007,07°Ta
04-09-2007,02°Pi	05-23-2007,05°Ar	07-06-2007,08°Ta
04-10-2007,02°Pi	05-24-2007,06°Ar	07-07-2007,08°Ta
04-11-2007,03°Pi	05-25-2007,07°Ar	07-08-2007,09°Ta
04-12-2007,04°Pi	05-26-2007,08°Ar	07-09-2007,10°Ta
04-13-2007,05°Pi	05-27-2007,08°Ar	07-10-2007,10°Ta
04-14-2007,06°Pi	05-28-2007,09°Ar	07-11-2007,11°Ta
04-15-2007,06°Pi	05-29-2007,10°Ar	07-12-2007,12°Ta
04-16-2007,07°Pi	05-30-2007,11°Ar	07-13-2007,13°Ta
04-17-2007,08°Pi	05-31-2007,11°Ar	07-14-2007,13°Ta
04-18-2007,09°Pi	06-01-2007,12°Ar	07-15-2007,14°Ta
04-19-2007,09°Pi	06-02-2007,13°Ar	07-16-2007,15°Ta
04-20-2007,10°Pi	06-03-2007,14°Ar	07-17-2007,15°Ta
04-21-2007,11°Pi	06-04-2007,14°Ar	07-18-2007,16°Ta
04-22-2007,12°Pi	06-05-2007,15°Ar	07-19-2007,17°Ta
04-23-2007,12°Pi	06-06-2007,16°Ar	07-20-2007,17°Ta
04-24-2007,13°Pi	06-07-2007,17°Ar	07-21-2007,18°Ta
04-25-2007,14°Pi	06-08-2007,17°Ar	07-22-2007,19°Ta
04-26-2007,15°Pi	06-09-2007,18°Ar	07-23-2007,19°Ta
04-27-2007,15°Pi	06-10-2007,19°Ar	07-24-2007,20°Ta
04-28-2007,16°Pi	06-11-2007,19°Ar	07-25-2007,21°Ta
04-29-2007,17°Pi	06-12-2007,20°Ar	07-26-2007,22°Ta
04-30-2007,18°Pi	06-13-2007,21°Ar	07-27-2007,22°Ta
05-01-2007,19°Pi	06-14-2007,22°Ar	07-28-2007,23°Ta
05-02-2007,19°Pi	06-15-2007,22°Ar	07-29-2007,24°Ta
05-03-2007,20°Pi	06-16-2007,23°Ar	07-30-2007,24°Ta
05-04-2007,21°Pi	06-17-2007,24°Ar	07-31-2007,25°Ta
05-05-2007,22°Pi	06-18-2007,25°Ar	08-01-2007,26°Ta
05-06-2007,22°Pi	06-19-2007,25°Ar	08-02-2007,26°Ta

08-03-2007,27°Ta	09-16-2007,23°Ge	10-30-2007,10°Ca
08-04-2007,28°Ta	09-17-2007,24°Ge	10-31-2007,10°Ca
08-05-2007,28°Ta	09-18-2007,24°Ge	11-01-2007,11°Ca
08-06-2007,29°Ta	09-19-2007,25°Ge	11-02-2007,11°Ca
08-07-2007,29°Ta	09-20-2007,25°Ge	11-03-2007,11°Ca
08-08-2007,00°Ge	09-21-2007,26°Ge	11-04-2007,11°Ca
08-09-2007,01°Ge	09-22-2007,26°Ge	11-05-2007,11°Ca
08-10-2007,01°Ge	09-23-2007,27°Ge	11-06-2007,11°Ca
08-11-2007,02°Ge	09-24-2007,27°Ge	11-07-2007,12°Ca
08-12-2007,03°Ge	09-25-2007,28°Ge	11-08-2007,12°Ca
08-13-2007,03°Ge	09-26-2007,28°Ge	11-09-2007,12°Ca
08-14-2007,04°Ge	09-27-2007,29°Ge	11-10-2007,12°Ca
08-15-2007,05°Ge	09-28-2007,29°Ge	11-11-2007,12°Ca
08-16-2007,05°Ge	09-29-2007,00°Ca	11-12-2007,12°Ca
08-17-2007,06°Ge	09-30-2007,00°Ca	11-13-2007,12°Ca
08-18-2007,06°Ge	10-01-2007,01°Ca	11-14-2007,12°Ca
08-19-2007,07°Ge	10-02-2007,01°Ca	11-15-2007,12°Ca
08-20-2007,08°Ge	10-03-2007,01°Ca	11-16-2007,12°CaRx
08-21-2007,08°Ge	10-04-2007,02°Ca	11-17-2007,12°CaRx
08-22-2007,09°Ge	10-05-2007,02°Ca	11-18-2007,12°CaRx
08-23-2007,10°Ge	10-06-2007,03°Ca	11-19-2007,12°CaRx
08-24-2007,10°Ge	10-07-2007,03°Ca	11-20-2007,12°CaRx
08-25-2007,11°Ge	10-08-2007,03°Ca	11-21-2007,12°CaRx
08-26-2007,11°Ge	10-09-2007,04°Ca	11-22-2007,12°CaRx
08-27-2007,12°Ge	10-10-2007,04°Ca	11-23-2007,12°CaRx
08-28-2007,13°Ge	10-11-2007,05°Ca	11-24-2007,11°CaRx
08-29-2007,13°Ge	10-12-2007,05°Ca	11-25-2007,11°CaRx
08-30-2007,14°Ge	10-13-2007,05°Ca	11-26-2007,11°CaRx
08-31-2007,14°Ge	10-14-2007,06°Ca	11-27-2007,11°CaRx
09-01-2007,15°Ge	10-15-2007,06°Ca	11-28-2007,11°CaRx
09-02-2007,16°Ge	10-16-2007,06°Ca	11-29-2007,11°CaRx
09-03-2007,16°Ge	10-17-2007,07°Ca	11-30-2007,10°CaRx
09-04-2007,17°Ge	10-18-2007,07°Ca	12-01-2007,10°CaRx
09-05-2007,17°Ge	10-19-2007,07°Ca	12-02-2007,10°CaRx
09-06-2007,18°Ge	10-20-2007,08°Ca	12-03-2007,10°CaRx
09-07-2007,18°Ge	10-21-2007,08°Ca	12-04-2007,09°CaRx
09-08-2007,19°Ge	10-22-2007,08°Ca	12-05-2007,09°CaRx
09-09-2007,19°Ge	10-23-2007,09°Ca	12-06-2007,09°CaRx
09-10-2007,20°Ge	10-24-2007,09°Ca	12-07-2007,09°CaRx
09-11-2007,21°Ge	10-25-2007,09°Ca	12-08-2007,08°CaRx
09-12-2007,21°Ge	10-26-2007,09°Ca	12-09-2007,08°CaRx
09-13-2007,22°Ge	10-27-2007,10°Ca	12-10-2007,08°CaRx
09-14-2007,22°Ge	10-28-2007,10°Ca	12-11-2007,07°CaRx
09-15-2007,23°Ge	10-29-2007,10°Ca	12-12-2007,07°CaRx

12-13-2007,07°CaRx	12-20-2007,04°CaRx	12-27-2007,01°CaRx
12-14-2007,06°CaRx	12-21-2007,04°CaRx	12-28-2007,01°CaRx
12-15-2007,06°CaRx	12-22-2007,03°CaRx	12-29-2007,00°CaRx
12-16-2007,05°CaRx	12-23-2007,03°CaRx	12-30-2007,00°CaRx
12-17-2007,05°CaRx	12-24-2007,02°CaRx	12-31-2007,00°CaRx
12-18-2007,05°CaRx	12-25-2007,02°CaRx	
12-19-2007,04°CaRx	12-26-2007,02°CaRx	

♃
Jupiter Ephemeris
2003–2007

2003	01-31-2003,13°LeRx	03-03-2003,09°LeRx
01-01-2003,16°LeRx	02-01-2003,13°LeRx	03-04-2003,09°LeRx
01-02-2003,16°LeRx	02-02-2003,13°LeRx	03-05-2003,09°LeRx
01-03-2003,16°LeRx	02-03-2003,12°LeRx	03-06-2003,09°LeRx
01-04-2003,16°LeRx	02-04-2003,12°LeRx	03-07-2003,09°LeRx
01-05-2003,16°LeRx	02-05-2003,12°LeRx	03-08-2003,09°LeRx
01-06-2003,16°LeRx	02-06-2003,12°LeRx	03-09-2003,09°LeRx
01-07-2003,16°LeRx	02-07-2003,12°LeRx	03-10-2003,09°LeRx
01-08-2003,16°LeRx	02-08-2003,12°LeRx	03-11-2003,08°LeRx
01-09-2003,16°LeRx	02-09-2003,12°LeRx	03-12-2003,08°LeRx
01-10-2003,16°LeRx	02-10-2003,12°LeRx	03-13-2003,08°LeRx
01-11-2003,15°LeRx	02-11-2003,11°LeRx	03-14-2003,08°LeRx
01-12-2003,15°LeRx	02-12-2003,11°LeRx	03-15-2003,08°LeRx
01-13-2003,15°LeRx	02-13-2003,11°LeRx	03-16-2003,08°LeRx
01-14-2003,15°LeRx	02-14-2003,11°LeRx	03-17-2003,08°LeRx
01-15-2003,15°LeRx	02-15-2003,11°LeRx	03-18-2003,08°LeRx
01-16-2003,15°LeRx	02-16-2003,11°LeRx	03-19-2003,08°LeRx
01-17-2003,15°LeRx	02-17-2003,11°LeRx	03-20-2003,08°LeRx
01-18-2003,15°LeRx	02-18-2003,11°LeRx	03-21-2003,08°LeRx
01-19-2003,14°LeRx	02-19-2003,10°LeRx	03-22-2003,08°LeRx
01-20-2003,14°LeRx	02-20-2003,10°LeRx	03-23-2003,08°LeRx
01-21-2003,14°LeRx	02-21-2003,10°LeRx	03-24-2003,08°LeRx
01-22-2003,14°LeRx	02-22-2003,10°LeRx	03-25-2003,08°LeRx
01-23-2003,14°LeRx	02-23-2003,10°LeRx	03-26-2003,08°LeRx
01-24-2003,14°LeRx	02-24-2003,10°LeRx	03-27-2003,08°LeRx
01-25-2003,14°LeRx	02-25-2003,10°LeRx	03-28-2003,08°LeRx
01-26-2003,14°LeRx	02-26-2003,10°LeRx	03-29-2003,08°LeRx
01-27-2003,13°LeRx	02-27-2003,10°LeRx	03-30-2003,08°LeRx
01-28-2003,13°LeRx	02-28-2003,09°LeRx	03-31-2003,08°LeRx
01-29-2003,13°LeRx	03-01-2003,09°LeRx	04-01-2003,08°LeRx
01-30-2003,13°LeRx	03-02-2003,09°LeRx	04-02-2003,08°LeRx

04-03-2003,08°LeRx	05-18-2003,10°Le	07-02-2003,18°Le
04-04-2003,08°Le	05-19-2003,11°Le	07-03-2003,18°Le
04-05-2003,08°Le	05-20-2003,11°Le	07-04-2003,18°Le
04-06-2003,08°Le	05-21-2003,11°Le	07-05-2003,18°Le
04-07-2003,08°Le	05-22-2003,11°Le	07-06-2003,18°Le
04-08-2003,08°Le	05-23-2003,11°Le	07-07-2003,19°Le
04-09-2003,08°Le	05-24-2003,11°Le	07-08-2003,19°Le
04-10-2003,08°Le	05-25-2003,11°Le	07-09-2003,19°Le
04-11-2003,08°Le	05-26-2003,11°Le	07-10-2003,19°Le
04-12-2003,08°Le	05-27-2003,12°Le	07-11-2003,19°Le
04-13-2003,08°Le	05-28-2003,12°Le	07-12-2003,20°Le
04-14-2003,08°Le	05-29-2003,12°Le	07-13-2003,20°Le
04-15-2003,08°Le	05-30-2003,12°Le	07-14-2003,20°Le
04-16-2003,08°Le	05-31-2003,12°Le	07-15-2003,20°Le
04-17-2003,08°Le	06-01-2003,12°Le	07-16-2003,20°Le
04-18-2003,08°Le	06-02-2003,12°Le	07-17-2003,21°Le
04-19-2003,08°Le	06-03-2003,13°Le	07-18-2003,21°Le
04-20-2003,08°Le	06-04-2003,13°Le	07-19-2003,21°Le
04-21-2003,08°Le	06-05-2003,13°Le	07-20-2003,21°Le
04-22-2003,08°Le	06-06-2003,13°Le	07-21-2003,22°Le
04-23-2003,08°Le	06-07-2003,13°Le	07-22-2003,22°Le
04-24-2003,08°Le	06-08-2003,13°Le	07-23-2003,22°Le
04-25-2003,08°Le	06-09-2003,14°Le	07-24-2003,22°Le
04-26-2003,08°Le	06-10-2003,14°Le	07-25-2003,22°Le
04-27-2003,08°Le	06-11-2003,14°Le	07-26-2003,23°Le
04-28-2003,08°Le	06-12-2003,14°Le	07-27-2003,23°Le
04-29-2003,09°Le	06-13-2003,14°Le	07-28-2003,23°Le
04-30-2003,09°Le	06-14-2003,14°Le	07-29-2003,23°Le
05-01-2003,09°Le	06-15-2003,15°Le	07-30-2003,23°Le
05-02-2003,09°Le	06-16-2003,15°Le	07-31-2003,24°Le
05-03-2003,09°Le	06-17-2003,15°Le	08-01-2003,24°Le
05-04-2003,09°Le	06-18-2003,15°Le	08-02-2003,24°Le
05-05-2003,09°Le	06-19-2003,15°Le	08-03-2003,24°Le
05-06-2003,09°Le	06-20-2003,15°Le	08-04-2003,24°Le
05-07-2003,09°Le	06-21-2003,16°Le	08-05-2003,25°Le
05-08-2003,09°Le	06-22-2003,16°Le	08-06-2003,25°Le
05-09-2003,09°Le	06-23-2003,16°Le	08-07-2003,25°Le
05-10-2003,10°Le	06-24-2003,16°Le	08-08-2003,25°Le
05-11-2003,10°Le	06-25-2003,16°Le	08-09-2003,26°Le
05-12-2003,10°Le	06-26-2003,17°Le	08-10-2003,26°Le
05-13-2003,10°Le	06-27-2003,17°Le	08-11-2003,26°Le
05-14-2003,10°Le	06-28-2003,17°Le	08-12-2003,26°Le
05-15-2003,10°Le	06-29-2003,17°Le	08-13-2003,26°Le
05-16-2003,10°Le	06-30-2003,17°Le	08-14-2003,27°Le
05-17-2003,10°Le	07-01-2003,17°Le	08-15-2003,27°Le

08-16-2003,27°Le	09-30-2003,07°Vi	11-14-2003,15°Vi
08-17-2003,27°Le	10-01-2003,07°Vi	11-15-2003,15°Vi
08-18-2003,28°Le	10-02-2003,07°Vi	11-16-2003,15°Vi
08-19-2003,28°Le	10-03-2003,07°Vi	11-17-2003,15°Vi
08-20-2003,28°Le	10-04-2003,07°Vi	11-18-2003,15°Vi
08-21-2003,28°Le	10-05-2003,08°Vi	11-19-2003,15°Vi
08-22-2003,28°Le	10-06-2003,08°Vi	11-20-2003,15°Vi
08-23-2003,29°Le	10-07-2003,08°Vi	11-21-2003,16°Vi
08-24-2003,29°Le	10-08-2003,08°Vi	11-22-2003,16°Vi
08-25-2003,29°Le	10-09-2003,08°Vi	11-23-2003,16°Vi
08-26-2003,29°Le	10-10-2003,09°Vi	11-24-2003,16°Vi
08-27-2003,29°Le	10-11-2003,09°Vi	11-25-2003,16°Vi
08-28-2003,00°Vi	10-12-2003,09°Vi	11-26-2003,16°Vi
08-29-2003,00°Vi	10-13-2003,09°Vi	11-27-2003,16°Vi
08-30-2003,00°Vi	10-14-2003,09°Vi	11-28-2003,16°Vi
08-31-2003,00°Vi	10-15-2003,10°Vi	11-29-2003,16°Vi
09-01-2003,01°Vi	10-16-2003,10°Vi	11-30-2003,17°Vi
09-02-2003,01°Vi	10-17-2003,10°Vi	12-01-2003,17°Vi
09-03-2003,01°Vi	10-18-2003,10°Vi	12-02-2003,17°Vi
09-04-2003,01°Vi	10-19-2003,10°Vi	12-03-2003,17°Vi
09-05-2003,01°Vi	10-20-2003,11°Vi	12-04-2003,17°Vi
09-06-2003,02°Vi	10-21-2003,11°Vi	12-05-2003,17°Vi
09-07-2003,02°Vi	10-22-2003,11°Vi	12-06-2003,17°Vi
09-08-2003,02°Vi	10-23-2003,11°Vi	12-07-2003,17°Vi
09-09-2003,02°Vi	10-24-2003,11°Vi	12-08-2003,17°Vi
09-10-2003,03°Vi	10-25-2003,11°Vi	12-09-2003,17°Vi
09-11-2003,03°Vi	10-26-2003,12°Vi	12-10-2003,17°Vi
09-12-2003,03°Vi	10-27-2003,12°Vi	12-11-2003,18°Vi
09-13-2003,03°Vi	10-28-2003,12°Vi	12-12-2003,18°Vi
09-14-2003,03°Vi	10-29-2003,12°Vi	12-13-2003,18°Vi
09-15-2003,04°Vi	10-30-2003,12°Vi	12-14-2003,18°Vi
09-16-2003,04°Vi	10-31-2003,12°Vi	12-15-2003,18°Vi
09-17-2003,04°Vi	11-01-2003,13°Vi	12-16-2003,18°Vi
09-18-2003,04°Vi	11-02-2003,13°Vi	12-17-2003,18°Vi
09-19-2003,04°Vi	11-03-2003,13°Vi	12-18-2003,18°Vi
09-20-2003,05°Vi	11-04-2003,13°Vi	12-19-2003,18°Vi
09-21-2003,05°Vi	11-05-2003,13°Vi	12-20-2003,18°Vi
09-22-2003,05°Vi	11-06-2003,13°Vi	12-21-2003,18°Vi
09-23-2003,05°Vi	11-07-2003,14°Vi	12-22-2003,18°Vi
09-24-2003,05°Vi	11-08-2003,14°Vi	12-23-2003,18°Vi
09-25-2003,06°Vi	11-09-2003,14°Vi	12-24-2003,18°Vi
09-26-2003,06°Vi	11-10-2003,14°Vi	12-25-2003,18°Vi
09-27-2003,06°Vi	11-11-2003,14°Vi	12-26-2003,18°Vi
09-28-2003,06°Vi	11-12-2003,14°Vi	12-27-2003,18°Vi
09-29-2003,06°Vi	11-13-2003,14°Vi	12-28-2003,18°Vi

12-29-2003,18°Vi	02-10-2004,16°ViRx	03-26-2004,11°ViRx
12-30-2003,18°Vi	02-11-2004,16°ViRx	03-27-2004,11°ViRx
12-31-2003,18°Vi	02-12-2004,16°ViRx	03-28-2004,11°ViRx
	02-13-2004,16°ViRx	03-29-2004,10°ViRx
2004	02-14-2004,16°ViRx	03-30-2004,10°ViRx
01-01-2004,18°Vi	02-15-2004,16°ViRx	03-31-2004,10°ViRx
01-02-2004,18°Vi	02-16-2004,16°ViRx	04-01-2004,10°ViRx
01-03-2004,18°Vi	02-17-2004,16°ViRx	04-02-2004,10°ViRx
01-04-2004,18°ViRx	02-18-2004,15°ViRx	04-03-2004,10°ViRx
01-05-2004,18°ViRx	02-19-2004,15°ViRx	04-04-2004,10°ViRx
01-06-2004,18°ViRx	02-20-2004,15°ViRx	04-05-2004,10°ViRx
01-07-2004,18°ViRx	02-21-2004,15°ViRx	04-06-2004,10°ViRx
01-08-2004,18°ViRx	02-22-2004,15°ViRx	04-07-2004,10°ViRx
01-09-2004,18°ViRx	02-23-2004,15°ViRx	04-08-2004,10°ViRx
01-10-2004,18°ViRx	02-24-2004,15°ViRx	04-09-2004,09°ViRx
01-11-2004,18°ViRx	02-25-2004,15°ViRx	04-10-2004,09°ViRx
01-12-2004,18°ViRx	02-26-2004,14°ViRx	04-11-2004,09°ViRx
01-13-2004,18°ViRx	02-27-2004,14°ViRx	04-12-2004,09°ViRx
01-14-2004,18°ViRx	02-28-2004,14°ViRx	04-13-2004,09°ViRx
01-15-2004,18°ViRx	02-29-2004,14°ViRx	04-14-2004,09°ViRx
01-16-2004,18°ViRx	03-01-2004,14°ViRx	04-15-2004,09°ViRx
01-17-2004,18°ViRx	03-02-2004,14°ViRx	04-16-2004,09°ViRx
01-18-2004,18°ViRx	03-03-2004,14°ViRx	04-17-2004,09°ViRx
01-19-2004,18°ViRx	03-04-2004,13°ViRx	04-18-2004,09°ViRx
01-20-2004,18°ViRx	03-05-2004,13°ViRx	04-19-2004,09°ViRx
01-21-2004,18°ViRx	03-06-2004,13°ViRx	04-20-2004,09°ViRx
01-22-2004,18°ViRx	03-07-2004,13°ViRx	04-21-2004,09°ViRx
01-23-2004,18°ViRx	03-08-2004,13°ViRx	04-22-2004,09°ViRx
01-24-2004,18°ViRx	03-09-2004,13°ViRx	04-23-2004,09°ViRx
01-25-2004,18°ViRx	03-10-2004,13°ViRx	04-24-2004,09°ViRx
01-26-2004,18°ViRx	03-11-2004,13°ViRx	04-25-2004,09°ViRx
01-27-2004,18°ViRx	03-12-2004,12°ViRx	04-26-2004,09°ViRx
01-28-2004,17°ViRx	03-13-2004,12°ViRx	04-27-2004,09°ViRx
01-29-2004,17°ViRx	03-14-2004,12°ViRx	04-28-2004,08°ViRx
01-30-2004,17°ViRx	03-15-2004,12°ViRx	04-29-2004,08°ViRx
01-31-2004,17°ViRx	03-16-2004,12°ViRx	04-30-2004,08°ViRx
02-01-2004,17°ViRx	03-17-2004,12°ViRx	05-01-2004,08°ViRx
02-02-2004,17°ViRx	03-18-2004,12°ViRx	05-02-2004,08°ViRx
02-03-2004,17°ViRx	03-19-2004,12°ViRx	05-03-2004,08°ViRx
02-04-2004,17°ViRx	03-20-2004,11°ViRx	05-04-2004,08°ViRx
02-05-2004,17°ViRx	03-21-2004,11°ViRx	05-05-2004,08°Vi
02-06-2004,17°ViRx	03-22-2004,11°ViRx	05-06-2004,08°Vi
02-07-2004,17°ViRx	03-23-2004,11°ViRx	05-07-2004,08°Vi
02-08-2004,17°ViRx	03-24-2004,11°ViRx	05-08-2004,08°Vi
02-09-2004,16°ViRx	03-25-2004,11°ViRx	05-09-2004,08°Vi

05-10-2004,08°Vi	06-24-2004,12°Vi	08-08-2004,19°Vi
05-11-2004,08°Vi	06-25-2004,12°Vi	08-09-2004,20°Vi
05-12-2004,08°Vi	06-26-2004,12°Vi	08-10-2004,20°Vi
05-13-2004,09°Vi	06-27-2004,12°Vi	08-11-2004,20°Vi
05-14-2004,09°Vi	06-28-2004,12°Vi	08-12-2004,20°Vi
05-15-2004,09°Vi	06-29-2004,13°Vi	08-13-2004,20°Vi
05-16-2004,09°Vi	06-30-2004,13°Vi	08-14-2004,21°Vi
05-17-2004,09°Vi	07-01-2004,13°Vi	08-15-2004,21°Vi
05-18-2004,09°Vi	07-02-2004,13°Vi	08-16-2004,21°Vi
05-19-2004,09°Vi	07-03-2004,13°Vi	08-17-2004,21°Vi
05-20-2004,09°Vi	07-04-2004,13°Vi	08-18-2004,21°Vi
05-21-2004,09°Vi	07-05-2004,13°Vi	08-19-2004,22°Vi
05-22-2004,09°Vi	07-06-2004,14°Vi	08-20-2004,22°Vi
05-23-2004,09°Vi	07-07-2004,14°Vi	08-21-2004,22°Vi
05-24-2004,09°Vi	07-08-2004,14°Vi	08-22-2004,22°Vi
05-25-2004,09°Vi	07-09-2004,14°Vi	08-23-2004,22°Vi
05-26-2004,09°Vi	07-10-2004,14°Vi	08-24-2004,23°Vi
05-27-2004,09°Vi	07-11-2004,14°Vi	08-25-2004,23°Vi
05-28-2004,09°Vi	07-12-2004,15°Vi	08-26-2004,23°Vi
05-29-2004,09°Vi	07-13-2004,15°Vi	08-27-2004,23°Vi
05-30-2004,09°Vi	07-14-2004,15°Vi	08-28-2004,24°Vi
05-31-2004,09°Vi	07-15-2004,15°Vi	08-29-2004,24°Vi
06-01-2004,10°Vi	07-16-2004,15°Vi	08-30-2004,24°Vi
06-02-2004,10°Vi	07-17-2004,15°Vi	08-31-2004,24°Vi
06-03-2004,10°Vi	07-18-2004,16°Vi	09-01-2004,24°Vi
06-04-2004,10°Vi	07-19-2004,16°Vi	09-02-2004,25°Vi
06-05-2004,10°Vi	07-20-2004,16°Vi	09-03-2004,25°Vi
06-06-2004,10°Vi	07-21-2004,16°Vi	09-04-2004,25°Vi
06-07-2004,10°Vi	07-22-2004,16°Vi	09-05-2004,25°Vi
06-08-2004,10°Vi	07-23-2004,16°Vi	09-06-2004,25°Vi
06-09-2004,10°Vi	07-24-2004,17°Vi	09-07-2004,26°Vi
06-10-2004,10°Vi	07-25-2004,17°Vi	09-08-2004,26°Vi
06-11-2004,10°Vi	07-26-2004,17°Vi	09-09-2004,26°Vi
06-12-2004,11°Vi	07-27-2004,17°Vi	09-10-2004,26°Vi
06-13-2004,11°Vi	07-28-2004,17°Vi	09-11-2004,27°Vi
06-14-2004,11°Vi	07-29-2004,18°Vi	09-12-2004,27°Vi
06-15-2004,11°Vi	07-30-2004,18°Vi	09-13-2004,27°Vi
06-16-2004,11°Vi	07-31-2004,18°Vi	09-14-2004,27°Vi
06-17-2004,11°Vi	08-01-2004,18°Vi	09-15-2004,27°Vi
06-18-2004,11°Vi	08-02-2004,18°Vi	09-16-2004,28°Vi
06-19-2004,11°Vi	08-03-2004,18°Vi	09-17-2004,28°Vi
06-20-2004,11°Vi	08-04-2004,19°Vi	09-18-2004,28°Vi
06-21-2004,12°Vi	08-05-2004,19°Vi	09-19-2004,28°Vi
06-22-2004,12°Vi	08-06-2004,19°Vi	09-20-2004,28°Vi
06-23-2004,12°Vi	08-07-2004,19°Vi	09-21-2004,29°Vi

09-22-2004,29°Vi
09-23-2004,29°Vi
09-24-2004,29°Vi
09-25-2004,00°Li
09-26-2004,00°Li
09-27-2004,00°Li
09-28-2004,00°Li
09-29-2004,00°Li
09-30-2004,01°Li
10-01-2004,01°Li
10-02-2004,01°Li
10-03-2004,01°Li
10-04-2004,01°Li
10-05-2004,02°Li
10-06-2004,02°Li
10-07-2004,02°Li
10-08-2004,02°Li
10-09-2004,03°Li
10-10-2004,03°Li
10-11-2004,03°Li
10-12-2004,03°Li
10-13-2004,03°Li
10-14-2004,04°Li
10-15-2004,04°Li
10-16-2004,04°Li
10-17-2004,04°Li
10-18-2004,04°Li
10-19-2004,05°Li
10-20-2004,05°Li
10-21-2004,05°Li
10-22-2004,05°Li
10-23-2004,05°Li
10-24-2004,06°Li
10-25-2004,06°Li
10-26-2004,06°Li
10-27-2004,06°Li
10-28-2004,07°Li
10-29-2004,07°Li
10-30-2004,07°Li
10-31-2004,07°Li
11-01-2004,07°Li
11-02-2004,08°Li
11-03-2004,08°Li
11-04-2004,08°Li
11-05-2004,08°Li

11-06-2004,08°Li
11-07-2004,08°Li
11-08-2004,09°Li
11-09-2004,09°Li
11-10-2004,09°Li
11-11-2004,09°Li
11-12-2004,09°Li
11-13-2004,10°Li
11-14-2004,10°Li
11-15-2004,10°Li
11-16-2004,10°Li
11-17-2004,10°Li
11-18-2004,11°Li
11-19-2004,11°Li
11-20-2004,11°Li
11-21-2004,11°Li
11-22-2004,11°Li
11-23-2004,11°Li
11-24-2004,12°Li
11-25-2004,12°Li
11-26-2004,12°Li
11-27-2004,12°Li
11-28-2004,12°Li
11-29-2004,12°Li
11-30-2004,13°Li
12-01-2004,13°Li
12-02-2004,13°Li
12-03-2004,13°Li
12-04-2004,13°Li
12-05-2004,13°Li
12-06-2004,14°Li
12-07-2004,14°Li
12-08-2004,14°Li
12-09-2004,14°Li
12-10-2004,14°Li
12-11-2004,14°Li
12-12-2004,14°Li
12-13-2004,15°Li
12-14-2004,15°Li
12-15-2004,15°Li
12-16-2004,15°Li
12-17-2004,15°Li
12-18-2004,15°Li
12-19-2004,15°Li
12-20-2004,16°Li

12-21-2004,16°Li
12-22-2004,16°Li
12-23-2004,16°Li
12-24-2004,16°Li
12-25-2004,16°Li
12-26-2004,16°Li
12-27-2004,16°Li
12-28-2004,16°Li
12-29-2004,17°Li
12-30-2004,17°Li
12-31-2004,17°Li

2005
01-01-2005,17°Li
01-02-2005,17°Li
01-03-2005,17°Li
01-04-2005,17°Li
01-05-2005,17°Li
01-06-2005,17°Li
01-07-2005,17°Li
01-08-2005,17°Li
01-09-2005,17°Li
01-10-2005,18°Li
01-11-2005,18°Li
01-12-2005,18°Li
01-13-2005,18°Li
01-14-2005,18°Li
01-15-2005,18°Li
01-16-2005,18°Li
01-17-2005,18°Li
01-18-2005,18°Li
01-19-2005,18°Li
01-20-2005,18°Li
01-21-2005,18°Li
01-22-2005,18°Li
01-23-2005,18°Li
01-24-2005,18°Li
01-25-2005,18°Li
01-26-2005,18°Li
01-27-2005,18°Li
01-28-2005,18°Li
01-29-2005,18°Li
01-30-2005,18°Li
01-31-2005,18°Li
02-01-2005,18°Li

02-02-2005,18°LiRx	03-19-2005,15°LiRx	05-03-2005,10°LiRx
02-03-2005,18°LiRx	03-20-2005,15°LiRx	05-04-2005,10°LiRx
02-04-2005,18°LiRx	03-21-2005,15°LiRx	05-05-2005,10°LiRx
02-05-2005,18°LiRx	03-22-2005,15°LiRx	05-06-2005,10°LiRx
02-06-2005,18°LiRx	03-23-2005,15°LiRx	05-07-2005,10°LiRx
02-07-2005,18°LiRx	03-24-2005,15°LiRx	05-08-2005,10°LiRx
02-08-2005,18°LiRx	03-25-2005,15°LiRx	05-09-2005,10°LiRx
02-09-2005,18°LiRx	03-26-2005,15°LiRx	05-10-2005,09°LiRx
02-10-2005,18°LiRx	03-27-2005,14°LiRx	05-11-2005,09°LiRx
02-11-2005,18°LiRx	03-28-2005,14°LiRx	05-12-2005,09°LiRx
02-12-2005,18°LiRx	03-29-2005,14°LiRx	05-13-2005,09°LiRx
02-13-2005,18°LiRx	03-30-2005,14°LiRx	05-14-2005,09°LiRx
02-14-2005,18°LiRx	03-31-2005,14°LiRx	05-15-2005,09°LiRx
02-15-2005,18°LiRx	04-01-2005,14°LiRx	05-16-2005,09°LiRx
02-16-2005,18°LiRx	04-02-2005,14°LiRx	05-17-2005,09°LiRx
02-17-2005,18°LiRx	04-03-2005,14°LiRx	05-18-2005,09°LiRx
02-18-2005,18°LiRx	04-04-2005,13°LiRx	05-19-2005,09°LiRx
02-19-2005,18°LiRx	04-05-2005,13°LiRx	05-20-2005,09°LiRx
02-20-2005,18°LiRx	04-06-2005,13°LiRx	05-21-2005,09°LiRx
02-21-2005,18°LiRx	04-07-2005,13°LiRx	05-22-2005,09°LiRx
02-22-2005,18°LiRx	04-08-2005,13°LiRx	05-23-2005,09°LiRx
02-23-2005,18°LiRx	04-09-2005,13°LiRx	05-24-2005,09°LiRx
02-24-2005,18°LiRx	04-10-2005,13°LiRx	05-25-2005,09°LiRx
02-25-2005,18°LiRx	04-11-2005,13°LiRx	05-26-2005,09°LiRx
02-26-2005,17°LiRx	04-12-2005,12°LiRx	05-27-2005,09°LiRx
02-27-2005,17°LiRx	04-13-2005,12°LiRx	05-28-2005,09°LiRx
02-28-2005,17°LiRx	04-14-2005,12°LiRx	05-29-2005,09°LiRx
03-01-2005,17°LiRx	04-15-2005,12°LiRx	05-30-2005,08°LiRx
03-02-2005,17°LiRx	04-16-2005,12°LiRx	05-31-2005,08°LiRx
03-03-2005,17°LiRx	04-17-2005,12°LiRx	06-01-2005,08°LiRx
03-04-2005,17°LiRx	04-18-2005,12°LiRx	06-02-2005,08°LiRx
03-05-2005,17°LiRx	04-19-2005,12°LiRx	06-03-2005,08°LiRx
03-06-2005,17°LiRx	04-20-2005,11°LiRx	06-04-2005,08°LiRx
03-07-2005,17°LiRx	04-21-2005,11°LiRx	06-05-2005,08°LiRx
03-08-2005,17°LiRx	04-22-2005,11°LiRx	06-06-2005,08°Li
03-09-2005,17°LiRx	04-23-2005,11°LiRx	06-07-2005,08°Li
03-10-2005,16°LiRx	04-24-2005,11°LiRx	06-08-2005,08°Li
03-11-2005,16°LiRx	04-25-2005,11°LiRx	06-09-2005,08°Li
03-12-2005,16°LiRx	04-26-2005,11°LiRx	06-10-2005,08°Li
03-13-2005,16°LiRx	04-27-2005,11°LiRx	06-11-2005,08°Li
03-14-2005,16°LiRx	04-28-2005,11°LiRx	06-12-2005,09°Li
03-15-2005,16°LiRx	04-29-2005,10°LiRx	06-13-2005,09°Li
03-16-2005,16°LiRx	04-30-2005,10°LiRx	06-14-2005,09°Li
03-17-2005,16°LiRx	05-01-2005,10°LiRx	06-15-2005,09°Li
03-18-2005,16°LiRx	05-02-2005,10°LiRx	06-16-2005,09°Li

06-17-2005,09°Li	08-01-2005,13°Li	09-16-2005,21°Li
06-18-2005,09°Li	08-02-2005,13°Li	09-17-2005,21°Li
06-19-2005,09°Li	08-03-2005,13°Li	09-18-2005,21°Li
06-20-2005,09°Li	08-04-2005,13°Li	09-19-2005,22°Li
06-21-2005,09°Li	08-05-2005,13°Li	09-20-2005,22°Li
06-22-2005,09°Li	08-06-2005,14°Li	09-21-2005,22°Li
06-23-2005,09°Li	08-07-2005,14°Li	09-22-2005,22°Li
06-24-2005,09°Li	08-08-2005,14°Li	09-23-2005,22°Li
06-25-2005,09°Li	08-09-2005,14°Li	09-24-2005,23°Li
06-26-2005,09°Li	08-10-2005,14°Li	09-25-2005,23°Li
06-27-2005,09°Li	08-11-2005,14°Li	09-26-2005,23°Li
06-28-2005,09°Li	08-12-2005,15°Li	09-27-2005,23°Li
06-29-2005,09°Li	08-13-2005,15°Li	09-28-2005,23°Li
06-30-2005,09°Li	08-14-2005,15°Li	09-29-2005,24°Li
07-01-2005,09°Li	08-15-2005,15°Li	09-30-2005,24°Li
07-02-2005,09°Li	08-16-2005,15°Li	10-01-2005,24°Li
07-03-2005,10°Li	08-17-2005,15°Li	10-02-2005,24°Li
07-04-2005,10°Li	08-18-2005,16°Li	10-03-2005,25°Li
07-05-2005,10°Li	08-19-2005,16°Li	10-04-2005,25°Li
07-06-2005,10°Li	08-20-2005,16°Li	10-05-2005,25°Li
07-07-2005,10°Li	08-21-2005,16°Li	10-06-2005,25°Li
07-08-2005,10°Li	08-22-2005,16°Li	10-07-2005,25°Li
07-09-2005,10°Li	08-23-2005,16°Li	10-08-2005,26°Li
07-10-2005,10°Li	08-24-2005,17°Li	10-09-2005,26°Li
07-11-2005,10°Li	08-25-2005,17°Li	10-10-2005,26°Li
07-12-2005,10°Li	08-26-2005,17°Li	10-11-2005,26°Li
07-13-2005,10°Li	08-27-2005,17°Li	10-12-2005,26°Li
07-14-2005,11°Li	08-28-2005,17°Li	10-13-2005,27°Li
07-15-2005,11°Li	08-29-2005,17°Li	10-14-2005,27°Li
07-16-2005,11°Li	08-31-2005,18°Li	10-15-2005,27°Li
07-17-2005,11°Li	09-01-2005,18°Li	10-16-2005,27°Li
07-18-2005,11°Li	09-02-2005,18°Li	10-17-2005,28°Li
07-19-2005,11°Li	09-03-2005,18°Li	10-18-2005,28°Li
07-20-2005,11°Li	09-04-2005,19°Li	10-19-2005,28°Li
07-21-2005,11°Li	09-05-2005,19°Li	10-20-2005,28°Li
07-22-2005,12°Li	09-06-2005,19°Li	10-21-2005,28°Li
07-23-2005,12°Li	09-07-2005,19°Li	10-22-2005,29°Li
07-24-2005,12°Li	09-08-2005,19°Li	10-23-2005,29°Li
07-25-2005,12°Li	09-09-2005,20°Li	10-24-2005,29°Li
07-26-2005,12°Li	09-10-2005,20°Li	10-25-2005,29°Li
07-27-2005,12°Li	09-11-2005,20°Li	10-26-2005,00°Sc
07-28-2005,12°Li	09-12-2005,20°Li	10-27-2005,00°Sc
07-29-2005,12°Li	09-13-2005,20°Li	10-28-2005,00°Sc
07-30-2005,13°Li	09-14-2005,21°Li	10-29-2005,00°Sc
07-31-2005,13°Li	09-15-2005,21°Li	10-30-2005,00°Sc

10-31-2005,01°Sc
11-01-2005,01°Sc
11-02-2005,01°Sc
11-03-2005,01°Sc
11-04-2005,01°Sc
11-05-2005,02°Sc
11-06-2005,02°Sc
11-07-2005,02°Sc
11-08-2005,02°Sc
11-09-2005,03°Sc
11-10-2005,03°Sc
11-11-2005,03°Sc
11-12-2005,03°Sc
11-13-2005,03°Sc
11-14-2005,04°Sc
11-15-2005,04°Sc
11-16-2005,04°Sc
11-17-2005,04°Sc
11-18-2005,04°Sc
11-19-2005,05°Sc
11-20-2005,05°Sc
11-21-2005,05°Sc
11-22-2005,05°Sc
11-23-2005,06°Sc
11-24-2005,06°Sc
11-25-2005,06°Sc
11-26-2005,06°Sc
11-27-2005,06°Sc
11-28-2005,07°Sc
11-29-2005,07°Sc
11-30-2005,07°Sc
12-01-2005,07°Sc
12-02-2005,07°Sc
12-03-2005,08°Sc
12-04-2005,08°Sc
12-05-2005,08°Sc
12-06-2005,08°Sc
12-07-2005,08°Sc
12-08-2005,09°Sc
12-09-2005,09°Sc
12-10-2005,09°Sc
12-11-2005,09°Sc
12-12-2005,09°Sc
12-13-2005,10°Sc
12-14-2005,10°Sc

12-15-2005,10°Sc
12-16-2005,10°Sc
12-17-2005,10°Sc
12-18-2005,10°Sc
12-19-2005,11°Sc
12-20-2005,11°Sc
12-21-2005,11°Sc
12-22-2005,11°Sc
12-23-2005,11°Sc
12-24-2005,12°Sc
12-25-2005,12°Sc
12-26-2005,12°Sc
12-27-2005,12°Sc
12-28-2005,12°Sc
12-29-2005,12°Sc
12-30-2005,13°Sc
12-31-2005,13°Sc

2006
01-01-2006,13°Sc
01-02-2006,13°Sc
01-03-2006,13°Sc
01-04-2006,13°Sc
01-05-2006,13°Sc
01-06-2006,14°Sc
01-07-2006,14°Sc
01-08-2006,14°Sc
01-09-2006,14°Sc
01-10-2006,14°Sc
01-11-2006,14°Sc
01-12-2006,15°Sc
01-13-2006,15°Sc
01-14-2006,15°Sc
01-15-2006,15°Sc
01-16-2006,15°Sc
01-17-2006,15°Sc
01-18-2006,15°Sc
01-19-2006,15°Sc
01-20-2006,16°Sc
01-21-2006,16°Sc
01-22-2006,16°Sc
01-23-2006,16°Sc
01-24-2006,16°Sc
01-25-2006,16°Sc
01-26-2006,16°Sc

01-27-2006,16°Sc
01-28-2006,16°Sc
01-29-2006,17°Sc
01-30-2006,17°Sc
01-31-2006,17°Sc
02-01-2006,17°Sc
02-02-2006,17°Sc
02-03-2006,17°Sc
02-04-2006,17°Sc
02-05-2006,17°Sc
02-06-2006,17°Sc
02-07-2006,17°Sc
02-08-2006,17°Sc
02-09-2006,18°Sc
02-10-2006,18°Sc
02-11-2006,18°Sc
02-12-2006,18°Sc
02-13-2006,18°Sc
02-14-2006,18°Sc
02-15-2006,18°Sc
02-16-2006,18°Sc
02-17-2006,18°Sc
02-18-2006,18°Sc
02-19-2006,18°Sc
02-20-2006,18°Sc
02-21-2006,18°Sc
02-22-2006,18°Sc
02-23-2006,18°Sc
02-24-2006,18°Sc
02-25-2006,18°Sc
02-26-2006,18°Sc
02-27-2006,18°Sc
02-28-2006,18°Sc
03-01-2006,18°Sc
03-02-2006,18°Sc
03-03-2006,18°Sc
03-04-2006,18°Sc
03-05-2006,18°ScRx
03-06-2006,18°ScRx
03-07-2006,18°ScRx
03-08-2006,18°ScRx
03-09-2006,18°ScRx
03-10-2006,18°ScRx
03-11-2006,18°ScRx
03-12-2006,18°ScRx

03-13-2006,18°ScRx	04-27-2006,14°ScRx	06-11-2006,09°ScRx
03-14-2006,18°ScRx	04-28-2006,14°ScRx	06-12-2006,09°ScRx
03-15-2006,18°ScRx	04-29-2006,14°ScRx	06-13-2006,09°ScRx
03-16-2006,18°ScRx	04-30-2006,14°ScRx	06-14-2006,09°ScRx
03-17-2006,18°ScRx	05-01-2006,14°ScRx	06-15-2006,09°ScRx
03-18-2006,18°ScRx	05-02-2006,14°ScRx	06-16-2006,09°ScRx
03-19-2006,18°ScRx	05-03-2006,14°ScRx	06-17-2006,09°ScRx
03-20-2006,18°ScRx	05-04-2006,14°ScRx	06-18-2006,09°ScRx
03-21-2006,18°ScRx	05-05-2006,13°ScRx	06-19-2006,09°ScRx
03-22-2006,18°ScRx	05-06-2006,13°ScRx	06-20-2006,09°ScRx
03-23-2006,18°ScRx	05-07-2006,13°ScRx	06-21-2006,09°ScRx
03-24-2006,18°ScRx	05-08-2006,13°ScRx	06-22-2006,09°ScRx
03-25-2006,18°ScRx	05-09-2006,13°ScRx	06-23-2006,09°ScRx
03-26-2006,18°ScRx	05-10-2006,13°ScRx	06-24-2006,09°ScRx
03-27-2006,18°ScRx	05-11-2006,13°ScRx	06-25-2006,09°ScRx
03-28-2006,18°ScRx	05-12-2006,13°ScRx	06-26-2006,09°ScRx
03-29-2006,17°ScRx	05-13-2006,12°ScRx	06-27-2006,09°ScRx
03-30-2006,17°ScRx	05-14-2006,12°ScRx	06-28-2006,09°ScRx
03-31-2006,17°ScRx	05-15-2006,12°ScRx	06-29-2006,09°ScRx
04-01-2006,17°ScRx	05-16-2006,12°ScRx	06-30-2006,09°ScRx
04-02-2006,17°ScRx	05-17-2006,12°ScRx	07-01-2006,09°ScRx
04-03-2006,17°ScRx	05-18-2006,12°ScRx	07-02-2006,09°ScRx
04-04-2006,17°ScRx	05-19-2006,12°ScRx	07-03-2006,09°ScRx
04-05-2006,17°ScRx	05-20-2006,12°ScRx	07-04-2006,08°ScRx
04-06-2006,17°ScRx	05-21-2006,11°ScRx	07-05-2006,08°ScRx
04-07-2006,17°ScRx	05-22-2006,11°ScRx	07-06-2006,08°ScRx
04-08-2006,17°ScRx	05-23-2006,11°ScRx	07-07-2006,08°Sc
04-09-2006,16°ScRx	05-24-2006,11°ScRx	07-08-2006,08°Sc
04-10-2006,16°ScRx	05-25-2006,11°ScRx	07-09-2006,08°Sc
04-11-2006,16°ScRx	05-26-2006,11°ScRx	07-10-2006,09°Sc
04-12-2006,16°ScRx	05-27-2006,11°ScRx	07-11-2006,09°Sc
04-13-2006,16°ScRx	05-28-2006,11°ScRx	07-12-2006,09°Sc
04-14-2006,16°ScRx	05-29-2006,11°ScRx	07-13-2006,09°Sc
04-15-2006,16°ScRx	05-30-2006,10°ScRx	07-14-2006,09°Sc
04-16-2006,16°ScRx	05-31-2006,10°ScRx	07-15-2006,09°Sc
04-17-2006,16°ScRx	06-01-2006,10°ScRx	07-16-2006,09°Sc
04-18-2006,16°ScRx	06-02-2006,10°ScRx	07-17-2006,09°Sc
04-19-2006,15°ScRx	06-03-2006,10°ScRx	07-18-2006,09°Sc
04-20-2006,15°ScRx	06-04-2006,10°ScRx	07-19-2006,09°Sc
04-21-2006,15°ScRx	06-05-2006,10°ScRx	07-20-2006,09°Sc
04-22-2006,15°ScRx	06-06-2006,10°ScRx	07-21-2006,09°Sc
04-23-2006,15°ScRx	06-07-2006,10°ScRx	07-22-2006,09°Sc
04-24-2006,15°ScRx	06-08-2006,10°ScRx	07-23-2006,09°Sc
04-25-2006,15°ScRx	06-09-2006,10°ScRx	07-24-2006,09°Sc
04-26-2006,15°ScRx	06-10-2006,09°ScRx	07-25-2006,09°Sc

07-26-2006,09°Sc	09-09-2006,14°Sc	10-24-2006,23°Sc
07-27-2006,09°Sc	09-10-2006,14°Sc	10-25-2006,23°Sc
07-28-2006,09°Sc	09-11-2006,14°Sc	10-26-2006,23°Sc
07-29-2006,09°Sc	09-12-2006,15°Sc	10-27-2006,23°Sc
07-30-2006,09°Sc	09-13-2006,15°Sc	10-28-2006,24°Sc
07-31-2006,09°Sc	09-14-2006,15°Sc	10-29-2006,24°Sc
08-01-2006,09°Sc	09-15-2006,15°Sc	10-30-2006,24°Sc
08-02-2006,10°Sc	09-16-2006,15°Sc	10-31-2006,24°Sc
08-03-2006,10°Sc	09-17-2006,15°Sc	11-01-2006,24°Sc
08-04-2006,10°Sc	09-18-2006,16°Sc	11-02-2006,25°Sc
08-05-2006,10°Sc	09-19-2006,16°Sc	11-03-2006,25°Sc
08-06-2006,10°Sc	09-20-2006,16°Sc	11-04-2006,25°Sc
08-07-2006,10°Sc	09-21-2006,16°Sc	11-05-2006,25°Sc
08-08-2006,10°Sc	09-22-2006,16°Sc	11-06-2006,26°Sc
08-09-2006,10°Sc	09-23-2006,17°Sc	11-07-2006,26°Sc
08-10-2006,10°Sc	09-24-2006,17°Sc	11-08-2006,26°Sc
08-11-2006,10°Sc	09-25-2006,17°Sc	11-09-2006,26°Sc
08-12-2006,10°Sc	09-26-2006,17°Sc	11-10-2006,26°Sc
08-13-2006,11°Sc	09-27-2006,17°Sc	11-11-2006,27°Sc
08-14-2006,11°Sc	09-28-2006,17°Sc	11-12-2006,27°Sc
08-15-2006,11°Sc	09-29-2006,18°Sc	11-13-2006,27°Sc
08-16-2006,11°Sc	09-30-2006,18°Sc	11-14-2006,27°Sc
08-17-2006,11°Sc	10-01-2006,18°Sc	11-15-2006,28°Sc
08-18-2006,11°Sc	10-02-2006,18°Sc	11-16-2006,28°Sc
08-19-2006,11°Sc	10-03-2006,18°Sc	11-17-2006,28°Sc
08-20-2006,11°Sc	10-04-2006,19°Sc	11-18-2006,28°Sc
08-21-2006,11°Sc	10-05-2006,19°Sc	11-19-2006,28°Sc
08-22-2006,12°Sc	10-06-2006,19°Sc	11-20-2006,29°Sc
08-23-2006,12°Sc	10-07-2006,19°Sc	11-21-2006,29°Sc
08-24-2006,12°Sc	10-08-2006,19°Sc	11-22-2006,29°Sc
08-25-2006,12°Sc	10-09-2006,20°Sc	11-23-2006,29°Sc
08-26-2006,12°Sc	10-10-2006,20°Sc	11-24-2006,00°Sg
08-27-2006,12°Sc	10-11-2006,20°Sc	11-25-2006,00°Sg
08-28-2006,12°Sc	10-12-2006,20°Sc	11-26-2006,00°Sg
08-29-2006,13°Sc	10-13-2006,20°Sc	11-27-2006,00°Sg
08-30-2006,13°Sc	10-14-2006,21°Sc	11-28-2006,00°Sg
08-31-2006,13°Sc	10-15-2006,21°Sc	11-29-2006,01°Sg
09-01-2006,13°Sc	10-16-2006,21°Sc	11-30-2006,01°Sg
09-02-2006,13°Sc	10-17-2006,21°Sc	12-01-2006,01°Sg
09-03-2006,13°Sc	10-18-2006,21°Sc	12-02-2006,01°Sg
09-04-2006,13°Sc	10-19-2006,22°Sc	12-03-2006,02°Sg
09-05-2006,14°Sc	10-20-2006,22°Sc	12-04-2006,02°Sg
09-06-2006,14°Sc	10-21-2006,22°Sc	12-05-2006,02°Sg
09-07-2006,14°Sc	10-22-2006,22°Sc	12-06-2006,02°Sg
09-08-2006,14°Sc	10-23-2006,23°Sc	12-07-2006,02°Sg

12-08-2006,03°Sg	01-20-2007,11°Sg	03-06-2007,18°Sg
12-09-2006,03°Sg	01-21-2007,12°Sg	03-07-2007,18°Sg
12-10-2006,03°Sg	01-22-2007,12°Sg	03-08-2007,18°Sg
12-11-2006,03°Sg	01-23-2007,12°Sg	03-09-2007,18°Sg
12-12-2006,03°Sg	01-24-2007,12°Sg	03-10-2007,18°Sg
12-13-2006,04°Sg	01-25-2007,12°Sg	03-11-2007,18°Sg
12-14-2006,04°Sg	01-26-2007,13°Sg	03-12-2007,18°Sg
12-15-2006,04°Sg	01-27-2007,13°Sg	03-13-2007,18°Sg
12-16-2006,04°Sg	01-28-2007,13°Sg	03-14-2007,18°Sg
12-17-2006,05°Sg	01-29-2007,13°Sg	03-15-2007,19°Sg
12-18-2006,05°Sg	01-30-2007,13°Sg	03-16-2007,19°Sg
12-19-2006,05°Sg	01-31-2007,13°Sg	03-17-2007,19°Sg
12-20-2006,05°Sg	02-01-2007,14°Sg	03-18-2007,19°Sg
12-21-2006,05°Sg	02-02-2007,14°Sg	03-19-2007,19°Sg
12-22-2006,06°Sg	02-03-2007,14°Sg	03-20-2007,19°Sg
12-23-2006,06°Sg	02-04-2007,14°Sg	03-21-2007,19°Sg
12-24-2006,06°Sg	02-05-2007,14°Sg	03-22-2007,19°Sg
12-25-2006,06°Sg	02-06-2007,14°Sg	03-23-2007,19°Sg
12-26-2006,06°Sg	02-07-2007,14°Sg	03-24-2007,19°Sg
12-27-2006,07°Sg	02-08-2007,15°Sg	03-25-2007,19°Sg
12-28-2006,07°Sg	02-09-2007,15°Sg	03-26-2007,19°Sg
12-29-2006,07°Sg	02-10-2007,15°Sg	03-27-2007,19°Sg
12-30-2006,07°Sg	02-11-2007,15°Sg	03-28-2007,19°Sg
12-31-2006,08°Sg	02-12-2007,15°Sg	03-29-2007,19°Sg
	02-13-2007,15°Sg	03-30-2007,19°Sg
2007	02-14-2007,16°Sg	03-31-2007,19°Sg
01-01-2007,08°Sg	02-15-2007,16°Sg	04-01-2007,19°Sg
01-02-2007,08°Sg	02-16-2007,16°Sg	04-02-2007,19°Sg
01-03-2007,08°Sg	02-17-2007,16°Sg	04-03-2007,19°Sg
01-04-2007,08°Sg	02-18-2007,16°Sg	04-04-2007,19°Sg
01-05-2007,09°Sg	02-19-2007,16°Sg	04-05-2007,19°Sg
01-06-2007,09°Sg	02-20-2007,16°Sg	04-06-2007,19°SgRx
01-07-2007,09°Sg	02-21-2007,16°Sg	04-07-2007,19°SgRx
01-08-2007,09°Sg	02-22-2007,17°Sg	04-08-2007,19°SgRx
01-09-2007,09°Sg	02-23-2007,17°Sg	04-09-2007,19°SgRx
01-10-2007,10°Sg	02-24-2007,17°Sg	04-10-2007,19°SgRx
01-11-2007,10°Sg	02-25-2007,17°Sg	04-11-2007,19°SgRx
01-12-2007,10°Sg	02-26-2007,17°Sg	04-12-2007,19°SgRx
01-13-2007,10°Sg	02-27-2007,17°Sg	04-13-2007,19°SgRx
01-14-2007,10°Sg	02-28-2007,17°Sg	04-14-2007,19°SgRx
01-15-2007,11°Sg	03-01-2007,17°Sg	04-15-2007,19°SgRx
01-16-2007,11°Sg	03-02-2007,17°Sg	04-16-2007,19°SgRx
01-17-2007,11°Sg	03-03-2007,18°Sg	04-17-2007,19°SgRx
01-18-2007,11°Sg	03-04-2007,18°Sg	04-18-2007,19°SgRx
01-19-2007,11°Sg	03-05-2007,18°Sg	04-19-2007,19°SgRx

04-20-2007,19°SgRx	06-04-2007,15°SgRx	07-19-2007,10°SgRx
04-21-2007,19°SgRx	06-05-2007,15°SgRx	07-20-2007,10°SgRx
04-22-2007,19°SgRx	06-06-2007,14°SgRx	07-21-2007,10°SgRx
04-23-2007,19°SgRx	06-07-2007,14°SgRx	07-22-2007,10°SgRx
04-24-2007,19°SgRx	06-08-2007,14°SgRx	07-23-2007,10°SgRx
04-25-2007,19°SgRx	06-09-2007,14°SgRx	07-24-2007,10°SgRx
04-26-2007,19°SgRx	06-10-2007,14°SgRx	07-25-2007,10°SgRx
04-27-2007,19°SgRx	06-11-2007,14°SgRx	07-26-2007,10°SgRx
04-28-2007,19°SgRx	06-12-2007,14°SgRx	07-27-2007,10°SgRx
04-29-2007,18°SgRx	06-13-2007,14°SgRx	07-28-2007,10°SgRx
04-30-2007,18°SgRx	06-14-2007,13°SgRx	07-29-2007,10°SgRx
05-01-2007,18°SgRx	06-15-2007,13°SgRx	07-30-2007,10°SgRx
05-02-2007,18°SgRx	06-16-2007,13°SgRx	07-31-2007,10°SgRx
05-03-2007,18°SgRx	06-17-2007,13°SgRx	08-01-2007,09°SgRx
05-04-2007,18°SgRx	06-18-2007,13°SgRx	08-02-2007,09°SgRx
05-05-2007,18°SgRx	06-19-2007,13°SgRx	08-03-2007,09°SgRx
05-06-2007,18°SgRx	06-20-2007,13°SgRx	08-04-2007,09°SgRx
05-07-2007,18°SgRx	06-21-2007,13°SgRx	08-05-2007,09°SgRx
05-08-2007,18°SgRx	06-22-2007,12°SgRx	08-06-2007,09°SgRx
05-09-2007,18°SgRx	06-23-2007,12°SgRx	08-07-2007,09°Sg
05-10-2007,18°SgRx	06-24-2007,12°SgRx	08-08-2007,09°Sg
05-11-2007,17°SgRx	06-25-2007,12°SgRx	08-09-2007,09°Sg
05-12-2007,17°SgRx	06-26-2007,12°SgRx	08-10-2007,09°Sg
05-13-2007,17°SgRx	06-27-2007,12°SgRx	08-11-2007,09°Sg
05-14-2007,17°SgRx	06-28-2007,12°SgRx	08-12-2007,09°Sg
05-15-2007,17°SgRx	06-29-2007,12°SgRx	08-13-2007,09°Sg
05-16-2007,17°SgRx	06-30-2007,12°SgRx	08-14-2007,10°Sg
05-17-2007,17°SgRx	07-01-2007,11°SgRx	08-15-2007,10°Sg
05-18-2007,17°SgRx	07-02-2007,11°SgRx	08-16-2007,10°Sg
05-19-2007,17°SgRx	07-03-2007,11°SgRx	08-17-2007,10°Sg
05-20-2007,16°SgRx	07-04-2007,11°SgRx	08-18-2007,10°Sg
05-21-2007,16°SgRx	07-05-2007,11°SgRx	08-19-2007,10°Sg
05-22-2007,16°SgRx	07-06-2007,11°SgRx	08-20-2007,10°Sg
05-23-2007,16°SgRx	07-07-2007,11°SgRx	08-21-2007,10°Sg
05-24-2007,16°SgRx	07-08-2007,11°SgRx	08-22-2007,10°Sg
05-25-2007,16°SgRx	07-09-2007,11°SgRx	08-23-2007,10°Sg
05-26-2007,16°SgRx	07-10-2007,11°SgRx	08-24-2007,10°Sg
05-27-2007,16°SgRx	07-11-2007,11°SgRx	08-25-2007,10°Sg
05-28-2007,16°SgRx	07-12-2007,10°SgRx	08-26-2007,10°Sg
05-29-2007,15°SgRx	07-13-2007,10°SgRx	08-27-2007,10°Sg
05-30-2007,15°SgRx	07-14-2007,10°SgRx	08-28-2007,10°Sg
05-31-2007,15°SgRx	07-15-2007,10°SgRx	08-29-2007,10°Sg
06-01-2007,15°SgRx	07-16-2007,10°SgRx	08-30-2007,10°Sg
06-02-2007,15°SgRx	07-17-2007,10°SgRx	08-31-2007,10°Sg
06-03-2007,15°SgRx	07-18-2007,10°SgRx	08-31-2007,10°Sg

09-01-2007,10°Sg	10-16-2007,16°Sg	11-30-2007,25°Sg
09-02-2007,10°Sg	10-17-2007,16°Sg	12-01-2007,26°Sg
09-03-2007,11°Sg	10-18-2007,17°Sg	12-02-2007,26°Sg
09-04-2007,11°Sg	10-19-2007,17°Sg	12-03-2007,26°Sg
09-05-2007,11°Sg	10-20-2007,17°Sg	12-04-2007,26°Sg
09-06-2007,11°Sg	10-21-2007,17°Sg	12-05-2007,26°Sg
09-07-2007,11°Sg	10-22-2007,17°Sg	12-06-2007,27°Sg
09-08-2007,11°Sg	10-23-2007,17°Sg	12-07-2007,27°Sg
09-09-2007,11°Sg	10-24-2007,18°Sg	12-08-2007,27°Sg
09-10-2007,11°Sg	10-25-2007,18°Sg	12-09-2007,27°Sg
09-11-2007,11°Sg	10-26-2007,18°Sg	12-10-2007,28°Sg
09-12-2007,11°Sg	10-27-2007,18°Sg	12-11-2007,28°Sg
09-13-2007,11°Sg	10-28-2007,18°Sg	12-12-2007,28°Sg
09-14-2007,12°Sg	10-29-2007,19°Sg	12-13-2007,28°Sg
09-15-2007,12°Sg	10-30-2007,19°Sg	12-14-2007,28°Sg
09-16-2007,12°Sg	10-31-2007,19°Sg	12-15-2007,29°Sg
09-17-2007,12°Sg	11-01-2007,19°Sg	12-16-2007,29°Sg
09-18-2007,12°Sg	11-02-2007,19°Sg	12-17-2007,29°Sg
09-19-2007,12°Sg	11-03-2007,20°Sg	12-18-2007,29°Sg
09-20-2007,12°Sg	11-04-2007,20°Sg	12-19-2007,00°Cap
09-21-2007,12°Sg	11-05-2007,20°Sg	12-20-2007,00°Cap
09-22-2007,13°Sg	11-06-2007,20°Sg	12-21-2007,00°Cap
09-23-2007,13°Sg	11-07-2007,20°Sg	12-22-2007,00°Cap
09-24-2007,13°Sg	11-08-2007,21°Sg	12-23-2007,01°Cap
09-25-2007,13°Sg	11-09-2007,21°Sg	12-24-2007,01°Cap
09-26-2007,13°Sg	11-10-2007,21°Sg	12-25-2007,01°Cap
09-27-2007,13°Sg	11-11-2007,21°Sg	12-26-2007,01°Cap
09-28-2007,13°Sg	11-12-2007,21°Sg	12-27-2007,01°Cap
09-29-2007,13°Sg	11-13-2007,22°Sg	12-28-2007,02°Cap
09-30-2007,14°Sg	11-14-2007,22°Sg	12-29-2007,02°Cap
10-01-2007,14°Sg	11-15-2007,22°Sg	12-30-2007,02°Cap
10-02-2007,14°Sg	11-16-2007,22°Sg	12-31-2007,02°Cap
10-03-2007,14°Sg	11-17-2007,22°Sg	
10-04-2007,14°Sg	11-18-2007,23°Sg	
10-05-2007,14°Sg	11-19-2007,23°Sg	
10-06-2007,15°Sg	11-20-2007,23°Sg	
10-07-2007,15°Sg	11-21-2007,23°Sg	
10-08-2007,15°Sg	11-22-2007,24°Sg	
10-09-2007,15°Sg	11-23-2007,24°Sg	
10-10-2007,15°Sg	11-24-2007,24°Sg	
10-11-2007,15°Sg	11-25-2007,24°Sg	
10-12-2007,15°Sg	11-26-2007,24°Sg	
10-13-2007,16°Sg	11-27-2007,25°Sg	
10-14-2007,16°Sg	11-28-2007,25°Sg	
10-15-2007,16°Sg	11-29-2007,25°Sg	

♄
Saturn Ephemeris
2003–2007

2003
01-01-2003,24°GeRx
01-15-2003,23°GeRx
01-29-2003,22°GeRx
02-12-2003,22°GeRx
02-26-2003,22°Ge
03-12-2003,22°Ge
03-26-2003,23°Ge
04-09-2003,24°Ge
04-23-2003,25°Ge
05-07-2003,26°Ge
05-21-2003,28°Ge
06-04-2003,00°Ca
06-18-2003,01°Ca
07-02-2003,03°Ca
07-16-2003,05°Ca
07-30-2003,07°Ca
08-13-2003,08°Ca
08-27-2003,10°Ca
09-10-2003,11°Ca
09-24-2003,12°Ca
10-08-2003,12°Ca
10-22-2003,13°Ca
11-05-2003,13°CaRx
11-19-2003,12°CaRx
12-03-2003,11°CaRx
12-17-2003,10°CaRx
12-31-2003,09°CaRx

2004
01-14-2004,08°CaRx
01-28-2004,07°CaRx
02-11-2004,06°CaRx
02-25-2004,06°CaRx
03-10-2004,06°Ca
03-24-2004,06°Ca
04-07-2004,07°Ca
04-21-2004,08°Ca
05-05-2004,09°Ca

05-19-2004,10°Ca
06-02-2004,12°Ca
06-16-2004,13°Ca
06-30-2004,15°Ca
07-14-2004,17°Ca
07-28-2004,19°Ca
08-11-2004,21°Ca
08-25-2004,22°Ca
09-08-2004,24°Ca
09-22-2004,25°Ca
10-06-2004,26°Ca
10-20-2004,27°Ca
11-03-2004,27°Ca
11-17-2004,27°CaRx
12-01-2004,26°CaRx
12-15-2004,26°CaRx
12-29-2004,25°CaRx

2005
01-12-2005,24°CaRx
01-26-2005,22°CaRx
02-09-2005,21°CaRx
02-23-2005,21°CaRx
03-09-2005,20°CaRx
03-23-2005,20°Ca
04-06-2005,20°Ca
04-20-2005,21°Ca
05-04-2005,22°Ca
05-18-2005,23°Ca
06-01-2005,24°Ca
06-15-2005,26°Ca
06-29-2005,27°Ca
07-13-2005,29°Ca
07-27-2005,01°Le
08-10-2005,03°Le
08-24-2005,04°Le
09-07-2005,06°Le
09-21-2005,08°Le
10-05-2005,09°Le

10-19-2005,10°Le
11-02-2005,10°Le
11-16-2005,11°Le
11-30-2005,11°LeRx
12-14-2005,10°LeRx
12-28-2005,10°LeRx

2006
01-11-2006,09°LeRx
01-25-2006,08°LeRx
02-08-2006,06°LeRx
02-22-2006,05°LeRx
03-08-2006,05°LeRx
03-22-2006,04°LeRx
04-05-2006,04°LeRx
04-19-2006,04°Le
05-03-2006,05°Le
05-17-2006,05°Le
05-31-2006,07°Le
06-14-2006,08°Le
06-28-2006,09°Le
07-12-2006,11°Le
07-26-2006,13°Le
08-09-2006,15°Le
08-23-2006,16°Le
09-06-2006,18°Le
09-20-2006,20°Le
10-04-2006,21°Le
10-18-2006,22°Le
11-01-2006,23°Le
11-15-2006,24°Le
11-29-2006,25°Le
12-13-2006,25°LeRx
12-27-2006,24°LeRx

2007
01-10-2007,23°LeRx
01-24-2007,23°LeRx
02-07-2007,21°LeRx

02-21-2007,20°LeRx	06-13-2007,20°Le	10-03-2007,03°Vi
03-07-2007,19°LeRx	06-27-2007,21°Le	10-17-2007,05°Vi
03-21-2007,18°LeRx	07-11-2007,23°Le	10-31-2007,06°Vi
04-04-2007,18°LeRx	07-25-2007,25°Le	11-14-2007,07°Vi
04-18-2007,18°LeRx	08-08-2007,26°Le	11-28-2007,08°Vi
05-02-2007,18°Le	08-22-2007,28°Le	12-12-2007,08°Vi
05-16-2007,18°Le	09-05-2007,00°Vi	12-26-2007,08°ViRx
05-30-2007,19°Le	09-19-2007,02°Vi	

♅
Uranus Ephemeris
2003–2007

2003	2004	2005
01-01-2003,26°Aq	01-14-2004,00°Pi	01-12-2005,04°Pi
01-15-2003,26°Aq	01-28-2004,01°Pi	01-26-2005,05°Pi
01-29-2003,27°Aq	02-11-2004,02°Pi	02-09-2005,05°Pi
02-12-2003,28°Aq	02-25-2004,02°Pi	02-23-2005,06°Pi
02-26-2003,29°Aq	03-10-2004,03°Pi	03-09-2005,07°Pi
03-12-2003,00°Pi	03-24-2004,04°Pi	03-23-2005,08°Pi
03-26-2003,00°Pi	04-07-2004,05°Pi	04-06-2005,08°Pi
04-09-2003,01°Pi	04-21-2004,05°Pi	04-20-2005,09°Pi
04-23-2003,02°Pi	05-05-2004,06°Pi	05-04-2005,10°Pi
05-07-2003,02°Pi	05-19-2004,06°Pi	05-18-2005,10°Pi
05-21-2003,02°Pi	06-02-2004,06°Pi	06-01-2005,10°Pi
06-04-2003,02°Pi	06-16-2004,06°PiRx	06-15-2005,10°PiRx
06-18-2003,02°PiRx	06-30-2004,06°PiRx	06-29-2005,10°PiRx
07-02-2003,02°PiRx	07-14-2004,06°PiRx	07-13-2005,10°PiRx
07-16-2003,02°PiRx	07-28-2004,05°PiRx	07-27-2005,10°PiRx
07-30-2003,01°PiRx	08-11-2004,05°PiRx	08-10-2005,09°PiRx
08-13-2003,01°PiRx	08-25-2004,04°PiRx	08-24-2005,09°PiRx
08-27-2003,00°PiRx	09-08-2004,04°PiRx	09-07-2005,08°PiRx
09-10-2003,00°PiRx	09-22-2004,03°PiRx	09-21-2005,08°PiRx
09-24-2003,29°AqRx	10-06-2004,03°PiRx	10-05-2005,07°PiRx
10-08-2003,29°AqRx	10-20-2004,03°PiRx	10-19-2005,07°PiRx
10-22-2003,29°AqRx	11-03-2004,02°PiRx	11-02-2005,06°PiRx
11-05-2003,28°AqRx	11-17-2004,02°Pi	11-16-2005,06°Pi
11-19-2003,28°Aq	12-01-2004,03°Pi	11-30-2005,06°Pi
12-03-2003,29°Aq	12-15-2004,03°Pi	12-14-2005,07°Pi
12-17-2003,29°Aq	12-29-2004,03°Pi	12-28-2005,07°Pi
12-31-2003,00°Pi		

2006
01-11-2006,08°Pi
01-25-2006,08°Pi
02-08-2006,09°Pi
02-22-2006,10°Pi
03-08-2006,11°Pi
03-22-2006,11°Pi
04-05-2006,12°Pi
04-19-2006,13°Pi
05-03-2006,13°Pi
05-17-2006,14°Pi
05-31-2006,14°Pi
06-14-2006,14°Pi
06-28-2006,14°PiRx
07-12-2006,14°PiRx
07-26-2006,14°PiRx
08-09-2006,13°PiRx
08-23-2006,13°PiRx
09-06-2006,12°PiRx

09-20-2006,12°PiRx
10-04-2006,11°PiRx
10-18-2006,11°PiRx
11-01-2006,10°PiRx
11-15-2006,10°PiRx
11-29-2006,10°Pi
12-13-2006,11°Pi
12-27-2006,11°Pi

2007
01-10-2007,11°Pi
01-24-2007,12°Pi
02-07-2007,13°Pi
02-21-2007,13°Pi
03-07-2007,14°Pi
03-21-2007,15°Pi
04-04-2007,16°Pi
04-18-2007,17°Pi
05-02-2007,17°Pi

05-16-2007,18°Pi
05-30-2007,18°Pi
06-13-2007,18°Pi
06-27-2007,18°PiRx
07-11-2007,18°PiRx
07-25-2007,18°PiRx
08-08-2007,17°PiRx
08-22-2007,17°PiRx
09-05-2007,16°PiRx
09-19-2007,16°PiRx
10-03-2007,15°PiRx
10-17-2007,15°PiRx
10-31-2007,15°PiRx
11-14-2007,14°PiRx
11-28-2007,14°Pi
12-12-2007,14°Pi
12-26-2007,15°Pi

♆ ♇

Neptune and Pluto Ephemeres

2003–2007

Neptune Ephemeris
2003
01-01-2003,09°Aq
02-01-2003,10°Aq
03-01-2003,11°Aq
04-01-2003,12°Aq
05-01-2003,13°Aq
06-01-2003,13°AqRx
07-01-2003,12°AqRx
08-01-2003,11°AqRx
09-01-2003,11°AqRx
10-01-2003,10°AqRx
11-01-2003,10°Aq
12-01-2003,10°Aq

2004
01-01-2004,11°Aq
02-01-2004,12°Aq

03-01-2004,13°Aq
04-01-2004,14°Aq
05-01-2004,15°Aq
06-01-2004,15°AqRx
07-01-2004,14°AqRx
08-01-2004,14°AqRx
09-01-2004,13°AqRx
10-01-2004,12°AqRx
11-01-2004,12°Aq
12-01-2004,13°Aq

2005
01-01-2005,13°Aq
02-01-2005,14°Aq
03-01-2005,16°Aq
04-01-2005,16°Aq
05-01-2005,17°Aq
06-01-2005,17°AqRx

07-01-2005,17°AqRx
08-01-2005,16°AqRx
09-01-2005,15°AqRx
10-01-2005,15°AqRx
11-01-2005,14°Aq
12-01-2005,15°Aq

2006
01-01-2006,15°Aq
02-01-2006,17°Aq
03-01-2006,18°Aq
04-01-2006,19°Aq
05-01-2006,19°Aq
06-01-2006,19°AqRx
07-01-2006,19°AqRx
08-01-2006,18°AqRx
09-01-2006,17°AqRx
10-01-2006,17°AqRx

11-01-2006,17°Aq
12-01-2006,17°Aq

2007
01-01-2007,18°Aq
02-01-2007,19°Aq
03-01-2007,20°Aq
04-01-2007,21°Aq
05-01-2007,21°Aq
06-01-2007,22°AqRx
07-01-2007,21°AqRx
08-01-2007,20°AqRx
09-01-2007,20°AqRx
10-01-2007,19°AqRx
11-01-2007,19°Aq
12-01-2007,19°Aq
01-01-2008,20°Aq

Pluto Ephemeris
2003
01-01-2003,18°Sg
02-01-2003,19°Sg
03-01-2003,19°Sg
04-01-2003,19°SgRx
05-01-2003,19°SgRx
06-01-2003,18°SgRx
07-01-2003,18°SgRx
08-01-2003,17°SgRx
09-01-2003,17°Sg
10-01-2003,17°Sg

11-01-2003,18°Sg
12-01-2003,19°Sg

2004
01-01-2004,20°Sg
02-01-2004,21°Sg
03-01-2004,22°Sg
04-01-2004,22°SgRx
05-01-2004,21°SgRx
06-01-2004,21°SgRx
07-01-2004,20°SgRx
08-01-2004,19°SgRx
09-01-2004,19°Sg
10-01-2004,19°Sg
11-01-2004,20°Sg
12-01-2004,21°Sg

2005
01-01-2005,22°Sg
02-01-2005,23°Sg
03-01-2005,24°Sg
04-01-2005,24°SgRx
05-01-2005,24°SgRx
06-01-2005,23°SgRx
07-01-2005,22°SgRx
08-01-2005,22°SgRx
09-01-2005,21°SgRx
10-01-2005,22°Sg
11-01-2005,22°Sg
12-01-2005,23°Sg

2006
01-01-2006,24°Sg
02-01-2006,25°Sg
03-01-2006,26°Sg
04-01-2006,26°SgRx
05-01-2006,26°SgRx
06-01-2006,25°SgRx
07-01-2006,25°SgRx
08-01-2006,24°SgRx
09-01-2006,24°SgRx
10-01-2006,24°Sg
11-01-2006,24°Sg
12-01-2006,25°Sg

2007
01-01-2007,27°Sg
02-01-2007,28°Sg
03-01-2007,28°Sg
04-01-2007,28°SgRx
05-01-2007,28°SgRx
06-01-2007,28°SgRx
07-01-2007,27°SgRx
08-01-2007,26°SgRx
09-01-2007,26°SgRx
10-01-2007,26°Sg
11-01-2007,27°Sg
12-01-2007,28°Sg
01-01-2008,29°Sg

APPENDIX B

RULERSHIPS

This list is by no means complete. Use these rulerships to find the extra layer of the story line when you're doing transits.

Accountants	Mercury, Virgo
Actors, actresses	Venus, Neptune, Leo, sun, fifth house
Advertising	Mercury, Gemini, third house
Agents	Mercury
literary	Mercury, third or fifth house
theatrical	Venus
travel	Mercury, third or ninth house
Aliens (E.T. variety)	Sagittarius, ninth house, Neptune, Uranus
Ambassadors	Jupiter, Mercury, ninth house
Animal trainers	Mercury, Virgo
Ankles	Aquarius, Uranus
Arms	Mercury, Gemini
Army officers	Mars, Aries, sun
Artists	Venus, Libra, Neptune, Mercury, Pisces
Bank teller	Venus, Taurus, Mercury
Beauticians	Venus, Libra
Blisters	Mars
Blood	Jupiter, Sagittarius
Blood circulation	Aquarius
Bones	Saturn, Capricorn
Bookkeepers	Mercury, Gemini, Virgo, third house
Booksellers	Mercury, Gemini, third house

Botanists	Venus
Brain	Mercury, Aries, moon
Builders	Saturn, Capricorn, Mars
Carpenters	Mars, Saturn, Capricorn
Cashiers	Venus, Jupiter, Mercury, second house
Cats	Virgo, Venus, fifth or sixth house
Celebrities	Sun, Jupiter
CEOs	Sun, Leo, tenth house
Chakras	Neptune
Childbirth	Moon
Children	Sun, Leo, fifth house, Venus
Chiropractors	Saturn, Capricorn, Uranus, Aquarius
Churches	Jupiter, Sagittarius, ninth house
Civil engineers	Mercury, Saturn, Capricorn
College students	Jupiter, Sagittarius, ninth house
Columnists	Mercury, third house
Computers	Uranus, Mercury
Contracts	Mercury, Gemini, Libra, seventh house, third house
Copyrights	Mercury, Jupiter
Counselors	
spiritual	Neptune
vocational	Saturn, Capricorn
Courts	Sagittarius, Jupiter, ninth house
Death	Pluto, Scorpio, eighth house, Mars, Saturn
Dentists	Saturn, Scorpio, Mars, sixth house
Department heads	Sun, Jupiter
Detectives	Pluto, Scorpio, Neptune, Pisces, twelfth house
Directors	Leo
Divination, diviners	Neptune, Pluto
Dogs	Mercury, Virgo, Sun, fifth or sixth house
Dolphins	Venus, moon
Drama	Venus, Neptune
Dreams	Neptune, Sagittarius, ninth or twelfth house

Drugs	Neptune, Pisces, twelfth house
Ducks	Moon
Ear (left)	Mars, Saturn
Ear (right)	Jupiter, Saturn
Editors	Mercury, Virgo, Gemini, Sagittarius, Jupiter
Eels	Moon
Elderly people	Saturn, Capricorn
Elections	Uranus
ESP	Neptune
Ethics	Jupiter
Exercise	Mars
Experts	Uranus
Eyes	Mercury, sun, Aries, first house
Eyesight	Mercury
Family	Moon, Cancer, fourth house
Father	Saturn, tenth house
Feet	Neptune, Pisces
Females	Venus, Moon
Fever	Mars, Aries, sun, Leo
Fiancé(e)	Venus
Fiction	Mercury, Neptune
Fingers	Mercury, Gemini
Fire	Mars, Aries, sun, Leo
Firebugs	Mars, Pluto
Fire engines	Mars, Uranus
Flight Attendants	Sagittarius, ninth house
Foremen	Sun, Leo
Freelancers	Uranus
Friends	Aquarius, eleventh house, Venus, Jupiter
Gamblers	Leo, sun, fifth house
Geese	Moon
Genius	Neptune
Government	Sun, Leo, Saturn
Grandparents	Saturn, first, third, fourth, seventh houses
Hands	Mercury, Gemini
Head	Aries, Mars
Hips	Jupiter, Sagittarius
Horses	Jupiter, Sagittarius, ninth house
Illusions	Neptune, Mercury

Inheritance	Pluto, ninth house, Scorpio
Interior decorators	Venus, Libra
Inventors	Uranus, Aquarius, Mercury
Journalists	Mercury, Gemini, third house
Juries	Jupiter, ninth house, Venus
Lawsuits	Libra, seventh house, Jupiter, ninth house
Lawyers	Jupiter, Sagittarius, Mercury, ninth house
Legs (lower)	Aquarius, Uranus
Legs (upper)	Jupiter, Sagittarius
Librarians, libraries	Mercury, Virgo, Gemini, third house
Love, lovers	Venus, Libra, fifth or seventh house
Luck	Jupiter
Lunatics	Moon, Pluto
Lungs	Gemini, Mercury
Magicians	Neptune, Uranus, Pluto, Scorpio
Males	Mars, Sun
Male relatives	Mars
Marriage (legal or otherwise)	Venus, Libra, seventh house
Mayors	Capricorn, tenth house
Mechanics	Uranus, Aquarius, Gemini
Mediumship	Neptune, Pisces
Memory	Mercury, Gemini, moon, third house
Meteorologists	Moon, Cancer
Midwives	Moon
Military	Mars, Aries
Ministers	Jupiter, Sagittarius, ninth house
Miracles	Uranus, Neptune
Mistress	Pluto
Monarchs	Leo, Sun, tenth house, Saturn
Mortician	Pluto, Scorpio, Mars, eighth house
Mothers	Moon, Venus, fourth house
Movies	Neptune, Venus, Uranus, Aquarius, Leo, fifth house
Music and musicians	Venus, Libra, Taurus, Neptune
Mystics, mysticism	Neptune, Pisces

Mythology	Neptune
Naturalists	Saturn, Neptune
Novelists	Mercury, Gemini, third house
Nuclear physicists	Uranus, Aquarius, Pluto
Nuns	Saturn, Pisces, twelfth house
Nurses, nursing	Moon, Cancer, Virgo, Neptune, sixth and twelfth houses
Nursing homes	Neptune, Pisces, twelfth house, moon
Occult	Scorpio, eighth or twelfth house, Neptune, Pisces, Uranus
Operations (surgical)	Mars, Aries, Scorpio
Ophthalmologists	Mercury, moon
Opticians	Mercury, moon, Aries
Oracles	Neptune
Owls	Moon
Pagans	Uranus, Neptune
Partners (marriage or business)	Venus, Libra, seventh house
Pathologists	Scorpio, Pluto, Mars, eighth or twelfth house
Pets	fifth or sixth house, sun, Venus, Jupiter
Physicians	Virgo, Mercury, Jupiter, sixth house
Piano, pianists	Venus, Libra
Pilots	Uranus, Aquarius, Sagittarius, ninth house
Plumbers	Neptune, moon, Cancer, Saturn, Pluto
Podiatry	Pisces, Neptune,
Poets, poetry	Venus, Neptune, Libra,
Police officers	Mars, Saturn, sixth or tenth house
Politicians	Saturn, Capricorn, Sun, Leo, tenth house
Pregnancy	Moon, Venus, fifth house
Prisoners	Neptune, twelfth house
Publishers, publishing	Jupiter, Sagittarius, ninth house
Real estate, realtors	Moon, Cancer, fourth house
Relatives	Mercury, Gemini, third house
Sadness	Saturn
Scholars	Mercury, Jupiter, ninth house

Schools	Mercury, Gemini, Jupiter, Sagittarius, third or ninth house
Séances	Neptune, Pisces
Secretaries	Mercury, Gemini, Virgo
Secret enemies	Twelfth house, Pisces
Self	Sun
Senate, senators	Jupiter, Aquarius
Senility	Saturn
Sexuality	Pluto, Scorpio, eighth house

CHARTS

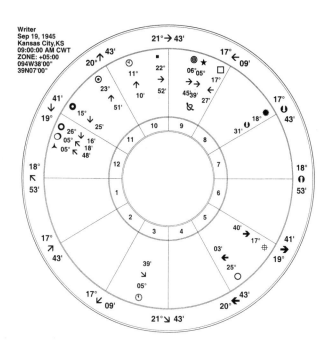

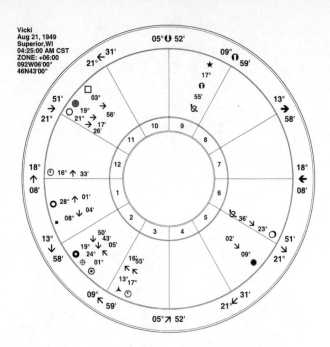

Vicki
Aug 21, 1949
Superior,WI
04:25:00 AM CST
ZONE: +06:00
092W06'00"
46N43'00"

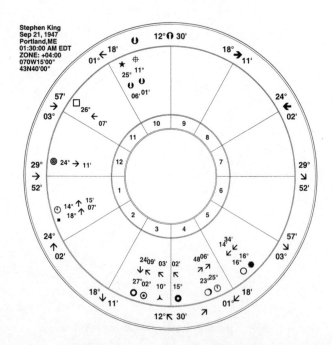

Stephen King
Sep 21, 1947
Portland,ME
01:30:00 AM EDT
ZONE: +04:00
070W15'00"
43N40'00"

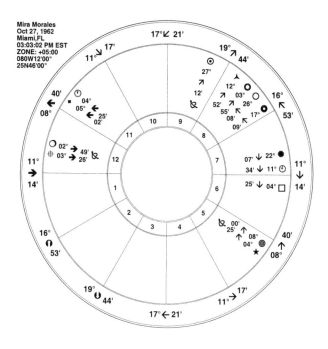

Mira Morales
Oct 27, 1962
Miami,FL
03:03:02 PM EST
ZONE: +05:00
080W12'00"
25N46'00"

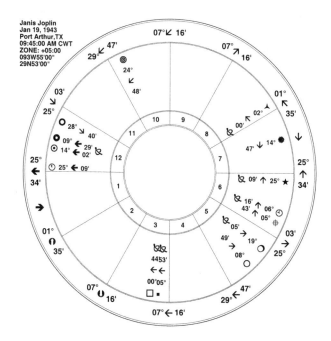

Janis Joplin
Jan 19, 1943
Port Arthur,TX
09:45:00 AM CWT
ZONE: +05:00
093W55'00"
29N53'00"

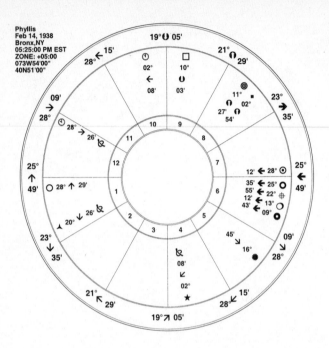

Phyllis
Feb 14, 1938
Bronx,NY
05:25:00 PM EST
ZONE: +05:00
073W54'00"
40N51'00"

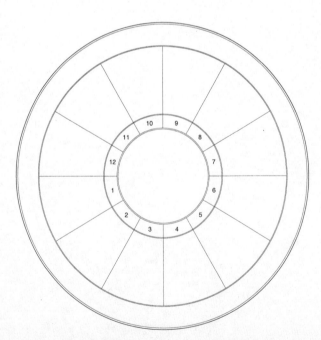

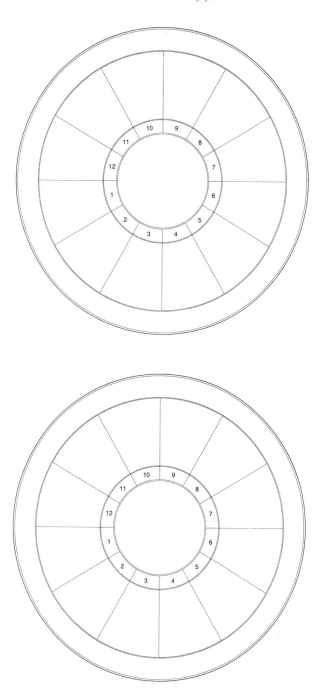

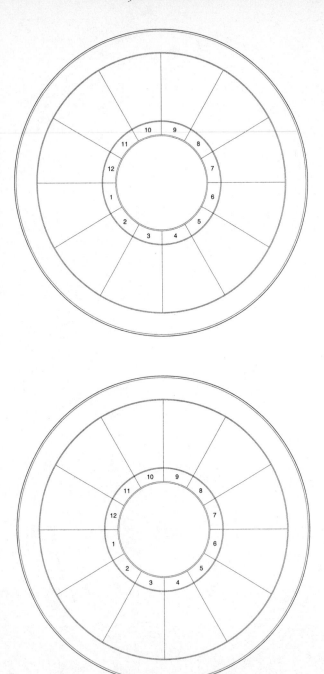

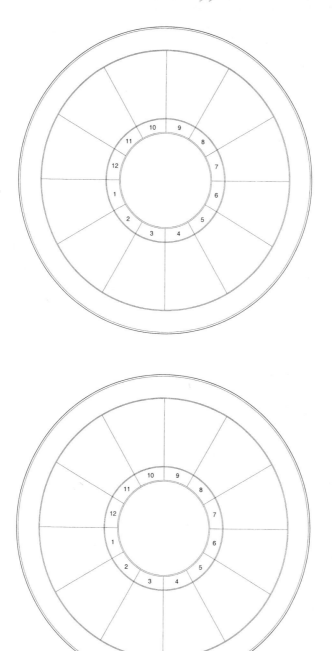

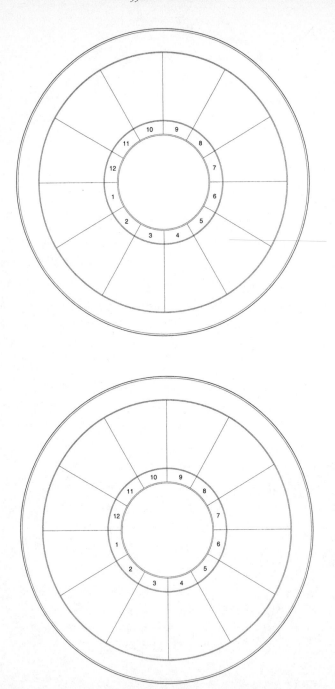

INDEX

Cancer (*continued*)
  Moon transits with, 68
  nurturer and intuitive, 118–19
  opposite sign, 42
  outer planets and, 126–27
  planetary plots for, 120–22
  Sun in, 118–29
  transits and timing for, 127–28
  a water sign, 14–15
Capricorn
  achiever and strategist, 194–96
  cardinal quality of, 15–16
  conjunctions and opportunities for, 240
  an earth sign, 13
  opposite sign, 42
  outer planets and, 89–90
  Sun in, 194–205
  transits and timing for, 204
cardinal quality, 15
career, 45. *See also* job
car purchase: Aquarius, 217; Cancer, 128;
      Capricorn, 205; Gemini, 117; Leo,
      140; Scorpio, 179; Virgo, 154
Castaway, 77
challenges, 60
change, sudden, 33
children, 25
Christine, 7
Clan of the Cave Bear, 12
college application: Pisces, 229
communication, 25, 45
computer or electronic device purchase:
      Aquarius, 217; Gemini, 117; Libra,
      167; Sagittarius, 192
confrontation, 62
conjunction, 57–59, 67
  and opportunities, 235–42
contacts
  challenging, 67–68
  positive, 67
contract, signing: Aries, 92; Cancer, 128;
      Gemini, 116; Leo, 140; Libra, 166;
      Pisces, 229; Sagittarius, 192; Scorpio,
      179; Taurus, 103; Virgo, 154
counseling, starting: Pisces, 230
courage, 141

course, taking a: Gemini, 116
Cowboy, 27
coworkers, talk with: Leo, 140
creative project, starting: Aries, 91; Cancer,
      128; Gemini, 116; Leo, 141; Taurus,
      103; Virgo, 154
creative project, submitting: Capricorn,
      205; Gemini, 116; Libra, 166; Pisces,
      229; Sagittarius, 192
creativity, 45
cruise, taking a: Gemini, 116
culmination, 62

daily bread, 45
dead, being, 117
Dead Again, 35, 80
dead people, vision of, 225–26
descendant, 43, 45
diet, starting: Aries, 92; Gemini, 116;
      Pisces, 229; Taurus, 103
direct motion, 23
Divine Secrets of the Ya-Ya Sisterhood, 68
divorce: Aquarius, 217; Aries, 91; Cancer,
      127; Capricorn, 204; Gemini, 116;
      Leo, 140; Libra, 166; Pisces, 229;
      Sagittarius, 191; Scorpio, 179; Taurus,
      103; Virgo, 153
The Dreamcatcher, 7
"*Dream of a Ridiculous Man,*" 77
dream recall: Pisces, 229
Du Maurier, Daphne, 56
Dune, 31

earth signs, 13
ease, 59
eclipse, solar, 24–25
Edison, Thomas, 206
Eighth house, 45
Einstein, Albert, 220
elements, the four, 12–15
  table of, 19
Eleventh house, 46
Ellen (case of), 225–27
employee, hiring and firing: Aries, 92;
      Scorpio, 179
The End of the Affair, 80